COMMUNITY CONFLICTS AND THE STATE
IN INDIA

This book comes out of a conference that was sponsored by the Joint Committee for South Asia of the Social Science Research Council and the American Council of Learned Societies.

COMMUNITY CONFLICTS AND THE STATE IN INDIA

Edited by

Amrita Basu
Atul Kohli

OXFORD
UNIVERSITY PRESS

OXFORD
UNIVERSITY PRESS

YMCA Library Building, Jai Singh Road, New Delhi 110001

Oxford University Press is a department of the University of Oxford. It furthers the
University's objective of excellence in research, scholarship, and education
by publishing worldwide in

Oxford   New York

Athens   Auckland   Bangkok   Bogota   Buenos Aires   Calcutta
Cape Town   Chennai   Dar es Salaam   Delhi   Florence   Hong Kong   Istanbul
Karachi   Kuala Lumpur   Madrid   Melbourne   Mexico City   Mumbai
Nairobi   Paris   Sao Paolo   Singapore   Taipei   Tokyo   Toronto   Warsaw

with associated companies in   Berlin   Ibadan

Oxford is a registered trade mark of Oxford University Press
in the UK and in certain other countries

Published in India
By Oxford University Press, New Delhi

ISBN   0 19 565214 2

Typeset at All India Press, Pondicherry 605001
Printed in India at Pauls Press, New Delhi 110020
and published by Manzar Khan, Oxford University Press
YMCA Library Building, Jai Singh Road, New Delhi 110001

Acknowledgements

Community Conflicts and the State in India originated under the auspices of the Joint Committee for South Asia of the Social Science Research Council (SSRC) and the American Council of Learned Societies in New York. Our colleagues on the committee encouraged us to organize a conference on the themes of the book and challenged us to rethink our initial proposal. Additional support from the United States Institute for Peace and the Five College Peace and World Security Studies Program enabled us to organize a conference on 'Political Violence in India: The State and Community Conflicts' at Amherst College on 23–4 September 1995. With the exception of the chapter by Sunita Parikh, which was written after the conference for this volume and a different paper by Christophe Jaffrelot than the one he presented at the Conference, all the other chapters were presented at the conference. Three of the chapters, by Atul Kohli, Jyotirindra Dasgupta and Mary Katzenstein et al., were first published as a special issue of the *Journal of Asian Studies* (vol. 56, no. 2, May 1997).

Each of us has received grants that have supported our research and writing for this project. Amrita acknowledges support from the John D. and Catherine T. MacArthur Foundation and from an Amherst College Faculty Research Grant. Atul is grateful to the Liechtenstein Research Program on Self Determination at the Centre For International Studies, Princeton University, and the Russell Sage Foundation in New York.

Several people contributed generously to the production of this book. At the SSRC, Itty Abraham, David Llelyveld, and Peter Szanton helped us organize, conceptualize and fund this project. Elora Shehabuddin helped compile and edit the final manuscript. We are also grateful to the editors of Oxford University Press, Delhi, for encouragement, support and helpful comments from outside reviewers.

The royalties from this book are being donated to the Suren Sova Memorial Trust, created in the memory of Amrita's grandparents. The Trust provides financial assistance for the higher education of some of the poorest young people in Calcutta.

AMRITA BASU
ATUL KOHLI

Contents

Conclusion
Reflections on Community Conflicts and the State in India

Contributors

AMRITA BASU teaches in the Departments of Political Science and Women's and Gender Studies at Amherst College.

JYOTIRINDRA DASGUPTA is Professor Emeritus of Political Science at the University of California, Berkeley, where he has also served as chairman of the Program in Development Studies.

CHRISTOPHE JAFFRELOT is a research fellow at the Centre National de la Recherche Scientifique and member of the Centre d'Etudes et de Recherches Internationales at the Fondation Nationale des Sciences Politiques in Paris. He teaches South Asian Politics at The Instit d'Etudes Politiques in Paris.

ZOYA HASAN is Professor at the Centre for Political Studies at the Jawaharlal Nehru University in New Delhi.

MARY FAINSOD KATZENSTEIN teaches in the Department of Government at Cornell University.

ATUL KOHLI is Professor of Politics and International Affairs at Princeton University.

UDAY SINGH MEHTA teaches Political Theory at the University of Pennsylvania. He has also taught at Princeton, Cornell, MIT and Chicago.

SUNITA PARIKH is Assistant Professor of Political Science at Washington University in Saint Louis.

ARUN R. SWAMY received his Ph.D. in political science at the University of California, Berkeley, in 1996.

USHA THAKKAR is Honorary Director of the Research Institute for Gandhian Thought and Rural Development in Mumbai.

STEN WIDMALM is currently lecturer in Comparative Politics in the Department of Government, Uppsala University in Sweden.

Abbreviations

ADMK	Anna Dravida Munnetra Kazhagam
BJP	Bharatiya Janata Party
CPI (M)	Communist Party of India (Marxist)
DK	Dravida Kazhagam
DMK	Dravida Munnetra Kazhagam
GOI	Government of India
JK	Jammu and Kashmir
JKLF	Jammu and Kashmir Liberation Front
LTTE	Liberation of Tamil Tigers Eelam
MLA	Member of Legislative Assembly
MNF	Mizo National Front
MNFF	Mizo National Famine Front
NC	Jammu and Kashmir National Congress
OBCs	Other Backward Classes
PMK	Pattali Makkal Katchi
RSS	Rashtriya Swayamsewak Sangh
UP	Uttar Pradesh
VHP	Vishwa Hindu Parishad

Abbreviations

Introduction

AMRITA BASU AND ATUL KOHLI

Political conflicts around religious, caste and regional identities have multiplied in India. Whether one views these 'million mutinies' as symptomatic of a growing crisis of governability or of a democratic revolution, analytical questions abound. Why is there apparently more violent conflict around identity politics in India today than at any time since Independence? To what extent do the character and intensity of recent conflicts differ from those of the past? What lessons can we learn from cases where community demands have been successfully accommodated? And on a related note, what measures might alleviate the widespread destruction of life and property, and create the sense of predictability on which all social order rests? The following essays analyse both the growing incidence of violent ethnic conflict in India and some of the conditions for its resolution.

It is difficult to overstate the contemporary relevance of community conflicts in India. The decade of the 1990s began with violence breaking out in many north Indian cities and towns, mainly in response to the government's decision to implement the Mandal Commission recommendations that provided quotas for employment and education to India's lower middle strata, the 'Other Backward Classes' (OBCs); anti-Mandal sentiment was an important element in the downfall of the central government in 1990 and in the subsequent growth of the Hindu nationalist Bharatiya Janata Party (BJP). In October 1990, the BJP organized a massive attempt to destroy the Babri Masjid, a mosque in the north Indian town of Ayodhya, that sparked off riots in which well over a thousand people died. But this was only a prelude to the more serious debacle in Ayodhya in December 1992 which resulted in well over two thousand deaths across India, including brutal killings in cosmopolitan Bombay. Violence in Kashmir has been severe for much of the first half of this decade.

The 1996 parliamentary elections provide further evidence of the growth of community identities. The two major victors were the Hindu nationalist BJP on the one hand, and the coalition of backward and lower caste groups that ultimately allied with Congress and formed the government on the other. The community conflicts that had earlier been played out in the streets have now found strong expression in the national electoral arena.

The chapters in this collection analyse the links between new expressions of community identity, growing ethnic conflict and the changing character of the Indian state. Our framing assumption is that contemporary conflicts reflect politically constructed antagonisms between communities. We then explore how an intensified sense of 'us versus them' comes into being, the particular forms it assumes—whether it involves one community against another, or a community against the state and its agents, or alliances amongst political parties, or, as is most often the case, some combination of all of these forces. Against the backdrop of this exploration, we focus on changes in expressions of community identity in relation to changes in the nature of the Indian state.

In this brief introduction, we first focus on our core concepts of the state and communities. It is the interaction between them that provides the cohering focus to the following essays.[1] In the conclusion, Amrita Basu will return in the conclusion to reflect on some of the main themes and findings.

THE STATE

Many of the most serious and violent conflicts that India has experienced in recent years have been directed against the state. Diverse groups do not simply vent their anger on the state but often also hold it responsible for the injustices they seek to redress. Hindu nationalists allege that the central government appeases the Muslim minority, upper caste youths who immolated themselves in 1990 accused the government of discriminating against the so-called forward castes by implementing the Mandal Commission recommendations, and regional movements demanding greater rights to self-determination have accused the national government of discriminatory allocation of resources and undue political interference at the state level.

The growth of community conflicts has coincided with a deinstitutionalization of the Indian state. Both the normative and organizational pillars of the post-Independence Indian state—secularism, socialism and nationalism of the Nehruvian type, as well as the Congress party and civil and political bureaucracies—have weakened. At the same time, the size of the electorate has multiplied, competition for state-controlled resources has increased, traditional social hierarchies have eroded, and the spirit of democratic competition has spread. The combination of a normative and organizational vacuum on the one hand and the intensification of demo-

---

[1] For a broader statement on the state–society approach that is consistent with these essays, see Migdal *et al*. (1994).

cratic politics on the other, has provided the opening for mobilization along multiple lines and thus the context for the outpouring of a variety of political conflicts.[2]

However, the state is not necessarily responsible for all the conflicts for which it is blamed. For example the BJP's contention that the Congress party's appeasement policy has damaged Hindu interests, thereby triggering the growth of Hindu nationalism and concomitant Hindu–Muslim conflict, represents a gross distortion and oversimplification of state policy; it is nonetheless a compelling discourse. So while we argue that the state's role is often critical to an understanding of the genesis and growth of community conflicts, we neither deny the influence of socio-economic conditions, nor of the understandings and discourses that undergird shifts in identity politics.

Further, our analysis of how the state influences community conflicts is not limited to those state policies that intentionally affect the communities that take to the streets in protest. The state's influence on ethnic conflicts may be powerful but indirect. Rajiv Gandhi, for example, no more intended to contribute to the BJP's growth by overturning the Supreme Court decision in the Shah Bano case than V. P. Singh intended to incite upper castes by implementing the Mandal Commission recommendations. We thus analyse the ways in which the state contributes to community conflict through its action as well as its inaction, through its passive and overt activities. And we also explore the relationship between what has increasingly become an electorally driven political system and the growth of community conflicts.

Just as we broaden our understanding of state policy by exploring its unintended consequences, we similarly challenge monolithic characterizations of the state by focusing on its diverse actions at the state and local levels. Many 'communal' riots have indeed been precipitated by discord between state and central governments and between local and national administrators. In other instances, however, community leaders and government representatives have worked together to prevent or contain violence. Such diverse examples warn against the dangers of overly simple characterizations of the state in situations of 'communal' unrest.

COMMUNITY CONFLICTS

The very task of specifying which community identities have been associ-

[2] Both the editors of this collection have worked on different aspects of this topic: Basu (forthcoming) explores popular participation in Hindu nationalist mobilization; Kohli has written extensively on the crisis of the state, including Kohli (1990 b).

ated with political conflict and violence is complex. People identify themselves in ways that often depart from the labels that scholars and administrators use to describe them. Moreover, what might appear to be a Hindu–
Muslim or a caste conflict may be infused with meanings other than the
terms 'communal' or 'caste' suggest.

It is often difficult to analyse simultaneously with adequate care the
complexity of identities and their social construction on the one hand, and
why identity-based political conflict has grown on the other hand. While
we as a group of political scientists agree that an adequate explanation of
ethnic conflict requires an understanding of the socially constructed nature of identities, given disciplinary proclivities, our 'comparative advantage' lies more in tackling issues of explanation than in unravelling complex social constructions.

Rather than exploring the whole range of community identities that
people embody, we focus on those identities that have become associated
with political violence in the recent past, especially religion, caste, language and region. In doing so we distinguish our approach from some
other prevailing approaches. While the debate on 'primordialism' versus
'instrumentalism' has by now been surpassed,[3] and most analysts agree
that ethnic identities are a product of complex strategic and cultural considerations, the conditions under which ethnic divisions within a political
community 'harden' or 'soften' remain far from clear. We hope to contribute to this analytical lacuna by specifying the 'political conditions'
that mould community identities. By 'political conditions' we refer both
to the nature and actions of the state on the one hand, and power competition and movement politics on the other hand. We thus seek political
explanations for such questions as why regional movements have apparently supplanted linguistic movements; why movements that made regional
demands have often found expression through religious idioms; and why
caste movements have ended up persecuting religious minorities.

We explore differences in people's expressions of their community
identities at the local, state and national levels. Since many of the movements we study are subnational or regional, 'victimization' of specific
groups by the central government figures as an important aspect of their
self-constitution as a movement. In other cases, however, the success of
movements masks the extent to which they have benefited from centre–state
conflicts. For example in the aftermath of events in Ayodhya, the BJP's
growth may deceptively appear to be the outcome of a groundswell of

---

[3] For a brief, good discussion of competing approaches to the study of ethnic politics,
see Young (1993: 21–5).

Hindu nationalist or 'communalist' sentiment. In fact, however, the BJP's growth in some states in which it is powerful may well result more from 'banal' political facts, such as the continuing decline of the Congress, centre–state conflict in these regions may help catapult the BJP into political prominence.

It is also important to contrast the ways in which local activists and national leaders define their identities and interests. Otherwise there is a risk of treating these movements as coherent, homogeneous entities. It is striking, for example, that local activists in secessionist, religious and caste movements often depict their actions as defensive. Assertions of victimization among relatively affluent, powerful groups that dominate along religious, caste or ethnic lines, have not prevented them from engaging in extreme brutality. Indeed their belief that they are victims of state policy is a common source of their frustration and aggression.

While we focus on religion, caste, language and region, we do not assume that these categories depict stably rooted identities. Rather, we are interested in how they acquire, transform and even lose political meaning. Take, for example, the Shiv Sena in Maharashtra: although it was initially depicted and described itself as a 'sons-of-the-soil' movement, today the Shiv Sena is commonly identified as a militant Hindu nationalist group. Similarly, the Akali Dal in Punjab was once considered a regional movement but has increasingly become known as a Sikh religious movement. In contrast, Tamil nationalism asserted itself as a regional force, won some victories, but later declined in intensity. These examples raise a series of questions: how do changes in identities of movements transpire?; what is the role of the state in renegotiating these identities?; what are the differences between the terms that leaders of these movements, 'ordinary' activists and the state use to describe them?; and what are the conditions that help us explain the rise and decline of such community-oriented movements?

The nine chapters that follow address the interaction between the state and politics on the one hand and the emergence, intensification, transformation and/or decline of community identities on the other hand. The opening essay by Atul Kohli explores the relationship of ethnic self-determination movements to changing state practices. He compares the trajectories of movements organized by Tamils, Sikhs and Kashmiri Muslims.

Sunita Parikh analyses caste and religious conflicts at the national level, focusing both on the interaction between political determinants and identity politics of caste and communal groups. Christophe Jaffrelot provides a useful historical overview of growing politicization of religious conflicts which culminate in riots. The remaining essays dissect a variety of regional situations. Zoya Hasan analyses how caste conflicts were transformed into religious conflicts in Uttar Pradesh, whereas Arun Swamy lays out a provocative argument for why mass violence is not as prevalent in some south Indian states such as Tamil Nadu as it is in the rest of India. Sten Widmalm focuses on the important case of Kashmir, suggesting that the conflict there is as much about politics as it is about religion. Jyotirindra Dasgupta then analyses ethnic conflicts in the north-east, emphasizing the latitude that exists for constructive resolution of subnational movements. Mary Katzenstein, Uday Mehta and Usha Thakkar explain the 'rebirth' of the Shiv Sena in Bombay by focusing on both institutional and discursive changes. The concluding chapter by Amrita Basu evaluates the different approaches the authors in this collection take in analysing the causes and consequences of the growth of community conflicts in India.

Can Democracies Accommodate Ethnic Nationalism?
The Rise and Decline of Self-Determination Movements in India

ATUL KOHLI[*]

Over the years, numerous ethnic movements have confronted the central state within India's multicultural democracy. India thus provides laboratory-like conditions for the study of such movements. In this paper I analyse three such ethnic movements—those of Tamils in Tamil Nadu during the 1950s and 1960s, of Sikhs in the Punjab during the 1980s, and of Muslims in Kashmir during the 1990s—with the aim of explaining both their rise and decline. The focus will be less on the details of these movements than on deriving some general conclusions.

I argue below that periodic demands for more control and power by a variety of ethnic groups—that is self-determination movements—ought to be expected in multicultural democracies, especially developing country democracies. The fate of these movements—that is the degree of cohesiveness these groups forge; whether they are accommodated or whether their demands readily escalate into secessionist movements; and their relative longevity—largely reflect the nature of the political context, although group characteristics around which movements emerge and the resources these groups control are also consequential. More specifically, two dimensions of the political context, namely how well central authority is institutionalized within the multicultural democracy and the willingness of the ruling groups to share some power and resources with mobilized

* I would like to thank the following for their helpful comments on earlier drafts: Amrita Basu, Ayesha Jalal, Pratap Mehta, Claus Offe, Pravesh Sharma, John Waterbury, and anonymous reviewers. The suggestions made by Ashutosh Varshney need to be singled out for acknowledgement because they were very useful; I incorporated many of them. The essay further benefited from comments of participants at the conference on Political Violence in India, at Amherst, Mass, 23–4 September 1995, and at a seminar I gave at the Department of Political Science, University of Toronto, 9 February 1996. A much earlier version of this paper was prepared with the financial help of the Liechtenstein Research Program on Self-Determination, Center of International Studies, Princeton University.

groups, appear to be especially relevant. Given well-established central authority and firm but compromising leaders, self-determination movements typically follow the shape of an inverse U-curve: a democratic polity in a developing country encourages group mobilization, heightening group identities and facilitating a sense of increased group efficacy; mobilized groups then confront state authority, followed by a more or less prolonged process of power negotiation; and such movements eventually decline as exhaustion sets in, some leaders are repressed, others are co-opted and a modicum of genuine power-sharing and mutual accommodation between the movement and the central state authorities is reached. Understood in this manner, self-determination movements constitute a political process whereby the central state and a variety of ethnic groups discover their relative power balances in developing country democracies.

This sweeping argument requires some qualifications and caveats that are best stated at the outset. First, in addition to the domestic political context, the comparative analysis of Indian material suggests that international factors can also alter the underlying power dynamics on which the predicted rise and decline of these movements rests. Second, the analysis is pitched at a fairly high level of generality. This not only obliterates complex details of individual movements but leads one to downplay important contrasts across movements: some identities (for example religion) may be better suited than others (for example language) to define ethnic boundaries and thus may be easier to mobilize and sustain in the cause of self-determination movements. Since no single essay can accomplish everything, I hope that the costs of aggregation are worth the benefits of generalizations that emerge. Finally, there is a need for a normative caveat. The focus on the state and the larger political context ought not to be read as endorsing the actions of state elites at the expense of the rights of ethnic movements. On the contrary, established states often trample on the rights of their minorities, sometimes ruthlessly. Whether a state or a demanding group has justice on its side is both important and controversial, and is best decided on a case-by-case basis.

The chapter is organized as follows. I first discuss some general issues, explaining why proliferation of group demands ought to be expected in a multicultural developing country democracy like India, and why the institutionalization of central authority and the nature of the leadership are especially important aspects of the political context that shape self-determination movements. Specific Indian material follows this general discussion, notably a comparison of self-determination movements of Tamils, Sikhs and Kashmiri Muslims. Towards the end, I not only summarize the analysis but elaborate on some general conclusions.

THE POLITICAL CONTEXT: SOME GENERALIZATIONS

Politicization in Developing Democracies

The introduction of democracy to a developing country setting nearly always exacerbates political conflicts over the short to medium term. Some observers are surprised by such outcomes because, extrapolating from the Western experience, they expect democracy to be a solution to existing, rather than a source of new, power conflicts. In the West, however, if one may overgeneralize, democracy evolved over a long time, and both suffrage and political competition expanded slowly within the framework characterized by centralized authority structures at the apex and growing popular pressures from below. Moreover, the question of which group constituted a 'nation' that was to be wedded to a specific state was often resolved prior to the introduction of mass suffrage. In this sense, democracy in the West indeed came to be a 'solution' to growing power conflicts in society, especially among economic elite and across class lines. By contrast, democracy comes to most developing countries in the form of imported ideas. As these ideas are translated into democratic institutions which, in turn, provide new incentives for political actors to organize and mobilize, the results over the short to medium term are often disquieting. Several state–society traits of developing country democracies help explain why this should be so.

First, prevailing cultural conditions in developing countries do not readily mesh with the imported model of political democracy. For example mass suffrage is introduced in a context where identities and attachments often tend to be more local than national; authority in society tends to be dispersed but, within dispersed pockets, quite rigid and hierarchical; and community norms often prevail over narrow individualism. As democracy is introduced and competing elites undertake political mobilization, old identities are rekindled and reforged. Modern technology hastens the process (for example the availability of the teachings of Khomeini on cassettes or the dramatization of the Ramayana on television), and the collision of mobilized identities with each other or with the state ought not to be totally surprising. The spread of democratic norms also threatens traditional elites, who are more than willing to join hands with all those who perceive the spread of individualism as disruptive of traditional lifestyles. Again, a variety of 'reactionary' movements ought to be expected.

Second, considerable state intervention is inherent in the overall design of 'late development' (Kohli 1990b: Conclusion). This structural trait in a low income setting generates special problems when democracy is introduced. For example ruling elites in developing country democracies cannot readily claim that distributive problems are social (private) and not political (public) problems; in other words, it is difficult in contemporary developing countries to establish the same separation between public and private realms that many Western democracies developed in the early stages. The accumulation of distributive claims on these states thus partly reflects the politicization engendered by the state's attempts to penetrate and reorganize socio-economic life. Relatedly, an interventionist state in a poor setting controls large proportions of a society's economic resources, thus attracting the competitive energies of many of those who seek economic improvement. Intense competition over the state's resources, in turn, politicizes numerous cleavages, adding to the problems of developing country democracies.

Third, since democracy comes to most developing countries as an import, and since the transitions to democracy are over relatively short time periods, democratic institutions tend to be weak in most follower democracies. There is some variation on this dimension, and I will return to the issue of relative institutionalization as a variable (India being more fortunate on this score). For the most part, however, such institutions as norms of electoral politics, political parties, parliaments, and constitutional separation of powers are not well established in developing country democracies. Competitive mobilization, in turn, that is unmediated by institutions tends to spell trouble for most states. Of the problems generated by this well-known condition, the most significant is that power in these settings often comes to rest in individuals rather than in institutions. Barring exceptional individuals, most leaders centralize personal power with long-term detrimental consequences. Because centralization of power in individuals nearly always weakens fragile institutions—strong institutions do constrain the power of individuals—there is a built-in incentive in developing country democracies for leaders to undertake periodic deinstitutionalization; weak institutions and personal power thus tend to create a mutually reinforcing, vicious cycle. Typically, therefore, developing country democracies tend to move towards situations in which a centralizing, personalistic ruling elite confronts a variety of oppositional elites, who mobilize that which is most readily mobilizable, namely community identities, and help transform them into rigid ethnic and group boundaries.

This brings the discussion to the fourth and last distinctive condition of developing country democracies. The introduction of competitive elections and mass suffrage amidst weak institutions will repeatedly generate expansionary political pressures in these democracies, that is pressures towards a more equal distribution of power in society. A movement towards genuine devolution of political and economic power could accommodate such tendencies, or establish a new 'equilibrium' between demands and governance, and help strengthen new democracies. Any such trend, however, is likely to run up against two pervasive global constraints, both manifest as near intellectual hegemonies. These are, first, a belief in strong, centralized states as a necessity for the welfare of nations and, second, in recent years, a widespread acceptance of orthodox economic models as appropriate models of economic development. Whereas the former privileges nationalists, the latter, in spite of the promised dismantling of the state and related decentralization, pushes centralizing technocrats to the forefront (for details, see Kohli 1993). In either case, devolution of power is a fairly low priority in most developing country democracies. A typical outcome is the evolution of these democracies towards two-track polities, with a democratic track in the sphere of electoral politics, and a not-so-democratic track in the state sphere, especially in the area of economic policy-making. The political society of many developing democracies is thus increasingly characterized, on the one hand, by 'too much democracy'—that is by a variety of conflicts, including ethnic conflicts—and, on the other hand, by 'not enough democracy,' as it increasingly insulates itself from social demands and conflicts.

The cumulative impact of these distinctive state–societal traits is that the introduction of democracy into developing countries rapidly politicizes the body politic. As a result, a variety of conflicts typically dot the political landscape of these democracies. Broad contextual conditions, of course, do not fully explain either the variations across such countries or the trajectories of specific conflicts; in the language of social science, a focus on the context provides necessary but not sufficient conditions of specific conflicts. What can be said at the general level, however, is that the four state–societal traits discussed above help explain why democracy in developing countries tends to be as much a source of, as a solution to, power conflicts.

These conflicts may precipitate along cleavages of class, interest groups, regions, or ethnic groups. Again, at a general level, it can be noted that ethnic and regional groups are more likely than classes or economic groups to demand 'self-determination', because they can more readily perceive themselves as 'total societies', that is as social groups with a sufficiently complex division of labor to sustain ambitions of territorial sovereignty. The possibility of a shared cultural heritage further encourages such 'imagining'. The more such groups exist in a developing country democracy, the more likely it is that movements for 'self-determination' will emerge. If this much is relatively clear, the next interesting question is: why are some such groups that demand greater power and control readily accommodated, while others are not, moving instead into a militancy–repression cycle, escalating their demands into secessionist movements, and threatening the territorial integrity of established states?

Institutionalization, Leadership and Self-Determination Movements

Continuing the discussion at a fairly general level, I hypothesize that two 'proximate variables' are especially important for understanding the varying trajectories of self-determination movements. The first of these is the level of institutionalization of the central state and the second concerns the degree to which the ruling strategy of leaders accommodates demands for self-determination. I use the concept of institutionalization in a fairly conventional sense (Huntington 1968)—it has both a normative and an organizational component—but my focus is more narrowly on central state authority than on a host of other norms and political structures that may be more or less institutionalized; also, I do not assume that state authorities are always agents of public order. The degree of institutionalization of the central state then influences the degree to which state authorities can 'impose' their preferred vision of the political order on the societies they govern. The vision, of course, may be more or less accommodating of opposition demands, and when pressed, the leadership strategy may be more willing in some instances than in others to devolve power. Degree of institutionalization and leadership strategies are thus two important variables, that is, two aspects of the broad political context discussed above that commonly vary within the developing world and influence the fate of self-determination movements. If one dichotomizes these two variables (an action which is clearly quite artificial), and if the mechanical quality of schematic depictions is excused, the resulting 2x2 matrix shown in Table 1 can help clarify some of the issues succinctly.

My main hypothesis is well depicted by the first quadrant. All other things being equal, the more the authority of the central state is institutionalized and the more accommodating the ruling strategy, the more likely it is that self-determination movements will traverse the shape of an inverse U-curve: they will first rise, because it is 'natural' for them to do so in the political context of developing country democracies discussed above, but, later, after a more or less prolonged period of power negotiation with the central state, they will inevitably decline in intensity as exhaustion

TABLE 1

DEVELOPING COUNTRY DEMOCRACIES: POLITICAL CONTEXT AND
THE TRAJECTORY OF SELF-DETERMINATION MOVEMENTS

Leadership strategy	Central authority	
	Well institutionalized	Weakly institutionalized
Accommodating	1. The inverse U-curve of ethnic politics (e.g. Tamils in India, 1950s and 1960s)	2. Peaceful breakup of the state (e.g. Czechoslovakia, 1990s)
Unaccommodating	3. Cycle of demands and repression (e.g. Sikhs in India's Punjab, 1980s)	4. Turbulence and/or breakdown (e.g. Nigeria, first and second republics)

sets in and some genuine compromise is reached. The logic underlying this proposition is that, on the one hand, a well-institutionalized state sets firm boundaries within which political movements must operate and, on the other hand, an accommodating leadership provides room—of course, within limits—for the movements to achieve some real gains.

The same logic can be readily extended to describe variations on the theme. Given space limitations, I will not belabour the point; a few examples will suffice. A state's leadership may turn out to be not very accommodating to self-determination movements. This may result from something as 'simple' as the type of leader in power or it may reflect something more complex, such as a different coalition on which the power of the leader rests. Whatever the underlying reasons, unaccommodating leaders in well-established states (that is quadrant 3) will often channel self-determination movements into cycles of escalating demands and repression. The reason is that a well-institutionalized democratic state both provides room for self-determination movements to emerge and possesses a fair amount of legitimate coercion to repress these movements. Unaccommodating leaders, who define the state's 'good' in terms of denying concessions to demanding groups, will typically repress such movements, only to push them further into more 'extreme' directions of secession as a goal and militancy as a tactic. The situation depicted in quadrant 3 is then ripe for prolonged, militant self-determination movements.

These situations are 'resolved' either when overwhelming force is used and/or when a more accommodating leader comes to power within the established state.

Self-determination movements are deeply threatening to weakly institutionalized states (quadrants 2 and 4). If the leaders of such states are relatively accommodating towards movements—such examples in the developing world are rare, suggesting that the institutionalization of authority structures and leadership strategies may not be entirely independent of each other—then the peaceful break-up or reorganization of the state is the most likely outcome. By contrast, unaccommodating leaders, especially those who control significant coercive resources, are likely to drive the situation towards, at minimum, considerable turbulence, and, at maximum, a civil war and possibly even the violent break-up of the state.

In sum, how well the authority of the central state is institutionalized and what the leadership strategy is are two important aspects of the political context that influence the pattern of self-determination movements. To repeat, the nature of the groups that are mobilized (that is what resources these groups control and whether the groups are organized around race, religion, or language), as well as how intensely such groups come to view their situation as unjust are issues that are by no means irrelevant to the fate of these movements; some of these issues are by their very nature specific to given situations and will emerge in the empirical discussion of specific cases. At a general level, it is my central hypothesis that the nature of the broader political context is quite important for understanding self-determination movements.

SOME EVIDENCE FROM INDIA

India is a noisy democracy which, over the years, has experienced a variety of political conflicts. Conflicts around cleavages of class, caste, parties, language, religion, and regions thus characterize India's political landscape. Elsewhere, I have analysed in detail why this should be so in India (Kohli 1990b); some of the theoretical generalizations stemming from that analysis were sketched out above in a highly condensed form. Within that context, the focus here is mainly on ethnic movements demanding self-determination.[1]

---

[1] As suggested above, I use the concept of self-determination movements fairly loosely. What I have in mind are mainly movements for greater power and control by groups which share some real or imagined characteristics and which are sufficiently large and complex to conceive of themselves as 'mini nations'. Within the Indian federation, then, demands of such minority groups have varied from minimum (i.e. for more

Again, India has experienced quite a few of these, especially by groups who define their regional distinctiveness along criteria of language or religion. Three of the most significant of these movements, namely those involving Tamils, Sikhs and Kashmiri Muslims are analysed below.[2] Since I have proposed that institutionalization of state authority and leadership strategies influence the pattern of these movements, prior to their analysis a few comments concerning how these contextual conditions have varied in India over time are in order.

In the 1950s, India was a relatively well-institutionalized polity, particularly in comparison with other developing countries. This was especially manifest in a fairly well-organized central state—reflected in a highly professional national civil service and armed forces—but also in a well-functioning national political party, the Congress, that generally controlled the state. In addition, India possessed such effective institutions as a parliament, an independent judiciary and a free national press. How and why India came to have such effective institutions is a complex issue, well beyond the scope of this paper. Suffice it to say that some state institutions were inherited from a colonial past and other more political ones were a product of a fairly prolonged and cohesive nationalist movement (Weiner 1967, 1989). India's rigid and segmented social structure—especially the elaborate caste hierarchies, organized over numerous, relatively isolated villages—kept levels of political mobilization low and, ironically, may have further helped new institutions to take root in the early, post-Independence phase.

Over time some of India's political institutions weakened. In terms of periodization, if the 1950s were a decade of relatively effective institutions, the 1960s are best thought of as a decade of transition during which the nationalist legacy declined, political competition and challenges to the hegemony of the Congress party increased, and a new type of political system—a more populist system—with non-institutional methods of securing electoral majorities was created by Indira Gandhi. During the following two decades, namely the 1970s and the 1980s, some of India's

power and resources within the federation and expressed through democratic channels) to maximum (i.e. for secession from the federation and expressed through militant means).

[2] I estimate the 'significance' of these movements by the following criteria: the number of people that were mobilized; the cohesiveness and longevity of the movement; and the degree to which they genuinely became a force that the central state could not ignore. It could be argued that this case selection is a little too convenient; that such other cases as in eastern India would be troubling to the argument of this paper. For an analysis of some eastern Indian material that is broadly consistent with the spirit of this essay, see the chapter by Jyotirindra Dasgupta in this volume.

established institutions were battered, especially by leaders in power.

Since levels of institutionalization are relative, it is important to remember that even during the 1970s and the 1980s, India's central state authority was relatively well institutionalized in comparison with most African and many Latin American countries. Nevertheless, in comparison with its own past, a fair amount of deinstitutionalization did occur: the Congress party was largely destroyed as an organization; the civil service, the police and even the armed forces became less professional and more politicized; parliament became less effective; and the the judiciary less autonomous. Once again, how and why these political changes occurred constitutes a complex story, far beyond the scope of this chapter. The only fact I will note is that growing personalization of power was at the heart of the story; growing political fragmentation in society privileged personalism and, in turn, personalistic leaders damaged the institutions that constrained their discretionary powers (Brass 1994; Kohli 1990b; Rudolph and Rudolph 1987).

As to the other variable of leadership strategy, India has had four main prime ministers who have ruled for more than two to three years each: Nehru ruled India for nearly seventeen years, from 1947 till his death in 1964; Indira Gandhi dominated India for nearly as long as her father (1966–77 and 1980–84); Rajiv Gandhi ruled from 1984 to 1989; Narasimha Rao took over in 1991 and ruled until 1996. To characterize the leadership strategies of these leaders in a brief space is to grossly oversimplify a fairly complex reality and I do so only reluctantly.

The main analytical concern here is how leaders typically respond to oppositional challenges, especially to demands of mobilized groups for greater self-determination. On a dimension of leadership strategy that varies from accommodating to unaccommodating, Nehru was closer to the accommodating end of the spectrum. This was both a function of his own personality and a reflection of his relatively secure power position; a concession from Nehru here or there enhanced his magnanimity rather than threatened his hold on power. The political situation during his daughter's rule, however, was quite different, as were her political instincts. The hegemony of the Congress had by then declined and Indira consolidated her power against considerable odds. Always suspicious of power challenges, she recreated a powerful political centre in India mainly by portraying herself as a champion of the poor. As her personal popularity soared, the opposition to her also became strident, culminating in her imposing the 'Emergency' in 1975, when democratic rights in India were suspended for about two years. When Indira Gandhi returned to power in 1980, she was less populist; nonetheless, needing to mobilize electoral pluralities, she started flirting with communal themes, occasionally courting India's Hindus (more than 80 per cent of India's population) by railing against religious minorities, especially Sikhs. This strategy made her increasingly less accommodating towards minorities, lest she be viewed as appeasing them. Overall therefore, in contrast to Nehru, Indira Gandhi was closer to the unaccommodating end of the leadership spectrum.

Both the subsequent leaders, Rajiv Gandhi and Narasimha Rao, have been more flexible than Indira Gandhi.[3] Rajiv Gandhi was especially accommodating towards self-determination movements during the first two years of his rule. As his political situation became less secure in the second half of his rule, he became more and more indecisive and unaccommodating. In the 1990s, Narasimha Rao portrayed himself as a nonpersonalistic, flexible leader who, at minimum, was not bent on a further centralization of power in his own hands. After the assassination of two prime ministers (both Indira and Rajiv were assassinated for political reasons), this ruling strategy appeared to calm an agitated polity.

The Nehru period in India, say, from 1950 to 1964, is best understood as a period when India's central state was relatively well institutionalized and leadership strategy, though firm, was flexible and accommodating to demands for self-determination. Subsequently, especially since the mid-1960s, India's political institutions have weakened, though they remain relatively effective by developing country standards. Leadership strategy over these last three decades, however, has varied. Whereas Indira Gandhi was quite unaccommodating towards demanding groups, both Rajiv and Rao appeared to be at least less threatening, if not actually more accommodating. With this context in mind, we are now in a position to turn our attention to a few specific self-determination movements within India.

Tamil Nationalism

Today, Tamil Nadu is one of India's important states, an integral part of the Indian federal system. Now, not even those who live in Tamil Nadu question whether they are fully a part of the Indian union. However, it was not always so. During the 1950s and the 1960s, arguing that Tamils were a distinct people, Tamil leaders mobilized considerable support for a 'Tamil Nation'; they demanded, at the very least, greater power and control over their own affairs *vis-à-vis* New Delhi or, at most, secession from India. A

---

[3] The contrast between these leaders and Indira Gandhi helps bolster the claim that leadership strategies are indeed somewhat independent of the degrees of institutionalization of state authority.

very brief recapitulation of the rise and decline of this movement will serve our broader analytical interests (see Barnett 1976; Swamy, this volume).

Tamil is a language, and Tamils as a social group, therefore, are mainly a linguistically defined group. Tamil, along with a few other languages in south India, but unlike most languages spoken in northern India, does not derive from classical Sanskrit with its Indo-Germanic roots; rather, it is a Dravidian language. Tamil nationalists also insisted that Tamils are a separate racial and cultural group, descended from a Dravidian society that was indigenous to southern India prior to the historic arrival of and domination by 'northern Aryans'. Brahmins in Tamil society could thus be viewed not as natural 'hegemons' of a caste society but rather as agents of northern domination. That some of the Tamil Brahmins were of lighter skin colour than much of the darker skinned Tamil society only added to the plausibility of such an interpretation. Two other sets of 'facts-on-the-ground' are important for understanding the dynamics of Tamil nationalism. First, Brahmins in Tamil society constitute a relatively small caste group: less than 5 per cent of the total (in comparison, say, to parts of northern India, where Brahmins often constitute nearly 10 per cent of total population). Second, for a variety of historical reasons, the area that is now Tamil Nadu was more urbanized by mid-century than many other parts of India.

The Congress party in this part of India, as elsewhere, built its pre-Independence base on Brahmins. That Brahmins were few in number and that non-Brahmin castes were already active in city life provided the necessary conditions for the early rise of an anti-Brahmin movement; in other words, democratization and related power conflicts came to this region of India relatively early. The first institutional manifestation of that movement was the Justice Party. Led by the elite of the non-Brahmin castes, it sided with the British against both Brahmins and Congress in the hope of securing concessions in government jobs and education. It was eventually delegitimized both because of its elitist nature and the rising tide of nationalism. This had significant consequences, especially because Congress became identified as a Brahmin party in a region where Brahmins had not been able to establish cultural and political hegemony. The early development of a cleavage between the Brahmin and non-Brahmin forces opened up the political space for subsequent anti-Congress developments.

The link between Congress and Brahmins became the target of Tamil nationalists in the post-Independence period. The Congress party in Madras could not easily break out of that mould. The continued Congress–Brahmin alliance enabled the regional nationalists to mobilize simultaneously against domination by both caste and north Indians. Hammering on the theme of the distinctiveness of the Tamil tradition and linking that with opposition to the rule of Hindi-speaking northerners and their allies, the southern Brahmins, the leaders of the Dravidian movement found a ready audience among the numerous backward castes that were already concentrated in the cities. To put it simply, Tamil nationalism and a 'petit bourgeois' base among the urban backward castes provided the core support for a regional nationalist movement.

The early demands of this self-determination movement were for greater power and control: over time, the broader movement came to include a separatist movement demanding a 'Dravidistan,' a land for the Dravidian people. A number of Indian states in the early 1950s argued for the reorganization of the Indian federation along linguistic lines. Most such demands, of course, were not separatist. Nevertheless, in the aftermath of partition, Nehru, in the early 1950s, was reluctant to consider a linguistic redesign, lest it strengthen secessionist tendencies and lead to a further breakup of India. Tamil nationalists and their mobilized supporters were a case in point, in so far as they pressed their identity politics hard through demonstrations that occasionally turned violent and included public burning of the Indian flag and the constitution. Under growing pressure from several states, Nehru realized that the dangers from not devolving power to linguistic groups were greater than of doing so. Fully in control at the national centre and widely accepted as India's legitimate leader, he set firm limits on what powers the newly constituted states would have and what would be controlled by New Delhi (which, by the way, was substantial). Within these limits then, India's federal system was reorganized into linguistic states in 1956. By granting Tamil nationalists a Tamil state, the reorganization took a fair amount of the separatist steam out of the movement.

Having gained a separate state of their own (first called Madras, subsequently relabelled Tamil Nadu, or the home of Tamils), the struggle of Tamil nationalists shifted to ousting Congress from power within the state. To that end, Tamil nationalists utilized a political party, the Dravida Munnetra Kazhagam (DMK), and set out to broaden their power base. Their party's radical rhetoric of land reform and eradication of the caste system further threatened the Brahmins, but attracted many intermediate and lower caste villagers. The DMK also used cultural themes to mobilize support. In this they were fortunate since many prominent Tamil nationalists were playwrights, literary figures and theatre and movie actors. In particular, the DMK used the emerging medium of movies with great skill and success to highlight such themes as the injustices of the caste system, the glories of Tamil history, and the societal need for Robin Hood-like heroes who would deliver the poor, the weak and the dispossessed from the clutches of the rich and the wicked.

As Tamil nationalism became more populist, it simultaneously became less coherent and more capable of winning elections. Following Nehru's death, for example, India's national leaders for a brief moment reattempted to impose Hindi as the national language on all states. Many states reacted negatively, but Tamil Nadu reacted the most violently. Well mobilized to confront precisely such national policy shifts, language riots broke out all over the state. Several students burned themselves to death, protesting the moves of the national government. For another brief spell, the national government used a heavy coercive hand to deal with protests. As matters got worse, the national government backtracked, conceding the principle that regional languages, such as Tamil, were 'co-equal' to the two national languages, namely Hindi and English. This represented a major victory for the DMK. Enjoying considerable popularity, the party ousted the Congress from power within Tamil Nadu in the 1967 elections. Since then, the Congress has not returned to power in that state.

The rise and consolidation of power by the DMK had a profound impact on Tamil Nadu's politics. The highest leadership posts in the state slipped out of the hands of Brahmins and went to the educated elite of the non-Brahmin castes. The intermediate and local leadership more accurately reflected the real power base of the DMK—the intermediate castes. Many of them gained access to more power and resources. As the DMK settled down to rule, the predictable happened. Over time, the DMK lost much of its self-determination, its anti-centre militancy, as well as its commitment to socio-economic reforms. The reasons for that deradicalization in Tamil Nadu were the same as elsewhere. Once national leaders made important concessions, though within firm limits, and the DMK achieved its major goal of securing increased power, *realpolitik* concerns took over, and mobilizing ideologies slowly lost their relevance for guiding governmental actions. Ethnic nationalism slowly declined, following the inverse U-curve discussed above.

Sikh Nationalism

Punjab is one of India's most prosperous states—the home of the green revolution—and Sikhs constitute about half of its population (the other half being Hindus). Sikh nationalism was a powerful political force in the state throughout the 1980s, with the demands of Sikh groups varying from greater political and economic control within the Indian federation to secession from India and the creation of a sovereign state, Khalistan. The national government under Indira Gandhi, especially during the 1980s, was not only *not* accommodating, but actively sought to divide and rule the Sikhs. The strategy backfired: some Sikh groups turned sharply militant and the central state, in turn, responded with considerable force. Conveniently situated on the border with Pakistan, Punjab's militant Sikhs were able to secure arms and support from that neighbouring nation. Militant nationalists and a repressive state thus confronted each other in a vicious cycle of growing violence. Political violence took a hefty toll throughout the 1980s—nearly 1000 people died every year—peaking in 1990 when some 4000 people were killed. Since then, however, the situation has changed. Brutal state repression 'succeeded' in eliminating many of the militants. A more politically flexible Rao allowed state-level elections in Punjab in the early 1990s. As an elected government settled down to rule, an exhausted state went back to work, and both militancy and state repression fell into the background. During 1993, only 73 people died in political violence, while, over the last few years, capital investments in Punjab have grown dramatically.

The underlying 'story' behind the rise and decline of Sikh nationalism is complex and cannot satisfactorily be retold here (for details, see Brass 1990). What follows, therefore, is only a bare bones account. The Sikhs are a religious group, concentrated mainly in the Indian state of Punjab. Sikh men are distinctive in that they have religiously prescribed long hair and wear turbans. Sikhs and Hindus lived side by side peacefully for several centuries. Like the Hindus—Sikhism was initially derived from Hinduism in the late medieval period—Sikhs are internally differentiated along caste-like groups. Most Sikhs are relatively prosperous agriculturalists; a sizable minority are urban traders and entrepreneurs. Until recently, intermarriage between these groups and their Hindu counterparts was common in Punjab. Sikhs also have their own version of 'untouchables', equivalent to the lowest Hindu castes that generally tend to be landless and very poor.

Prior to the political turmoil that arose in the 1980s, caste and community divisions in Punjab had given rise to easily identifiable political divisions. In the past, the Hindus generally supported the Congress party, though a significant minority had also been loyal to a Hindu nationalist party. The Akali Dal, by contrast, had consistently counted on the Sikh vote, but had seldom succeeded in mobilizing all the Sikhs as an ethnic political bloc. Given internal divisions among Sikhs, the Congress was often in a position during the 1960s and 1970s to form a government in Punjab with the help of Hindus and a significant Sikh minority. The Akalis, by contrast, could only form a coalition government, and that only with a seemingly unlikely partner: the pro-Hindu party. These basic political and community divisions provide the essential background for understanding the intensified political activities of the Sikhs during the 1980s. Akali militancy was aimed at mobilizing as many Sikhs as possible around a platform of 'Sikh nationalism.' The analytical issue is—why did such fairly normal political ambitions generate so much chaos and turmoil?

The Akali Dal as a political party has always exhibited a mixture of religious fervour and hard-nosed political realism aimed at capturing power. Since it is mainly a Sikh party, it has always had a close relationship with Sikh religious organizations. The Sikh political elite thus periodically utilizes religious organizations to influence the political behaviour of the laity. Over the years, the Akalis have been in and out of power. They first came to power in 1966 when they spearheaded a successful movement for a separate 'Punjabi Suba' (or the land where Punjabi is spoken), and the current boundaries of the state of Punjab were drawn. Given the electoral arithmetic, however, the power position of the Akalis was never secure. Sikhs barely constituted a majority in the state and Congress party leaders consistently sought to draw away part of the Sikh vote through one machination or another. Unlike Tamil Nadu, therefore, where Tamil nationalists came to power around the same time, consolidated their hold, and settled on a slow but steady road towards deradicalization, Akalis in Punjab have consistently needed to whip up religious and nationalist issues that would keep Sikhs politically united.

During the early 1970s, as Indira Gandhi's popularity grew across India, Congress party leaders in Punjab undertook aggressive efforts to divide Sikhs and to consolidate their own hold over state politics. A threatened Akali Dal had little choice but to raise the ante; they started demanding even greater control over the affairs of Sikhs, coming closer and closer in their formal statements to demanding a sovereign state for the Sikhs that they could control. Indira Gandhi countered with a combination of repression—labelling secessionists as seditious—and further attempts to divide Sikhs. During the 'Emergency' many Sikh leaders were imprisoned. When Indira Gandhi returned to power in 1980 and another round of elections was held in the Punjab, Congress won a clear majority, with the Akalis securing only 27 per cent of the popular vote. Congress leaders considered themselves the legitimate, elected rulers. The Akalis, by contrast, viewed Punjab as 'their' state, which they ought to control. The Akalis, cornered in their own state, decided they had to fight for their political life. Much of what followed— some of it anticipated but most of it not—makes sense mainly from this retrospective logic of competitive mobilization.

The battle lines were drawn. Indira Gandhi had popular support. She decided to use her position of advantage to launch a political offensive and consolidate her position vis-à-vis the Akalis. If she could use Sikh militants to split the ranks of the Akalis still further between the moderates and the extremists, victory would be hers. And this is precisely what she attempted.

The Akali Dal possessed another set of political resources, however, whose efficacy Indira Gandhi apparently underestimated. Close as they were to the Sikh religious organizations, the Akalis could still organize around the issue of Sikh nationalism like no other party in the Punjab. The chain of Sikh *gurudwaras*, moreover, provided a ready organizational network with money, personnel, and the proven ability to sway opinion. A populist, centralizing, and unaccommodating central leader, Indira Gandhi, thus came to be pitted against the Akali Dal, a regional party with considerable potential to mobilize the forces of religious nationalism.

Both Indira Gandhi and the Akalis assembled militant forces for political ends. In retrospect, it is clear that over the next several years, the militancy led to civil disorder that took on a political life of its own, and increasingly went out of the control of both the Akalis and the national government. Whether that was simply not foreseen or was brazenly ignored under the short-term pressure to seize political advantage may never be known.

What we do know is that, once mobilized, Sikh militants very quickly gained political advantage over moderate Sikh leaders. If the political aim was indeed to create Khalistan, a separate Sikh state, then moderate Sikh leaders had little to contribute towards achieving such ends. For most moderate Akalis, a move towards secession was mainly a political ploy. Having shifted the political discourse in that direction, however, any and all efforts to work with New Delhi simply undermined the legitimacy of this moderate leadership; normal politics made the moderates look like opportunists not worthy of the mantle of leadership. Instead, true believers became heroes of the day and gained public sympathy. Flush with arms that often came from Afghanistan via Pakistan, Sikh militants then unleashed a holy war aimed at establishing a sovereign Sikh state. Indira Gandhi countered with increasing governmental repression. As a cycle of militancy and repression set in, Punjab, one of India's most prosperous states, became engulfed in violence for a decade.

There were at least two important occasions during the 1980s when Congress and Sikh moderates came close to a compromise. Among the demands of Akalis were a number of concrete 'bread and butter' issues that fell well short of secession: control over river waters, the capital city of Punjab, and agricultural subsidies. From 1982 to 1984, Indira Gandhi refused these compromises, lest she be viewed nationally as appeasing minorities. This weakened Sikh moderates and privileged those who wanted to use more militant tactics. A second and more important occasion arose when Rajiv Gandhi came to power in 1985. Flushed with victory and committed to resolving the Punjab conflict, Rajiv offered broad compromises to the Akalis. The results were dramatic. Elections were held in the state, the Akalis came to power, and political violence came down sharply during 1985. Unfortunately, all this was short-lived. Very quickly Rajiv Gandhi found it impossible to implement the compromises he had offered to the Akali leaders. While the details are complex, the major obstacle to implementation was Rajiv's own growing political vulnerability: as his popularity declined, beginning sometime in 1986, he was increasingly pressed within his own party to not make any 'further' concessions to minorities. Once it became clear that concessions from Delhi were more apparent than real, the position of the elected Akali leaders was again undermined, and the cycle of militancy and repression recurred.

Had India been a weaker state during this period, it is conceivable that Sikh secessionists would have succeeded in establishing yet another state on the subcontinent. As it was, however, even though its political institutions had weakened considerably over the last few decades, India remained a relatively well-established state. The national legitimacy of elected leaders, an effective civil and police bureaucracy and, most important, loyal armed forces are critical components of this state and were all utilized—brute force, in particular—to contain and repress Sikh militants. Over time, the militants also became marginalized as they lost popular support. Repression and political marginalization led to a dwindling number of Sikh militants undertaking violent acts in order to accomplish secessionist goals.

Rao finally called elections in the Punjab in 1992. The Akalis boycotted the election, and a Congress government led by a Sikh chief minister came to power. When municipal elections were called later, even the Akalis joined in. For now, therefore, the militancy and repression of the 1980s has receded into the background.

To sum up, Sikh nationalism in Punjab also traversed the inverse U-curve discussed above, but the top of the curve turned out to be like a plateau. Among the important underlying contrasts with the earlier Tamil movement were the different approaches of Nehru and Indira Gandhi: Nehru was accommodating and Indira was not. Of course, there were other factors at work: Tamils totally dominate Tamil Nadu, whereas the Sikhs constitute only half of Punjab's population; Tamils are a linguistic group, whereas Sikhs are a religious group, and, given the close marriage of politics and religion in Sikhism, Sikh religion probably provides a more encompassing identity than does attachment to a language; the threat posed by rapid socio-economic change in Punjab to Sikhism as a religious community was more serious than that to the linguistically defined community of Tamils; and Tamils did not have as easy an access to arms and across-the-border sanctuaries as did Sikh militants. All of these factors played some role, but none of them on their own varies as neatly with the rise and decline of movements as do the relative degrees of institutionalization of state authority and the contrasting strategies of national leaders. Within a more turbulent polity, Indira Gandhi's commitment to dominate Punjab politics pushed Akalis into aggressive mobilization. Once they were mobilized, professional politicians lost control and militants took over. Finally, over time, militants were repressed out of existence, and a tired population was relieved to accept some concessions from a more accommodating national leadership and to re-elect the provincial government.

Muslim Nationalism in Kashmir

Since 1989, the state of Jammu and Kashmir, especially its northern valley of Kashmir, has been gripped by a militancy–repression cycle. The main protagonists in the conflict are, on the one hand, Islamic groups that do not want Kashmir to be part of India and, on the other, a variety of Indian security forces. The dimensions of the conflict are quite startling: in a relatively sparsely populated state of about 8 million people (of whom approximately 65 per cent are Muslim), at least 10,000 people (some estimates go as high as 40,000) have died as a result of political violence over the last five years; security forces deployed in the state by now consist of more than 300 paramilitary companies and several army divisions; and at least 100,000 Hindus have migrated from the Muslim-dominated Kashmir valley, mainly to Jammu, the southern, Hindu-dominated part of the state. At the time of this writing, India's central government is pursuing a two-pronged strategy: it is coming down quite hard on recalcitrant Islamic militants and it is openly calling for elections in the 'near future', thereby strengthening the hands of those leaders who are willing to respect 'constitutional boundaries' and participate in electoral politics. Whether this will generate a result similar to that in the case of Sikhs in Punjab, namely a return to normalcy, is not yet clear.

Once again, the full 'story' behind this specific Indian case of ethnic politics need not be recalled here (Varshney 1991; Widmalm, this volume). The condensed account below suggests that this case does not fit as neatly into the inverse U-curve argument developed above. I explain this partial anomaly as the result of the fact that the conflict is, first, more internationalized than the two cases discussed above and, second, still relatively 'young'; as predicted, the decline of ethnic militancy and the related fratricide may still set in over the next few years. Whatever the eventual outcome, some elements of how and why ethnic conflict flared up in Kashmir are still broadly consistent with the propositions developed above.

Ever since India and Pakistan emerged as sovereign states in 1947, Kashmir has been a focus of dispute. As a Muslim-majority state that was contiguous with Pakistan, Kashmir, arguably, should have become a part of Pakistan. The Hindu head of the Kashmiri state instead chose to join India. Pakistan contested the 'legality' of this decision and, as often happens in interstate relations, it was not legality but might that determined what was right. A large part of Kashmir was incorporated into India and India and Pakistan have fought two wars over the issue. What is important for our analytical purposes is that, in spite of these international problems, for much of this period—say 1950 to 1980—ethnic nationalism in Kashmir remained relatively mild. The memory and stories of ethnic injustices, however, were probably kept alive. Kashmir was accorded a 'special status' within the Indian constitution, giving it considerable autonomy within India's federal system; India's central government also provided a substantial financial subsidy to facilitate the 'economic development' of Kashmir. This seemed to have done the 'trick.' While both New Delhi and Kashmiri, especially Muslim, leaders viewed each other with suspicion, a working arrangement of sorts operated well into the early 1980s.

Several new factors came into play in the early 1980s. As discussed above, the Indian polity as a whole was by now relatively more turbulent. Old nationalist institutions like the Congress party were in decline. A whole new post-nationalist generation demanded a greater share of political and economic resources. In her post-populist phase in the early 1980s, Indira Gandhi increasingly flirted with pro-Hindu themes to recreate a new national electoral coalition. This strategy did not bode well for states with considerable non-Hindu populations, such as Punjab and Kashmir. Given her centralizing and unaccommodating instincts, moreover, states like Kashmir came under increasing political pressure.

Kashmir's 'founding father' and much revered leader, Sheikh Abdullah, died in 1982. His son Farooq Abdullah moved into the resulting political vacuum, both as leader of the state's main non-Congress political party, the National Conference, and as head of the state government. State-level elections in 1983 turned out to be quite important. Farooq successfully campaigned on an anti-Congress, anti-Delhi, pro-Kashmiri autonomy platform. The campaign caught the imagination of a large majority, especially Kashmir's Muslim majority. Indira Gandhi herself campaigned in Kashmir on behalf of the state Congress party, often appealing to the fears of the Jammu Hindus. Communal polarization, while hardly new to Kashmir, grew under increasing sponsorship by the competing elites. Farooq's platform was well short of secessionist demands; nevertheless his emphasis on regional autonomy for Kashmir turned out to be very popular, propelling the National Conference to a handsome electoral victory over the Congress.

Farooq had to tread a thin line between emphasizing Kashmiri autonomy on the one hand and not appearing as an anti-national, Muslim Kashmiri secessionist on the other. In order to bolster this precarious position, he joined hands with other non-Congress heads of state governments. Hoping to be perceived as one of the many members of the 'loyal opposition', Farooq hosted a well-publicized conference in Kashmir of major opposition leaders. Unfortunately this was precisely the type of move that threatened Indira Gandhi. With the intention of clipping Farooq's growing political wings, she appointed Jagmohan, a close and tough personal aide, to be Kashmir's governor. Jagmohan, in turn, initiated a series of machinations whereby a number of National Conference legislators defected to the Congress, threatening Farooq's position. Finally, in 1984, Jagmohan dismissed Farooq as Kashmir's chief minister by claiming, without proof, that Farooq had lost the support of a majority in the legislature.

Farooq's dismissal—very much a part of an all-India pattern woven by a threatened Indira Gandhi, bent on centralizing and weakening India's federal institutions—turned out to be a critical turning point. While public opinion data is not available, it appears that the dismissal sent a strong message—especially to Kashmiri Muslims—that their democratic and legitimate efforts to create greater political spaces within India may well be thwarted.[4] This growing alienation of Muslims, particularly urban youth, was strengthened by ensuing political events. As the 1987 state elections approached (Indira Gandhi was by now dead and her son Rajiv was prime minister), Farooq Abdullah, both politically pressed and sufficiently opportunistic, formed an electoral alliance with the Congress party. This seemingly innocuous electoral opportunism had the profound impact of eliminating any major democratic outlet for Kashmiri Muslims who sought greater autonomy from Delhi. A number of Muslim groups hurriedly came together under an umbrella organization, the Muslim United Front. They, in turn, mobilized the urban youth and grew in popularity. The elections themselves and their aftermath turned out to be bitter; mobilized and angry youth were confronted, even assaulted, by security forces. Further alienated, some went across the border to Pakistan, where they were trained as militants; they returned armed with Kalishnikovs. The National Front–Congress alliance victory at the polls were met with widespread charges of

[4] See, for example, the essays by George Fernandes (a well-known Indian political leader who directly participated in Kashmiri affairs) and Riyaz Punjabi (a Kashmiri professor who lived through these events) in Thomas (1992).

electoral fraud. Whatever the reality, Kashmir was engulfed by a serious legitimacy crisis.

Meanwhile the Soviet Union intervened in Afghanistan the United States again armed Pakistan; and Pakistani rulers regained the sense of confidence *vis-à-vis* India that they had lost after the 1971 war. There is ample evidence to indicate that Pakistan trained alienated Muslim youths from Kashmir and provided them arms and resources. Even when the Pakistani government was not directly involved, India's hostile neighbour became both a staging ground and a sanctuary for Kashmiri militants. It is estimated that, to date, several thousand Kashmiris have been trained in Pakistan.[5]

Following the 1987 elections, Kashmiri Muslims, especially those in the valley (Muslims in Jammu tend to be ethnically distinct), confronted governments in Kashmir and in New Delhi simultaneously as hostile parties. Kashmiri militants and security forces increasingly met each other in a growing cycle of militancy and repression. The occurrence of human rights abuses must have further alienated the Muslim population. When elections were called again in 1989, militant groups boycotted them quite successfully. The more the democratic political process lost its meaning, the more a full-scale insurgency came to be unleashed.

Factionalism among Islamic militants has also increasingly come to the fore. The Jammu and Kashmir Liberation Front (JKLF)—an immensely popular and nominally secular group under Muslim leadership—argues for a sovereign state of Kashmir, including the part of Kashmir controlled by Pakistan. The Hizbul Mujahideen are modelled after the Mujahids in Afghanistan and demand the accession of Kashmir to Pakistan. Although less popular than the JKLF, the Mujahideen receive more support from Pakistan and are better trained and armed. The popular JKLF faces the enormous obstacle that neither India nor Pakistan supports the idea of a sovereign state of Kashmir. In contrast, the militant Mujahideen, though a potent armed force, are politically not so popular. With increasing Hindu migration out of the Kashmir valley, the struggle has come to be regarded as one of Kashmiri Muslims versus India. Most Kashmiri Muslims, however, want a sovereign state; they do not want to join Pakistan. Apart from the fact that neither India nor Pakistan favours such an outcome, Kashmiri Muslims face another major hurdle: there are nearly 100 million Muslims in India, of which Kashmiri Muslims constitute only about 5 per cent.

[5] George Fernandes in 1990 estimated this figure to be in the range of 3000 to 5000. Since in his former capacity as India's Minister for Internal Affairs (Janata Dal government, 1989), he had access to all of Indian and other intelligence services data, and since this estimate was provided in a public lecture at Harvard University, one is inclined to give some credence to these estimates. See Thomas (1992: 289).

Fearing for their own welfare in India if a Kashmiri Muslim state were established by force (such a move would be bound to encourage anti-Muslim sentiments and propel the pro-Hindu Bhartiya Janata Party [BJP] party to the political forefront across India), Indian Muslims have generally refrained from openly supporting the cause of Kashmiri Muslims. The overall situation is thus a near stalemate: most Kashmiri Muslims are by now deeply alienated from India; while divided among themselves, a majority among the Muslims would probably opt for a sovereign state of Kashmir; however, not only would the powerful Indian state not let go of it, but Pakistan also would not support such an outcome; finally, Pakistani-trained militants, with arms left over from the Afghanistan civil war, remain a powerful force, though one which Indian security forces have successfully fought to a standstill. Whether the state elections of 1996 will help break this stalemate remains hard to predict at the time of writing.

Leaving the details of the tragic 'story' aside, what are its analytical implications? It is clear that the roots of the militancy–repression cycle in Kashmir can be traced back to a power conflict in which a centralizing Indira Gandhi dislodged the elected government of Farooq Abdullah, precipitating a long-term legitimacy crisis. Had political institutions like parties been stronger in Kashmir or the Indian federal system, one leader could not have pursued such centralizing antics except with great difficulty, and even if she had, they would certainly have been easier to weather. The combination, however, of weakening institutions and an unaccommodating national leader helped push normal power struggles into a cycle of militancy and repression. The early trajectory of the Kashmir conflict thus broadly fits the analytical scheme developed above; however, the obvious fact that the conflict in Kashmir continues to this day clearly defies the predicted journey—given certain conditions—of ethnic conflicts along an inverse U-curve. Since India's democratic institutions, in spite of some attenuation, remain relatively strong, and since the leadership of Rao was more flexible than that of Indira Gandhi, how does one explain the persistence of a high intensity ethnic conflict in Kashmir?

Three different answers (or three components of one answer) are possible to this question, each with different implications for the analytical argument proposed in this chapter. The first answer, and the one least compatible with the thesis of this essay, would focus on the distinct values and discourse of Islam, possibly suggesting that political identity based on Islam is felt both more intensely and more comprehensively, and thus one cannot expect an Islam-based ethnic movement to follow a trajectory similar to that followed by Tamil or Sikh nationalist movements. Such an argument, however, would have the burden of explaining why Muslim nationalism flared up primarily in Kashmir (and not in other parts of India) and why mainly in the 1980s and 1990s.

A second answer would focus on the role of Pakistan in the Kashmir crisis. One could argue that unlike in Tamil Nadu and even more so than in Punjab, Pakistan's continuing involvement in Kashmir has prolonged the conflict. While I have not emphasized this explanation, such an argument is compatible with the thesis of this essay in so far as the logic of the argument developed here is essentially political: ethnic movements in developing country democracies constitute a political process whereby the central state and mobilized groups discover their relative power balances. Intervention by an external actor affects the balancing process, at least prolonging, if not altering, the overall trajectory.

Finally, the simplest answer and one that is most readily compatible with this essay's thesis is that it is still too early to predict how the Kashmir crisis will end; if Pakistan's role diminishes and if the United Front government maintains a firm but flexible set of policies—that is if following the state elections it grants the promise of 'maximum autonomy' within the Indian federation—ethnic conflict in Kashmir may well decline over the next few years.

The argument of this chapter ought not to be taken too literally. It merely suggests that in an established multicultural democracy in the developing world, ethnic conflicts will come and go. Well, of course! The real message of the essay is thus not so much its literal interpretation but rather some of the implications that flow from it. In conclusion, therefore, I wish to spell out a few of these implications.

The first set of implications concerns analytical issues. Indian material suggests that ethnic conflicts are best thought of as power conflicts. Ethnic conflicts are thus a subset of the larger set of political conflicts that include conflicts along class, caste, or party lines that are characteristic of the political landscape of developing country democracies. While one can readily emphasize the distinctiveness of ethnic from other types of political conflicts, there are also certain similarities: mobilized ethnic groups, like other mobilized groups, seek greater power and control, either as an end in itself or as a means to secure other valued resources. Such a perspective, in turn, also suggests what ethnic conflicts are not: they are not inevitable expressions of deep-rooted differences; they are not anomic responses to the 'disequilibrium' generated by 'modernization'; and, while ethnic identities are indeed contingent, the process of identity formation and ethnic conflict is also not so indeterminate as to defy a causal, generalizing analysis.

If ethnic conflicts are mainly power conflicts then how power is organized in state and society becomes important for understanding their patterns. I have suggested that in developing country democracies, when state authority is well institutionalized and when national leaders act in a firm but accommodating manner, ethnic conflicts typically follow the shape of an inverse U-curve. Both national leaders and leaders of ethnic movements may be quite calculating, and thus their strategies and counterstrategies may be amenable to a bargaining type of rationalist analysis. The shifts in values and discourses of the broader membership of an ethnic group that inevitably emerge during ethnic mobilization are, in turn, best understood from a close, anthropological type of research. As micro approaches, however, neither the rational choice nor the anthropological approach readily aggregates into macro generalizations.[6] Generalizations about the conditions that help explain the rise and decline of ethnic movements, therefore, are best derived from a direct, macrofocus on state and societal conditions. The emphasis on the degree of institutionalization of state authority in society and a focus on leadership held up fairly well in the preceding discussion on ethnic movements in India. If persuasive, or at least suggestive, such an approach and hypothesis may be worth examining against ethnic movements in countries other than India.

A second set of implications concerns normative and policy issues. To the extent that ethnic conflicts are power conflicts, it is often difficult to identify the true heroes and villains in these conflicts. It is difficult, on an *a priori* basis, to hold whether established states are more right or wrong than demand-making ethnic groups. A lot depends on the situation. As a scholar it is as important to eschew the conservative bias that states necessarily act to preserve the public good, as it is to resist the temptation that all groups seeking self-determination have justice on their side. What is clearer is that leaders—especially national leaders, but also leaders of ethnic movements—who persistently choose to be unaccommodating will channel normal power conflicts down a destructive path, where calculating leaders drop off and true believers take over, utilizing militant tactics because the cause becomes worth dying for. The true villains of ethnic conflicts are thus those leaders who refuse to see that the failure of timely compromise can only produce and exacerbate political problems.

Finally, I turn to the question posed in the title of the chapter, namely can democracies, especially developing country democracies, accommodate ethnic nationalism. Indian material suggests that the answer has to be a

---

[6] For a quick review of theoretical debates in the study of, and for further references to, the literature on politics of ethnicity, see Young (1993: 21–5).

qualified 'yes'.[7] It is ironical that democracy and democratization in a developing country setting first encourages the emergence of ethnic demands. A well-institutionalized state can put some limits on how far these demands may go. Of course, if the state itself is not well institutionalized, then democracy and multiethnic competition spell great political problems; that constitutes a set of cases not discussed here. Given an institutionalized state, however, if some of these demands are not accommodated, the sense of exclusion and injustice may well turn demanding groups towards militancy. That is why democratic leaders with inclusionary, accommodating ruling strategies fare better at dealing with ethnic conflicts. In sum, democracy in a developing country setting both encourages ethnic conflict and, under specific circumstances, provides a framework for its accommodation.

---

[7] An important book that after a great deal of valuable empirical work reaches a conclusion that, though not identical, is broadly consistent with this conclusion is Horowitz (1985)

Religion, Reservations and Riots: The Politics of Ethnic Violence in India

SUNITA PARIKH

In recent years the worldwide incidence of violent conflict within and across states has appeared to grow rather than diminish, and both lay observers and scholars have been quick to attribute the increase to 'primordial' identities. From the former Soviet Union and the former Yugoslavia to Rwanda, old ethnic, religious, and nationalist attachments are said to be reemerging after decades of internal quiescence or repression from above, and they have been blamed for causing violent conflicts that have led to the deaths of hundreds of thousands of people. As a consequence, ethnicity as a causal variable has once again been thrust into the limelight both in popular political debate and in academic scholarship in the social sciences.

Among countries in which ethnicity has been considered to be resurgent, India occupies a special place. Despite the bloody nature of the partition of British India into independent India and Pakistan, the country has often been hailed as an exemplar of how diverse religions, nationalities, and ethnicities can coexist in one political unit. Nehru and the Congress party consistently asserted their vision of a secular, tolerant India in which many cultures would be welcomed but none would dominate. Since the early 1980s, however, this vision of India has increasingly come under siege, in terms of both rhetoric and reality. The rise of extremist separatist movements in Punjab and Assam in the early 1980s were amongst the early challenges to central government authority, but since then conflicts have broken out across India and have been attributed to religious, nationalist, and caste identities.

This chapter is part of a larger project in which I examine two sets of conflicts in India and ask the question, were these conflicts caused by the caste and religious factors to which they have been ascribed, or were other forces at work as well? The cases being analysed are the 1990 riots over the V. P. Singh government's decision to implement affirmative action at the national level for middle castes, and the 1992 riots sparked off by the demolition of a mosque in Ayodhya, in north India.

In this chapter I draw on evidence from four states: Bihar, Delhi, Gujarat, and Karnataka. These four states vary in a number of important dimensions. They have different histories of caste and Muslim–Hindu relations. They differ in their economic endowments and patterns of economic development. They have different political histories, with the Bharatiya Janata Party (BJP), Congress, and Janata Dal having differential success across them. At the same time, they also have key similarities: in all cases caste and religious conflict have ebbed and flowed, and reservation policies have been extremely important politically.

At first glance the two sets of conflicts seem unconnected, and they also seem motivated by quite different factors. The 1990 disturbances were attributed to caste tensions that were exacerbated by the government's decision to implement a controversial caste-based policy, while the 1992 disturbances seemed to be the direct result of Hindu–Muslim tensions and the rise of Hindu nationalist sentiment within India.

When we examine these cases more carefully, however, a number of factors become apparent that run counter to these interpretations. For example in the case of the caste riots, the pattern of conflict is not consistent with previous instances of violence over similar issues. And as far as the Ayodhya conflict is concerned, we might expect that riots over religion would be more likely to occur in those areas where Hindu–Muslim conflict has traditionally been greater or where Hindu nationalism is particularly strong, but there is no straightforward correlation of this type either. In order to understand more clearly the connection between these religious and caste issues and the violence that appears to have been generated by them, I use theories of ethnic conflict and of political violence more generally to interpret the cases and shed light on their causes. In particular, I examine the role of political factors in generating or exacerbating conflict.

Drawing on these theories, I hypothesize that just as the reservation riots were not entirely about reservation policies, the religious riots were not entirely about religion. This is not to say that such identities are unimportant; people resort to collective action over issues that have high salience for them, and few issues have higher salience in India than caste and religion. However, the role of identity differs from the way it has been conceptualized in the old primordialist literature and the way it is invoked today to explain, for example, the conflict in the former Yugoslavia. Ethnic hatreds are neither immutable nor unchanging. Ethnic attachments can be invoked and their salience increased under certain conditions, but this fluidity is precisely the opposite of the notion of primordialism. Sometimes, conflict over reservation policies may be part of a larger struggle for power in which caste, religion, and nationalism are invoked singly or together to achieve specific political goals.

The resurgence of caste, religious, and ethnic conflict can best be explained by analysing concurrent political, social, and economic developments taking place in the affected communities. Theories of political violence offer several hypotheses, some competing and others complementary, which purport to link factors and explain variations across cases.

COMPETING AND COMPLEMENTARY EXPLANATIONS OF CONFLICT

Ethnic Conflict

In the 1960s and the 1970s, there were many first-rate studies of the role of ethnicity in social conflict. Substantively, the breakup of colonial empires created heterogeneous nation states in which ethnic issues were frequently at the forefront, while theoretically the process of modernization in these new nations was a major focus of research for social scientists. The debate over the role of ethnicity in nation building soon revolved around two presumptions: first, that ethnic attachments were inherent, or 'primordial,' in citizens and became salient in heterogeneous cultures because of the necessity of interaction between fundamentally opposed groups; and second, that ethnic attachments were used instrumentally by elites to further their own goals. The first view explained ethnic violence as an affective response to feelings of threat and prejudice, while the second directed attention to the material interests of elites and their followers, such as economic mobility, political power, and the like.

In writings on ethnonationalism, Walker Connor presents an articulate and operationalizable position of ethnic attachment as a bond that has a 'psychological and emotional hold ... upon the group' (1994: 73). He deplores instrumental approaches as having 'a continuing tendency of scholars to harbor what we termed earlier "an unwarranted exaggeration of the influence of materialism upon human affairs"'. He argues that while these theories can also be criticized empirically, 'they can be faulted chiefly for their failure to reflect the emotional depth of ethnonational identity and the mass sacrifices that have been made in its name' (1994: 74). Connor does not deny the role of economic and political factors in stirring up ethnic passions, citing especially the role of arbitrary (i.e. ethnically insensitive) borders in the creation of new nation states in Africa and Asia. He agrees that economic inequality arguments play a major role in ethnonationalist debates: 'Economic arguments can act as a catalyst or exacerbator of national tensions. But this is something quite different than acknowledging economic deprivation as a necessary precondition of ethnonational conflict' (1994: 153). Connor insists that the fundamental driving force is a psychological and emotional attachment to ethno-national identity, which he compares to an individual's attachment to family and kin groups. Ethnic identity is defined as drawing on the myth of common descent, which 'would explain why nations are endowed with a very special psychological dimension—an emotional dimension—not enjoyed by essentially functional or juridical groupings, such as socioeconomic classes or states' (1994: 74).

For Connor, then, affective attachments provide inherently stronger motivations than those based on material interests. But while he makes a good case that variations in economic inequality do not regularly correspond to variations in ethno-nationalist conflict, he is less convincing when stating that variations in ethno-nationalist conflict correspond with the affective measures to which he assigns such weight. He asserts that 'the sense of kinship, which lies at the heart of national consciousness, helps to account for the ugly manifestations of inhumanity that often erupt in the relations among national groups' (1994: 206). But he does not relate the two in any systematic way, and he goes on to recognize that 'not all relations among nations are so hate-filled. Popular attitudes held by one nation toward another are quite positive' (1994: 206), which seems to contradict the idea that a sense of 'us v. them' can explain conflict (no cause can explain both the presence as well as the absence of a condition).

At the other extreme, Paul Brass provides an excellent example of arguments that interpret ethnic conflict as essentially instrumental. In work that spans more than two decades, Brass has been one of the preeminent spokesmen for the position that ethnicity is socially constructed and conflict that appears to be ethnic in nature is actually the result of manipulation of symbols by the elite for their own benefit. In a celebrated debate over whether ethnicity is primordial or instrumental, he and Francis Robinson put forth opposite explanations of the factors driving Muslim mobilization around the issue of the official status of Urdu in the nineteenth century (Taylor and Yapp 1979). While Robinson asserted that the Muslim view of Urdu as a symbol of religious and cultural identity predated the Hindi–Urdu competition of the late nineteenth century, Brass countered that Urdu, and indeed many symbols of Hindu and Muslim cultural identity, became important in the elite competition for economic and political advantage (Brass 1991: 84).

According to Brass, while it is true that people have emotional attachments of language, religion, culture, and kinship, 'a sense of identity based on attachment to one's region or homeland usually does not become a politically significant matter for those who remain there unless there is some perceived discrimination against the region and its people in the larger society' (1991: 71). And while the myth of common descent clearly does unite some people, its 'fictive character presumes variability by definition. Consequently, even "the facts of birth" are either inherently of no political significance or are subject to variation' (1991: 71).

For Brass, then, the key factor creating ethnic consciousness is not emotional or psychological, but political: 'The study of ethnicity and nationality is in large part the study of politically-induced cultural change' (1991: 75). He acknowledges that the emotional attachments to which primordialists attribute so much importance have value, but only because they 'may remain available in the unconscious to be revived by some appeal that strikes a sympathetic psychic chord' (1991: 70). They provide the palette from which leaders of ethnic movements select 'those aspects that they think will serve to unite the group and which will be useful in promoting the interests of the group as they define them' (1991: 74).

The instrumental approach as articulated by Brass leaves very little room for a strong emotional attachment to cultural or ethno-nationalist symbols and markers. In the case of the Hindi–Urdu script controversy, Brass concludes that Muslim insistence on the Persian–Arabic script came from a combination of instrumental factors: the desire of Muslims to force Hindus to learn a difficult script in order to get government jobs, the use of a differentiating feature to cleave two communities who spoke the same language, and the use of Persian-based Urdu to give Muslims a common and distinct form of communication (1991: 83–6). Brass acknowledges that for religious practices Hindus learned Sanskrit and Muslims learned Persian and/or Arabic, and all three of these contributed to the development of Hindu–Urdu. But even though 'they may have used different languages to communicate with their deity, they used a common language to communicate with each other' (1991: 85). Brass pays no attention to the possibility that as languages were being standardized and codified in official usage, each community might have wanted, for affective reasons, a language script that shared features with its own religious practices. He implicitly privileges everyday secular communication over intimate religious communication in setting Hindus' and Muslims' preferences. This choice may in fact be correct, but evidence in its support is missing.

Connor and Brass provide clear examples of the positions at the extremes of the ethnic conflict literature. In this essay I propose a middle ground, one that accepts the institutional focus of Brass while paying attention to Connor's emphasis on the importance of non-material attachments. There may well be times when conflict is the expression of emotional or psychological attachments rather than a method of achieving rational or instrumental goals. At the same time, some riots are difficult to attribute to affective attachments alone. It has been said that no spontaneous riot lasts more than three days; after that people get tired, go home, resume their responsibilities. In the 1990 and 1992 riots, I contend that while religious or caste feelings may well have provided the impetus to riot, sustained violence can only be explained through the analysis of institutional, especially political, factors.

MANDAL AND MANDIR

Mandal

The 1990 riots are usually referred to as the Mandal riots. They derive their name from the commission that recommended the implementation of affirmative action (known in India as 'reservations') at the national level for middle castes, or 'Other Backward Classes' (OBCs) as they are called in the Indian constitution. The Mandal Commission and its report were not new to the political landscape; indeed, the report had been delivered in 1980 and had eventually gone out of print since no government action was taken. This neglect was due primarily to the potentially explosive issues raised by reservation policies in general and the difficulties of implementing such policy at the national level in particular.

Affirmative action and quotas in the form of reserved seats have existed at the national and regional levels for untouchables, or scheduled castes, since before India attained Independence. Reservations for scheduled castes have historically not been the most controversial or problematic; the percentage of places reserved in education and government employment is set at the state level according to the percentage of scheduled castes in each state. These reservations have several political advantages. They were agreed upon in a famous compromise in 1932 between Mahatma Gandhi and the B. R. Ambedkar, leader of the Depressed Classes, in a document called the Poona Pact and then written into the Indian constitution, so their legitimacy is rarely questioned. They signal the government's commitment to scheduled caste concerns, but they do not cause much antagonism on the part of other Indians because the full quota of reservations is almost never utilized, so competition over scarce resources is rarely a problem.

Reservations for OBCs are more problematic. Southern Indian states, which have tiny upper caste populations, almost no middle castes, and vast numbers of low castes, instituted state-level reservations well before

Independence and have continued them into the present. But greater difficulties arise in northern and western India, where there is no analogous history of elite Brahmin domination and where there are large numbers of aspiring middle castes who are too high to be considered OBCs but who perceive their economic, social, and political position to be inferior to that of the highest castes. As a result, the extension of reservations to OBCs in these states has regularly been challenged by the other castes.

Under Nehru's Congress this potential conflict was avoided by refusing to consider OBC reservations in northern and western India. The central government had briefly debated OBC reservations at the national level in the 1950s, but Parliament soon tabled the discussion when it became clear that there were extremely volatile issues involved. But after Nehru's death, and the untimely death of his successor, L. B. Shastri, the situation changed. The Congress party old guard had attempted to continue their nearly complete domination of Indian politics by choosing as their next Prime Minister Nehru's daughter, Indira Gandhi, on whose lineage they hoped to capitalize and whose inexperience they mistook for acquiescence. By the end of the 1960s Mrs Gandhi had broken away and was heading her own Congress party I faction, and she swept the Parliamentary and state elections of 1971. During the campaign she directly appealed to the low caste and scheduled caste vote and made reservation policy part of her election manifesto.

However, while new Congress-I governments in northern and western states such as Gujarat and Madhya Pradesh began to appoint commissions to establish OBC reservations, the federal government continued to lag behind. Regional variations, the difficulty of compiling a national list of OBCs, and the political problems inherent in pushing a national policy combined to keep Congress from actively pursuing their implementation in national-level educational and employment opportunities. In 1977 the Janata Party, which had defeated the Congress-I after India's experience with the Emergency, in trying to expand its elite electoral base and capture some of Congress' support, established the Mandal Commission. By the time the Commission reported back to the government in 1980, Indira Gandhi's party, popularly called Congress-I, had been returned to power.

By 1990 the Mandal report had been languishing for ten years. Because of its symbolic and practical importance to the critical middle caste vote blocs, every major political party acknowledged its existence, and almost all party platforms supported its implementation. But it was in no party's interest to antagonize its equally significant high caste vote blocs by carrying out this promise, and therefore a gentleman's agreement had apparently been established according to which everyone supported

Mandal in theory and ignored it in practice. It was broken in August 1990, when Prime Minister, V. P. Singh announced that his government would actually implement the policy.

V. P. Singh came to power in 1989 after Rajiv Gandhi's Congress government was defeated in the national elections. Singh's Janata Dal party did not command a majority, but he was able to gain support from the Hindu-nationalist BJP and form a government. His majority, however, was still slim, and it was dependent within his National Front coalition on the continued cooperation of ambitious regional political leaders who had previously led smaller parties of their own. Singh's initial decision to implement the long dormant Mandal Commission recommendations was almost certainly motivated by the loss of Devi Lal, an important north Indian leader who commanded strong voter support.[1]

Devi Lal brought into the National Front a critical and highly coveted vote bloc: lower caste small-scale farmers in north India. He had been a difficult coalition partner, because he had Prime Ministerial aspirations himself. But he was necessary because of his demonstrated ability to deliver his vote banks. When Devi Lal defected, there was no leader, either within the National Front or outside the party who could be coopted, and who could take his place. V. P. Singh himself was an aristocratic north Indian who commanded respect but lacked the personal appeal or background characteristics that might appeal to Devi Lal's constituency. Implementation of the Mandal Commission report offered a concrete way to demonstrate his commitment to that electoral group.[2]

There were no initial indications that V. P. Singh's decision would precipitate a major crisis for the government and for the country. All major parties had consistently included support for the Mandal Commission recommendations on their platforms, so the Prime Minister may not have anticipated the political firestorm that erupted after he announced on 7 August 1990 that the government would immediately begin implementing the Mandal recommendations on OBC reservations. However, the reactions across northern India were unprecedented in their scope and intensity. The initial violence, which began in Bihar, was not totally unexpected given Bihar's history of violent response to previous attempts to extend reservation policies. But conflict spread from Orissa in the east to western Uttar Pradesh and into New Delhi. And in addition to riots and destruction of property, which had occurred in similar circumstances before, it also took uncommon forms, including mass student strikes and acts of self-

---

[1] Interview with Sitaram Kesri, New Delhi, December 1992.
[2] *India Today* , 1 September 1990.

immolation. These protests, which continued for over two months, severely undermined the strength and credibility of the government and contributed to its fall later in the year.[3]

The other members of the coalition government, notably the BJP and members of Singh's own party, were in an awkward position. They could not denounce the idea of OBC reservations because they all depended on the vast OBC vote and they all supported implementation of the Mandal recommendations in their platforms. So they were left with various contradictory responses. Rajiv Gandhi condemned Singh's action in Parliament but the Congress party as a whole failed to repudiate it. The BJP contended that Singh had not consulted with them before making such an important policy decision and therefore while they did not disagree with the principle of OBC reservations they opposed the specific instance and the way the policy had been chosen. Individual political and other critics drew on expert opinion and argued that while *some* OBC reservations might be acceptable, the specific recommendations of the Mandal Commission were flawed because the data gathering techniques and data analysis were not up to social science standards; therefore there should be no implementation.[4]

In the face of sustained protests and strikes by students within the capital city, V. P. Singh withdrew the plan for implementation of OBC reservations in higher education and limited them to central government employment. This concession was not enough to bring the unrest to an end, however, and the tenor of the conflict took on a horrifying new aspect as teenagers and college students began to burn themselves alive and cited the Mandal policy as their motivation. The extent to which Mandal was the true reason for their actions is debatable, but the connection was widely accepted. At the same time the Indian press, which is arguably the best in the developing world, continued its unrelenting opposition to V. P. Singh's actions.

Finally the BJP, which had been particularly outraged by V. P. Singh's policy decision, retaliated. Perceiving the Mandal policy as cutting across its own attempt to unite Hindus regardless of caste, the party sought to mend the caste cleavages it had revealed. The BJP announced that it would make the demolition of a mosque at Ayodhya, in UP, a major priority. There had been periodic conflicts between Muslims and Hindus over the legitimacy of the mosque, and it was contended that a Hindu temple had been destroyed in order to build the mosque. That the supposed destruction had taken place hundreds of years ago carried little weight with militant

---

[3] *India Today* , 15 November 1990.
[4] *India Today* , 15 September 1990.

Hindus; they contended that the site was holy for Hindus and therefore must be reclaimed. The additional conflict generated by this new crisis proved to be too much for the frail National Front government. Bereft of BJP support, Janata Dal was unable to hold its coalition together, and V. P. Singh lost a no-confidence vote in Parliament. He was replaced by a former ally, Chandra Sekhar, who had led 60 Janata Dal MPs in a breakaway and who made a pact with Rajiv Gandhi's Congress party so that he could achieve his ultimate goal: to be Prime Minister. Meanwhile, the Mandal policy was put before the Supreme Court which could rule, as *India Today* noted at the time, in a matter of months or a matter of years.[5]

An intriguing aspect of this controversy, which contributed to the fall of the V. P. Singh government, is that the majority of Indian public opinion supported implementation of the Mandal report. The influential newsmagazine *India Today* was vehemently opposed to the report, the Commission, and the government actions—indeed, its reporting during the crisis editorialized blatantly—but its own polls showed that the Indian public was, on balance, supportive.[6] V. P. Singh's problem was that he needed more than a simple majority, he needed that majority to be composed of a stable and internally consistent coalition of interests. He undoubtedly failed to gauge the depth of hostility of high and middle caste groups to the extension of OBC reservations to central government level, a hostility that made the policy of enormous importance to them. Given this animosity, no party could afford to support his actions, even though they could not afford to condemn them too vigorously either.

The results of this process are ironic. The controversy over the Mandal report helped to bring down V. P. Singh's government, but the Supreme Court upheld the report's constitutionality in November 1992. The party in power at that point was Congress, and Prime Minister Narasimha Rao announced that he would abide by the Court's decision and begin implementation as soon as it was practicable. Neither the Court's verdict nor the Congress party's announcement of its intention to comply set off much conflict; there were a few scattered attempts at protest, but these soon fizzled out. Perhaps the opponents were tired, perhaps they were deflated by the Court's strong endorsement of the report, or perhaps their attention was focused on the religious tensions that had arisen between 1990 and 1992. These tensions centred primarily around the legitimacy of an old, decrepit and little used mosque in the north Indian town of Ayodhya, which is reputed to be the birthplace of the Hindu god Ram.

[5] Ibid.
[6] Ibid.

Mandir

Hindu–Muslim conflict is hardly a new form of violence in India. Scholars debate how much of the recent conflict is generated by the two communities and how much was brought about by British policies during the colonial period (Ludden 1996, Singh A.I. 1987). But however blame is assigned, there is no question that the differences between Hindu and Muslim interests, at least at the elite level, were thrown into sharp relief during the Independence movement, especially in the final years. The culmination of these conflicts in the horrors of the Partition of India and the creation of Pakistan, when hundreds of thousands of Hindus and Muslims were killed, sometimes in barbarous ways, is a vivid memory for Indians of both religions, and its ramifications continued after the event. For many Indian Muslims, the creation of Pakistan drastically reduced their power in India and effectively entrenched them in a dependent position. For many Hindus, the creation of Pakistan left a lingering suspicion that Indian Muslims were more attached to Pakistan than to India.

In the two decades that followed Partition, the determinedly secular approach of Nehru dominated both national and Congress party politics. The repercussions of Partition lingered, especially for Muslims: for example while language, region, and even caste were acceptable identities around which to mobilize, religion was not. As a result, disadvantaged Muslims were often unable to demand compensatory treatment along the lines obtained by other disadvantaged groups because they could not use their religious identity as a mobilizing tool. But by the same token, Hindu nationalism could not be used as a justification for mobilization and strongly nationalist Hindu groups such as the RSS were even banned for a time. The association of Mahatma Gandhi's assassin with the RSS led in large part to its ban for a number of years and cast a shadow over Hindu nationalism more generally.

In the 1950s and 1960s, the suppression of Hindu nationalist sentiment seemed unproblematic to many Indians. Partition had rendered the Muslims who remained in India leaderless and disproportionately poor, while Hindus had 'won'. In practice, symbols of Muslim rights were probably protected to a greater extent than their Hindu counterparts, with religious law being a case in point (Basu 1994, Hasan 1989). Within two decades Hindu family law had been largely secularized and Westernized, while Muslim family law remained traditional.

For a time after Nehru's death the secular orientation of the Congress party remained intact, but as the party splintered into different factions in the late 1960s each group looked for new ways to appeal to pre-existing constituencies known as 'vote banks'. When Indira Gandhi campaigned on her 1971 slogan, 'abolish poverty', she appealed to untouchables, to low castes, and to Muslims as disadvantaged groups. Nevertheless, it took time for religious appeals to become entrenched as an enduring political strategy. Electoral appeals were not made to Muslims only, but also to groups on the basis of their caste or regional identities. And while these tactics were unwelcome to middle and high caste Hindus who also made up part of the Congress vote bloc, Indira Gandhi's personal status overrode much of the increasing dissatisfaction.

After Mrs Gandhi's assassination, however, the Congress party's control of its electorate began to slip considerably. Rajiv Gandhi never commanded the personal and party loyalty accorded his mother, and a combination of growing Congress weakness and specific incidents that highlighted Congress' interest in the Muslim vote alienated Hindu voters and created opportunities for other political parties. Two factors stand out in this process. First, the decline of Congress party was accompanied by the growing deprofessionalization and corruption of the Congress party that had begun under Indira and continued under Rajiv, and which undercut electoral loyalty. Second, highly publicized decisions such as the Shah Bano case—in which Muslim law was upheld even though it clearly violated secular norms by allowing a 70-year-old Muslim wife to be abandoned by her husband without provision for alimony—and Rajiv Gandhi's subsequent support of the Muslim Women's Bill, made Congress look as if it were pandering to the Muslim elite in order to capture votes. In these circumstances, a pro-Hindu party, which would have seemed an unlikely candidate for success in the 1970s, started to look quite viable. The Rashtriya Swayamsevak Sangh had returned from its banishment much weaker, and the latest Hindu nationalist party was retooling itself to stress good government rather than explicitly Hindu goals.

The BJP is a successor to the old Jana Sangh party. Its aggressively pro-Hindu orientation has ebbed and flowed since the early 1980s. When it first reappeared on the political scene it played down its earlier, 'fundamentalist' roots and stressed its commitment to clean and effective government to distinguish itself from the Rajiv-led Congress party. However, in the aftermath of the Shah Bano case, which alienated Hindus from the Congress, and Rajiv's assassination, which weakened the electoral connection between the Congress and the Nehru family, the BJP has re-emphasized its Hindu antecedents. And as other parties, especially V. P. Singh's core party in the National Front, the Janata Dal, and the Congress, have targeted untouchables, Muslims, and low castes, the BJP has sought to unite the Hindu vote through an appeal to Hindu nationalism (Jaffrelot 1996).

It is in this political context that the demolition of the mosque at Ayodhya needs to be placed. The Congress and the Janata Dal had developed a high versus low caste strategy. The BJP challenged this approach by attempting to build a coalition whose orientation was around their common religion and which ignored the divergences within the religion. Muslims and scheduled castes were excluded, but that still left a sizable electoral bloc. The BJP leadership saw at once that the V. P. Singh decision to implement the Mandal Commission constituted a major threat to its political coalition, because reservations had always split the Hindu electorate on caste lines. In September 1990, when the Mandal riots were just beginning to subside, the party consciously settled on a strategy that would emphasize Hindu nationalist symbols and themes in order to put this fragmented coalition back together. In 1991 L. K. Advani, a BJP leader who seemed relatively secular and Western in his outlook, turned in his beautifully cut suits for native garb and inaugurated a *yatra* , or pilgrimage, from Somnath to the town of Ayodhya, in the northern state of UP, to protest the existence of the mosque on, a site which it has been argued, is god Ram's birthplace. The pilgrimage attracted thousands of spectators on the route, occasionally precipitated religious clashes, and correlated strongly with many of the locations where riots were most intense after the demolition of the mosque.

The 1992 gathering at Ayodhya was the culmination of a two-year campaign to make Hindu issues the centrepiece of the BJP's political message. By this time the BJP had succeeded in becoming a major political force in north India and was ruling in four states, including UP. The Indian Supreme Court had denied a petition to allow Hindus to demolish the mosque, but the BJP had continued to place the issue on the front burner. It organized a large rally at Ayodhya which was scheduled to take place on 6 December 1992. Responding to concerns from the national government, which was still controlled by the Congress party, both Advani and the UP government gave assurances that the meeting would be orderly and non-violent.

However, the events that transpired were exactly the opposite of what the BJP had assured they would be. After a week during which thousands of men and women chanting Hindu slogans descended on Ayodhya from every corner of India, the mosque was demolished in the space of a day by zealots wielding picks and tridents. As news of the mosque's destruction spread throughout the country, riots began to break out. Some arose in areas that were noted for previous instances of religious conflict, while others sprang up in localities that had rarely experienced communal violence in the past.

There is no doubt that the events at Ayodhya incited religious passions in Hindus and Muslims. While the English-language press deplored the demolition, many Hindus privately expressed a marked lack of regret and even outright approval. They saw Muslims as having received special privileges from political parties other than the BJP, especially from Congress, and they considered the BJP's approach as an extreme but defensible response to these abuses. At first it was difficult to gauge the consequences for the BJP. It becomes relatively clear, however, that they had condoned, through inaction, the initial efforts of some extremists who began the destruction, and this inaction had led the violence at Ayodhya to become more general.

At present the BJP's fortunes in particular and those of Hindu nationalist sentiment in general appear to be somewhat mixed. The BJP was, for the first time, asked to form a government after the 1996 elections, but no major party would join it, which gives credence to observers who argue that secular nationalism is still alive and well in India. They won spectacular electoral victories in the prosperous western Indian states of Gujarat and Maharashtra in the March 1995 state assembly elections, winning outright in the former and forming a coalition government, albiet as 'junior' partner, in the latter. The Maharashtra government, in which the BJP joined the Shiv Sena party that makes its own Hindu platform seem underpowered, is particularly frightening. At the same time, however, the BJP managed a short coalition with a low caste party in UP that did little but confirm critics' suspicions that its ideological goals were less important than its pragmatic ambitions. It cannot be denied, nonetheless, that the BJP's success has been matched by decreasing reticence on the part of Hindus to declare emphatically that India is a Hindu state, contrary to the early days of Independence when Nehru set the secular tone.

In both Mandal and Mandir, the role of politics looms large. Specific decisions taken by specific leaders in response to electoral or party demands led to policies that erupted in controversy and violence. Therefore, the institutional dimension of the conflict is not difficult to see. The collapse of Congress hegemony and the rise of authentic party competition made parties reach for policies that would solidify their constituent bases. At the same time, however, the changing perceptions of the Hindu and high and middle caste majorities are keys to understanding the increasing unpopularity of policies that might, twenty years ago, have been somewhat less problematic. The actual position of Hindus *vis-à-vis* Muslims has not worsened since party competition increased. But the inability of any party to take votes for granted (as well as some bad decisions at key moments by party leaders) meant that parties pursued strategies that appeared to make Hindus feel that Muslims were gaining power. Encouraged by BJP strategies, they struck back.

Changing attitudes towards caste politics are also dominated by the perception of threats, but the political ascendancy of middle and low castes is very real. In the early years of the Indian republic scheduled caste reservations could be accepted because they infringed so little on caste Hindus and their oppression had been so great. But the consistent extension of reservations to low castes all over India and the groups that M.N. Srinivas has referred to, made dominant castes in the south upper, and especially middle castes, feel very squeezed. In particular, middle castes see high castes retaining their favoured positions while low castes get greater government protection than before. In an increasingly competitive environment with scarce resources, this is seen as a grave threat indeed, and the eagerness with which political parties court low caste vote banks exacerbates this sense of lost ground.

The preceding discussion by focusing on how the events transpired at the national level, gives a misleading impression of homogeneity. As most observers of India are well aware, there are subnational exceptions to almost any statement made about India as a whole, and the Mandal and Mandir cases are no exception. Variations at the state level are critical for understanding both the success and failure of party strategies at the national level and the eventual form that policies can take. It is to these state-level experiences that I now turn.

INCIDENTS OF VIOLENCE ACROSS INDIAN STATES

In the larger project I examine patterns of political violence, specifically riots, across five Indian states and the former union territory (now state) of Delhi, the capital, to determine the extent to which riots which are attributed to caste and religious cleavages are in fact based on those issues. I do not wish to engage in a debate over whether these attachments are essentially deep and affective or superficial and manipulated, as the extremes of the literature posit. It seems evident that they possess aspects of both. If these issues were not intrinsically salient then participation would be much more difficult to achieve, but it is also unlikely that conflict could spread quickly without considerable prior organization. At the same time, an explanation that relies on the primordial nature of these identities cannot explain the timing or the intensity of conflict, that is why there is conflict in some places and not others, and why some events and not others trigger such conflict.

The larger project seeks to provide a way to examine and ultimately explain the variation that can be observed in the development of both sets of riots by focusing on several different areas within India. I compiled a list of states and localities that varied in two dimensions: level of violence in 1990 and 1992, and reasonable expectations of violence based on previous riots. I found several examples of areas that varied in these dimensions, some of which I had previously analysed in a project on the formulation and implementation of reservation policies in different parts of India. For the 1990 riots I selected the following states and localities for analysis: Gujarat (expected violence did not occur), Bihar (expected and occurred), Karnataka (not expected and not occurred), and the union territory of Delhi (with a different political structure than the states; not expected and occurred). I found that essentially the same states could be utilized to examine the Mandir riots as well. For 1992 the predictions were: Gujarat (expected and occurred), Bihar (expected and did not occur), Karnataka (not expected and occurred), and Delhi (expected and did not occur).

The logic behind this research design is straightforward. These states vary on a number of variables relevant to the theories discussed above, including economic and social conditions, political organization, level of violence in general, and religious and caste demographics. If we find that the variation in riots matches the variables of a particular theory, then our cases can provide support for that theory. Conversely, if the correlation fails to exist, then the theory seems unlikely to capture the factors behind the presence or absence of conflict. While I have compiled quantitative (crime, census and election data from 1970 to 1992) and qualitative (newspaper reports, interviews, local histories in selected districts of the three states) data for the larger study, here I provide an overview of events in three states—Gujarat, Bihar and Karnataka—and Delhi.

EXAMINING THE EVIDENCE

Gujarat

Although Gujarat in western India, is the birthplace of Mahatma Gandhi and one of the cradles of the non-violence movement, it has had a history of both communal (religious) and caste-based violence. Riots were usually precipitated by religious festivals and involved Hindus and Muslims in the state's largest city, Ahmedabad, and some of the secondary cities such as Baroda. But beginning in the 1980s, the state government's implementation of reservation policies for 'Other Backward Classes' (OBCs) led to the political rise of low castes and the emergence of violence over reservations, with the most sustained riots taking place in 1981 and 1985. These conflicts were sparked each time by the state government's decision to extend reservations for OBCs. To try and force the government to reverse its decision, opponents of reservations took to the streets.

It is sometimes difficult to categorize the motivations behind these riots because they undergo transformations as they develop. For example analyses of these riots by several scholars' suggest that while the initial protests were about reservations, in both 1981 and 1985 the violence was sustained by other issues, especially religious tensions (Yagnik and Bhatt 1984, Spodek 1987, Brass 1994, Kohli 1990b). One hypothesis put forward is that the sustained violence was fuelled by political entrepreneurs, who used the situation to develop political power and gain new allies. A second conjecture is that Hindu–Muslim violence that grew out of the conflict over reservations was incited by political actors who used the initial tension over reservations to rekindle dormant religious disputes.

While it may be difficult to sort out single causes for specific instances of conflict, it seems clear that Gujarat provides a good case for examining the presence or absence of the Mandal and Mandir riots. The results, however, are somewhat surprising. Gujarat erupted in 1992 after the demolition of the mosque, but it was relatively quiescent in 1990 after the Mandal policy was announced. If we had been forced to predict, we would probably have expected the opposite to occur, since the pattern has been for reservation conflicts to metamorphose into religious strife, while religious riots have become less common.

In 1990, when it became apparent that the government's decision on Mandal was leading to tension and violence, Gujaratis braced themselves for outbursts in their own state. After all, the 1985 riots, which had been triggered by a state government decision to increase reservations for OBCs had resulted in months of strife in which hundreds had been killed and millions of rupees lost as businesses and schools were closed. But there was no repeat of these incidents, and the disturbances which engulfed other parts of India remained distant. To be sure, the potential was evident; the leader of the 1985 anti-reservation riots, Shankarbhai Patel, still commanded considerable loyalty among his followers. But while Patel and other anti-reservation policy activists made initial attempts to mobilize their supporters and take to the streets, these efforts fizzled out fairly quickly.

In 1992, however, the scene in Gujarat was quite different from what it had been in 1990. The riots that swept India in the wake of the destruction at Ayodhya engulfed the state. The city of Ahmedabad, which had seen reservation riots become religious conflicts in the past, was once again shaken by communal strife as dozens were killed and the old city was put under curfew for more than a week. The city of Surat had not previously been the site of much violence, but was now one of the hardest hit, with over half the state's deaths occurring there. And perhaps most frightening, because they raised memories of Partition, were incidents in which passengers were pulled of trains and hacked to death.

How can we account for these events? The difference in the political environment appears to explain why there were no riots in 1990. In 1985, as Yagnik and Bhatt demonstrate, dissolving political coalitions created conditions in which both the reservation policies and the riots that followed were used by different political factions to strengthen their own positions and weaken their rivals. But in 1990 the government was dominated by the very groups that had previously incited conflict. Their new power could only be threatened by the political instability that inevitably accompanied violence, and so they refused to support it. Low caste groups supported Mandal, and consequently they too had no reason to agitate for its withdrawal.

The occurrence of riots in 1992 is slightly more complex. In absolute terms Hindus in Gujarat were still much more powerful than Muslims. But over the preceding decade, Hindus had come to see Muslims as receiving greater shares of political attention and sympathy. Most of this attention was symbolic rather than substantive. Nevertheless, for those Hindus who already harboured suspicions about Muslim loyalty to India after the creation of Pakistan, the political concern they seemed to attract from political parties, especially the Congress, seemed both unwarranted and unfair. The symbolic importance to Hindus of this party focus on Muslim issues becomes evident when in conversation after conversation Hindus cite the same incidents and anecdotes to describe Muslim disloyalty to India and politicians' pandering to them. None of these events or policies are substantively important, but they resonate as markers of the growing sense of resentment and injustice.

In this climate the BJP's championing of Hindutva and a Hindu India has had increasingly receptive treatment. The share of BJP supporters in Gujarat has been estimated to be as high as 25 per cent, which even if inaccurate suggests that the party's support has a very solid base. Given that Hindu nationalism is a core ideology of the party, it is difficult to be a supporter without subscribing at least in part to this view. And with the elevation of the Mandir issue, BJP loyalty and Hindu nationalism became fused with anti-Muslim sentiment. While there were many Gujarati Hindus who were unwilling to endorse the demolition of the mosque, there were equally few who were willing to be completely condemnatory. The BJP's strategy had two consequences: it has given voice to the sense of threat that some Hindus have been feeling from Muslims and it has legitimated the political expression of that attitude.

Without a sense of grievance on the part of Hindus over perceived favoritism towards Muslims, Hindu–Muslim conflict would be much more difficult to generate. But without the BJP providing a concrete point of friction between the two groups and endowing that point with political legitimacy, it is unlikely that violence would have erupted with the same scope and intensity. In addition, the representation of Muslims as the 'other' opened up space to characterize non-Muslim groups in the same way. In Surat, for example, violence was directed not only at Muslims, but also at immigrant workers from Bihar and Orissa, who were considered to have taken jobs away from native Gujaratis.

Bihar

Bihar is notorious throughout India for its poverty, its political corruption, and its violence. Therefore, when the 1990 riots over the Mandal controversy began in Bihar, few observers were surprised. The state had previously been the site of bloody riots over attempts to implement state-level reservation policies for low castes in 1977, and the opposition to Mandal had intensified since then. However, Bihar was surprisingly peaceful in 1992. What explains this variation?

Bihar is a very poor state with few economic opportunities. The lack of a vibrant private sector makes government employment almost the only game in town, and civil service positions are highly sought after. In 1977 the Janata government had attempted to implement OBC reservations at the state level, but the widespread violence that greeted this decision helped to bring down the government and made it very difficult for its successors to use reservations as a mobilizing tool to appeal to low caste voters.

By the late 1980s tension over reservations had grown even greater because while the economic situation in Bihar remained discouraging, low caste groups had become more mobilized and more demanding. The government in Bihar at the time of Mandal reflected this new political reality, with chief minister Laloo Prasad Yadav being a member of the increasingly powerful backward classes. These groups had formed an alliance with high caste Rajputs to share power. Mandal drove a wedge through this alliance because it benefited Yadavs at the expense of Rajputs. At the same time, the worst off OBCs knew that under the Mandal formula most of the reservations would go to intermediate OBCs, and so they were unenthusiastic. The chief minister's decision to wholeheartedly support the implementation of the Mandal report thus drew fire from both high castes and lower OBCs and precipitated severe, violent conflict. Yet there was little else he could do: his support base was exactly the group that Mandal targeted, and he was better off risking the break-up of his alliance with high castes than rejecting a policy that was essentially a litmus test for his core constituency. As a result heavy rioting took place throughout Bihar, but the government did not fall.

In 1992 the situation was quite different. Bihar, notable throughout India for its propensity to violent action, was one of the quietest states in the wake of the demolition of the mosque at Ayodhya. This restraint can be attributed to two factors: the relative lack of support for the BJP in Bihar and the specific actions taken by chief minister Laloo Prasad Yadav. Despite long-standing conflicts between different caste and religious groups in Bihar, the BJP has not been very successful at mobilizing a pan-Hindu coalition there. This is probably because caste is a stronger identity than religion, that is the divisions that caste has engendered in Bihar make low castes very suspicious of alliances with high castes. And in recent years, the increasing political power of middle and low caste groups has exacerbated these tensions. As a result, for many Biharis the call to Hindu nationalism sounds uncomfortably like a return to the bad old days when Brahmins and Rajputs dominated all other Hindus.

The chief minister exploited these suspicions as tensions rose by arguing to his low caste supporters that the BJP was a high caste Hindu party regardless of its inclusive rhetoric. At the same time he reached out to the Muslim elite and promised to protect them if they could keep their followers from rioting. And finally, he ordered his police forces to do everything possible to curtail any outbreaks of violence, including shooting anyone who fomented violence. Thus by a combination of political accommodation and police ruthlessness, the death toll in India's most violent state was kept at two dozen, less than a tenth of the toll in Gujarat.

The growing political power of intermediate OBCs has exacerbated tensions between these groups and those above and below them in the caste hierarchy. The high castes see their traditional power eroding and the low castes feel even more excluded. Under these conditions it is not surprising that violence had occurred over reservation policies. At the same time, however, the stakes for the ruling party differ in the two cases. Laloo Prasad Yadav's political base required him to strongly support Mandal despite the potential for conflict, and his choice proved to be astute. After Ayodhya, by contrast, he had everything to lose and nothing to gain if violence broke out. By calming Muslim fears and emphasizing caste differences within the Hindu fold, he was able to keep Muslims in the coalition and perhaps even strengthen that coalition by reminding his low caste core constituency that the BJP could not be counted on to look after its interests.

Karnataka

Karnataka has a demographic distribution that is markedly different from northern and western states. It has a tiny Brahmin population, no middle castes, and a huge low caste population. Reservations were begun in employment and education for low and scheduled castes under the Maharajah of Mysore in 1922. The deal struck then was to include all castes except Brahmins in the list of those eligible for reservations. Today 96 per cent of the population continues to be eligible for over 60 per cent of the available seats. In recent years there have been attempts to exclude the best off of the dominant castes, but this strategy creates problems for almost every political party because they all include both dominant castes and other low castes in their coalitions. In 1986, when a Backward Class Commission recommended using stricter criteria, there was an immediate outcry and organized public protests. While this response was mild by the standards of other states, it was enough to cause the government to shelve the report. In 1992 the most recent commission 'implicitly acknowledged the problems inherent in designing a reservation policy that excluded any part of the government's electoral coalition' (Parikh 1997: 177). Therefore reservations continually violate Supreme Court guidelines, but are politically manageable. It is not surprising, therefore, that when the Mandal riots swept the country, there was little reaction in Karnataka. The extension of reservations to central government positions was opposed only by a tiny minority who had long since grown used to being excluded from reservation policy politics.

Hindu–Muslim conflict is more common in Karnataka. Historically, Bangalore, Mysore, and smaller regional towns in north Karnataka have been sites of ugly communal clashes. In addition, Karnataka is one of the few southern states in which the BJP has had some success. The BJP has attempted to build a grass roots organization in the state, relying as usual on RSS organizational strength. The party reached its high water mark in 1991, when it received 20 per cent of the vote. In addition, the BJP was active in regional towns like Hubli and Bijapur, and used small outbursts of communal violence to its advantage. In Hubli, for example, it asserted its right to raise an Indian flag on Independence Day at a *maidan* (large open space) that the government had granted to Muslims. Ordinarily this might have been unproblematic, but since the occasion coincided with Id, it became a communal flashpoint. With this conflict simmering since 1991, it is not surprising that Hubli was a site of violence after the Ayodhya demolition.

Similarly, in Bangalore and Mysore there were unusually strong outbreaks of Hindu–Muslim conflict in 1992. Closer inspection revealed that much of the violence occurred in areas where the BJP had been most successful in organizing. In particular, those parts of Bangalore where the BJP had been especially active suffered heavy casualties. The importance of the BJP factor can be gathered from the fact that areas with large Muslim populations where the BJP was less well organized were much calmer.

Delhi

Until very recently Delhi was administratively considered a union territory, not a state. It is governed by a municipal corporation structure, but is also greatly influenced by the central government apparatus that dominates the city. Delhi has been the site of religious conflict at various times over the years, but caste conflict has been rare. It was all the more surprising, therefore, when Delhi became one of the focal points of the 1990 riots.

The development of conflict in Delhi appeared to follow the general pattern of student-led movements. Students began to organize spontaneously without waiting for direction from official organizations such as youth party wings, unions, and so on. For many college students who participated, it was their first act of protest. And at first, the agitations were non-violent. However, the conflict soon took a horrifying turn, as first college students and then even pre-collegiate youth began immolating themselves to protest the Mandal report.

What explains this apparently spontaneous protest and the particular forms it took? The initial negative reaction of students to the implementation of the Mandal policy arose from the perceived and perhaps real threat it presented to their futures. Not coincidentally, the most intense condemnations came from Bihari students. Given the limited availability of elite career choices in that state, any extension of reservations has ramifications for members of non-targeted groups. Mandal reserved seats for OBCs in higher education and government employment, both of which are coveted by middle class upwardly mobile Indians.

While the sense of grievance on the part of these students was real, there was also a purely political component to the protests. For reasons given previously, no political party could afford to publicly oppose V. P. Singh's decision. But both Congress and the BJP were considered to have instigated and helped sustain the Delhi riots covertly, through their youth wings. They provided expertise and organization that the students did not have, and they made it possible for the conflict to look more consensual than it probably was. Both students and the parties benefited—students because their protests were more effective and more widespread, and the parties because the students' agitation seemed less calculated and therefore more compelling than a party-led demonstration would have been.

It is more difficult to account for the wave of self-immolations. From where did this phenomenon arise? Was there just a sub-group for whom hatred of Mandal was especially intense and expressed in this way? While such an answer has some intuitive appeal, it does not hold up on closer inspection. For one thing, some of the victims were not planning to go to college or embark on government careers, in which case Mandal would have had little or no direct effect on their futures. Instead, the phenomenon appears to have been initiated for strategic reasons and then adopted as a mean of expressing alienation and disaffection for youths unconnected in any other way with the Mandal protests. The first case was by a college student who was at the forefront of the protests and was seeking a means of drawing attention to the issue. By all accounts his immolation was initially intended to be quite limited, with his friends on hand to extinguish the fire immediately. But the fire grew out of control before they could stop it and he was critically injured.

The reaction of students had a genuinely spontaneous aspect to it, and their protests were motivated by a strong sense of grievance against the government for adopting a policy that seemed to them to be blatantly unfair. But without expert political assistance it is unlikely that their protests would have been as sustained or as effective. And finally, the self-immolation of young people appears to have been due to forces quite removed from feelings about the Mandal policy.

The 1992 riots ran truer to expectations in Delhi. While there was rioting in the old city, most of this violence took place at sites that had previously experienced communal violence. Again, the presence of the national government and political parties was evident, as the BJP threatened to call general strikes and hold protests. Unlike other centres of conflict, in Delhi there was almost as much tension arising from fears of impending conflict as there was from actual violence.

These cases provide convincing evidence that the caste and religious conflicts that have frequently gripped India in the last four years have motivations that cannot be solely attributed to caste and religious feelings. The extent to which such feelings were translated into conflict and violence varied according to the political environment in which individuals participated. At the same time, however, the salience of identity cannot be ignored, as the instrumentalists are sometimes accused of doing. In almost every case discussed, the presence of feelings of relative deprivation fuelled conflict, and the violence was more intense in those areas with a history of conflict over these issues.

The riots that swept India in 1990 and 1992 have generated considerable debate over the importance of caste and religious identity in India, and they have raised fears about the future of secular democracy there. But the reality is considerably more complex. Caste and religious attitudes play an important role in fomenting conflict between groups, but the political environment is equally important in this process. The preferences of political parties and organizations, and the political context in which caste and religious identities are located, are necessary to explain the timing and intensity of the increasing violence that has engulfed India.

Returning to the theoretical frameworks described above, it seems clear that the evidence from these cases supports Brass to a greater extent than Connor. However, it would be premature to dismiss Connor's argument entirely. While there is little evidence of the deep primordial attachments and hostilities that he emphasizes, the Brass approach should be amended to include a greater sensitivity to groups' attitudes and emotions. Political interests and strategies shaped the course of the Mandal and Mandir riots, but they were successful because they struck a chord.

In the 1980s and early 1990s, Hindus began to fear that their religious identity was increasingly coming under threat, and therefore was in greater need of protection than before. This sense of threat was a result of changing electoral strategies by parties, socio-economic transformations in terms of urbanization and differential upward mobility at the local and state levels, and the introduction of new policies that emphasized religion and caste. At the same time, for their own benefits, political parties across the spectrum began to speak out about religious and caste identity, giving public voice to Hindu and high caste fears and exacerbating them. Therefore an increased sense of threat combined with parties and politicians who tapped these feelings for political gains. The mosque strategy of the BJP not only gave credence to Hindu concerns about Muslims, it used civil disobedience and ultimately violence, which increased the legitimacy of both on the public stage.

The 1990 reservation riots were what might be called the old-fashioned kind by Indian standards. Caste violence has a long history in India, and in the twentieth century it has been influenced by party politics. As in previous instances, where there was a history of caste antagonism, oppression of low castes, competition over scarce opportunities, *and* encouraging political elites, riots occurred. The 1992 riots were somewhat different. They were not most severe in those places where government supported them, but rather where the BJP was strong, whether at the state level or within a particular city, such as Surat. Bihar, where the BJP is weak, had almost no riots despite its history and its position as India's most lawless and violent state.

There is no question that caste and religious tensions are reaching critical levels in India today, and that they present a threat to secularism and democracy. But by labelling these tensions as primordial we both fail to explain them accurately and we abdicate our responsibility to uncover solutions to the problems they create. The BJP has succeeded where previous Hindu-centric parties did not in part because of the political choices made by other parties, especially the Congress. The mobilization of new political vote blocs, the loss of Congress hegemony, and the ensuing scramble for votes has made caste and religion ready and popular issues around which to mobilize voters, and politicians and lay observers have been unwilling to acknowledge the costs of these strategies. Religious and caste tensions can be reduced, but it will require a reformulation of political strategies by the so-called secular parties.

The Politics of Processions and Hindu–Muslim Riots*

CHRISTOPHE JAFFRELOT

> Why should we not be able to convert large religious festivals into political mass rallies? Would it not be possible for the political activities to in this way penetrate the most humble village?
>
> editorial of the *Kesari* in 1896, cited in Cashman 1975: 79.

The series of communal riots which broke out in the late 1980s and early 1990s amidst the Ayodhya controversy were, judged by the number of casualties, the worst since Partition. Many of these explosions of violence originated in Hindu processions. The fact that religious processions could be a vector of tension and even violence between communities is not new. In his essay on the prehistory of communalism, C. A. Bayly shows that riots occurred because of, or in the wake of, religious processions in the late eighteenth and early nineteenth centuries (Bayly 1985: 198–9). Nor is such a phenomenon peculiar to India, as Natalie Davis's account of the sixteenth–seventeenth century conflicts between French Catholics and Protestants demonstrates. According to Davis, 'Much of the religious riot is timed to ritual, and the violence seems often a curious continuation of the rite' (Davis 1987: 170); baptisms and religious services are two common occasions for riots. She underlines, however, that 'these encounters are nothing compared to the disturbances that cluster around processional life' (Davis 1987: 171).

There is no doubt that the correlation between processions and riots results from certain features of this social and ritual institution. First of all, processions are one of the procedures by which a community delimits its territory. In her study of nineteenthth century British India, Sandria Freitag convincingly argues that religious processions define the 'sacred space' of the community. This attribute was naturally conducive to violence in certain contexts, since 'when one group's space overlapped another's...these circumstances often prompted riots' (Freitag 1990: 134–5). In his study of the 1893 riots in Bombay, Jim Masselos also shows that

---

* A shorter version of this article has been published in French in Vidal, Tarabout and Meyer, 1994.

communal violence pitched in opposition groups whose territories had previously been demarcated by religious festivals (Masselos 1993:187). Second, processions also constitute potential vehicles of communal violence because of their capacity for homogenizing identities. The participants in a procession necessarily downplay the internal divisions of their community and place more value on their sense of belonging to a religious group.

Though each group of participants might remain distinct from its neighbours, they shared involvement in the same observance for the same ostensible object. Community connections must have been felt at their most tangible and concrete, fostered by these very specific influences which were physical, spatial and temporal in nature. As long as the impact of all these influences still operated, the overarching nature of group identification based on religious community appeared utterly convincing. *Threats to community values during these occasions of integrative collective activities could prompt immediate and vehement response.* (Freitag 1990:138, emphasis added.)

Freitag's analysis is drawn from the concept of *communitas* as elaborated by Victor Turner to designate circumstances, such as processions, in which a social 'structure,' necessarily heterogeneous in terms of status, constitutes an *undifferentiated whole* (Turner 1974: 237). These notions appear to be particularly applicable to the Hindu milieu, given its extreme social differentiation along caste and other lines, and the manner in which religious processions transcend such distinctions.[1] The procession, by virtue of its encompassing and homogenizing qualities, will be particularly apt to oppose itself to the 'other,' primarily the Muslims.

This approach has recently been taken by Sudhir Kakar (1996; see also 1990: 143) in a book based on the 1990 Hindu–Muslim riot in Hyderabad. One of the key concepts Kakar uses is that of 'physical group' which he defines as 'a group represented in the bodies of its members rather than in their minds, a necessary shift for a group to become an instrument of actual violence' (1996: 45). Further elaborating on this notion, he writes:

The individual is practically wrapped up in the crowd and gets continuous sensual pounding through all avenues that one's body can afford. The consequence is a blurring of the body image and of the ego, a kind of self-transcendence that is reacted to by panic or exhilaration as individuality disappears and the 'integrity', 'autonomy' and 'independence' of the ego seem to be wishful illusions and mere hypothetical constructs. (1996: 45.)

[1] This process is never entirely realized, however, because 'the Brahmin excludes from his procession Untouchables and excludes himself (or is excluded) from theirs ... Only partial totalisations occur' (Herrenschmidt 1989: 193).

According to Kakar, religious processions 'perhaps produce the most physical of all groups' (1996: 46):

Rhythms of religious ritual are particularly effective in breaking down social barriers between the participants. They produce a maximum of mutual activation of the participants and a readiness for action, often violent. This is why violence, when Muslim-initiated, often begins at the end of Friday afternoon prayers when congregants, who have turned into a congregation, stream out of the mosque into the street in a protesting procession. Processions at Muharram for the Muslims and Dusshera (and increasingly Ganesh Chaturthi) for the Hindus are almost certain recipe for violence when they are preceded by a period of tension between the communities and when a precipitating incident has just occurred.

The idea that a religious procession is an 'almost certain recipe for violence' implies that certain communal riots find their origin in crowd psychology. Such an interpretation echoes the well-known approach of Gustave Le Bon in *La Psychologie des Foules* (1895). By studying communal violence from this perspective, one tends to exaggerate the spontaneity and the autonomy of the crowd involved in rioting. Moreover, when he considers the role leaders can play in a crowd, Kakar highlights their restraining influence. According to him, 'Without the rituals which make tradition palpable and thus extend the group in time by giving assurances of continuity to the beleaguered ego, and without the permanent visibility of leaders whose presence is marked by conspicuous external insignia and who replace the benign and loving functions of the superego, religious crowds can easily turn into marauding mobs' (1990: 143).

Other students of religious riots, however, have often emphasized the role of leaders in triggering violence. Thus when writing about the riots between Catholics and Protestants, Davis highlights the role of clerics and local notables whose premeditated involvement is demonstrated by the manner in which they identified targets in advance (Davis 1987: 182, 184). She logically concludes that 'crowds do not act in the mindless way' (1987: 186). Similarly in his study of South Asia, Stanley Tambiah notes that processions often degenerate into rioting as a result of manipulation by leaders who wish to bring about ideological and political mobilization:

Processions can be precursors of violence as well as actually develop into riots, and both politicians and religious leaders, who are often both, know their histrionic value as well as their instrumental efficacy in defining and inscribing the region or territory being claimed as an ethnic group's homelands (1996: 241).

The notion of premeditation is not unknown either. The houses of the targeted 'others' are sometimes marked in advance. In fact, riots caused by processions constitute the *modus operandi* of what Paul Brass calls

' "institutionalized riot systems" in which known actors specialize in the conversion of incidents between members of different communities into "communal riots" ' (Brass 1997: 9). As we shall see, processions can easily offer such 'incidents' to these 'known actors', whom Brass defines as 'a network of persons who maintain communal, racial, and other ethnic relations in a state of tension, of readiness for riots' (1997: 126), and among whom Hindu nationalists figure quite prominently. Mass processions can entail a loss of rationality when they drift towards a status of *communitas*, but it is precisely for this reason—notably for the sociological homogenization inherent in this phenomenon—that leaders can attempt to utilize them as striking forces or potential instruments. Kakar recognizes this fact but chooses not to pursue it:

That the physical and cultural groups sometimes coincide and that it is the endeavor of those who use and manipulate symbols of cultural identity to bring the cultural group closer to the psychological state of a physical group is a subject which I will not pursue here. (Kakar 1996: 45)

By contrast, I advance the hypothesis that the instrumentalization of religious processions by ideologically minded leaders largely explains the way these rituals have become conducive to communal riots. To overlook this fact is to miss the key aspect of the complex relationship between processions and communal violence. Indeed, Kakar's interpretation based on crowd psychology itself implies the intervention of ideological factors: it presupposes that religious processions do not comprise members of more than one community although traditional Hindu processions included Muslims and vice versa. Just as Hindu groups often participated in Muharram, Muslims would perform as musicians at certain Hindu festivals. The gradual (and partial) exclusion of these 'others' is a political process which evolved over an extended period of time.

The manipulation of religious processions by political leaders is an old phenomenon. On the Hindu side, on which I focus in this chapter, it appears along with the crystallization of militant Hinduism in the late nineteenth century. It was primarily aimed at mobilizing the Hindu community against what was perceived by some Hindu leaders as the Muslim 'threat'. I shall explore this claim by looking at some of the most important examples. Tilak's re-interpretation of processions in honour of Ganesh beginning in the 1890s, represented an anti-Muslim unitarian mobilization. In the 1920s, following the Khilafat Movement, the same logic operated.

However, processions also became vehicles of violence when local power politics was at stake. The relative democratization of the political system, which followed the Government of India Act of 1919, favoured the emergence of a political class which was attentive to the sensibilities of the electorate and was concerned, therefore, with defending religious institutions such as processions. Over the years, a twofold pattern of procession-based riots has emerged, for ideological and electoral reasons. The growing importance of elections in a democratic framework and the increasingly tense relations between Hindus and Muslims from the 1970s onwards largely explain this development. In the late 1980s and early 1990s, however, the two aspects of the politics of procession were increasingly integrated: Hindu nationalist leaders used processions and riots to mobilize supporters more and more frequently, especially at the time of elections, when it was particularly useful for them to polarize the electorate along religious lines.

RELIGIOUS PROCESSIONS AND RIOTS IN BRITISH INDIA

The 'New' Hindu Processions as Anti-Muslim Mobilizations

I have attempted to show elsewhere (Jaffrelot 1996: chap. 1) that a sense of cultural vulnerability was prompted in certain Hindu circles by the activities of Christian missionaries after the 1820s. Even though they criticized them publicly, members of the Hindu elite took to imitating these *firangis* (foreigners) in order to resist them more efficiently. In order to cope with the missions' proselytizing, the Arya Samaj adapted the Christian notion of conversion through the reinterpretation of a traditional ritual of purification called *shuddhi*. In other words, some of the most militant Hindus developed a strategy of stigmatization and emulation of the so-called 'threatening others'. Starting in the late nineteenth century, and especially in the early twentieth century, at the time of the Khilafat movement, they came to regard Muslims as the main threat to Hindus. Some Hindu leaders, more or less consciously, began to imitate the congregational aspects of Muslim festivals, deliberately using processions as a means of mobilizing their community. While these aspects of communal relations have been amply examined by historians, the fact that a large number of Hindu–Muslim riots found their origin in processions must be emphasized and explored in greater depth.

The Ganesh Festival Reinterpreted

The capacity of Hindu processions to transcend certain social distinctions constituted a valuable asset for those who deplored divisions within the majority community, a weakness to which they imputed the boldness with which Muslims assaulted Hindus. Such considerations formed the background of the reinterpretation of the Ganesh festival in the late nineteenth century.

In 1893, a procession organized in Yeola in honour of Balaji was attacked by Muslims as it passed by a mosque; the Muslims had been disturbed by the music. Seeking a means to strengthen Hindu communitarian consciousness, B. G. Tilak, one of the chief Hindu traditionalist leaders of the Indian National Congress in Bombay Presidency, called upon all Hindus to desist from participating in Muharram processions. It was in this context that he decided to reinterpret Ganesh Chaturthi, the festival that is organized every year on the occasion of the birth anniversary of Ganesh (or Ganapati) (Kelkar 1967: 182). Tilak thus transferred the celebration from the private sphere to the public domain in order to mobilize and unite Hindus.[2]

This reinterpretation of the Ganesh festival is a good illustration of the strategy of stigmatization and emulation of 'threatening others' that militant Hindus adopted. Tilak, faced with the Muslim 'threat,' envisaged the incorporation into Hinduism of a practice he perceived as a strength of Islam—assembly and worship as a community of equals. Moreover, as an editorial in *Kesari*, one of Tilak's newspapers, shows, he did not conceal the mimetic dimension of this approach:[3]

Religious thoughts and devotion may be possible even in solitude, yet demonstration and *eclat* are essential to the awakening of masses. Through this nationalist appeal, the worship of Ganapati spread from the family circle to the public square. The transition is noteworthy since (despite some exceptions) Hindu religious worship is largely a matter of individual or family worship. Congregational worship as that in Christianity or Islam is not common. But nationalism provided the necessary social cement in this case. (Quoted in Jog 1979: 44–5.)

The Ganesh festival henceforth consisted of a long celebration of ten days which coincided with Muharram and concluded with a procession in

---

[2] Numerous editorials by Tilak in *Kesari* bear witness to this. For instance on 3 September 1895, he wrote: 'If Hindus, even in one province, unite to worship the same God at least for ten days every year, it is an event of no mean significance' (quoted in Karandikar 1957: 124).

[3] His lieutenant, the editor of *Kesari*, said: 'Tilak himself admitted that the arrogance of the Moslems gave rise to the idea of the festival which was obviously intended to draw all the Hindus around a central national function. Tilak often justified it by remarking that there was nothing wrong in providing a platform for all the Hindus of all high and low classes to stand together and discharge a joint national duty' (Kelkar 1967: 284).

the course of which militant chants were sung before the idol of the god was immersed.[4] The pageant held during the new Ganesh festival included choirs of young men clad in the uniform of Shivaji's soldiers; their main 'patriotic' themes were directed as much towards the British as towards the Muslims. In Poona in 1894, Tilak's supporters defied the orders of the District Magistrate not to take a procession past a mosque, and thereby precipitated a riot. The following year, the procession again ignored the route fixed by the authorities to take the same 'detour'; this time, however, 400 Muslims had stocked weapons in the mosque and were awaiting its arrival (Michael 1986: 191–2). These events mark the emergence of a particular pattern of communal rioting which has subsequently been repeated and amplified. Initially, this model was composed of three sequential elements: (i) the development of a sentiment of vulnerability among Hindu militants following an outbreak of rioting, the initiative of which was attributable to the Muslims; (ii) a unitarian reaction involving a recourse to processions which comprised only one community by excluding Muslims from the Hindu processions; (the purpose of the processions was to symbolize Hindu solidarity and, thereby, serve as instruments of political mobilization); and finally, (iii) the instigation of a riot following a change of route by the new Hindu procession, which the Muslims perceived as blatant incitement. This pattern retained several elements of earlier procession-based riots. The change of route, for instance, has long served as a provocation; it is designed to assert one's presence over a large territory or to infringe on the other community's space. Since the late nineteenth century, however, with the construction of communal identities, the processions have been reinterpreted and used as provocation by the new, ideologically-oriented leaders. Over time, the protagonists became accustomed to preparing for the rioting, notably by arming themselves; this gradually became characteristic of this pattern of violence. While this schema took shape in the late 19th century, a period marked by one of the first waves of communal violence, it became more prevalent in the 1920s during the series of riots which broke out in conjunction with the Khilafat movement.

---

[4] The first public celebration took place in Girgaum, near Bombay, under the auspices of, among other personalities, the father of Bal Thackeray, the founder of the Shiv Sena. It was there that the centenary of this institution was celebrated with great pomp in 1992 (*Sunday*, 20-6 September 1992: 47–9).

Processions and Riots in Nagpur in the Context of the Khilafat and Hindu Sangathan Movements

In the early 1920s, Hindu sentiments of vulnerability *vis-à-vis* the Muslims were reactivated by the Khilafat Movement. This Muslim mobilization degenerated into riots on several occasions, in particular on the Malabar coast, where the Mapillas (or Moplahs), Muslim tenants who had in the past led numerous peasant revolts (Dale 1975: 85–97), attacked the British administration and Namboodari landowners (some of whom had been forcibly converted).[5]

This rioting appears as the first (and among the most significant) of a series which continued up to 1927. A number of these violent acts were incited when a Hindu procession insisted on playing music while passing in front of a mosque—a practice which Muslims, especially those participating in the Khilafat Movement, did not tolerate.[6] The bloody rioting in Calcutta in 1924 and, above all, in 1926, broke out over the same issue.[7]

Muslim sensitivity to this problem was to be used by militant Hindu members of the Indian National Congress to mobilize their community. A number of them, associated with the Hindu Mahasabha, which acted as a kind of pressure group in the Congress, had viewed the Hindu–Muslim riots in the early 1920s as cause for deep concern.[8] This was true in the case of B. S. Moonje, a former lieutenant of Tilak (who died in 1920) in Nagpur.[9]

[5] The number of Hindus forcibly converted would have been between 1000 and 1500 (Wood 1987: 215; see also Hardgrave 1977: 82).

[6] In Akola, in the Central Provinces, Muslims obtained in 1924 the banning of Ganesh processions, introduced in 1907 and accompanied by music only since 1923, without doubt under the influence of the local Hindu Sabha, which militated in vain for a lifting of the prohibition by the British authorities. National Archives of India, New Delhi, Home Political Department, F-179 & KW (1926).

[7] *Indian Quarterly Register (IQR)*, 1924, vol. 2, p. 30; and Dutta (1990: 38–47). The violence in Calcutta in 1926 caused 110 deaths and left 975 wounded.

[8] See, for instance, the reaction of the Arya Samajist Lajpat Rai (Rai 1966: 173).

[9] Moonje established himself in Nagpur in 1901 as a surgeon specializing in ocular problems (*Dharmaveer Dr. B.S. Moonje Commemoration Volume*, 1972: 26). The first organization which he introduced locally was the Rashtriya Mandal, a circle of Brahmin intelligentsia founded in 1906, which supported the cause of the 'Extremists' until they were banned by the British in 1909. From 1917, Moonje was considered to be the dominant figure in the Provincial Congress Committee in the Central Provinces (Baker 1979: 54). Although a Deshastha Brahmin, he ate meat and was devoted to hunting (NMML, microfilm section, Moonje Papers, roll n. 7, letter of 30 October 1927 to Maharajah Scindia). He said of himself that he was 'perhaps Kshatriya by temperament' (*ibid.*, roll n. 11, letter of 18 May 1936 to Rajah Ichalkarang). In addition, he developed shooting clubs which were intended to actualize the *akhara* traditions

After having investigated the violence in Malabar, Moonje wrote a report in which he underlined the necessity of strengthening the Hindu community by removing caste distinctions, by restoring the Vedic practice of animal sacrifice to recapture the physical courage displayed by the Muslims and by establishing congregational forms of worship, also practised by Muslims. The latter represented one of the axes of the 'Hindu Sangathan' (literally, Union/Organization of Hindus) movement which was launched by the Hindu Mahasabha in 1922 (Prakash 1938). Moonje's strategy of simultaneous stigmatization and emulation of the Muslims had an aggressive dimension, as his tactics in Nagpur testify.

In September 1923, the small Muslim minority in Nagpur, as elsewhere, protested that Hindu processions, accompanied by music, were being taken past their mosques. On 30 October 1923, the authorities prohibited all processions. To challenge this decision, Moonje orchestrated a protest movement which rallied approximately 20,000 persons (Andersen and Damle 1987:32). Having proved his point, in November, he organized a procession which involved music and passed several mosques. Since both camps had been armed beforehand, the subsequent riot entailed heavy casualties. The following year, the local Hindu Sabha claimed the right for its participants to carry *lathis* (sticks) in the Ganesh Chaturthi procession.[10]

The Rashtriya Swayamsevak Sangh (RSS, Association of National Volunteers) was founded in 1925 in Nagpur by one of Moonje's lieutenants, K. B. Hedgewar, who shared his concern for strengthening the Hindu *vis-à-vis* the Muslims. As a veteran of the Nagpur RSS, Vasant Rao Oke, who joined the movement shortly after its formation, explains, the aggressive defence of processions occupied a major place in the RSS strategy:

In 1927 there were riots in Nagpur. Hindus were defensive. [In the past], Muslims stopped the Ganesh processions when they passed before a mosque with music. However, in 1927 Dr. Hedgewar came in front of the [Ganesh] procession, from the beginning, on the mosque road till the tank while beating the drums. Because of him all the others also came along beating the drums. They had the courage then [to follow the procession].[11]

---

during the Second World War for the massive enlisting of Hindus in the British army, because the training of his community in military techniques was more important than anti-colonial non-cooperation.

[10] Baker (1979:101) and NMML, Moonje Papers, sub-file n. 13 Letter of the General Secretary of the Hindu Sabha of Nagpur to local papers, 3 September 1924.

[11] Interview with V. R. Oke, 12 August 1992, in New Delhi.

Political leaders with Hindu militant leanings invested this procession with the purpose of strengthening the majority community *against* the Muslims. It was a matter of confirming its collective identity by establishing the Hindus' claim on urban space—aggressively, if need be—and of exploiting the mobilizing virtues of the procession to rally followers. The procession as a technique of mobilization was thus increasingly employed by political leaders, precisely *because* potential violence made it possible to assert in the streets the dominant status of the Hindu community with regard to the minorities. A further dimension to inter-communal conflict was provided by the representative politics which developed around electoral and parliamentary institutions provided under the Government of India Act of 1919. The political system then became increasingly influenced by the role of elections and factionalism.

Political Competition, Processions and Riots: The Case of the Ram Lila in Allahabad

The political framework of British India was significantly transformed in 1919 when the Montague–Chelmsford Reform extended the right to vote to new strata of the population and stimulated political competition by endowing provincial governments with new power. Party leaders bent upon appealing to the voters tended to resort to arguments drawn from the religious repertoire.

As Bayly has shown, until the turn of the century, local politics had been dominated by *rais* (notables), who typically belonged to merchant or landlord milieus, and were considered by the British to be 'natural leaders'. Their patronage of religious institutions represented an important source of social respect, and it was with these leaders that the British negotiated the route to be followed by processions. The 'patrons' used educated young men, whose learning gained them acceptance as intermediaries with the British (Bayly 1973: 349–88). However, from the time of the constitutional reform of 1909, these publicists began to emancipate themselves from the tutelage of the *rais* and to use the Indian National Congress as a vehicle for their political ambitions. This process was accentuated following the 1919 reforms (Bayly 1975: 273). Politicians of the 'publicist' type then became rivals of the *rais*, not only for elected posts, but also for more symbolic functions providing prestige such as the patronage of religious ceremonies like processions. 'Publicists' inducted into politics vied with them for this office and then endeavoured to arrogate it to themselves, sometimes for electioneering purposes (Freitag 1990: 76, 200).

In Allahabad, the political game was dominated during the 1920s by the rivalry between Motilal Nehru and Madan Mohan Malaviya, who were poised to supplant the local *rais*. The former called for a secularism of British inspiration, while the latter, who came from a very orthodox family,[12] valued the defence of Hindu interests. Since 1880, Malaviya had participated in the Hindu Samaj, an organization formed under the patronage of *rais* in reaction to the threat which Christian missionaries brought to bear on the annual Magh Mela (Bayly 1975: 106). Above all, since 1904, he had worked towards the foundation of a Benares Hindu University which finally opened in 1916 and, in his eyes, was to be the vehicle of a Hindu renaissance (Sundaram 1942: XLI). The first public clashes between Nehru and Malaviya took place in 1915–16, after the former supported a law which accorded Muslims in the United Provinces a separate system of electorates at the municipal level (Robinson 1973: 427–32). In response, Malaviya then participated in a major agitational campaign[13] and in the formation of a regional Hindu Sabha (Gordon 1975: 151). In 1923, the conflict between the two factions took a more radical turn after the Swaraj Party, newly constituted by Motilal Nehru and C. R. Das, gained a majority in the Allahabad municipal council, and won thirty-one seats in the legislative council as opposed to six by Malaviya's group. Malaviya exploited the tense relations between Hindus and Muslims to regain ascendancy at the local level.[14]

The Malaviya family, traditionally versed in the Vedas and known for its strict observance of *smarta* (traditional, orthodox) rites, enjoyed a particular prestige by virtue of which it bore responsibility for the annual Ram Lila (festival celebrating various events of Ram's life) which assumed notable eminence in Allahabad (Parmanand 1985, vol. 2: 684). After its electoral defeat at the local level, Malaviya's group[15] sought to reassert its sway over the Allahabad Hindus by offering itself as the defender of Hinduism and probably, also, exploiting communal tensions. A serious riot broke out in 1924 after members of the Ram Lila procession engaged

[12] His father was accorded the title of 'Vyas' in recognition of his knowledge of the *Bhagawata* (Chaturvedi 1972: 1).

[13] Meston Papers, Mss Eur F (IOLR) and Home Political Department, file n. 56, Deposit Fortnightly Report of UP (Sept. 1915).

[14] Studying 'the connection between political ambitions at the provincial level and the growth of communal antagonism in the localities' (Page 1982: 77), David Page underlines that in Allahabad, 'Malaviya's party exploited religious passion as a means of displacing their opponents' (Ibid., 80–1).

[15] The distinction between M.M. Malaviya and his group, more involved than himself in the riots of 1924–6, is underlined by the local British authorities (Parmanand 1985, vol. 2: 678).

in provocative behaviour. The exclusion of Muslim musicians from the procession, for which Malaviyas's followers were were probably responsible, prepared the ground for this communal flare up in which twelve were killed and hundreds injured. Whereas in the past, the presence of Muslim musicians had ensured that music was not played before mosques, on this particular occasion, the Hindu processionists organized a demonstration in front of the Jama Masjid or local Grand Mosque. The Malaviyas' strategy became clear during the 1925 Ram Lila, which occurred a few weeks prior to municipal elections: they refused to commit themselves to desisting from music when their procession passed before the Jama Masjid. The District Magistrate, who banned the Ram Lila procession, stated that he was convinced that their objective was 'to show the Nehru family that they do not rule the Allahabad Hindus' (Parmanand 1985, vol. 2: 83; Pandey 1978: 119–20). Indeed, the Malaviyas regained control of the municipal council in the subsequent elections.

In 1926, the electoral stakes were much higher, as approximately 1.3 million voters were called upon to send new representatives to the legislative council of the United Provinces. With this contest in mind, Malaviya formed a new political group within the Congress, the Congress Independent Party, and was more zealous than ever in his defence of the Ram Lila procession. The British authorities, however, made their approval of the procession dependent on a guarantee from the organizers that no music would be played when the marchers were passing a mosque. Presiding over a meeting of 10,000 people on 5 October, Malaviya indignantly retorted: 'If music is to be stopped before every one of the sixteen or seventeen mosques it will be a mourning procession, not a Ram Dal (group celebrating Ram)' (quoted in Parmanand 1985: 688). He then addressed a telegram to the British authorities which began thus:

The Hindu residents of Allahabad assembled at a public meeting, record their strong protest against the attitude of the district authorities in refusing licences even this year for the Ram Lila procession in conformity with the long-established local custom (*IQR* 1926, vol. 2: 104).

Malaviya called for a show of determination even though rioting had broken out the previous month in the centre of Allahabad on the occasion of the Dadkhando (anniversary of Krishna), causing two deaths, and the situation remained tense (*IQR* 1926, vol. 2: 81). The defence of processions at the risk of precipitating a riot appears here to be doubly connected with electoral competition. On the one hand, processions played a part in political propaganda, promoting Malaviya as the protector of 'his' community and disqualifying the adversary;[16] on the other hand, communal tensions (and even violence in 1924) dramatically divided the electorate along religious lines, in such a manner that the Hindu voter valued this particular identity and voted in conformity with it.[17] The procession assumed a key function here as a vehicle of rioting. The Allahabad *Leader*, founded by Malaviya, read:

The religious processions ... ha[ve] in recent years ... been devoted largely to the display of weapons and physical force by both Mohammedans and Hindus.... Weapons and ammunitions were purchased in large quantities by the inhabitants [of Allahabad] in September [1924]. (Quoted in Freitag 1980: 202.)

The Ram Lila procession was banned in Allahabad by the British administration during 1925–36. In 1937, however, when the first elections under the 1935 Act were held, one observes in Allahabad as in many other towns, an attempt to establish this ritual as a show of force. The Hindu Mahasabha campaigned not only for the lifting of the ban on the Ram Lila but also for the right to play music before mosques at any time (Kesavan 1990:13). Eventually, a riot occurred in 1938 after participants of the Holi procession (celebrated at the end of winter, during the Holi festival) indulged in provocative colour throwing. According to Kesavan, 'the Holi procession was evidently looking for trouble because it counted two to three hundreds lathis in it, vastly more than normal' (1990: 16).

During the colonial period, militant Hindus found in the religious processions of their community an institution which would prove most useful for their ideological project of promoting Hindu interests. It was a means of mobilizing the majority community in the face of so-called Muslim 'threats' and an ideal instrument for instigating violence with the aim of reasserting Hindu supremacy in a most radical manner. It was not difficult, amidst tensions, to transform the fervour of the procession into aggression, even to add to it an armed gang. In the 1920s, in addition to this strategy, the politics of processions acquired an electoral dimension in the framework of growing political competition. A new element of election-oriented religious populism came to exacerbate communal tensions at the local level. The pattern of procession-based riots initiated by the new Ganesh festival, with its three sequences identified above persisted, but

---

[16] In 1926, Motilal Nehru wrote to his son: 'Publicly I was denounced as an anti-Hindu and pro-Mohammedan, but privately almost every individual voter was told that I was a beef-eater in league with the Mohammedans to legalise cow-slaughter in public places at all times' (Nehru 1960).

[17] The ICP took twelve seats, as against sixteen for the Swaraj Party (which amounted to scarcely half its result in 1923).

the motivations of the political entrepreneurs orchestrating them changed. The Hindu leaders who used the processions to mobilize their community against the Muslims were no longer alone. Growing political competition and the increasingly important role of elections in determining leadership led some political leaders to consider processions and riots as resources.

TOWARDS THE ROUTINIZATION OF A PATTERN

After Independence and the riots related to Partition, communal violence became a marginal phenomenon. On average, there were fewer than 100 riots a year between 1954 and 1964 (Jaffrelot 1996: 552). The trauma of 1947 and Nehru's vigilant secularism are among the main explanations for this state of things. The frequency of communal riots began to increase in the late 1960s and again in the late 1970s. The model we have used so far remains relevant in explaining certain forms of this communal violence as suggested by isolated cases, such as the riot of Bhiwandi in 1970 and Jamshedpur in 1979. Similarly, some of the procession-based riots of the early 1980s retain features of the anti-Muslim mobilization of the 1920s. The ever-increasing politicization of processions, however, gradually introduced one significant difference: in the end, the religious element almost disappeared from them; they were converted into demonstrations of strength, pure and simple.

From Bhiwandi to Jamshedpur

In the 1970s, two instances of violence, the magnitude of which justified the appointment of commissions of inquiry, bear testimony to the persistence of the old pattern of procession-led riots but also of its progressive transformation into a more blatantly political phenomenon.

In Bhiwandi, relative communal harmony still prevailed in the early 1960s partly because of socio-economic reasons. While the textile mills, the main source of employment in the town, belonged primarily to Muslims, their suppliers and moneylenders were mainly Marwaris (Hindu merchant caste from Marwar); the working force comprised Muslims as well as Hindus. This economic interdependence made possible an arrangement whereby Hindu and Muslim representatives alternated as heads of the Municipal Council. The deterioration in relations between the two communities in the second half of the 1960s, may be attributed to the organization of processions of a political nature. Indeed, Hindu nationalist activists gave an aggressive turn to Shiv Jayanti (the festival celebrating the anniversary of Shivaji).

Tilak had initiated this festival to celebrate the birthday of Shivaji. While the purpose of the procession was not to attract devotees, the distinctive features of the religious procession had been preserved: the image of Shivaji was conveyed on a palanquin and the march was accompanied by the same musical instruments. It was a political procession in religious garb. However, since the time of Tilak, Shiv Jayanti had not been used to mobilize Hindus in the street as systematically as the Ganesh procession which appeared to be more suited to this purpose because of its religious appeal.[18] Until 1964, this festival continued to be celebrated privately in Bhiwandi by members of the RSS. That year, however, the members of this movement and of its political front, the Jana Sangh, constituted a 'Shiv Jayanti Utsav Samiti' (committee for Shiv Jayanti) which would be responsible for organizing a public commemoration of Shivaji's anniversary. Three thousand people, including many young men, marched, throwing *gulal* (a coloured powder used during Holi) and chanting provocative slogans, in particular, 'Akhand Hindusthan Zindabad' (Long live Undivided India!) and 'Hindu Dharmacha Vijay Aso' (Let the

---

[18] In 1927 the celebration of the tricentenary anniversary of Shivaji in Surat was an interesting exception. The procession of *Shiv Jayanti*, which was led by leaders of the local Hindu Sabha, was under close scrutiny by the District Magistrate who gave the following account:

> When the procession consisting of about 1000 persons and with five parties of *bhajanwallas* [singers and musicians] playing *manjiras* [cymbals] and singing religious songs, came to Parsi Sheri, it came to a halt owing to the menacing attitude of about 20 to 25 Muhammedans with *lathis* in front. A parley took place between the few Muslims and the advanced guard of the procession led by Dr Raiji [leader of the Hindu Sabha] and others. The Muslims requested that the music should stop near the mosque. It appears that either Dr Raiji definitely refused to accept such a request, or that his attitude was interpreted to mean that. The Muslims got excited. Brickbats and pieces of road metal were flourished in the air ... the City Magistrate asked the leaders of the procession to disperse the procession or to change the route as the attitude of the Muslims was threatening. It however appears that the leaders were divided over the question ... when the armed party had been lined up across the road, the constables as well as the procession advanced a little towards the mosque. This was immediately interpreted by the Muslims as the decision of the police to conduct the procession past the mosque with the protection of the armed constables, and with music playing. This was unfortunate as it led to an infuriate attack.... (Report of K.L. Panjabi, District Magistrate of Surat, to the Secretary to the Government of Bombay, Government of Bombay, Confidential Proceedings in the Political Department for the year 1927, P/Conf/73, India Office Library and Records.)

This narrative, if one accepts it as a reliable source, illustrates the key role played by Hindu nationalist leaders within processions directed against the Muslims.

Hindu religion be victorious!) (Madan nd:163–4). A similar demonstration involving 6000 people passed in front of the Grand Mosque of Nizampura. In 1966, *gulal* was thrown at a mosque in an expression of greater militancy. The 1967 procession reproduced the same scenario, but with still greater ostentation: two images of Shivaji, one showing him mounted on horseback and the other surrounded by his court, were carried in the procession (Madan nd: 166–71). The impending municipal elections were not irrelevant to this elaboration of the demonstration; furthermore, all those who took an active part therein—some of them from the newly created Shiv Sena—were elected.

In 1968, the more moderate elements in both communities went to great lengths to marginalize the radicals in the Shiv Jayanti Utsav Samiti and organized a Shiv Jayanti procession which reintegrated numerous Muslims. It was the same in 1969, but that year nineteen militant Hindus, fifteen of whom belonged to the Jana Sangh, resigned from the Shiv Jayanti Utsav Samiti to form a 'Rashtriya Utsav Mandal' (National Festival Circle) (D. P. Madan: 179). The latter took charge of the organization of the Shiv Jayanti and the procession, to which it attracted, between 3000 and 8000 villagers from the surrounding areas (out of a total of roughly 10000 participants) (Madan nd: 145). The processionists were armed with *lathis* at the end of which hung saffron flags. At one point, the procession struck up anti-Muslim slogans, compelling the Muslim participants to walk out. Then, it slowed its progress while traversing Muslim quarters, provoking retaliation in the form of stone throwing. Members of the procession immediately attacked Muslim stalls and dwellings, as well as their inhabitants. On 7 May, rioting caused 43 deaths—15 Hindus and 28 Muslims. Despite a curfew, the rioting continued the next day leaving 22 dead, 8 Hindus and 14 Muslims, and for the four following days, during which 8 Muslims were killed.

This violent outcome reveals the increasing politicization of the pattern initiated by the 'new' Ganesh festival. First, the procession used for mobilizing Hindus in the street did not have a religious character; it no longer seemed necessary to make instrumental use of the devotees' emotion as had been done earlier in celebrating the Ganesh festivals. Second, the Shiv Jayanti procession was manipulated with political and even electoral objectives in mind. The Jana Sangh, evidently eager to promote the idea that its local branch sought to defend the Hindu community, was prepared to encourage activism within the procession even at the risk of causing a riot. In fact, the Shiv Jayanti procession provided the Jana Sangh and the Shiv Sena with a vehicle for communal aggression. The testimony of one of its militants after the violence of 1970 is most revealing in this respect:

Every organisation which demands public support always tries to make a show that it has a following.... It is true that by collecting so many villagers for the Shiv Jayanti procession, the constituents of the RUM, namely, the Jana Sangh-minded and the Shiv Sena-minded leaders thereof wanted to show their strength. (Cited in Madan nd: 157–8.)

Another element of the original model, the Hindu feeling of vulnerability, which amounted to a paradoxical inferiority complex on the part of the majority community, is also to be found in the Bhiwandi riots. Shortly after the events, *Sobat*, a Marathi weekly of Hindu nationalist inspiration published in Poona, carried an article in which the following point was made:

A Hindu boy grows up hearing the news of terrible atrocities done by the Muslims. Feelings of inferiority complex are created in his mind throughout his life, directly or indirectly. The boy growing today at Ahmedabad, Baroda or Bhiwandi-Thana will not grow to be of that type. He has seen Hindus thrashing Muslims, he has seen and heard Hindus destroying the Dargahs and mosques wherein arms were kept hidden. (Cited in Madan nd: 113.)

The other large riot resulting from a Hindu procession in the 1970s took place in Jamshedpur in 1979. This iron and steel centre in Bihar, where the Muslim minority represents roughly a fifth of the population, had already experienced communal tensions in April 1978, when the Ramnavami procession deviated from the authorized route to pass through Muslim quarters. In March–April 1979, the *akhara* (gymnasium, generally attached to a temple) responsible for this annual procession asked the authorities for permission to follow the same route. The District Commissioner refused and entered into negotiations with the representatives of the two communities with the intention of reaching a compromise. But on 7 April, a leaflet was distributed in town announcing the determination of the Hindu militants to pass through Muslim quarters; this threat was carried out, forcing the police to intervene and arrest some of the activists. The RSS, which in Jamshedpur numbered between four and five hundred regular members divided into fifteen *shakhas* (literally, branches), was clearly at the root of these initiatives, acting through an organization known as the Ramnavami Akhara Samiti. Moreover, Deoras, the head of the RSS, had arrived on 1 April to preside over a meeting in Jamshedpur; in front of an audience of 2000 persons, he denounced the fact that Hindus could not freely organize processions in their own country.

The direct involvement of local Hindu nationalists was evident throughout this crisis. On 10 April, while negotiations between representatives of the two communities were being pursued at a police station in the town, the Muslims gave way so as to defuse the Hindu mobilization. This unanticipated concession perceptibly upset the plans made by the Hindu nationalists: there was now a chance that the procession would pass through the Muslim quarters without clashes. The following day, the procession had covered half its planned route when Dina Nath Pandey, a former Jana Sanghi, stopped it near a Muslim quarter; he demanded that the authorities immediately release sympathizers arrested on 7 April. This demand, which had not been made earlier in such terms, was unacceptable to the Superintendent of Police. The impasse exacerbated latent tensions, particularly as 2000 persons armed with knives suddenly joined the procession. The Muslims then began to throw stones at the marchers, precipitating a riot in the course of which militant Hindus used home-made bombs, confirming the premeditated character of the violence. Of the 108 dead, according to official estimates, 79 were Muslims. The report drawn up by the commission of inquiry concluded without circumlocution that Hindu nationalists in general, and Pandey in particular, were responsible for what had transpired.[19]

In contrast to the Bhiwandi riot, the Jamshedpur disturbance proceeded from the manipulation of a traditional religious procession. However, one again finds therein the determining role of Hindu nationalists acting *ex officio* or through an *akhara*. By and large, these two case studies bear testimony to the persistence of the politics of procession in which the psychology of crowds is less decisive than the part played by political leaders. The procession-based riots of the early 1980s recall even more precisely the communal violence of the 1920s.

Processions and Riots as Means of Transcending Caste Barriers

The early 1980s were marked by a reactivation of a feeling of vulnerability within Hindu nationalist circles. The process was probably set in motion by the conversion to Islam of about 3000 Untouchables in Tamil Nadu in 1981 (Mathew 1982: 1028–31). This presented an opportunity to transform their sense of ineffectiveness induced Hindu nationalists by caste divisions into a struggle for unity in communal conflicts with Muslims. This was the chain of reaction, similar to the Sangathan movement, that the Hindu nationalists were trying to create in the 1980s. From 1981 to 1983, the RSS and its offshoot, the Vishva Hindu Parishad (VHP), organized 'Hindu

[19] *Report of the three-member Commission of Inquiry headed by Shri Jitendra Narain, former judge, Patna High Court, to inquire into the communal disturbances that took place in April 1979, in and around Jamshedpur*, Patna, Superintendent Secretariat Press, 1981, p. 41.

Solidarity Conferences', which culminated in rioting on several occasions. Although some violent acts affected Christians,[20] most were directed towards Muslims.

In Poona, a fifteen-day campaign orchestrated by the RSS concluded on 14 February 1982 with a procession named 'Vishal Hindu Aikya Yatra' (Pilgrimage of Hindu Unity). The route of this procession had been fixed by the local authorities but was changed so as to enter a Muslim quarter where militants of the VHP trigerred off acts of violence; hotels and shops, for example, were set on fire. The procedure was repeated the following day in Sholapur when a similar procession became a show of force with cries of *'Ek dakha aur do, Pakistan tor do'* (Give another shove and shatter Pakistan) and *'Bande Mataram gana hoga nahin to Hindustan chorna hoga'* (Sing the Bande Mataram, or leave India). Shops in the Muslim area were also set on fire. The procession in Poona carried three large bells which were supposed to 'symbolically toll for the death of Untouchability'[21] and giant portraits of Ambedkar, Phule, Gandhi and Golwalkar, as well as a copy of the 'Laws of Manu' (Engineer 1984: 135). They, therefore, seem to have appeared as a means of reinforcing the cohesion of the Hindu community *against* the Muslim Other.

The 1982 riot in Meerut Muslims and Bhangis (sweepers, removers of night-soil), whom Hindu nationalist propaganda encouraged to consider themselves as descendants of Valmiki, the legendary author of the Ramayana (Engineer 1982: 1003). This participation by the Bhangis would certainly have resulted from some sort of negotiation; according to testimonies gathered by Engineer, Rs 200 were paid for each crime committed. This tactic was effective during the 1987 riots in Meerut when 'Chamars and Bhanghis joined upper-caste Hindus to loot and burn down' Muslim shops and houses in return for money and alcohol (Engineer 1988: 29). It was also employed in riots in Ahmedabad and Delhi.

In the 1980s, the policy of reservations implemented by the Gujarat government hardened social relations in Ahmedabad. In 1981, the granting of additional quotas to Untouchables for certain classes of medical colleges provoked violent acts of retaliation on the part of the upper castes. These developments favoured a rapprochement between the movements of the Untouchables and Muslims (Bose 1981: 713–16). In 1985, the announcement of an increase in quotas prompted new acts of particularly fierce violence—180 people were killed—directed first against the lower

[20] One example is Kanyakumari, a district in which the RSS had developed some hundred *shakhas* so as to better combat the influence of Christianity (Mathew 1983: 415).

[21] *Organiser,* 28 February 1982, p. 7.

castes and then the Untouchables (Patel 1985: 1175). However, VHP militants were soon dispatched to the quarters of Untouchables affected by the rioting in order to distribute funds and dissuade those who threatened to convert to Islam.[22] Above all, Ahmedabad represented a favourable context for the strategy of forging Hindu unity using violence instigated through processions.[23]

Slogans advocating caste unity were written on walls in the Untouchable quarters. The *Rath Yatra* (procession of the Hindu festival of Lord Jagannath during which his image is taken in a chariot for a bath in the sea) soon provided an occasion to actualize these appeals. The procession numbered 100,000 participants and was one and a half kilometres in length. It was intended as a show of Hindu force and the customary involvement of Untouchables in the *Rath Yatra* provided an ideal vehicle for the sentiment of *communitas*. The ten-hour procession passed through seven Muslim quarters, shouting disparaging, indeed obscene, slogans. Stones were thrown at the procession, inciting a riot which many Untouchables, who had been brought in lorries, joined.

Thus the first half of the 1980s, as earlier in the 1920s, was the setting for the reaction of militant Hindu movements to the 'Muslim threat'. The former aimed at strengthening the cohesion of the majority community, notably by means of the procession as a form of *communitas* and the violence which such shows of force, sometimes inevitably, provoked. It was a matter of creating Hindu unity (including Untouchables) against the Muslim Other. In the second half of the decade, the upsurge of rioting responded to an analogous logic but once again electoral considerations played an important part.

AN ALL-INDIA ANTI-MUSLIM, ELECTION-ORIENTED POLITICS OF PROCESSIONS?

The most important change affecting the politics of procession and rioting probably took place in the late 1980s to early 1990s, during the wave of riots induced by the Ayodhya affair. At that time, the two dimensions of the communal use of processions—anti-Muslim mobilization and election

---

[22] *India Today*, 31 May 1986, p. 35.

[23] The local VHP paper, *Vishwa Hindu Samachar*, stated in July 1985: 'All Hindus should unite against *vidharma* [those who practise another religion]. Outmoded feudal values still prevail in our villages which have kept the caste pollution intact and has thus resulted in friction within the Hindu fold.... Savarna Hindus [upper castes] should now become alert and not widen the gap between the castes and compromise with *dalit* and should not continue to remain selfish' (quoted in Engineer 1986: 1343).

oriented use of shows of strength and violence—merged to a great extent. The Hindu nationalist strategy still entailed the use of processions and riots as a means to react to so-called Muslim threats; however, communal violence was also utilized to polarize voters along communal lines. That such politics came to acquire an all-India dimension was also a new phenomenon.

From the mid-1980s, relations between Hindus and Muslims in the public sphere were dominated by the controversy site of the Ayodhya. In 1984, the VHP started an agitation campaign for the 'liberation' of a site which Hindu nationalists claimed to be Ramjanmabhoomi (the birthplace of Ram) where a mosque had been erected under the auspices Babar, founder of the Mughal dynasty (van der Veer 1987: 298). This step was intended to rally 'the Hindu nation' around a common symbol. The agitation attained its peak in 1989, when the number of riot victims reached levels unprecedented in India since 1947. The major riots occurred because of, or in the wake of, pseudo-religious processions organized by the VHP on the occasion of *Ram Shilan Puja* (literally, worship of the Ram bricks). Even though the Bharatiya Janata Party (BJP) was not at the forefront, its leaders, especially at the local level, took part in the *Ram Shilan Puja* in order to gain political advantage from these popular mobilizations before the campaign for the Lok Sabha elections which were scheduled to take place in late 1989.

The *Ram Shilan Puja* and the 1989 Elections

The VHP had announced in January 1989 that it would lay the foundation stone of a temple dedicated to Ram at the site of his birth on 9 November, that is to say, with great likelihood, in the middle of the electoral campaign. In the meantime, beginning that summer, the VHP undertook to consecrate bricks stamped with the name 'Ram' (*Ram Shila*) in as many urban quarters and villages as possible. This ceremony comprised a *puja* (Hindu ceremony of worship)—during which militants or officiating priests collected donations—and a procession carrying the 'sanctified' bricks. We find here the utilization of ritual forms borrowed from Hinduism to raise the value of a political symbol in a pre-electoral context. These processions became increasingly similar to shows of force as the election date drew closer, rapidly fostering a cycle of rioting.

The appeals surrounding the *Ram Shilan Puja* contained some strong language and invited the audience to think in terms of confrontation and aggression. A typical example is the following extract from the text contained in a standard propaganda cassette:

The blood of foreigners, of traitors who do not venerate the ancestors, will flow....
The *Ram Shila* will be the protectors of Hindu culture.... The foreign conspiracies
[an allusion to conversions allegedly financed with money from Arab countries]
will no longer succeed. The *Ram Shila* will be the death of those who call Mother
India by the name of sorceress.[24]

According to official estimates, 706 riots took place in 1989.[25] One reliable
source claims that '1,174 people died in different parts of the country in
riots that followed the passage of *Ram Shila* processions through the
states'.[26] Violence was particularly fierce in Gujarat, Rajasthan, Madhya
Pradesh, Uttar Pradesh and Bihar, but some southern states, mainly
Karnataka and, to a lesser extent, Andhra Pradesh were also affected. The
typical development of the riots is very clearly illustrated by those that
occurred in Bhagalpur which, by far the most violent, saw about 1000
people dead, of whom 900 were Muslims.[27] In October 1989, the VHP
organized *Ram Shila* processions which were to pass through the rural
parts of Bhagalpur district for a period of five days before converging on
24 October in the town. On that day, the procession—which initially
numbered from 1000 to 3000 persons,[28] but after a few kilometres swelled
to 10000 participants—struck up such slogans as '*Hindi, Hindu,
Hindusthan, Mullah bhago Pakistan*' (Hindi, Hindu, for India; Muslim
clerics must flee to Pakistan) (Bharti 1989: 2643). It was stopped by roughly
300 Muslims at the approach to the Muslim-dominated area of Tartarpur
'which was not on the route sanctioned by the official licence issued to the
procession'.[29] Marchers, among whom were VHP, BJP and RSS members
according to witnesses audited by the subsequent inquiry commission,
then started to shout slogans such as 'Long live mother Kali [a Hindu
goddess], Tartarpur will be empty' and 'We will avenge the insult inflicted
by Babar on her children' (Engineer 1996: 1729). At that stage, according
to the majority report of the inquiry commission: 'a large portion of the
majority of the processionists were peaceful and totally devotional in their
attitude and were dedicated to the task they were performing but there
were also persons who were armed and there were persons who were
shouting slogans' (cited in Engineer 1996: 1730).

---

[24] A cassette in Hindi, signed 'VHP—New Delhi' and entitled 'Ram Shila Pujan'.
[25] *Muslim India* 103, December 1991, p. 557.
[26] *Economic and Political Weekly*, 4 May 1996, p. 1055.
[27] K. Chaudhuri, 'A Commission Divided: Who Was Behind the Bhagalpur Riots?'
Frontline, 11 August 1995, p. 33.
[28] *India Week*, 3 November 1989, p. 2; *Times of India*, 4 November 1989, p. 1.
[29] *Economic and Political Weekly*, 4 May 1996, p. 1058.

The procession in this case had grown beyond expectations and the crowd was behaving in a hysterical manner. One participant described what had happened in the following terms:

There seemed to be some sort of a madness in the procession of Mahadev Singh. It was as if everyone believed that it would be a great victory for Hinduism if the procession passed through Chattarpur [sic]. The crowd seemed to be intoxicated with its power and was shouting anti-Muslim slogans with fervour.[30]

This group followed its route with police escort when a home-made bomb exploded, triggering off the riot. It lasted several days and spread to 250 villages spanning 15 of the 21 blocks of Bhagalpur district. The duration and intensity of the violence were partly the responsibility of the police who, along with BJP activists, participated in rioting and looting. A mosque was partially destroyed and residents belonging to certain student hostels figured among the victims of the first day of violence. Rioting continued more or less sporadically for over a month and spread to the rural periphery of Bhagalpur where the pattern of communal violence resembled that of the urban areas.

Thus the wave of rioting in the autumn of 1989 was provoked by militant Hindu nationalists employing processions to mobilize their community and instigate communal violence. The novel features concern the organization of pseudo-religious processions such as the *Ram Shilan Puja* the triggering of pre-electoral riots and the pan-Indian use of this strategy. First the Hindu nationalist movement has invented pseudo-religious processions from the *Ekatamata Yatra* in 1983 to the *Rath Yatra* in 1990. For the *Sangh Parivar* (the Hindu nationalist combine), it obviously makes more sense to design their own rites in order to promote their ideology; it is also easier to use them as they wish, including as vehicles of aggressive behaviour. The invention of new political rites, however, does not imply major changes in the inner logic of these processions: many of them combine people motivated by ideology with devotees following their religious emotion, as was evident in the case of the *Ram Shilan Puja* of Bhagalpur.

Second, the hypothesis that communal riots tend to polarize the electorate in such a way that the Hindu majority, feeling 'more Hindu', would be more inclined to vote for the BJP, is confirmed by the outcome. Out of eighty-eight constituencies in which the BJP won in the 1989 Lok Sabha election, forty-seven were in areas where there had been rioting during the autumn, thus confirming that 'an atmosphere of communal polarization contributed to the strength of the party's showing'

[30] Quoted in *India Week*, 3 November 1989, p. 3.

(Chiriyankandath 1992: 69). In their interviews with Paul Brass after the 1991 elections, both BJP and Janata Dal leaders in Uttar Pradesh acknowledged 'that the fomenting of violence both to win votes and to ward off defeat by arousing communal sympathy and animosities is part of the standard repertoire of contemporary political practices in north India politics' (Brass 1993: 274).

Third, for the first time, riots broke out simultaneously in all the northern states on the basis of the same issue. In the past, rioting remained more or less localized, and was most often caused by particular socio-economic rivalries and political conflicts, while the pretexts for violence would usually be specific to the place concerned. The unleashing of communal violence on a general scale was made possible by the use of the pan-Indian symbol of Ram by a Hindu nationalist network which could itself cover the entire Indian territory to organize *Ram Shilan Pujas*. These were performed in 297,705 different places.[31]

The Ayodhya movement alone, however, did not account for the riots. The nationalization of communal violence, remained incomplete. Riots probably occurred for both national as well as local reasons. In the villages around Bhagalpur which were affected by communal riots, local economic rivalries partly explain the violence, even though the *Ram Shilan Puja* was a catalyst. As Tambiah suggests, the process of nationalization needs to be complemented by an analysis in terms of 'parochialization' since local configurations (socio-ethnic and caste cleavages, the outcome of local history, etc.) give different meanings to issues such as the Ayodhya movement (Tambiah 1996: 257). Nevertheless, the nationalization of communal conflicts had probably never had such an impact relative to the local factors. There were certainly local explanations for most of the riots but they were generally less important than national explanations for communal violence.

The endeavour to 'nationalize' Hindu–Muslim antagonism by organizing processions with violent implications undoubtedly reached its height on the occasion of the *Rath Yatra* of L. K. Advani in the autumn of 1990. In fact, in the early 1990s, the politics of procession acquired a new shape, that of 'yatra politics,' which was characterized primarily by an attempt to cover larger territories.

Yatra Politics and Communal Riots:
Rath Yatra, Ram Jyoti Yatra and Asthi Kalash Yatra

For the president of the BJP, the *Rath Yatra* entailed covering 10,000 kilometres in the space of one month, from the Somnath temple in Gujarat to Ayodhya in

---

[31] *Hindu Vishwa* 25 (12), August 1990, p. 62.

Uttar Pradesh, where the VHP had announced that the construction of the temple—called *kar seva*, literally service action—would commence on 30 October 1990. Advani stood in a DCM-Toyota, decorated to replicate the model of Arjun's chariot which had appeared in the televised version of the Mahabharata broadcast from 1988 to 1990. He covered between 100 and 250 kilometres each day, halting time and again to hold meetings.

The distance travelled and the nature of the point of arrival evokes the comparison of the *Rath Yatra* with a pilgrimage, rather than with a procession. Thousands of people went to witness the passing of the *Rath Yatra* through their quarters or their villages, greeting it with marks of religious fervour and joining it as if it were a procession; women, for example, offered their *mangalsutra* (the necklace received by a woman upon marriage and meant to be worn at all times) and coconuts, or performed the *Rass Garba*, a dance characteristic of Krishna and his *gopis* (milkmaids; in the Mahabharata, they are Krishna's lovers).

Parallel to this enormous procession, the VHP organized the *Ram Jyoti Yatra* (pilgrimage of light in honour of Ram) also in preparation for the *kar seva* due to commence on 30 October: 'the *ramjyoti* (*yatra*) was conceived as a surrogate for Advani's *Rathyatra*, and was intended to help form processions wherever he personally could not go' (Chakravarti *et al.* 1992: 952). The plan of action, beginning on 29 September, involved lighting with a torch from Ayodhya other torches in Mathura and Varanasi and, from there, in all districts in order to symbolize the reawakening of the worshippers of Ram—potentially all Hindus. Once again, processions were the medium of choice; this time, the object being carried was a flame. In Karnail Ganj, a small town in the district of Gonda, adjacent to Faizabad district where Ayodhya is located, the *Ramjyoti Yatra* forcibly joined the Durga Puja (festival in honour of the Hindu goddess Durga) procession, despite efforts by the police to keep the two apart; and it was the larger procession thus formed which broke into anti-Muslim slogans when passing through sensitive parts of town. This resulted in stones and Molotov cocktails being thrown; the riot later spread to Muslim quarters. Five days of violence caused the death of forty-five persons.[32] Hindu zealots had taken advantage of the fervour of the participants in the *Durga Puja* procession to turn it against the Muslims.[33]

---

[32] *Frontline*, 27 October 1990, pp. 31–4.

[33] In Gujarat, militant Hindu nationalists had made use of the processions associated with the Ganesh festival, which occurred shortly before the *Ramjyoti Yatra*. In five towns (above all in Baroda, Anand and Surat), they organized processions with insult

The riots connected with the *Ramjyoti Yatra* confirmed the increasingly all-India character of communal violence: they occurred in many different settings, including localities in Karnataka. At Channapatna, located 70 kilometres south-west of Bangalore, the *Ramjyoti Yatra* proceeded without incident under heavy police escort. Five days later, however, the local procession commemorating the birth anniversary of Muhammad came under attack; thirteen of the seventeen victims were Muslims. In another town in Karnataka, Davangere, the *Ramjyoti Yatra*, numbering 15,000 to 20,000 participants, provoked a riot after successfully negotiating with local authorities to deviate from the original route and enter a Muslim quarter.[34]

Advani was arrested when his *Rath Yatra* entered Bihar. Hindu nationalists immediately declared a 'Bharat Bandh' which soon degenerated into rioting, notably in places through which Advani had passed—in the same way that reprisals would occur when a local procession was attacked. In two days of violence, prompted sometimes by the unwillingness of some Muslim merchants to close their shops, 42 people died in Rajasthan, 7 in Gujarat, 6 in Karnataka, 5 in West Bengal and 1 in Andhra Pradesh.

In spite of massive arrests and severe controls at the borders of Uttar Pradesh, tens of thousands of VHP militants appeared on 30 October at the mosque in Ayodhya to accomplish the announced *kar seva*. They assaulted the site twice, obliging the forces of law and order to open fire in order to repel them. This provoked anti-Muslim riots in nearly all the states; in five days the violence caused, 66 deaths in Karnataka, 63 in Gujarat, 50 in Uttar Pradesh, about 20 in Madhya Pradesh and in Bihar, and at least 10 in Andhra Pradesh.[35]

---

ing slogans directed against Muslims. Officially, the riots caused sixteen deaths (Engineer 1990: 2234–5). For more on the rioting in Baroda, where hundreds of thousands of persons took part in a procession and *gulal* was thrown at a mosque, see 'Communal Riots in Baroda,' *Economic and Political Weekly*, 24 November 1990: 2584–5.

[34] A similar phenomenon was observed in Madras, when the decision by V.P. Singh to recognize the birth anniversary of the Prophet Muhammad as a holiday provoked the anger of the militant movements of the Hindu Munnani (Hindu Front formed after the conversions of 1981). On 2 September, the Vinayak (Ganesh) Chaturthi procession slowed in front of a mosque at the time of prayer. According to official sources, the ensuing riot, in which *dalits* took part, resulted in three deaths (Geetha and Rajadurai 1990: 2122–3).

[35] These figures and orders of magnitude were provided by police reports issued to the press at the time of the events (*vide*, for example *Indian Express*, 1–5 November 1990). Either the government did not take this wave of riots into account when it drew

The *kar sevaks* who died in Ayodhya were immediately hailed as martyrs by the *Sangh Parivar*. Urns containing their ashes became the object of further processions (the *Asthi Kalash Yatra*), which travelled through several districts. These corteges no longer retained anything but the form of Hindu processions, with the object of veneration being related even more indirectly to a religious ritual than in the case of the *Ram Shilas*. Once again, however, it was a matter of arousing the fervour of *communitas* through discourses which combined songs and speeches.[36] As such, the *Asthi Kalash Yatra* served to incite new outbreaks of rioting. A procession in Agra, apparently comprising no more than fifty persons, ignored the guidelines of the local authorities and entered a Muslim quarter. Stone-throwing in those areas precipitated a new riot in which militant Hindu nationalists made use of more sophisticated arms than usual: later searches found one of the militants in possession of sixty high powered home-made bombs and 80 litres of acid.[37]

Conclusion

Scholars such as Sandria Freitag and Sudhir Kakar argue that religious processions are occasions which lend themselves to the outbreak of communal rioting because the participants have an intricate relation to space and an exceptionally strong sense of belonging to their community. However, available evidence suggests that these conditions that are necessary but not sufficient for collective aggression. In most of the cases cited in this chapter, such potential energy exploded when it was directed and even sparked off by ideologically minded leaders. Indeed, as processions have become increasingly politicized, they have become more directly correlated with riots.

The pattern of procession-based riots which emerged in the late nineteenth century with the reinterpretation of the Ganesh festival was initiated by Hindu leaders eager to unify and mobilize Hindus—allegedly in reaction to Muslim assaults. This type of ideological procession, as a vehicle for recurrent acts of violence, was to be found again in the 1920s

---

up the balance of violence for the year in the Rajya Sabha (*Muslim India*, 103, July 1991, p. 323), or it was deliberately underestimated, since it certainly could not have been ignored; the rioting in Jaipur, then, must have resulted in about 100 deaths (*Frontline*, 10 November 1990:106) and not fifty-one as officially indicated.

[36] Field observations made at Shivpuri (Madhya Pradesh), corroborated by reports published in the press.

[37] *India Today*, 15 January 1991, pp. 28–9.

in Nagpur. At that time, the democratization of the political system brought forth a small political class which, divided as it was into parties and factions, was all the more inclined to exploit the religious sentiments of the electorate. In this context, the defence of processions became an issue in electoral contests that zealots such as Malaviya promoted at the risk of inciting riots. In fact, the transformation of Hindu processions into shows of force and the triggering of communal violence were sometimes seen as a means of polarizing the voters along religious lines. Thus in the cases of pre-Independence riots that I have selected, Hindu processions were related to communal antagonism from two points of view, as anti-Muslim mobilizations and as elements of political, or even electoral, strategies. In both situations, local leaders, Hindu nationalist activists or politicians, played a crucial part. This twofold pattern persisted after Independence; more precisely, it was one of the scenarios followed by communal riots when Hindu–Muslim conflicts became virulent. Initially, the dimension of mobilization had been more significant than the electoral one. One of the main changes to come about in the late 1980s and early 1990s involved the manner in which both aspects combined, many procession-based riots serving as anti-Muslim mobilizations in the framework of electoral campaigns. Another significant change lay in the partial nationalization of the Hindu–Muslim conflict, as promoted by 'yatra politics'.

In concluding, three additional questions might be raised. Do communal riots find their origin only in *Hindu* processions? What has been the response of the state to these kinds of riots and to riots in general? Is it still relevant to study the procession-related riots in the 1990s given that, first, the 1992–3 communal violence did not follow this pattern and, second, the incidence of not only procession-based riots but all sorts of communal riots is on the wane?

The Politics of Riots and Processions

The outburst of communal violence which followed the demolition of the Babri Masjid in Ayodhya on 6 December 1992 and which was responsible for about 1250 casualties was not 'instigated' by processions: there was no need to mobilize people in that manner because Hindu–Muslim antagonism had already been sufficiently exacerbated. This does not mean that this cycle of violence was not orchestrated in a ritualized way: often in reaction to Muslim protests in the streets, Hindu nationalist activists (from the *Sangh Parivar* or the Shiv Sena) led the offensive and resorted to processional forms, using 'rituals of confrontation', to borrow a phrase coined by Marc Gaborieau (1985). Sudhir Chandra remarks that the activities of the rioters who took part in the communal violence which occurred in Surat after the demolition of the Babri Masjid were indeed 'like rituals':

The arson they indulged in then resembled the community bonfire organised on the occasion of the Holi festival. It bore an even more bizarre resemblance—one with sacrificial *yajnas*—as some of the rioters threw into the rising flames, as oblation, live human beings, including children. (Chandra 1996: 84)

In Bombay in January 1993, the Shiv Sena organized *Maha Aartis* (a grand version of the Hindu ritual of worship performed at sunset) which, in contrast with the usual *aartis* performed in the temples, assumed a mass congregational character (see chapter by Katzenstein *et al.* in this volume for a discussion of these patterns in Bombay). They were intended to compete with the Muslims' *namaz* (literally, prayers; in this context, congregational prayers held in mosques) in which the Shiv Sainiks probably saw impressive gatherings and which they criticized for spilling out from the mosque onto the streets. Once again, the stigmatization of the Other is associated with an effort to emulate him. These *Maha Aartis* prepared the ground for riots in a way similar to the processions, as suggested in the following account by Masselos:

The experiences enforced ideas of separate identity from Muslims and bonded those present to activity of antagonism.... [T]hey provided physical gathering points and emotional rallying spaces from which gangs moved out to attack Muslim targets. (Masselos, 1996: 116)

Since early 1993, the number of communal riots has steeply declined from 1601 (with 1681 people killed) in 1992 and 2292 (952 killed) in 1993 to 179 (78 killed) in 1994.[38] According to Engineer, sixty-two people died in such violence in 1995 and twenty-four in 1996 (Engineer 1995a, 1995b, 1997). This pattern clearly stems from several contradictory factors: militant Hindus believe that the Muslims have been 'taught a lesson' (to quote a phrase often heard in the *Sangh Parivar*) with the demolition of the mosque and the subsequent riots; secular activists have worked against communalism at the grass-roots level and large sectors of the population are aware of the manner in which such turmoil can affect their daily lives and businesses. In 1993, especially after the electoral defeat of the BJP in Uttar Pradesh, Madhya Pradesh and Himachal Pradesh, the Hindu nationalist organizations realized that communal violence had alienated

[38] These figures come from the Ministry of Home Affairs' Note for Consultative Committee Meeting on Communal Situation (*Muslim India* 156, December 1995, p. 558.)

many voters, especially in the rural constituencies; they began to soft-pedal the issue of Ayodhya and relinquished the idea of mobilizing Hindus against Muslims through politico-religious processions. A major reason for the declining number of riots no doubt lies in this altered strategy.

Yet this pattern of communal mobilization has not disappeared, as conditions in several south Indian cities testify. In Hyderabad and Madras, Ganesh processions still lead to riots, as in 1995 when the processionists deliberately slowed down in order to pass by mosques at the time of the Friday prayer. In Hyderabad, the riot left five people dead. In Madras, the Hindu Munnani, an RSS affiliate clearly orchestrated such provocation.[39] Indeed, riots related to Hindu processions are probably more numerous in south India today possibly because some members of the RSS combine feel the need to crystallize a militant identity within the majority community of that region—something that has already been partly accomplished in the north.

Muslim Processions and Riots

While Hindu processions are more often at the origin of a communal riot since they fit well in the Hindu nationalist strategy of ethno-religious mobilization used by the *Sangh Parivar* in the late 1980s–early 1990s, Muslim processions can also be used for similar purposes. Instances of this are available as far back as in Penderel Moon's testimony in the 1940s[40]

---

[39] *Frontline*, 6 October 1995, pp. 30–2.

[40] The testimony of this British administrator illustrates the parallel that one can establish between the situation created by Hindu processions and Muslim processions:

The last day of the festival (of Muharram)...was always an anxious one for the police. The whole city turned out to see the *taziyas*; sightseers crowded streets and the roofs of the houses. The mourners, excited by the onlookers and fortified with drugs, worked themselves up to a final pitch of fervour and frenzy, which the most trifling incident might turn to blind fury. It was during the early part of the day, when the *taziyas* were still moving about in the crowded walled city, that the danger was the greatest. At some places rival processions had to pass close to one another; the routes of several lay right through the centre of the Hindu quarter of the city. An angry word or a slight mischance might easily precipitate a riot... there was a long tale of Muharram riots.... One year the top of a large *taziya* stuck against a telegraph wire; a small bit was broken off and fell on the ground. In a few minutes a rumour spread through the crowds that a Hindu had thrown a stone at a *taziya*. Hindus and Muslims fell upon one another; hooligans set fire to buildings, houses were looted, and for several days there was an orgy of bloodshed. On another occasion, just as the *taziyas* were being lined up on the circular road, it was heard that four Muslims had been stabbed by Hindus on the other side of the city. Dropping their *taziyas* on the road, the mourners and bearers rushed back into the city to loot the Hindu shops and murder any Hindu they might meet on their way. (Moon 1944: 88) as well as in some of the most recent riots. In May 1996, for example, Calcutta was affected by a riot resulting from a controversy about the Muharram procession:[41] one of the processions bearing a *taziya* (replica of the cenotaphs of Hasan and Hussain, the grandsons of the Prophet Muhammad) insisted on passing through a Hindu area, whose inhabitants mobilized to such an extent that they pelted the procession with stones. The ensuing riot was responsible for five casualties and the army had to intervene to restore peace and order. As usual, politicians were involved: although this Muslim pocket of Calcutta has traditionally been a stronghold of the Left Front—Kalimuddin Shams, one of Jyoti Basu's ministers had been elected from there in the past—a Congressman had won the recent elections and become the champion of the local Muslims. 'The heretic voters deserved punishment', commented M. K. Dhar in *The Hindustan Times*. In addition, the local mafia was looking for an opportunity to have the local administrators transferred because they had stopped several illegal constructions and put bootleggers behind bars. Thus one finds the same ingredients in this riot originating from a Muslim procession as in those deriving from Hindu ones.

Today, Hindus and Muslims are engaged in fierce competition over processions. Since 1978 in Hyderabad, a large procession has been organized in honour of Muhammad to coincide with the Ganesh procession (Engineer 1991: 273–4). Also to be observed, on the part of the Hindus, is a multiplication of processions. In Maharashtra, sixty-eight *Rath Yatras* alone were registered in the first half of 1986, compared to four in 1985, and 944 Shivaji Jayanti celebrations were held, compared with 656 in 1985 (Rajgopal 1987: 133). What can the state do about this disturbing development?

The Role of the State

The fact that a growing number of processions serve as vehicles of communal rioting will no doubt be difficult to counter, as the authorities have inherited from the Raj the principle of non-interference in religious celebrations.[42] N. S. Saksena, a veteran of the Indian police, gives an interesting testimony in this respect:

In all Police Training Colleges the trainees are told about the main festivals of

---

[41] As usual, everybody gave different versions but three press reports converge: *The Sunday* and *The Hindustan Times*, cited in *Muslim India* 163, July 1996, pp. 323–4 and *India Today*, 15 July 1996, p. 17.

[42] Regarding British policy, see Robb (1986: 285–319).

Hindus and Muslims; then they are told as to what precautions have to be taken to maintain peace. One important aspect of this instruction is to explain to them how all religious processions have to be regulated and controlled. In order to do this job successfully it is incumbent on all Station House Officers to maintain an exhaustive record of all religious processions—the route which is customarily followed by them, the equipments, including ceremonial weapons, which are carried, the timings of the start and finish of the procession, etc. *No one ever contemplated or should contemplate banning of these processions.* (Saksena 1990: 84, emphasis added.)

There has been a general failure to ban even ideologically motivated processions for very long. Shiv Jayanti, banned in Bhiwandi subsequent to the 1970 riots, resurfaced at Kalyan (located 10 kilometres from Bhiwandi) in 1982. The participation of Bal Thackeray, head of the Shiv Sena, and of Congress ministers from Maharashtra, suggests that the party in power can expect a certain recognition from the electorate for this symbolic gesture.[43] In 1984, Shiv Jayanti was the occasion of a new riot in Bhiwandi, where the procession had once again received authorization.

The attitude of the state towards processions needs to be analysed within the broader context of its policy *vis-à-vis* communal mobilizations and conflicts at large. Today, the agencies of the government rarely remain neutral during communal riots. Ideally, the government, the administration and the police should aim only at re-establishing civil peace through repression and, possibly, negotiation; most of the time they have other things in mind. Several scenarios illustrating the role of the state, or some of its agencies, in communal riots need to be analysed.

Let us first consider the situation which arises when a political group aims to discredit the government in a particular state. It may choose to foment or exploit a communal riot to support the claim that the ruling faction (or party) is incapable of maintaining law and order. Such a chain of events developed in Madhya Pradesh in 1989, when the *Ram Shilan Puja* led to a riot in Indore. Reliable informers alleged that supporters of the head of one of the Congress factions had orchestrated the outbreak of violence in order to cause trouble for the incumbent chief minister, Motilal Vora, the head of another Congress faction. The primary objective of his opponents was to undermine his efforts to win endorsement for his followers as the party's election candidates.[44] While taking *Ram Shilas* in procession had generated a lot of communal tension, the magnitude of the 1989 riot in Indore can be partly explained by factional fights within the

---

[43] *Organiser*, 9 May 1992.
[44] *Dainik Bhaskar*, 21 October 1989.

ruling party. A similar situation arose in Hyderabad with the riot which occurred in December 1990 in the wake of the *Rath Yatra* and led to the death of 120 people. It was alleged that members of the chief minister's own party, the Congress, had instigated the rioting in order to discredit him, and he felt obliged to resign from office shortly after the disturbance.

In such cases, however, state power is involved only to the extent that it is coveted by dissidents in the ruling party. The state can of course play a part on its own. Obviously, a government may often interfere with the action of the security forces. In some cases, its main aim is to delay their intervention in order (i) to 'teach a lesson' to a community whose vote was 'misguided' in the past; (ii) to let the victims suffer in order to appear as its protector—a stratagem which the Congress is alleged to have used *vis-á-vis* the Muslims; (iii) or even to let a minority which has just been subjected to severe humiliation or even violence, take its revenge in the streets. (This would explain the duration of the 1990 Hyderabad riot, given the fact that the aggressors were primarily Muslims of the old town.) The two other scenarios can be illustrated by the riots of Meerut. In 1982 and 1987 Congress leaders, including the then chief minister, are alleged to have let the riot develop against the Muslims partly because they did not vote the right way in the previous elections (Engineer 1982: 1804; see also 1988: 22). According to some press reports, the management of communal violence was especially in evidence in Congress-ruled states before the 1989 elections. At that time, the Congress(I) used riots to appear as the saviour of the Muslims and to divide the opposition since the BJP and the Left could less easily work together in the context of communal polarization. And it was more difficult to foment riots in opposition-ruled states.[45]

Police officers often invoke political interference to explain the duration of riots, whether they have been provoked by processions or not. In early 1995, a senior police officer of Uttar Pradesh completed a study on the 'Perception of Police Neutrality during Communal Riots' at the National Police Academy of Hyderabad. From a study of ten major riots, he reached the conclusion that 'no riot can last for more than 24 hours unless the state administration wants it to continue'.[46] Yet he admitted that the prolongation of riots was not only due to the (in)action of governments; he found a deep anti-Muslim bias within the police itself. In Uttar Pradesh, such bias is on a par with the under-representation of Muslims in the state police, especially the Provincial Armed Constabulary (PAC), where they account

[45] Smita Gupta, 'Riots and Election Strategy', *The Independent*, 12 October 1989.
[46] Interview in *Communalism Combat*, February 1995.

for a mere 4 per cent, as against 17.3 per cent in the state population.[47] This imbalance partly explains why Hindu–Muslim riots have increasingly tended to pitch Muslims against the police since the late 1970s. One of the first examples of this evolution is probably to be found in the Varanasi riot of 1977 (Banerjee 1990: 56).

While the police is vulnerable to such criticism, it is not prevented, not even dissuaded from reprehensible behaviour by the State. After the 1987 Meerut riot, which can well be described as a police assault on Muslims, the only government sanction consisted of suspending the local chief of the PAC. Amnesty International then objected that such leniency would suggest that the police enjoyed complete impunity (Noorani 1987: 2140).[48] Similarly, after the beginning of the Bhagalpur riot in 1989, Rajiv Gandhi visited the place and cancelled the transfer of the local Superintendent of Police, whose anti-Muslim prejudice had publicly found expression during the events; this was obviously because the man was very popular with the Hindu community, which the Congress party could not afford to alienate before the elections.[49] Many of the worst crimes took place after that; it was as though the rioters had gained total immunity.

The capacity of the state administration, even in Bihar, to control the communal bias of the police has been illustrated by the way Laloo Prasad Yadav, as soon as he took over as chief minister in 1990, successfully threatened police officers with systematic sanctions in case of riots in their district. However, the state administration has not really penalized police officers who have been found guilty by the majority report of the inquiry commission about the Bhagalpur riot: the Inspector General of Police in Bhagalpur at the time of the riot has simply been transferred. Nonetheless, the situation in West Bengal—an obvious degeneration since the late 1980s notwithstanding—suggests that communal peace does, to a great extent, depend on political will. Despite the high proportion of Muslims (23.1 per cent in 1991), Hindu–Muslim tensions are very rare, except in districts where Bangladeshi immigration is high (such as Murshidabad) and in parts of Calcutta. Surely such an exceptional situation must be attributed to the secular policies of West Bengal's Left Front

[47] *India Today*, 31 January 1993, pp. 31–7.

[48] When he was Chief Minister of Uttar Pradesh, Mulayam Singh Yadav, true to his reputation for conspicuous concern for the Muslims, 'asked the CID to launch prosecution against 19 PAC and other police personnel who had been indicted for involvement in the killing of innocent persons in May 1987 in Meerut,' but 'nothing has happened beyond the order to the CID to prosecute the accused' (*PUCL Bulletin*, 15(8), August 1995, p. 1).

[49] On this point, see the comments of retired police officer N. S. Saxena (1990: 20).

government, which has been dominated by the CPI (M) since it attained power in June 1977.

Largely because of the state governments' attitude—whatever the party in command—the inquiry commissions investigating communal riots are rendered ineffectual. Most of the time, politicians interfere with their work; as a result, their reports tend to be delayed and, in any case, there is seldom any follow-up by the criminal justice system. After the Bhagalpur riot in 1989, the Congress government of Bihar appointed a one-man commission of inquiry whose communal bias appeared so apparent that Laloo Prasad Yadav, who became chief minister in 1990, felt compelled to add two more members to the commission; the original member remained chairman. Five years after the event, the chairman finally submitted a minority report exonerating the Hindu nationalist forces and the police officers while his colleagues produced a completely different report. Parallel to that, the judiciary, whose work is independent of that of the inquiry commission, has not achieved very much in its treatment of riots related to the Ayodhya controversy. The 142 cases filed in the court accused 1392 people of participating in incidents of violence and looting. Six years later, 87 cases against 901 accused are still pending. Of the 55 cases decided, 11 have ended in convictions in which 50 people have been punished. Of the 142 cases, 38 cases relate to murder of which 12 cases have been decided and 1 resulted in conviction. Of the 406 people accused in murder cases, the court has decided on 95 people, of whom 94 have been acquitted.[50]

[50] 'Recalling Bhagalpur—Aftermath of 1989 Riots', *Economic and Political Weekly*, 4 May 1996, p. 1057.

Community and Caste in Post-Congress Politics in Uttar Pradesh

ZOYA HASAN

Much recent writing on community conflicts has argued that the social internal conflicts confronting most Third World societies, including India, are the products of internal forces and processes that have been significantly influenced by the cultural specificities of these societies. Thus communal and ethnic conflicts which rocked India's secular and multicultural democracy in the early 1990s were attributed to primordialism and a wider alienation of culture from the state that was tearing people away from their local communities and civilization. In this interpretation of India's recent political history, communalism expresses primordial loyalties set free by the collapse of the centralized state. Religiosity is seen as a natural eruption of people's cultural identity suppressed by Nehruvian socialism. The Ayodhya movement and the destruction of the Babri Masjid could well be seen as a cultural movement and religious nationalism as an expression of cultural-cum-primordial loyalties unleashed by the crumbling of the Indian state in the 1980s.

In this chapter, I focus on the dynamics of intercommunity conflicts in Uttar Pradesh, and the links between community identity, growing political violence and the changing fortunes of the Bhartiya Janata Party (BJP). I intend to explore how an intensified sense of community came to occupy centre stage, and how the communally divisive expression it assumed in the wake of the Ayodhya and anti-Mandal movements involved the pitting not only of caste and community against one another but also of the Hindu community against the state. The decisive role in precipitating conflicts around community and caste was played by political parties. This strengthened community identities suggesting thereby that these identities were not culturally given or unchanging, rather they were sharpened in response to the changing nature of state policies and party strategies. The Ayodhya movement played a central part in this process. Attention is paid to this movement because the BJP achieved through it an appeal and support that goes much beyond its organizational and electoral strength in UP. In other words, the Ayodhya movement helped the BJP reach by a shorter route what would otherwise have been a long drawn out process of party building and mobilization to displace the Congress and non-Congress formations. More than anything else, the Ayodhya movement provided the BJP with a dominant issue of public debate, an ideological movement calculated to appeal to differing audiences in urban and rural areas. The Ayodhya movement should not be mistaken for a religious movement: its motivations were principally political and electoral. The important questions of why the Ayodhya *masjid–mandir* could become such a contentious issue in the first place, and can or why Hindu nationalism has acquired mass support and whether this can be attributed to the bankruptcy of secularism or modernity are not addressed here (Basu 1996; Davis 1996; year; Fox Freitag 1996; van der Veer 1996). Rather this chapter focuses on a crucial period of transition, between 1984 and 1991, from secular to communal politics, which the BJP deftly used to establish a major presence in UP and to realign the balance of forces in national politics by redefining some of these issues in UP.

State-level politics is crucial to the understanding of community conflicts in India, the supra-regional nature of the politics of such conflicts notwithstanding. Indeed, that the BJP's political discourse from Kashmir in the north to Karnataka and Kerala in the south is supra-regional is evident from the issues that have formed the staple of the party's campaign for power at the centre: Ayodhya, a uniform civil code, ban on cow slaughter, abolition of Article 370 of the constitution which accords special status to Kashmir. These issues, however, are mainly popular in north and west India which have a history of Hindu opposition to Muslim rule and Hindu–Muslim antagonism.[1] Unlike the states of south India, those of the north have lacked regional identities and have also not had any vibrant broad-based democratic movements that could transcend sectarian boundaries and incorporate large sections of people. Instead, recent years have witnessed the emergence of a politics centred around community identity, which finds expression in religious nationalism abstracted from region, class and caste. This identity tends to define social boundaries in terms of mutually exclusive communities and in relation to the Us–Them divide. It frequently reinforces itself by defining the Us, not in terms of the positive attributes of the community, but in opposition to the Other; thus it invariably takes the form of Hindus versus Others.

Uttar Pradesh is the great success story of Hindu nationalism and of the BJP's rapid growth. Bruce Graham argues that the Jana Sangh failed to become a significant force in UP in the 1960s because its convictions

---

[1] The BJP won the bulk of its seats, i.e. 74 per cent, from the Hindi heartland and another 20 per cent from Maharashtra and Gujarat in the 1996 elections.

were not shared by even a substantial minority of Hindus (Graham 1990: 225). But only a few decades later, the BJP won the bulk of its seats from UP in 1991 and formed the government in that state. What helped elect the BJP to power was the sustained Ramjanmabhoomi campaign to build a temple in Ayodhya; however, its success cannot be attributed solely to the Ayodhya movement. In fact, at least three other factors should be credited with creating an atmosphere of communal differentiation conducive to the growth of the BJP—the Urdu–Hindi controversy, communal violence and the upper castes opposition to the government's decision to implement the Mandal report. The elimination of Urdu, for example, played a particularly important role in the emergence of a collective Hindi–Hindu identity in contradistinction to a composite identity. Together the Hindi–Urdu controversy, Ayodhya movement and Mandal issue contributed to an overlapping consensus to preserve the interests of upper castes.

The Ayodhya movement was not conceived for UP alone, but the heart of the movement lay in UP. The Vishwa Hindu Parishad (VHP) launched its Ayodhya campaign in 1984 at a congregation on the banks of the Saryu. This was a prelude to the larger agenda of incorporating the disputed shrines issue into the main plank of communal mobilization. Neither the support nor the pressure built up by the VHP were initially remarkable, yet the Congress government, both at the centre and in UP, chose to capitulate to these pressures (Jaffrelot 1996). Gauging the Congress mood, the VHP pressed forward with its campaign which culminated in February 1986 in the unlocking of the gates of the Babri mosque in Ayodhya for the *darshan* of the Ram idols.[2]

Many new developments in civil society were responsible for energizing the communal project from the early 1970s. Backed by the urban lower middle classes, the VHP organized a series of public meetings, demonstrations and processions against conversions to Islam in Meenakshipuram in order to create Hindu unity (Gold 1991). Religious pilgrimage and processions were the foremost instruments of socio-political mobilization. UP figured prominently in these programmes (van der Veer 1994:653), which made use of a repertoire of rituals and symbols like the sacredness of the water of the Ganges to enunciate the message of Hindu

[2] A Citizens' Tribunal on Ayodhya set up by non-governmental organizations which investigated events leading to the demolition of the Babri Masjid, indicted the UP government for its complicity: 'Senior functionaries of the Government .... have suggested that the Government was instrumental in facilitating the unlocking of the Masjid.' Citizen's Tribunal on Ayodhya, *Report of the Inquiry Commission*, pp. 116–17.

unity. During these marches, VHP leaders repeated the theme of 'save Hinduism', condemned conversions, warned against concessions to Urdu and, most importantly, criticized politicians who pampered Muslim vote banks. These ideas were supported by the lower and middle classes; their receptivity was built upon both religious sentiment and socio-economic changes in UP towns triggered by Gulf remittances and the new wealth acquired by Muslims that clearly disturbed the traditional patterns of dependence between Hindu traders and Muslim artisans. The VHP cashed in on the new markers of Muslim affluence, particularly the mushrooming of mosques, to create a sense of insecurity in the majority community. Its propaganda efforts strongly underlined differences between Hindus and Muslims which became abundantly clear after the VHP launched its project to 'liberate' Ramjanmabhoomi. Fairly soon it became apparent that the VHP endeavour was to extend the conflict beyond the takeover of the disputed site to emphasize Hindu–Muslim contention on many other issues.

The important thing is that in many districts these *yatras* were welcomed.[3] In eastern UP, Congress Committees received them. Both local and state-level Congress leaders participated in the campaign even though they could not assume leadership of the movement; it was primarily to thwart increasing challenges to their social dominance from castes and classes below them that they tried to identify with the campaign. Moreover, many local Congress leaders, who were prominent members of the VHP, felt that the Congress ought to support Hindu claims precisely because of Ayodhya's religious significance; at the same time, senior Congress leaders regarded the party's involvement in the campaign as a short-term strategy that could offset the party's reduced appeal engendered by serious oppositional challenge from the mid-1980s. For the BJP, Ayodhya—and, through it, the control of UP—was essential for capturing power at the centre.

The Ayodhya dispute dramatically altered the balance of politics in UP as it quickly became the most important symbol and site of competitive struggle and mobilization. Ashok Singhal, president of the VHP, had predicted in early 1986: 'You will soon see a vertical divide within each political party—those who accept Hindu nationalism and those who don't.'[4] The home ministry acknowledged five years later, that 'no single issue so adversely affected communal harmony between Hindus and Muslims as the Ramjanmabhoomi–Babri Masjid controversy'.[5] Intercommunity

[3] *Pioneer* (Lucknow), 20 January 1986.
[4] Quoted in *India Today*, 31 October 1989.
[5] Ibid.

conflicts escalated in the wake of the Ayodhya controversy, sparking off violence in Barabanki, Varanasi, Lakhimpur Kheri, Meerut, Rampur, Moradabad, Kanpur, and Allahabad. Very quickly the conflict at Ayodhya turned into a turbulent political confrontation in which, according to official estimates, 349 people were killed in 1990.[6]

This issue generated a rift within the Congress as district leaders took advantage of the rapid change in favour of majoritarianism to marginalize Muslim leaders even in constituencies with large Muslim population. Most senior leaders chose to remain silent in the face of clear signs of Muslim alienation. Congress strategy was inspired by its own crisis of hegemony: challenges from above and below undermined its dominance; new rural elites from the backward castes pressed for more power outside the Congress party; Dalits and Muslims were disenchanted with Congress failure to address their problems and were inclined to press ahead with their agenda both within and outside the Congress. In this situation of steady decline, the party re-oriented its strategy along new lines, not through massively organized public events, demonstrations, processions, and media spectacles, but largely through back-room scheming and alliances made along communal lines in elections. Though the Congress did not have a communal platform, its pragmatic communalism upset the consensual basis of the political system that had so far functioned along lines of accommodation of minorities and collaboration amongst and coalition of groups (Frykenberg 1991: 233–52). Consequently, communal and religious organizations came to exercise a new influence on everyday life ranging from dictating what Hindu or Islamic symbols were important for unity or identity, to promoting an expanded use of Sanskritized Hindi or Persianized Urdu, to offering opinions on family planning. It was clear, however, that not all the forces seeking to commandeer religious symbols to advance their social and political goals were equally suited to that purpose. The introduction of the Ayodhya issue propelled certain ideas and compromises that both benefited and harmed the Congress as well as the BJP in widely different ways.

The VHP's mobilizational efforts met with considerable success but largely because the government was prepared to appease it (Jaffrelot 1996: 361; Datta 1993). As the 1989 general elections approached, the central government acceded to religious sentiment under pressure from VHP activists, by allowing them to lay the foundation stone of the proposed Ram temple at the disputed site. This was a major political achievement for the VHP and a critical strategic surrender on the part of the Congress.

---

[6] Figures from report in *India Today*, 15 January 1991.

The Muslim community was taken by surprise. The *shilanyas* reinforced its misgivings that the ruling party was paying only lip-service to secularism. Government action provoked strong protest from Muslim leaders who vitiated the political atmosphere by launching a strident campaign for restoration of the status quo in Ayodhya. The All India Babri Masjid Action Committee, formed at the initiative of Muslim leaders and *ulema* from UP, organized strikes and demonstrations in Lucknow and other cities of UP to exhibit their clout. Several Muslim MLAs were arrested in the course of these political protests which lasted for nearly a year. Two attempts were made to begin a march to Ayodhya. The first had to be called off because of Meerut riots which alerted Muslims to the irreparable damage done by the dispute. The second fell through when thousands of Bajrang Dal volunteers descended on Ayodhya to stop the Babri Masjid Action Committee (BMAC)-sponsored march.[7]

Congress leadership realized, rather belatedly, that the political energies released by the Ramjanmabhoomi–Babri Masjid controversy had created widespread friction and strife within the state. Central Congress leadership sought to contain the damage by shifting the issue on to legal terrain; but the conservative Brahmin Congress leaders of UP were not convinced and they used the interregnum of political uncertainty to regain their hold on state politics. This was a significant move because such leaders were largely responsible for the marginalization of secular politics, and the adoption of a majoritarian position by the Congress and its subsequent decline. They had estranged vast sections of the electorate, largely on account of their policy of denying political power to the Other Backward Classes (OBCs) and Dalits. More importantly, the Brahmin group in the UPCC resisted any attempt to oppose religious sentiment. The political moves of the UP Congress and the administrative actions of the state and central governments were inspired by these considerations. The Congress party's appropriation of the 'Ayodhya strategy' in order to reverse its weakening and waning proved disastrous, contributing to its downfall by drawing it into an uneven contest with the BJP on the issue of religious nationalism.

Two consequences of this process were a groundswell of support for political Hinduism on the one hand, and a point of no recovery for the Congress on the other. This upsurge crested during a period of marked shift in Congress strategies; the greatest beneficiary of this upsurge, however, was not the Congress but the BJP. At no point before the 1991 elections had the BJP won even a quarter of votes or seats in the UP

---

[7] Based on reports in the *Pioneer* (Lucknow), 17 May 1988.

Assembly.[8] This stands in sharp contrast to Madhya Pradesh, for example, where the BJP has maintained a high vote level of 30 per cent since 1967, which increased to 40 per cent in 1989-90. Christophe Jaffrelot's study highlights the specificity of the party-building pattern in Madhya Pradesh which has relied heavily on Rashtriya Swayamsevak Sangh (RSS) party discipline and network since the early 1950s. The BJP's impressive political expansion in UP is intricately linked to the Ayodhya movement. From the moment Ayodhya reached centre stage, the BJP's political agenda was tied to the VHP. In no other state did the VHP play such an important role in bringing about political change as it did in UP. This clearly differentiates BJP strategy in UP from that in Madhya Pradesh and Rajasthan, where the party was building upon social and political networks established by the RSS over several decades of social and political mobilization.

Disputed shrines provided the primary vehicle of mobilization in UP and gave the VHP a premier role. But the primacy of the VHP does not mean that the Ayodhya movement in UP was religious and the emotions aroused by it spontaneous or primordial. No doubt the major actors were an assortment of *sadhus* who dominate religious life in north India and the principal arena of whose activities is pilgrimage centres. But the VHP's concerns were essentially political. Its paramount objective of communalizing the polity was served by promoting an exclusive and competitive Hindu identity (Bhattacharya 1991: 124–6). The Hindu assertion was built upon a carefully constructed anger against minority appeasement which was attributed to Hindu tolerance and passivity.[9] Thus it was claimed that, by granting religious freedom to the minorities, the Indian state was bestowing 'privileges' on the Muslim minority denied to the majority community by virtue of the pseudo-secular ethos which had changed Hindu laws but not dared to change the laws of the minority community.

There is no doubt that in order to solicit the support of Muslim leaders,

---

[8] The highest vote of 21 per cent was achieved in 1967. But the party could not maintain this level in subsequent elections; the average vote (excluding 1967) was around 10 per cent.

[9] 'Yes for too long I have suffered affronts in silence.... My numbers have dwindled. As a result, my adored motherland has been torn asunder.... My temples have been desecrated, destroyed...you get my vote but you pamper those who attack me...even the Haj pilgrims are subsidised from my money.... For so long—for too long—I have been in a deep coma.... Hereafter I will sleep no more. I will not remain dumb. I will speak out.... I will not run away from the challenge.... Really speaking, I am more angry about myself than about others.' *Angry Hindu! Yes, Why Not?*, 1988. Delhi: Suruchi Prakashan.

the Congress was prepared to stall moves for reform of Muslim personal law. It was giving them concessions in the hope of recouping its electoral reverses in the by-elections of 1985–6. The principal charge levelled by Hindu communalists against the Congress government was its preferential treatment of Muslims—exemplified by the Muslim Women's (Protection of Rights on Divorce) Bill. They argued that this bill represented an unwarranted compromise with the minority community and constituted a violation of the principles and procedures of secularism and equality before law. Described by L. K. Advani as a 'watershed event',[10] the Hindu right saw in this controversy their main opportunity to occupy the political space created by the deep contention on secularism and the concomitant ideological and organizational vacuum in the high ground of Indian politics. Nationally, it gave them a remarkable opportunity to press their claims on the disputed mosque site in Ayodhya. Assuming a militant stance, the BJP sought to exploit the potential of the disputed shrines issue by assiduously combining non-parliamentary activism with parliamentary politics. This was reflected at the all-India level in the 'process of reintegration of the BJP into the RSS complex'.[11]

The Ayodhya movement had clearly struck an emotive chord among Hindus, overriding, for the moment, divisions of class and caste. Taking advantage of this sentiment, the VHP quickly stepped up its campaign, emphasizing that Muslims were insensitive to Hindu sentiments on Ayodhya. New religious networks—the Ramjanmabhoomi Mukti Yagna Samiti, Ramjanmabhoomi Trust and a Sant Sammelan—were established for this purpose. Ramanandacharya Shri Shivaramacharya, who was head of the Ramanandis of Varanasi and commanded considerable influence in Vaishnavaite circles, was made chairman.

The Ayodhya movement heightened the friction between state and society, with the latter being increasingly dominated by the RSS–VHP through its congregational politics linking the home, the street and the temple (Jaffrelot, this volume). This new style of congregational politics linked both large-scale congregations and processions in various towns of UP with the Ayodhya site and with Lucknow by bringing to public attention the ideological bonding around pivotal symbols. It was specifically built around a calendar of religious festivities demanding public participation, culminating in a procession winding through the major streets of towns. Mobilization for the Ramjanmabhoomi temple was the most spectacular aspect of congregational politics which was punctuated by a series of rituals

---

[10] *Times of India*, 14 October 1990.

[11] Ibid., p. 378.

and *yatras* invented to encompass all aspects of community. The VHP identified a list of seventy-two festivals, and attempted not only to take over the celebration of these festivals in neighbourhoods, but also to occupy the largest spaces in towns. Apart from using existing festivals, there was a sustained effort to enter everyday life, primarily through the use of temple premises as organizational centres for political activism and for the propagation of Hindu aspirations (Chakravarti *et al.* 1992). The emphasis on public celebration of festivals attempted to bring homes and communities into a Hindu orbit. In this way, the politics of Hindu nationalism was inserted into the everyday life of towns.

Two distinct phases can be discerned in the growth of this movement in UP. The first phase, dominated by the VHP's Ramshila campaign in 1989–90, involved the worshipping of bricks at the local level before dispatching them for *kar seva* to Ayodhya. This broad-based and localized effort created an upheaval in UP, often leading to violent confrontations (Chatterji 1994). Towns like Meerut, Khatauli, Gonda, Basti, Gorakhpur, Sambhal, Moradabad and Bijnor became flashpoints for religio-political activity and also for riots, arson and violence. The *Ram Shila* crusade and later the *Rath Yatra* blurred the distinctions between the BJP, VHP and RSS and this was used to build an ideological stance by combining local and national issues.

The second phase of the movement was directed mainly against the state government, in particular the communal harmony rallies organized by chief minister Mulayam Singh Yadav and police action against of the *kar sewa* ordered by him. These rallies which were the only instance of organized resistance to communalism were condemned by the BJP combine as being provocative. Consequently, these rallies were turned into an occasion for counter-actions by the Sangh combine. Both the rallies and the aborted *kar seva* on 30 October 1990 brought into the open community identity that had sprouted as a result of mobilization; its precise political characteristics were specified by opposition to police action which transformed the Ayodhya struggle into a mass movement against the prevention of *parikrama* (ritual circumambulation) and *kar seva*.[12] The widespread perception of state insensitivity to Hindu sentiments played a crucial part in the consolidation of community identity. But barring this single instance of government intervention, there is no evidence of state opposition to the movement. In fact a great deal of the Ayodhya movement's energy derived from its ability to draw upon the co-operation of the state

[12] Interview with Ashok Priyadarshi (Lucknow), District Magistrate of Lucknow during 1990–3, 7 April 1995.

machinery. The administration and security personnel were more than willing to assist *kar sevaks* whom they recognized as partners in the advancement of Hindu nationalism.

Support for the BJP swelled after the police firing, as did opposition to the Janata Dal government; neither of these reactions was, however, unconscious (Nandy *et al* . 1995). Rather they were arbitrated by the political networks of the BJP combine and the social spadework done by the VHP for over a decade. The process of communal consolidation, however, sowed seeds of disunity in the Hindu community which was divided in its support for temple construction and its long-term support for Mulayam Singh Yadav who was forging an OBC–Muslim alliance to displace the upper castes from power, and was thus committed to the protection of the mosque and the secular–plural fabric of UP.

The demonization of Mulayam Singh Yadav was connected to upper caste anxieties over the shift of power to the OBCs. The significant modification in the composition of the legislative assembly, revealed in the dramatic increase in the representation of OBCs from 5 per cent in 1980 to 30 per cent in 1993, is an indication of changing power equations in the state.[13] Until the late 1980s bureaucratic power in UP was the monopoly of upper castes and after Mandal that too was under threat. The hegemonic hold of the upper castes was gradually being broken: between 1984 and 1993 the proportion of non-upper castes in the bureaucracy increased to one-third (Varma 1993). These changes gave the BJP combine the opportunity to capitalize on the discontent of upper castes who began to shift support to the BJP to regain privileges that they were likely to lose if the OBCs were allowed to further strengthen their hold on power. Political and economic change hastened by Mandalization contributed to middle class perception of itself as disadvantaged. The BJP, the prime vehicle for the expression of these feelings, directed this anger against Muslims who became a trope for a much wider alienation from the state over reduced employment opportunities for the middle classes and induction of OBCs into the government.

The social solidarity forged in the course of the Ayodhya movement was clearly frustrated by the controversy over Mandal. The turning point was V. P. Singh's decision to implement the Mandal Commission recommendations on reservation of jobs for the OBCs in public employment. Although the Mandal announcement did not apply to government posts in states, this decision had a profound impact on UP politics. The national importance of the decision focused attention on

[13] This figure is derived from fieldwork in Lucknow in 1995 and 1996.

reservations as the principal issue in the political arena. Mulayam Singh Yadav was a strong votary of reservations. Thoroughly disillusioned by Congress politics of patronage and failure to implement the Mandal Commission recommendations, OBCs rallied in full force behind the new coalition of OBCs, Dalits and Muslims forged by Yadav to outwit the BJP. His government promulgated an ordinance providing 15 per cent reservations in government service for the OBCs in July 1989 even before the central government's reservation policy was announced.[14] The quota was increased to 27 per cent in November 1990, thus raising the total reservations to 52 per cent. This announcement, made at the height of the Ayodhya crisis, was an attempt to give precedence to caste over communitarian issues.

Caste was the cornerstone of Mulayam Singh Yadav's politics. Indeed, he was the first politician to advocate the empowerment of OBCs on the principle of exclusion of upper castes and inclusion of Muslims and Dalits in a coalition to fight the upper castes. The new OBC politics was not the routine politics of vertical mobilization but a more assertive politics of horizontal aggregation as for the first time it explicitly challenged the caste hierarchy. For its supporters, Mandal was an idea whose time had come. Its powerful temptation for the OBCs set the stage for a process of retaliatory moves by the upper caste political elite who wanted to contain the threat to their monopoly over political and bureaucratic power. Mandal made visible existing divisions and tensions in Hindu society and exposed the difficulties of forging Hindu unity. By reinforcing alternative social allegiances, Mandal was able to partially offset the pull of a composite unified Hinduism. The problem was a particularly serious one for the BJP as the party had clearly made significant inroads among the OBCs in large parts of the state and could not afford to alienate them by opposing reservations. This process has been reinforced by the significant representation given to the OBCs in the BJP which in turn has contributed to a dilution of the Brahminical core of Hindutva politics in UP. This is in contrast to Madhya Pradesh where the BJP is dominated by the upper castes. The reasons for the OBC support for the BJP are not far to seek: these groups have a much longer history of political involvement in Awadh; in addition, the BJP has always nominated a large number of OBC candidates from this region to the assembly. For instance, the BJP fielded

[14] As in the case of central government policy, the UP government's decision was criticized for being modulated by electoral considerations. It was also seen as an effort to pull the rug from under the feet of the National Front government which was planning to implement the Mandal recommendations. See 'Wooing Backward Vote', *Patriot*, 3 July 1989; 'Yadav Tries to Carve a Constituency', *Times of India*, 11 August 1990.

26 per cent OBC candidates in 1991. And yet many OBCs were not convinced of the BJP's OBC credentials largely because the ideology of Hindutva is marked by a clear upper caste bias.

The Ayodhya movement was quite strong in eastern and central UP, most notably in the districts of Basti, Gorakhpur, Gonda, Bahraich, Barabanki, Faizabad, Sitapur and Deoria, all of which are very near Ayodhya and also have large OBC populations. Indeed, among the most enthusiastic supporters of the movement in this region were the OBCs, particularly the Kurmis and Lodhs who are generally against the Yadavs. Their active participation in the Ramjanmabhoomi campaign is revealed by several surveys of the social background of participants in the campaign and in the demolition of the Babri Masjid (Chibber and Misra 1993). Vaishnav belief and practice heavily influenced the nature and pattern of social mobilization on the Ramjanmabhoomi issue (Pinch 1990: 85–6). The Ayodhya site as the birthplace of Lord Ramchandra and Ram *bhakti* (devotion) occupy a significant place in the popular imagination of the majority of Vaishnavs of eastern and central UP. Three prominent *jatis* articulating this identity are the Keoris, Kurmis, and Goalas. Critical to the process was the strong urge among them for a broader Hindu identity to cope with socio-economic transformation. Loss of power on account of land transfers from upper castes to OBCs could be mitigated by ideological appeals that drew contending groups together.

Reservations for OBCs placed the BJP in a dilemma. The party formally supported Mandal recommendations, but at the local level it encouraged upper castes to oppose it. Its most effective retaliation was a renewed attention to the liberation of the Ramjanmabhoomi temple in Ayodhya which alone could 'transcend class and caste barriers and force Hindu society to think and act as one'.[15] The decision to launch a *Rath Yatra* to Ayodhya at this juncture rapidly changed the political discourse from reservations to Hindu nationalism and Hindu unity. Fairly quickly, caste conflict turned into Hindu–Muslim polarization followed by rioting in which Muslims were the main victims. A pamphlet circulated in Khurja district of western UP exhorted the upper castes to unite against the divisive tactics of Mandal and the government's concessions to minorities which were described as singularly exploitative of the upper castes.[16] The BJP accordingly assumed an overtly anti-Mandal stand in western UP, but in eastern UP where Mandal was popular it skirted the issue by focusing on

[15] *Organiser*, 11 October 1990.

[16] Chowdhary Ameer Singh, *Sarkar ke Suvarno ke virudh Shadyantra, Suvarna Hit Rakshak Dal*, September 1990.

the Ayodhya campaign. It succeeded in weaning away Kurmis and Lodhs
in central and eastern UP and secured their support by increasing their
presence in the party. As part of this strategy, it gave greater prominence
to Kurmi and Lodh leaders, most conspicuously Vinay Katiyar from
Faizabad and Kalyan Singh from Aligarh. The vertical divisions between
Yadavs, and Kurmis and Lodhs helped the BJP to stave off the challenge
posed by the cohesion of backward castes under the Mandal platform.

Both the Ramjanmabhoomi and anti-Mandal mobilization spotlighted
their attention on dislodging the OBC-oriented Janata Dal government.
This master goal was achieved by turning the anti-reservation agitation in
a communal direction by emphasizing the anti-national role of caste politics.
Underscoring Hindu–Muslim conflict was significant in this context
because it took the heat off the Mandal issue by removing it from the
intra-community to the intercommunity context. Soon caste conflict turned
into Hindu–Muslim polarization and rioting in which Muslims were the
main victims. Communal violence promoted a Hindu militancy that
encouraged an *en bloc* shift of upper castes to the BJP. Political violence
and ideology was thus effectively used by the powerful to define and limit
the social boundaries of state power to upper castes. The anti-Mandal and
Ramjanmabhoomi schemes were conflated in the service of an implicit
class strategy of domination.[17]

A significant feature of escalating communal violence in UP was the
incorporation within its ambit of hitherto peaceful towns and surrounding
rural areas. As the intensity of communal politics increased, there was a
marked increase in communal violence and rioting. The state witnessed
several months of confusion and disorder from August 1990 to June 1991
marked by communal frenzy and 169 deaths from 7 to 20 December in
1990.[18] From November 1990 onwards the greater proportion of violence
was concentrated in UP—34 towns in UP and another 36 across the country
were under curfew (Chakravarti *et al* . 1992). There was respite from
violence only after the collapse of the V. P. Singh government at the centre.
Mulayam Singh Yadav survived as chief minister only because he decided
to support the new prime minister Chandrasekhar who had split from the
Janata Dal. The proposal to begin a second round of *kar seva* in Ayodhya
on 7 December, after the fall of the Janata Dal government saw another
round of widespread violence. Western UP saw the area of maximum
incidence both in areas with long histories of communal violence as well

[17] For a discussion of a very similar situation and agitation in Gujarat see Kohli
(1990b: chap. 9). Also see Wood (1984).

[18] 'Anatomy of a Carnage', *India Today*, 15 January 1991.

as those without (Engineer 1991). Another striking feature was the outbreak of riots simultaneously in different cities and towns throughout UP. Many cities like Etah and Agra had no history of violence since Independence. Although not BJP strongholds, these were areas where processions and marches were taken out and became a form of Hindu assertion through their use of militant slogans and gestures. Riots created a deep wedge between communities and invented a political constituency for the BJP in Khurja and Bijnor, for instance, where the BJP had very little support before the riots of 1990. By comparison central and eastern UP did not experience the same scale of rioting; they witnessed a lot of VHP activity instead.

Communal militancy weaned away the upper castes from the Congress and sliced off the OBCs from the Janata Dal in central UP. The BJP gained fresh support from Brahmins and expanded its following among Ahirs, Kurmis and Lodhs of eastern UP. It took the BJP and the upper castes who were veering towards it only a short time to appreciate that the Mandal recommendations could rewrite the rules of electoral politics in a way that would displace the upper castes from positions of dominance. Besides the capacity of the established elite to command the support of the lower strata had gradually diminished throughout the 1970s and 1980s. The upper castes could no longer mobilize majorities in the way they had done in the past, and especially not when confronted with the mass mobilization and assertions of the hitherto marginalized majority.

The Ayodhya movement claimed that it could transcend a variety of differences; it could unite popular and high culture, reach out to urban and rural people alike, and could potentially unite the backward and lower castes with the upper castes. But this Hindu homogenization project was confronted and contested by backward caste–Dalit politics in UP which perceived in it an effort to counter lower caste aspirations. Indeed, the strident efforts to forge an inclusive national/Hindu identity was a clear attempt to bring the OBCs and Dalits back under Brahminical domination since the crucial ideological and organizational initiatives in the reconstruction of the polity have come from hitherto marginalized classes and castes. Thus the main challenge to the BJP's politics of Hindus versus Others has come from the cross-cutting political strategy of the Samajwadi Party (SP) and the Bahujan Samaj Party (BSP). The significant gains made by the SP–BSP alliance in the 1993 assembly elections de-emphasized communal mobilization and at the same time signalled the coming of age of backward caste politics in the changed context of competitive politics. The installation in February 1997 of a BJP–BSP coalition government based on a novel system of power sharing that gives BSP and BJP an equal number of cabinet positions even though the BJP is the much larger of the two parties is emblematic of the new leverage exercised by lower castes.

The rise to power of the OBCs accompanied simultaneously by an autonomous mobilization of Dalits constitutes the biggest impediment to the ideological and political expansion of Hindu nationalism. This socio-political churning partly accounts for the inability of the BJP to overpower the caste politics of the OBCs and Dalits. The BJP combine has to contend with the variance between notions of a permanent majority defined solely on the basis of the census definition of a Hindu and the democratic determination of electoral majorities (Sarkar 1996: 272). The assertions of lower castes have certainly divided Hindu society but this has not weakened Hindu nationalism. Lower caste politics has succeeded in putting its own political parties in government; however, their rise to power did not mean that the battle against communalism in UP has been decisively won.

Parties, Political Identities and the Absence of Mass Political Violence in South India

ARUN R. SWAMY

The southern states of India have in recent years acquired a reputation for resisting a general trend towards increasing political violence seen in the country at large. It is not always easy to see why: riots over the redrawing of state boundaries in Andhra Pradesh and language policy in Tamil Nadu were among the earliest instances of large-scale political violence in independent India, while the last decade has witnessed conflicts between castes in Tamil Nadu, between religious communities in Andhra Pradesh and Karnataka, and over the sharing of river waters between Karnataka and Tamil Nadu. If the south appears exceptional, it is because of the absence of *mass* political violence—large-scale rioting, *occurring simultaneously in many urban centres.* Since at least two states in the south lead the country in literacy and transport infrastructure, attributes that should lend themselves to coordinated political violence, this is surprising.

Recent political events and scholarly treatment suggest two explanations. First, the south's distinctive cultural traits and political history might make the region less receptive to issues that have caused friction in the north—conflicts over the Babri mosque in Ayodhya, and central government reservations ('affirmative action quotas') for other backward classes (OBCs). While there are reasons to believe this is the case, southern exceptionalism does not explain why the issues that do cause violent conflict seldom spread. Second, the south might be better endowed with institutions capable of coping with conflict. The second explanation, however, leaves some anomalies: the south's state governments have not been noticeably less prone to corruption or assaults on legal institutions than other states, while its political parties have, if anything, exemplified the 'populist' tendencies blamed for 'deinstitutionalization'.

There is, however, a different aspect of party competition which might provide an answer. This relies on treating party *systems*—the ways in which parties define the ideological space of a polity and incorporate the electorate—as institutions in their own right. This view has a long pedigree in political science, but has tended to be neglected for a more formal understanding of institutions that focuses on organizational integrity. The connection between party systems and political violence is necessarily indirect. Any contribution this chapter can make to an understanding of political violence is dependent on the validity of certain other hypotheses about the causes of certain kinds of mass political violence in India.

There are two routes that can be imagined, both of which assume that institutionalization through a party system is enhanced by having competing parties with the prospect of their alternating in power. One route focuses on the behaviour of voters. By providing newly mobilized voters with an identity and an electoral vehicle for their aspirations, a party system might prove a more flexible way of incorporating new waves of voters as what Deutsch (1961) has termed 'social mobilization' progresses. The second route focuses on the behaviour of parties. Specifically, the possibility of alternating in power might affect the conditions under which parties might turn to violence; its relevance is contingent upon the accuracy of the claim made by others that parties are indeed responsible for instigating and coordinating certain kinds of violence. My hypothesis is that parties with a significant political base will do this only when their prospects for victory at elections appear to be bleak.

Both arguments suggest that a competitive party system is more stable than a one-party dominant one, provided parties can both build stable coalitions and have a realistic chance of winning. Given India's first-past-the-post electoral system, this is likely to require a two-party system, at least for each state. This in turn depends on whether there is 'space' for two parties to build stable near-majoritarian coalitions.

It is here that conventional explanations about the pattern that electoral competition should follow becomes a handicap. Scholars have typically bemoaned the absence of any logic to the contest between parties in India. Parties have been viewed as ideologically incoherent collections of personal factions, vehicles for a single leader or, at best, coalitions of specific caste groups without a coherent programme. I will argue below that these characterizations have missed an important regularity in Indian party systems, one that is exemplified by the contest between the Dravida Munnetra Kazhagam (DMK) and Anna Dravida Munnetra Kazhagam (ADMK) in Tamil Nadu but is now also emerging in the rest of India. This is a contest between parties espousing two distinct rhetorical styles, with associated differences in electoral coalition and programme, styles that I term *empowerment populism* and *protection populism*.[1]

[1] I first developed this distinction in 1988 for a research proposal approved by the American Institute of Indian Studies and the Government of India. At that time, I termed 'empowerment populism' 'privilege populism'. Similar labels—'assertive' and 'paternalistic' populism—have since been employed by Subramanian (1993).

I use the term *empowerment populism* to refer to a style of political rhetoric that describes society as a conflict between 'the common people' and a narrow elite, demanding greater privileges for out-groups on behalf of 'the people'. By *protection populism*, on the other hand, I mean a rhetoric that emphasizes themes of vulnerability, offering to protect 'the weak' and 'truly needy'. Although they often coexist in the same movement or rhetoric, there is a tension between the themes of empowerment and protection as visions of social justice that allows them to be championed by rival parties under competitive conditions. This can occur either as an original movement splits, or when defensive elites use 'sandwich tactics' to outflank insurgent counter-elites by forming a coalition with the most disadvantaged.

The potential for 'sandwich coalitions' always exists because of vertical differentiation within the constituencies claimed by the rising social groups who typically articulate themes of empowerment populism, and because those with the greatest uncertainty and deprivation are likely to be more responsive to such measures as social insurance and the provision of basic needs. Sandwich tactics can be pursued in one of two ways: by seeking to *target* benefits toward 'the truly needy' or by *substituting* measures that provide for the needy in place of those which claim to shift power downward.

This model of Indian party competition as revolving around a centrist 'populist' axis with empowerment and protection as the poles draws and builds upon a considerable body of literature on the electoral bases of Indian parties. It fits descriptions of the Congress coalition in UP as consisting of upper castes, Dalits and minorities, as opposed to the middle and 'backward' castes mobilized by the Lok Dal, the socialists and the Janata Dal, as well as the more general thesis that Congress draws from the very poor (e.g. Brass 1994). As we shall see, it fits the contest between the ADMK and the DMK in Tamil Nadu, despite their very different histories.

I see the competing populisms model as an improvement on existing formulations, however, for a number of reasons. It is difficult, in the first place, to make much sense of parties' electoral coalitions if one treats them as built out of determinate social groups. These building block models suggest a far sharper difference in voting behaviour than can actually be sustained and have difficulty accommodating variations in voting patterns over space and time. More importantly, they are unable even to address one of the most important predictors of voting behaviour in India—gender.

Second, and on a related note, by focusing purely on the coalitional aspect of parties' constituencies without reference to the nature of the political appeal, or by superimposing these appeals on a 'left–right' spectrum, existing accounts of these coalitions often leave us with no way to understand what draws diverse groups together, or what to expect in the area of policy. The second of these problems is especially marked when it comes to issues that are not necessarily 'organically' linked to the place of a social category in the division of labour. The possibility of substituting welfare policies and other policies intended to ameliorate rather than remove the structural causes of poverty are difficult even to envision, much less explain.[2] Similarly the possibility that parties might be able to divide the constituency they face by limiting benefits through means-testing or other targeting mechanisms is always greeted with surprise even though by now students of Indian politics should have learned to anticipate such tactics. Thus to illustrate with reference to all-India politics, conceiving of Indira Gandhi's 'populism' as 'radical' or 'socialist' not only makes us gloss over real differences between her 'socialism' and the Lohiaite variety, but also makes recent changes in the Congress' approach to distributional issues seem far more discontinuous than it actually is: while the Jawahar Rozgar Yojana, or the recently announced school lunch programme are clearly not very 'socialist', when set against the context of the policy debates of the period, there is far more continuity between these and the targeted 'poverty *alleviation*' measures of the 1970s, and even the Karachi Resolution of 1931, than is implied by loose references to 'socialism'.[3]

These gaps in the conventional picture of how parties are supposed to function probably explain why Tamil Nadu seems so strange to observers both within the state and outside it. The state's two parties, the DMK and the ADMK appear to some authors (Washbrook 1989) to be indistinguishable factions of a single party, and to thrive on exotic issues and practices. Yet, as we will see, they have more often than not anticipated trends in the rest of India.

In this chapter I present Tamil Nadu as a paradigmatic instance of the stability afforded by an increasingly competitive party system, and argue that the nature of this competition indicates the direction in which the rest of India is moving. The key to this stability has been the emergence of a pattern of party competition in which two centrist parties differentiate

---

[2] This is not to suggest, of course, that the difference has not been recognized; Kohli's (1987) distinction between 'distributional' and 'redistributional' policies would be sufficient to refute that charge. The issue is which policy we think of as normal or exemplifying the 'logic of history'.

[3] These arguments about the nature of all-India party competition are developed in my dissertation (Swamy 1996b) where I also argue that Congress resembles the well-established tradition of European conservative paternalism.

themselves from each other by championing different kinds of distributive issues. In Tamil Nadu, several decades of competing populisms have resulted in parties *outflanking* rather than outbidding one another. Over time, the result has actually been a rather stable party system and, despite reports to the contrary, a rather good development record. This pattern emerged out of the contradictions in the kinds of broad majoritarian coalitions of farmers and backward classes adopted by the Janata Dal and other like minded parties in northern India, and that some authors have anticipated would come to dominate in India. Thus contrary to the views of many (e.g. Frankel 1990), it is likely that Bihar is now merely entering a phase that Tamil Nadu (and some other states) entered upon decades ago and, in the future, is likely to experience a similar return to protection populism. I present my argument in two major sections, the first addressing the relationship between parties and institutionalization, the second seeking to explain the success of protection populism under M. G. Ramachandran (MGR) as a function of his policies and performance on developmental issues.

PARTIES AS INSTITUTIONS AND IDENTITIES

Tamil Nadu has witnessed two-party competition for longer than any other region in India. Since 1916, when the Justice Party was founded, the state has witnessed a series of contests, first between the Justice Party and the Congress, then between the Congress and the DMK, and finally between the DMK and the ADMK. Each of these contests can be understood as an instance of an evolving competition between empowerment and protection populism, although the specific coalitions shifted with the changing boundaries of the franchise and increasing levels of social mobilization. With MGR's rise, stable party identities with distinct coalitional features crystallized around the DMK and the ADMK, with the ADMK coalition incorporating the very poor and, crucially, women, by opening up a gender gap in voting. This relatively well-institutionalized party system helped to counteract the effects of the assaults on institutions undertaken by the ADMK. This section discusses these developments through subsections dealing with the rise of a two-party system, the crystallization of the MGR constituency and the assault on other institutions.

The Emergence of a Two-Party System

In November 1916, a small group of men founded the South Indian People's Association, later renamed the South Indian Liberal Association, and popularly known as the Justice Party. This event marked the formal birth of the Dravidian movement and of electoral competition in the area later renamed Tamil Nadu. Over the next twenty years, the Justice Party actively challenged the Indian National Congress for political hegemony in Madras Presidency. The party's message centred around the charge that Brahmins had acquired an illegitimate monopoly of power and privilege in south Indian society and that non-Brahmins, as a single collective entity, needed special measures to redress this imbalance. In effect, the party was the electoral expression of a non-Brahmin movement which sought to erode the ritual hegemony of Brahmins, through such cultural changes as performing marriages without Brahmin priests.[4]

The Justice Party's programme itself was oriented towards counteracting the more temporal aspects of Brahmin dominance. The most notable legacies of this period were the enactment of fixed quotas for different caste groups in government employment, and establishment of control over the fiscal management of Tamil Nadu's large, well-endowed temples, the elected local boards of which had become important centres of patronage (Presler 1987; Washbrook 1973). Under the very limited franchise granted by the political reforms of 1920, the Justice Party won elections and formed provincial governments in every triennial election from 1923 to 1934 but one—that of 1926. This was the sole election contested by segments of the Indian National Congress under the banner of the Swaraj Party, which emerged as the largest party in the legislature (Pande 1985).

The Justice Party's inability to win elections when the Swaraj Party contested them proved to be a harbinger of its fate under an expanded franchise (Irschick 1986: 126–42; Arnold 1977). During the 1930s, nationalist agitations emphasizing concerns over land taxes, untouchability and prohibition helped the Congress to expand its base. In the provincial elections of 1937, following the expansion of the franchise in 1935, the Congress won 74 per cent of the seats, a larger majority than in any other province (Brown 1985: 287). After 1937, many Justice Party politicians joined the Congress, while the rest were absorbed by a movement that had initially challenged the Justice Party 'from below'.

The Self-Respect movement of Periyar E. V. Ramasami had emerged in the 1920s to articulate a more radical version of the non-Brahmin

---

[4] Madras Presidency, of course, contained many areas that were not Tamil-speaking, although the Tamil districts which, unlike Telugu, Malayalam and Kannada areas, were almost entirely contained in the province, dominated politically. The Justice Party drew support from all the regions, but other aspects of the non-Brahmin movement appear to have been heavily Tamil in their cultural orientation.

doctrine than that of the Justice Party—in part because the latter addressed itself mainly to the concerns of elite non-Brahmins. According to this doctrine, which I refer to as Dravidianism, all non-Brahmin speakers of the Dravidian languages of southern India were culturally and racially distinct from northern 'Aryans' and Hinduism was an alien imposition of 'Aryan' Brahmins. The Self-Respect movement sought to erase all caste distinctions (not merely those between Brahmins and elite non-Brahmins), eliminate discrimination against women in Hindu society (identified as a legacy of Brahminism) and abolish religion in the name of 'rationalism'— rather than merely removing Brahmins from the rituals (see Barnett 1976: 34–8; Hardgrave 1979; Irschick 1986: 89–90; Subramanian 1993; Swamy 1996a: 212–14; 1996b: 164–74).

The importance of the new doctrine's regional—rather than merely caste—aspirations became clear in 1938 when Periyar and his principal lieutenant, the future DMK chief minister Annadurai, led protests against Congress policy requiring all schoolchildren to learn Hindi. In 1944 Periyar formally inaugurated the secessionist phase of the Dravidian movement by founding the Dravida Kazhagam (DK) or Dravidian Association which demanded an independent state in southern India for the Dravidians. This demand was, of course, never met. Following Independence in 1947, the DK split with one faction, the Dravida Munnetra Kazhagam or Dravidian Progress Association, eventually emerging, under Annadurai, as the electoral vehicle of Tamil nationalism.

Although one interpretation of the DK/DMK split is that Annadurai wished to take advantage of the new opportunities afforded by Independence, the DMK did not immediately contest elections, preferring, initially, to remain a 'non-political' social movement like the DK. It made its presence felt in a number of ways: it sponsored agitations; it produced popular films with Tamil nationalist and anti-Brahmin themes; in the general elections of 1952, it supported parties opposed to the Congress, in particular the Communist Party of India and two others representing specific 'backward' caste clusters. Only when the latter 'betrayed' the alliance by joining the Congress government did the DMK decide to seek electoral office.

By this time two changes had altered the context in which the DMK had to compete. First, the redrawing of state boundaries along linguistic lines, compelled by the demands of Telugu-speaking Dravidians, left the DMK without a rationale for secession—the Tamil districts were considered too small to constitute a viable nation—but with a more culturally homogeneous political arena, in which the distinctly Tamil content of the DMK message would no longer be a handicap. Second, the rise of K. Kamaraj to the position of Congress leader and chief minister in the state largely defused the charge that Congress was a Brahmin vehicle. Kamaraj, a member of the formerly 'backward', but upwardly mobile Nadar community presided over a regime that was characterized both by extraordinarily successful efforts at industrial development, and some quite notable innovations in the area of social insurance (to be discussed later). Additionally, he was able to capture in some part of the mantle of Tamil regional pride and win support from the DK. The DMK began to emphasize distributional issues, notably backward class reservations, to expand its base. Around this time, the themes of DMK films began to emphasize issues of poverty as much as anti-Brahminism, and in these films starred future chief minister MGR.

Contesting elections in 1957, the DMK rapidly established itself as principal challenger to Congress in the state. From winning under 13 per cent of the vote in 1957, while contesting half the seats, the party grew to win over a quarter of the vote in 1962, while contesting over two-thirds of the seats. Furthermore, a DMK–Communist alliance won municipal power in the state's two largest cities in 1959, while a DMK alliance with the Brahmin-led Swatantra Party in 1962 demonstrated that it was willing to be quite pragmatic in its quest for power.

The party's growth concerned the Congress leadership enough for Kamaraj to volunteer to resign as chief minister in an effort to rejuvenate the Congress organization as president of the state unit. The panic may have been unnecessary: the 1962 elections showed the popularity of Congress to be undiminished; the DMK's expansion thus came mostly at the expense of minor parties and independent candidates. For the DMK to replace Congress, it needed to undermine the latter's claim to represent Tamil aspirations and the poor. Two events in 1965 and 1966 allowed this to happen. First, in 1965, riots erupted in the state over the central government's decision to replace English entirely with Hindi for official purposes—and in examinations. Second, and more importantly, the drought and crop failures of 1965–6 caused widespread food shortages.

The political consequences of food shortages require no explanation. A word on the salience of the language issue in Tamil Nadu, however, is in order. The impact of this decision on the job prospects of educated Tamils would have been devastating: along with one of the highest rates of literacy in the country, Tamil Nadu also had a wider gap between bilingualism in English and Hindi in favour of English than any other state (Swamy 1996b: 395). The state government's decision under Kamaraj's successor Bhaktavatsalam to order the police to fire on the demonstrators leaving hundreds of middle class students dead, compelled a retraction by the central government, and permanently damaged the prestige of Congress (Das Gupta 1970: 236–7; Barnett 1976: 131–4).

Ironically, the impact of these events was magnified by the prominent position occupied by leading Congressmen in national politics. Kamaraj, elevated to president of the national Congress organization in 1964, was the reputed kingmaker of the party in the mid-1960s; his rival, C. Subramaniam, chosen by Indira Gandhi to serve as food minister, was to become the architect of the Green Revolution. That Kamaraj, who had demonstrated the power to choose who would be prime minister, was powerless to prevent a policy he knew would be anathema to his state only underscored the complicity of the state Congress in the debacle. That the Union food minister could not provide his own state with food heightened the party's impotence.

In 1967, the DMK joined a grand anti-Congress coalition and campaigned on three issues—preserving English as an official language, increasing state autonomy in economic decision making and providing cheap rice. The rice issue was critical: the party's main plank was a promise to provide three measures of rice for one rupee, and DMK slogans mocked Kamaraj and Subramaniam by name for their inability to provide their home state with food. The DMK alliance won in a landslide, even though the Congress vote fell by only 4 percentage points, and both Kamaraj and Subramaniam lost their parliamentary seats.[5]

TABLE 1

PERFORMANCE OF CONGRESS AND DMK IN TAMIL NADU
ELECTIONS, 1957–1967

| | 1957 | | 1962 | | 1967 | |
	Congress	DMK	Congress	DMK	Congress	DMK
% of vote received	45.3	12.8	46.1	27.1	41.4	40.6
% of seats contested	100	58.8	100	69.4	100	74.4
% of seats won	73.7	6.3	67.5	24.2	21.4	59.0

SOURCES: Barnett (1976:41, 149; Tables 6–2; 6–6), Singh and Bose (1988: 42–4).

[5] These slogans included 'Kamaraj Annachi, Arasi Ennachi' ('Elder Brother Kamaraj, what happened to the rice?') and 'Subramania...Coru Podu' ('Subramaniam give us food.') For an overview of the campaign see Barnett (1976: 136–7). I am indebted to my late father, P. M. Swamy, for these long forgotten slogans.

The DMK moved rapidly to make good on many of its long-standing promises. These included getting the state renamed from Madras to Tamil Nadu, hosting the first World Tamil Conference, appointing a commission to recommend reservations for the backward classes, and forcing the central government to accept its decision not to have Hindi taught, even as a second language. The promise to sell cheap rice was also implemented, although in a diluted form: rice was sold at one measure for one rupee.

The party, however, appears to have had difficulty holding on to lower caste groups and the very poor from the beginning. Conflicts between middle status 'backward class' groups and former 'untouchables' are one frequently cited instance of such tensions.[6] Annadurai's death of cancer in 1969 cast even greater doubt on the party's hold on the poor. His successor M. K. Karunanidhi, the party's organizational genius, was popular within the party and among the backward classes, but did not have the mass appeal enjoyed by Annadurai or MGR.

It is interesting to speculate about what might have happened to the DMK after Annadurai's death had it faced a united Congress in the following elections. Fortunately for Karunanidhi, the Congress party split the same year. With the leading Congressman in the state, Kamaraj, aligning himself against Indira Gandhi, and the latter being left with a minority government at the centre, the DMK was presented with an opportunity to support the governing party in Delhi against a common foe. When, in 1971, Indira Gandhi called early elections and campaigned on the famous slogan, 'Remove Poverty,' she supported the DMK without putting up a single candidate for the Tamil Nadu Assembly: the DMK was able to sweep the 1971 state elections, winning 48.6 per cent of the total vote and 184 seats in a house of 234.[7]

As with later landslides, this supermajority only heightened internal fissures. In 1972 MGR, the film actor who was the DMK's principal campaign draw as well as its treasurer, resigned from the party, charging its top leaders with corruption and with betraying Annadurai's ideals. He formed a new party, the Anna Dravida Munnetra Kazhagam dedicated to

[6] The most notorious instance was the massacre of scheduled caste labourers by landlords in Kilvenmani (Barnett 1976: 257–60) to which the DMK government responded tepidly. While the DMK's unwillingness to confront landlords was not more marked than that of other non-Communist parties. This ambivalence was in sharper contrast to its claim to represent all lower caste groups.

[7] The Congress (R) did not contest a single seat in the state assembly elections, and put up candidates for only nine of the thirty-seven parliamentary seats in the state.

the ideology of 'Annaism!'[8] Soon thereafter Sathiavani Muthu, the only woman and Dalit in the party's top leadership, broke with the DMK accusing Karunanidhi of promoting a personality cult and charging the party with having betrayed the scheduled castes. She later joined the ADMK (Barnett 1976: 299–300; Forrester 1976: 293).

Initially, observers underestimated the ADMK. Although the party demonstrated its strength in by-elections in 1973 and 1974, it was not until the state assembly elections of 1977 that it became clear that the ADMK had become the most popular party in the state.[9] In a four-way contest between alliances led by the DMK, the ADMK, Indira Gandhi's Congress (R), and Kamaraj's Congress (O), now merged into the Janata Party, the ADMK won a majority with just over a third of the vote.[10]

TABLE 2

PERFORMANCE OF MAJOR PARTIES IN THE 1977 TAMIL NADU
ASSEMBLY ELECTIONS

	ADMK	DMK	Congress	Congress(O)/ Janata
No. (%) of seats contested[a]	200 (85.5%)	230(98.3%)	198 (84.6%)	233 (99.6%)
% of total vote received[a]	30.4	24.9	17.5	16.7
Vote % in seats contested[b]	35.8	25.9	20.6	18.6
Vote % in 4-way races[b]	34.5	24.7	20.5	17.7
No. of total seats won[a]	126	48	27	10
% of contested seats won	63%	21%	13.6%	4.3%

SOURCES: (a) Thandavan 1987: 133; (b) Calculated from Government of Tamil Nadu, Public (Elections) Dept., Results on General Elections to Tamil Nadu Legislative Assembly, 1977, 1980, 1984.

[8] For details on the split, including on DMK factional disputes, see Barnett (1976: 295–7) and Forrester (1976). 'Annaism!' is the title of an undated manifesto released by the party at the time of the split.

[9] In the Dindigul parliamentary by-election in 1973, the ADMK won with over 52 per cent votes against the Congress (O), DMK and Congress (R). The following year, in alliance with the Communist Party of India, it won an assembly by-election in Coimbatore (West), a parliamentary by-election in the Tamil-speaking former French enclave of Pondicherry, and the elections to the Pondicherry assembly (Thandavan 1987: 125–30). Even more significantly, the DMK came in third behind Kamaraj's Congress (O) in all the by-elections.

[10] During the 1977 general elections held several months earlier, the ADMK had been allied with Mrs Gandhi's Congress (R) and the alliance had swept the state. The Congress (I)'s defeat at national level caused the ADMK to abandon the alliance.

The elections also point to the weakness of the DMK and the continued survival of a considerable Congress coalition in the state. With the DMK receiving barely a quarter of the vote to the ADMK's one-third, and the two claimants to the Congress mantle together polling more votes than the ADMK, one does wonder whether without MGR's intervention Congress might not have won the state back. In the event, Congress was reduced to a third force in the state—with the defection of many former Congress (O) leaders to the Congress (I) largely eliminating Janata and its successors from the state, while MGR went on to dominate Tamil Nadu politics until his death in 1987, winning elections in 1980 and 1984 decisively.

Institutionalizing a Protection Populist Constituency

MGR's accession to power marked a shift in the politics of Tamil Nadu from one characteristically associated with issues relating to upward mobility to one in which social welfare policies became the hallmark of the state. MGR's personal background is often said to have been responsible for this shift: although from a high caste background, he had grown up poor owing to his father's early death, and repeatedly pointed to his mother's plight to explain his special concern for widows and abandoned women. Additionally, one can speculate, his background may have made him more receptive to an economic understanding of disprivilege as opposed to one emphasizing ascriptive origins.

MGR used both targeting and substitution to shift the emphasis of social policy in the state. His administration displayed far greater ambivalence toward backward class reservations and such key intermediate social groups as farmers than had the Karunanidhi administration, in both cases attempting to limit benefits to the poorer members of the constituency, while downplaying the DMK's historic animus toward Brahmins and the north. The policies with which his administration was associated were, instead, prohibition, conceived of as a policy to help poor women; the extension of minimal social security provisions aimed at particular groups with whom he had identified himself in his films—fishermen, rickshaw-pullers, abandoned wives and widows; and a massive feeding programme that came to be known as the Noon Meal Scheme.

These patterns, however, were not uniform through his ten years in office. The elections of 1980, which dealt MGR both his biggest setback and his most impressive triumph, signalled a significant shift in strategy. As in many Indian states, the elections of 1980 were actually held in two stages. In national elections held in January, an alliance of the Congress and DMK won all but two of the state's thirty-nine parliamentary seats.

However, in state assembly elections held a few months later, after Indira Gandhi dismissed state governments opposed to her, the ADMK returned to power, defeating the combined efforts of the next two largest parties in the state with only minor allies. The ADMK's votes by the constituencies it contested increased by almost 8 points, suggesting to many observers that there was a sizable swing vote which preferred Congress at the national level and the ADMK at the state level.

Table 3

PERFORMANCE OF MAJOR PARTIES IN THE 1980 PARLIAMENTARY AND STATE ELECTIONS

	ADMK	DMK	Congress
LOK SABHA[a] (Total Seats: 39, Turnout: 66.8%)			
Number of seats contested	24	16	22
Percentage votes polled[a]	25.4	23.0	31.6
Number of seats won[a*]	2	16	20
Percentage votes received in seats contested	*42.9*	*54.0*	*48.4*
ASSEMBLY[b] (Total Seats: 234, Turnout: 64.8%)			
Number of seats contested	177	114	112
Percentage votes polled	38.9	22.5	20.5
Number of seats won (%)	128	38	30
Percentage votes received in seats contested	*50.6*	*49.1*	*47.6*

SOURCES: (a) Butler et al. 1991:253–62; (b) Singh and Bose 1988:44–5, 560–610.

*One Lok Sabha seat was won by an Independent.

The 1980 elections had several long-term repercussions, all stemming in part from the insecurity MGR experienced on losing the 1980 parliamentary elections. First, they resulted in a long-term alliance between the ADMK and Congress based on a seat-sharing that allowed the ADMK to dominate at the state level, while reversing the position for the national elections. As a consequence, the elections of 1984 and 1991—the second of these held after MGR's death—resulted in huge, lopsided victories, in the latter case virtually eliminating the DMK from the legislature. Second, the years following 1980 saw a reduced willingness to directly challenge empowerment constituencies, and also increasing charges of corruption and administrative arbitrariness. MGR stepped up the social welfare component of his policies inaugurating some of his best-known programmes during this period, and his administration also began to preside over an impressive economic turnaround.

It is at this point that the question of who exactly constituted MGR's constituency becomes critical. Annual opinion polls conducted by the Statistics Department of Madras Christian College demonstrate that, in keeping with MGR's film image and his distinctive approach toward distributional policy, the ADMK developed an electoral support base markedly different from that of the DMK's support base, drawing greater support from women and from the poorest segments of the population.

TABLE 4

PER CENT CITING MGR AS THE 'LEADER ... YOU SUPPORT WITH YOUR WHOLE HEART' FEBRUARY. 1983

Men	Women	Age 21–30	Age 51–60	Illiterates	College-educated
40	50	52	34	57	29

SOURCE: *Statewide Surveys on Public Opinion,* Dept of Statistics, Madras Christian College

Another important factor in MGR's success, however, was Karunanidhi's unpopularity. Opinion polls taken during MGR's lifetime indicate some interesting patterns. MGR, of course, was the most popular leader in the state, consistently viewed favourably by 70 per cent of respondents, with at least 40 per cent expressing 'strong support'. Karunanidhi was actively 'opposed' by half the electorate. As we will see, the DMK leader's high negative ratings are confirmed by other data, and appear especially marked among women voters. This suggests that MGR's constituency was not simply alienated from his film image but was already attracted to the DMK.

TABLE 5

PUBLIC ATTITUDES TOWARDS MAJOR LEADERS, MGR PERIOD

Date of Opinion Poll and View Expressed	MGR	Indira/Rajiv Gandhi	Karunanidhi
February 1983			
Strongly Support	46	19	20
Good Opinion	24	50	19
Oppose	25	20	52
February 1986			
Strongly Support	40	28	17
Good Opinion	30	54	26
Oppose	20	6	46

SOURCE: Statewide Surveys on Public Opinion, Dept of Statistics, Madras Christian College.

The Persistence of the Coalitions

MGR's death in December 1987 put to the test the question of whether his popularity could outlast him. For several years the party had been publicly riven by factional disputes between MGR's former co-star Jayalalitha, the party's most popular public spokesperson, and his principal lieutenant and organizational right-hand man R. M. Veerappan.[11] Shortly after MGR's death, the party split into two camps, one headed by Jayalalitha and the other effectively controlled by Veerappan but formally headed by MGR's widow Janaki.

The ADMK split encouraged the Congress party to contest the elections on its own for the first time since 1977, so that the state elections in January 1989 were fought between four alliances, one led by the DMK and three by parties that had been in the MGR coalition in 1984—Congress, and the Janaki and Jayalalitha factions of the ADMK. As a result the DMK alliance returned to power in a landslide with only a little over 30 per cent of the vote.

[11] Based on many news reports at the time. e.g. 'Mayhem in Madras', *Sunday,* 7–13 February 1988, pp. 16–18; 'The Last Journey', *Aside,* 1–15 January 1988, pp. 14–23; 'Curtain!: Chaos in AIADMK', *The Week,* 3–9 January 1988, pp. 11–23; 'Wives and Lovers', *Sunday,* 17–23 January 1988, pp. 26–34; and reports in *The Hindu,* esp. 'Who will succeed MGR', 30 December 1987.

TABLE 6

PERFORMANCE OF MAJOR PARTIES IN THE 1989
ASSEMBLY ELECTIONS

	DMK	ADMK (Jayalalitha)	Congress	ADMK (Janaki)
% of total Votes	33.4	21.7	20.2	9.1
Average vote % per candidate	37.9	24.5	21.5	11.6
Seats contested	202	201	215	177
Seats won	151	27	26	1
Second place in	47	91	62	11

SOURCE: *The Hindu* (International Edition), 4 February 1989, p. 9.

The real story of the 1989 elections, however, lay in the stability of the vote patterns and the establishment of a clear heir to MGR's mantle. Neither the DMK nor the Congress was able to improve significantly over its earlier vote base. More importantly, the Jayalalitha faction of the ADMK established clear dominance over the Janaki faction, and edged out Congress to become the second largest party in the state. The stability of the ADMK coalition, divided though it was between rival claimants, is demonstrated by the pre-election opinion poll conducted by *The Hindu.*

There are three noteworthy facts about this opinion poll. First, there is very little difference between the vote percentages predicted for different parties when those parties are identified by party name, symbol and leader, indicating a high degree of awareness of the relevant configurations. Second, when the poll is compared to the actual results (above) it appears that undecided voters largely swung to the Jayalalitha faction of the ADMK—the one party whose predicted vote differed markedly from the actual outcome. Finally, whereas few of those polled volunteered a party other than the four main choices, many responded with a different chief ministerial preference, suggesting that party identity is stronger than leadership preference.

TABLE 7

PARTY PREFERENCES PRIOR TO THE 1989
ASSEMBLY ELECTIONS

Preference for alliance led by	When identified by	Total	Men	Women
DMK	party name	35.6	40.0	30.0
	CM candidate	37.6	42.2	31.7
	party symbol	35.5	40.0	29.7
ADMK Jaya	party name	15.7	14.0	17.72
	CM candidate	17.0	14.9	19.59
	party symbol	15.5	13.7	17.8
CONGRESS	party name	25.1	24.9	25.5
	CM candidate	24.8	24.8	23.5
	party symbol	25.4	25.1	25.6
ADMK Janaki	party name	11.9	10.9	13.2
	CM candidate	12.3	10.8	14.2
	party symbol	12.3	11.3	13.5
Undecided	party name	9.8	8.17	11.86
	CM candidate	0.02	0.0	0.0
	party symbol	8.9	7.4	10.8
Others	party name	1.9	2.0	1.8
	CM candidate	8.92	7.27	10.96
	party symbol	2.5	2.5	2.5

SOURCE: Hindu/APT Research Group, Public Opinion Poll, January 1989. Data used by courtesy of
Mr N. Ram, Editor, *Frontline*.

As this poll shows it was the Jayalalitha faction which inherited the
gender gap opened up by MGR. Even more important is the strong evidence
of a relative *antipathy* among women voters to the DMK which was even
stronger than the preference of women for either ADMK faction. Both
findings are borne out by booth-level voting data from sex-segregated
booths gathered for two districts.

TABLE 8

MEAN ADVANTAGE AMONG WOMEN VOTERS BY
PARTY JANUARY 1989 ELECTIONS*

	ADMK–Jaya	Congress	DMK	ADMK–Janaki
Madurai–Rural	5.4 (6/6)	0.7 (6/6)	–5.5 (6/6)	–1.0 (4/6)
Madurai–Urban	7.2 (4/6)	1.5 (6/6)	–8.1 (5/6)	–2.3 (4/6)
Tirunelveli	5.9 (4/8)	1.2 (6/8)	–5.6 (6/8)	0.2 (7/8)

* Vote in women's booths minus votes in men's booths. Figures in parentheses indicate number of constituencies contested, and number of constituencies for which data were available, respectively.

Source: Booth–level results gathered from collectorates of Madurai and Tirunelveli Kattabomman districts, with permission from Public (Elections) Dept, Govt of Tamil Nadu. For constituency-wise details, see Swamy (1996b).

Following these elections, Janaki retired from politics; the ADMK reunited under Jayalalitha's leadership and re-established its alliance with Congress in time to sweep the November 1989 Lok Sabha elections, as well as the 1991 elections. The inability of the DMK to use its period in power to expand its base requires explanation. Of particular importance here are votes of women and the rural poor who, as opinion polls indicate, continue to be the strongest supporters of the ADMK since Jayalalitha's return to power. Indeed, in the case of female voters, the gap appears to have widened even further.

With respect to women, an important part of the explanation is clearly the extraordinarily skilful use Jayalalitha made of a notorious incident in the state assembly, when she was physically assaulted by a DMK member. Jayalalitha used the incident in her campaign to depict the DMK as condoning violence against women, asking, in effect, 'If this can happen to me in the assembly, is any woman safe?' This appears to have resonated with a general perception among women of the DMK as a misogynist party of 'lumpen' elements.[12] Additionally, the DMK sought to recoup

[12] The incident occurred when, following a heated discussion on the assembly floor, Jayalalitha chose to stage a protest walk-out. One DMK legislator grabbed at the end of her sari, which was attached to her blouse by a safety pin, causing the blouse to tear slightly. During the campaign ADMK posters drew an analogy to a famous scene in the Hindu epic, the Mahabharata, in which the evil Kaurava princes attempt to strip the Pandava queen Draupadi in court. For discussions of the effect on the 1991 campaign, see Manivannan (1992: 167); Suresh (1992: 2315).

revenue by lifting prohibition. It did also attempt to protect the poor from the effects of the policy by establishing a government monopoly over the production of native liquor to ensure its quality and sell it cheaply through government shops.[13] While brilliant as a policy solution, the picture of the government actively engaging in producing and selling liquor to the working class—rather than merely allowing it—was a public relations disaster, and appears to have contributed dramatically to the collapse of the party's support, particularly among women.[14] Reviving prohibition on country liquors was one of Jayalalitha's first acts in office, shortly followed by a demand that the central government compensate Tamil Nadu for the loss in revenue.[15]

More generally, the DMK's efforts to cut back on some of MGR's policies may have backfired. During its eighteen months in power, the DMK sought desperately to co-opt the ADMK's support among the poor and women, while also pursuing its own agenda. Thus the party tabled the recommendations of the second Backward Classes Commission appointed by MGR, added eggs to the Noon Meal diet, and announced a number of social welfare programmes; however, the party also cut back on a number of measures intended to help the most vulnerable groups, particularly relating to food security.[16]

In addition to these difficulties, the DMK faced two handicaps in the June 1991 elections. The first was the growing unpopularity of the Sri Lankan Tamil militant group, the Liberation of Tamil Tigers Eelam (LTTE), which was increasingly running criminal activities out of its camps. Charges that the DMK was allied with the LTTE led to the government's dismissal. Second, and closely related, was Rajiv Gandhi's assassination in Tamil Nadu by LTTE militants. Given the fact that all opinion polls indicate that Rajiv had enjoyed considerable personal popularity in the state, the assassination is often held to have hurt the DMK even more and helped the Congress–ADMK alliance. Finally, there was the rise of a new party, the Pattali Makkal Katchi (PMK), a vehicle for the 'backward' Vanniyar caste which demanded separate affirmative action quotas for itself. This replicated a recurring source of tension in the Dravidian movement, and

---

[13] See reports in *Indian Express*, 29 March 1990; and *The Hindu*, 11 March, 5 May and 15 June 1990.

[14] Among women, of course, this represents the 'further erosion' of support. Both Congress and the ADMK led protests against the policy. See *The Hindu*, 23 March, 1 April, 3 October and 29 November 1990, and *Indian Express*, 24 April 1990.

[15] See *The Hindu*, 16 July and 19 July 1991.

[16] For details see Suresh (1992: 2313–15).

foreshadowed similar conflicts within the backward class category in northern India.[17]

As a consequence of all these factors, the DMK won only one assembly seat in the 1991 elections—Karunanidhi's. By December 1991, according to opinion polls, the party was at its weakest in a decade, and the ADMK appeared as strong as the DMK and Congress combined. While almost 30 per cent of the electorate continued to declare themselves DMK supporters, well over half were now actively opposed to the party. By contrast the ADMK's support levels exceeded 43 per cent with an additional 22 per cent declaring themselves sympathetic to the party.

TABLE 9

ATTITUDE TOWARDS MAJOR PARTIES DECEMBER 1991

% of respondents in the poll sample	ADMK	Congress	DMK
Support	43.1	17.19	29.59
Have sympathy for	22.1	51.14	11.72
Oppose	31.1	21.79	52.78

This erosion in the DMK's support was most marked among women: support for the DMK was almost 14 percentage points lower among women than men, while for the ADMK it was 17 points higher among women.

TABLE 10

SUPPORT FOR MAJOR PARTIES BY GENDER DECEMBER 1991

	Percentage supporting		
	ADMK	Congress	DMK
Men	36.8	16.6	34.5
Women	53.2	18.3	20.8

SOURCE: *Statewide Surveys on Public Opinion*, Dept of Statistics, Madras Christian College.

[17] For the origins of this movement, see 'Caste Clash,' *India Today*, 15 October 1987. For the impact of the PMK on the DMK vote see Suresh (1992: 2316–17 and Table 1).

Levels of party support across other kinds of classifications demonstrate that ADMK support continued to be strongest among the weakest and most marginalized demographic categories in every dimension, while the DMK's support was strongest in the middle categories, again in every dimension. Some variation appears at the relatively privileged end of the various categories, with the ADMK's support sometimes dominant in some, while in others, it is the Congress which appears to have captured the 'top' of the sandwich coalition.

Thus, for example, the DMK's support is strongest in small towns, while the ADMK is strongest in villages and hamlets.

TABLE 11

SUPPORT FOR PARTIES BY RESIDENCE DECEMBER 1991

	Percentage supporting		
Residents of	ADMK	Congress	DMK
Cities	33.3	27.8	22.2
Large towns	43.2	21.1	24.2
Small towns	36.2	19.3	33.0
Villages	42.3	17.6	29.4
Hamlets	48.9	12.4	30.1

SOURCE: *Statewide Surveys on Public Opinion,* Dept of Statistics, Madras Christian College.

Similarly the ADMK draws its strongest support among the illiterate and those with less than an eighth grade education, while the DMK is weakest among the illiterate.

TABLE 12

SUPPORT FOR PARTIES BY EDUCATIONAL LEVEL

Level of education	Percentage supporting		
	ADMK	Congress	DMK
College	35.2	14.4	31.2
9th–12th grade	36.0	19.1	32.3
Upto 8th grade	45.7	15.1	30.7
Illiterate	52.8	17.5	22.5

SOURCE: *Statewide Surveys on Public Opinion,* Dept of Statistics, Madras Christian College.

Along similar lines, using voters' source of information as an indicator of socio-economic status suggests that the elite, those who rely exclusively on English sources of information, overwhelmingly supported Congress. Among those who read Tamil papers, with or without English, support for the DMK and ADMK was on a par, but the ADMK's vote increased on the lower rungs of the socio-economic scale while the DMK's decreased.

TABLE 13

SUPPORT FOR PARTIES BY SOURCE OF INFORMATION
DECEMBER 1991

Primary source of information	Percentage supporting		
	ADMK	Congress	DMK
English papers	13.6	36.4	13.6
English & Tamil papers	36.5	20.6	29.9
Tamil papers	39.2	16.4	33.5
Radio	52.3	16.8	23.2
None of the above	59.0	14.5	20.7

SOURCE: *Statewide Surveys on Public Opinion*, Dept of Statistics, Madras Christian College.

Finally, support for parties by occupation likewise show a pattern of increasing support with declining social status for the ADMK, with DMK support concentrated in the middle.

TABLE 14

SUPPORT FOR PARTIES BY OCCUPATION DECEMBER. 1991

Occupation	Percentage supporting		
	ADMK	Congress	DMK
Business	43.2	22.7	25.0
Professional	31.4	22.9	24.2
Trader	39.4	15.9	34.1
Agriculturist	37.3	16.9	35.3
Office work	31.2	18.3	34.4
Self-employed	42.8	14.5	29.0
Landless labourer	57.5	14.9	22.3
Others	33.2	18.2	25.8

SOURCE: *Statewide Surveys on Public Opinion*, Dept of Statistics, Madras Christian College.

With the DMK suffering yet another split in 1992, and Jayalalitha increasingly appearing to adopt a Hindu nationalist stance, militant Tamil nationalism appeared spent, at least as an electoral force.[18] As it turned out, however, in the 1996 elections, an alliance between a breakaway Congress faction and the DMK presented the ADMK, which was allied with the official Congress, with an electoral debacle comparable to the defeat suffered by the DMK in 1991.

There appear to be two major reasons for the collapse of ADMK support. One was the break between Congress and the ADMK. Although the ADMK had succeeded in defeating an alliance of the DMK and Congress in the state elections in 1980, it was, as we have seen, a close election: the Congress–DMK alliance had swept parliamentary elections only a few months earlier. It is likely that the Congress provided at least the 'top slice' in the ADMK's sandwich coalition and, given its own protection populist tendencies, might also have brought in new voters. Indeed, Jayalalitha's efforts to publicly humiliate local Congressmen may have alienated Congress voters to the extent that when the latter broke away, rather than follow the national leadership's directive to renew the alliance prior to the 1996 elections, it is likely that they took most of their voters with them.[19]

A second factor is clearly the public displays of arrogance and corruption for which Jayalalitha became notorious.[20] Although allegations of arrogance and corruption were also levelled at MGR—as indeed at most successful Indian politicians—these acts were never performed in public. During her five-year period in power, by contrast, Jayalalitha became noted for the public sycophancy displayed by her party members, and some younger leaders with their own support bases left the party to found a rival ADMK once again.[21] Jayalalitha also attracted international attention only a few months before the election with a massive gala wedding for her adopted son, for which the entire city of Madras was festooned. While it was plausible to view this as a logical extension of the 'bread and circuses' aspect of protection populism, and news reports did indicate

[18] For the background of the most recent DMK split, see Geetha and Rajadurai (1993). On the other matters, Manivannan (1992) and Suresh (1992).

[19] For an account of the rift, see 'Divorce Proceedings', India Today, 28 February 1993. For the impact of the rupture on voters, see the India Today–MARG opinion poll reported in India Today, 15 April 1993. For the split preceding the 1996 elections and its consequences, I have relied on daily reports from the online edition of The Hindu, and reports can be found in any Indian newspaper or magazine of this period.

[20] Details of the corruption charges levelled by different parties can be found in 'Memo of Corruption,' Frontline, 9 October 1988.

[21] For example see "Larger than Life," India Today, 15 November 1994.

that poor voters had been brought into the city to enjoy the festivities, there is reason, at least in retrospect, to wonder whether a sizable segment of the ADMK voter base was not alienated.

Corruption and Personalism

The most troubling aspect of the ADMK's legacy is perhaps its dealings with political institutions. There can be little doubt that ADMK governments under both MGR and Jayalalitha undertook a systematic assault on legal and political institutions. The MGR period was characterized by the well-publicized censorship of political critics,[22] systematic police abuse and a remarkably well-coordinated system of massive kickbacks from the liquor industry. Authoritarianism and intimidation of opponents became even more pronounced under his successor. Early in Jayalalitha's administration, the government took measures to limit certain kinds of political expressions that, while outwardly oriented toward public safety, were read by many observers as designed to limit her opponents' ability to spread their message.[23] The notorious acid attack on a female civil servant by the name of Chandralekha, was alleged by many to have been instigated by the ruling party after Chandralekha questioned orders regarding the sale of shares of a joint sector firm. This was followed by threats of criminal prosecutions against newspapers for printing the charges.[24] And under Jayalalitha, the use of police harassment was greatly expanded with the help of anti-terrorist measures enacted to enable her government to remove Sri Lankan rebels from Tamil Nadu. More than these various kinds of assaults on civil liberties, however, it was the cult of personality encouraged by both MGR and Jayalalitha that set them apart from many other state governments in India.

The high degree of personalization of the regime perhaps accounts for

[22] These were especially associated with ADMK Speaker of the Legislative Assembly, P.H. Pandian. In 1987 Pandian jailed the editor of a respected Tamil weekly for publishing a cartoon that likened state legislators to pickpockets and state ministers to bandits ('In the Wake of a Cartoon', *Frontline*, 18 April 1987; 'Arresting Affair', *India Today*, 30 April 1987). A few months earlier he had disqualified three DMK legislators from the Assembly for participating in an anti-Hindi demonstration in which a copy of the constitution was burned ('Controversial ways of a Speaker', *Frontline* 13–26 December 1986).

[23] For details see 'One Year of Jayalalitha Rule', *Frontline*, 11 September 1992, pp. 5–12. Some of the specific measures included one to make political parties financially responsible for damage inflicted by the rallies they sponsored, and a bill prohibiting the posting of posters or bills on walls in the city confines.

[24] 'L' Affaire Chandralekha', *Frontline*, 4 December 1992.

the most spectacular failings of ADMK governments—the massive and almost institutionalized level of corruption. While corruption in India is hardly limited to Tamil Nadu, the ADMK may well have regularized the solicitation of kickbacks in a way that was matched only by the Congress party at the centre. More importantly, the uses to which at least some of this money was put appear to have been integral to the functioning of the party. Specifically, with the (partial) lifting of prohibition, the MGR government appears to have begun to receive a fixed cut of every unit of liquor sold in the state in exchange for which taxes on liquor were kept relatively low, while liquor prices were higher than in other states.[25] In effect, that is, MGR—or the ADMK—privatized a portion of the effective excise tax on liquor in the state. In wondering where the money went, one of the newspapers pointed to MGR's reputation for personal generosity. While it is speculative, I would like to suggest that the point could be generalized: a great deal of funds siphoned off from private contributors in this and other areas could well have funded the informal social insurance and charitable functions the ADMK is said to have engaged in (Dickey 1993). This pattern, too, appears to have been expanded in the Jayalalitha period: while the lavishness of her foster son's wedding attracted international attention, it is less often noted that much of the expense involved lavish gift giving. Reports in the *New York Times* that poor villagers were brought into Madras at Jayalalitha's (or the party's) expense only underscore the fact that the ADMK required money to carry out its self-appointed role as champion of the poor.

It should be noted that these events do not negate the viability of a protection populist strategy. Pre-election opinion polls, which accurately predicted the outcome, also indicated that poor voters, and especially women voters, continued to support Jayalalitha, who greatly expanded the policies aimed at them. It does remind us, however, that the strength of electoral democracy as an institution lies precisely in the possibility of losing. Electoral setbacks in 1980 indeed sharpened MGR's protection populism, although they also made him less willing to challenge powerful social groups.

[25] *India Today*, 31 January 1987.

EXPLAINING PROTECTION POPULISM
STRUCTURE, CULTURE, POLICY DIFFERENCES AND
DEVELOPMENTAL PERFORMANCE

What accounts for the success of the ADMK coalition forged by MGR? There are two aspects to this question: why did the DMK, with its seemingly powerful rhetorical appeal to common folk fail to hold on to the poor; and what attracted the poor to the ADMK?

The common belief that India's idiosyncrasies render it unfit for comparative analysis is matched by an analogous proposition put forward by various authors that Tamil Nadu's politics are the result of a social and cultural history that renders it distinctive *within* the Indian context. These arguments point, in particular, to the importance of MGR's film career in elevating him to power, the heightened salience of charity measures over structural reforms, and the importance of women voters to the party's support base. In contrast, I argue that Tamil Nadu's socio-economic structure made it more susceptible to protection populism, and that vertical conflict within empowerment constituencies made them vulnerable both to sandwich tactics and to the substitution of social welfare policies. These claims are substantiated below where I first trace the susceptibility of the politics of backward class reservations and sectoral agrarianism to sandwich tactics within these constituencies, including MGR's use of these tactics to contain their demands, and then describe the major welfare policies initiated by the MGR regime.

It should be noted at the outset that the policies of the MGR regime towards empowerment constituencies do not constitute a perfect case for the argument. Following his defeat in the 1980 national election, MGR reversed some of his efforts to target electricity subsidies to poor farmers; now electricity is provided virtually free to all farmers in the state at great cost to the State Electricity Board. Likewise, MGR reversed his attempts to eliminate certain castes from the backward classes list, but did maintain the policy of compartmentalizing reservations for the 'most backward'. These shifts, however, do not appear to have been necessitated by the logic of electoral competition, since MGR did win the 1980 state elections. Rather, they appear to have been an exaggerated response, stimulated in part by the direct pressure tactics adopted by these constituencies rather than by their electoral strength. On the other hand, it was after the 1980 elections that many of the most important social welfare policies were launched, and that economic development appears to have become a more important goal for the government.

Culture and Structure

One attempt to give content to the notion of Tamil 'exceptionalism' in this regard is the idea that Tamil culture was historically more oriented towards a 'kingly' model of political behaviour, suggesting that MGR's popularity stemmed from the historic association between kingship and public largesse in the popular mind (Price 1989).[25] It is possible to accept the characterization and even the proposition that this cultural model may resonate with the poor in Tamil Nadu without believing that it explains much of anything: associating kingship with paternalistic obligation is hardly unique to Tamil Nadu, probably not even within India. It does not explain why a style of politics based on this kingly role arose in Tamil Nadu alone.

Similarly, while the role of MGR in DMK politics has inspired scholars and journalists alike to attribute to the film medium alone quite extraordinary powers of hypnosis (e.g. Hardgrave 1971), his rise cannot be attributed simply to the transfer of film popularity to politics. In the first place, MGR carefully crafted his screen persona to match the role he would eventually adopt as a politician: that of heroic fighter against injustice, saviour of the poor and, above all, a gallant protector of women. Moreover, at least in public, MGR went to great lengths to live his screen role in real life. From the 1950s on, MGR was associated with highly publicized acts of charity which reinforced—and were reinforced by— his film image.[26] Further, as we will see later, if the image persisted through his political career, it was in part because his policies sought to live up to it. That MGR's popularity stemmed from the receptiveness of the audience to his message is made even more clear when we consider the nature of his films.

The details of MGR's film career have been discussed by Pandian (1992) and more briefly by Hardgrave (1973: 298–300). My intention here is to summarize the picture generally drawn of MGR films before adding a few caveats of my own; I then do the same with Jayalalitha's films. These are suggested as hypotheses only. In general, three recurring

[25] A fuller exposition of this model—derived from the work of George Hart— suggests that the institution of kingship was unusually important in Tamil society. One interesting, if irrelevant, piece of evidence for this, according to Hart (personal communication), is that even the words for god—*andavan, kadavan, iraivan*—are essentially a projection of the words for 'king'. To some extent this overlaps with the importance of Murugan worship to Tamil culture. (Murugan, depicted as the son of Shiva, is normally identified with Karthik, but the differences in characteristics ascribed to the two, and in the importance attached to them, are so profound as to be meaningless.)

[26] See, for example, N. Krishnaswamy, 'From Hero to Messiah, Step by Step', *Indian Express*, 9 January 1988.

themes in MGR movies have been seen as politically significant: MGR as crusader against tyranny; MGR as champion of the poor—often combined with the first through a Robin Hood-style social bandit role—and MGR as the protector of women—as loyal son or husband, and chivalrous champion of women's virtue. One additional theme, however, that is seldom commented on is the frequency with which MGR is depicted *not* as a member of the working class himself, but as a member of the natural aristocracy to whom common folk look for leadership against usurpers (as in *Ayarathil Oruvan*), or even a dispossessed king of a blighted country out to rescue and restore a Golden Age (as in *Nadodi Mannan*).

The theme of dispossession lends itself to two possible interpretations: that it is consistent with DMK ideology, representing the dispossession of Dravidians and that it represents MGR himself as dispossessed of his legitimate status as a high caste (non-Brahmin) Menon whose family had been reduced to poverty. In either case it would appear that MGR's film role was less about resistance from below than about *noblesse oblige*, and may have resonated for that reason.[27]

By contrast, I offer a somewhat different hypothesis about Jayalalitha's role. As many observers have remarked, Jayalalitha is an unusual choice to lead the dominant faction of what was once the 'Dravidian Movement'. Her background is urban upper middle class and Brahmin. That Jayalalitha's close association with MGR was essential for her success is obvious. However, MGR had many heroines. Why was she the most popular—as it is generally acknowledged, she was becoming the highest paid female star in the 1960s and 1970s—and it would appear, the most memorable? Her political career was launched more than a decade after her retirement from films. To answer this, it might be worthwhile to look at her film character.

One hypothesis, suggested to me by a few films starring MGR and Jayalalitha is that this actress was particularly popular, especially among women, because she was almost always depicted as assertive, even if in a traditional role.[28] One remarkable movie that bears this out is *Adimai Penn*

---

[27]In this context it is worth noting again that even in the archetypal DMK movie, *Parasakthi*, the non-Brahmin hero is depicted not as a member of the 'subaltern' classes but as the scion of a wealthy trading family.

[28] This interpretation was first suggested to me by a group interview with working class women associated with the Madras-based credit collective, Working Women's Forum, in January 1989. In the view of many of these women—almost all of whom admitted to being MGR fans and ADMK partisans—Jayalalitha was preferable to Janaki because the latter was merely a 'doll' (*bommai*), providing a front for strongman Veerappan, while Jayalalitha was her own woman.

(Slave Women). In this movie MGR, the true heir to the throne has been imprisoned from childhood and is a mute. Most of the women in the country have been put to slave labour. Jayalalitha, a member of an underground resistance movement which rescues him, is given the task of making a man out of him. She initially nurtures him—literally cradling his head in her arms and mothering him—then actually teaches him to fight and sends him to rescue the slave women. Later in the film the two are trapped by an evil queen—played by Jayalalitha in a 'double role'—whose hissing machinations they defeat together.

With these observations in mind, I propose that a better explanation for the early salience of social insurance and welfare programmes for Tamil women, is that they are objectively more vulnerable to loss of income owing to their greater exposure to market forces. Specifically, Tamil Nadu's economy is characterized by monetization and wage labour to a greater degree than most Indian states, as well as by an extraordinarily high rate of participation by women in the wage labour force. This suggests that with the expansion of wage labour, particularly as Indian agriculture becomes more monetized, the welfare populist or social insurance issues that make Tamil Nadu seem so distinctive, will become more salient in other parts of India.

TABLE 15

WAGE EMPLOYMENT AMONG RURAL WOMEN IN TAMIL NADU,
INDIA AND UTTAR PRADESH

	Year	% of rural women classified as main workers	% of rural women classified as main workers and as agricultural labourers
Tamil Nadu	1981	27.9	16.7
	1991	32.9	19.7
India	1981	16.0	8.0
	1991	19.1	9.1
Uttar Pradesh	1981	5.9	2.2
	1991	9.4	3.6

SOURCE: Census of India, 1991.

Policies 1: Vertical Conflict and Targeting

One important precondition for the rise of protection populism is the existence of vertical conflict within empowerment constituencies and the use of sandwich tactics to exploit them. Efforts to split empowerment constituencies are most evident in the signature issue of the Dravidian movement—reserved quotas for the backward classes. Tamil Nadu has had a long history of providing preferential treatment for communities considered 'backward' in the race for entry into English-language education and government jobs, beginning with tuition subsidies ('fees concessions') for Muslims and Oriya speakers in 1872 (Radhakrishnan 1990: 509). By 1880 a dozen Hindu 'backward communities' were being granted similar concessions, a number expanded to forty-five in 1903–4. By 1913 proposals were being made to extend educational concessions to a much larger list of 'backward classes' encompassing half the population (Irschick 1986: 46).

These concessions were sufficiently alluring to prompt changes in identity in order to gain access to the concessions. A number of caste groups whose associations had been claiming Brahmin status redefined their status objectives in favour of 'backwardness', while the 1891 census reported a mysterious increase in the proportion of respondents declaring Oriya as their mother tongue (Irschick 1986: 47–9; Radhakrishnan 1990: 509–19). The impact of the fees concessions, however, paled in comparison to the effects of caste-based quotas for entry into universities, professional colleges and public service. Demands for the latter were also qualitatively different in that they were explicitly directed *against* a particular segment of the population, Brahmins, who had come to dominate government service and the professions.

The introduction of caste-based quotas by the Justice Party in 1927 inaugurated what was to become a recurring battle over defining who was truly 'backward' enough to merit compensatory discrimination. The Justice Party fixed quotas by caste category for appointment to all grades of government positions, allotting five out of twelve seats, or 42 per cent, for 'non-Brahmin Hindus' collectively, and a maximum quota for Brahmins of two seats out of twelve; there were no 'open competition' seats. The 1927 quotas also seriously underrepresented the Depressed Classes or 'Untouchable' groups, allotting them only one out of twelve seats, and assigned quotas to two minority communities, Muslims and Anglo-Indians (GOI 1989: 164). By the early 1930s, however, the Justice Party's preferential policies had come under attack from within the non-Brahmin category for being monopolized by elite non-Brahmin castes. In 1934 legislators belonging to lesser agricultural caste clusters formed the Madras Provincial Backward Classes League, and presented to the government a memorandum seeking to demonstrate the need for limiting preferential quotas to 'Backward' as opposed to 'Forward' non-Brahmin Hindus (Irschick 1986: 74–7; Barnett 1976: 56–65). In 1947 this demand was finally granted in a revised 'Communal Government Order' which allotted two out of twelve seats to 'Backward non-Brahmin Hindus' and doubled the share of the Depressed Classes, largely at the expense of Muslims and Anglo-Indians. Shortly thereafter, however, the Supreme Court decreed that the practice of fixing quotas for all groups was unconstitutional; reserved quotas were permissible only on the grounds of compensation for disadvantage, thus a substantial proportion of all seats would have to be allotted on the basis of open competition. A revised government order in 1954, accordingly, made provision for reservation only for 'backward classes' and the constitutionally specified 'scheduled castes and tribes,' who were given 25 per cent and 16 per cent respectively. All others, including the 'Forward' non-Brahmin Hindu castes were henceforth assigned to the open competition category (GOI 1980: 165).

Following the declaration that only 'backward' castes could be given preferential quotas, vertical conflicts turned on whom to include in the 'backward' category, and whether to further compartmentalize this category by creating quotas for the 'most backward' castes. Here the DMK, which has championed 'backward caste' reservations since the 1950s, has been notably resistant to the further compartmentalization of the category. By contrast, both the Congress and the ADMK have consistently shown willingness to target reservations within the backward category, on both income and caste criteria. Thus the Kamaraj government introduced separate reservations for the 'most backward' castes by dividing large clusters into 'forward' and 'backward' subcastes. In 1970, the DMK, which had appointed the first Tamil Nadu Backward Classes Commission rejected its recommendation that access to reserved quotas be limited to those with an annual family income under Rs 9000 but accepted a proposal to expand the overall quota. The income cut-off was subsequently implemented by MGR in 1979 but withdrawn in the wake of DMK-led demonstrations. Two years later the administration appointed a second Backward Classes Commission. The report submitted by this body was ignored by the MGR government and finally submitted to the legislature by the second Karunanidhi government of 1989–91 (Radhakrishnan 1989: 1265).

Internal conflicts within the 'backward class' category, however, continue to undermine the DMK. As we have seen, an important reason for the drop in the DMK vote in 1991 was the emergence of the PMK or

'Common People's Party'. Supported principally by the members of the same Vanniyar caste cluster whose earlier electoral vehicles had a short-lived alliance with the DMK in the 1950s, this party's principal demand is for compartmentalizing 'backward class' reservations and for granting Vanniyars separate quotas nationwide.[29]

A similar trajectory appears with farmers' movements. The Tamil Nadu Agriculturists Association (TNAA), which arose in the cotton-growing district of Coimbatore, an area dominated, like Haryana and western UP, by progressive farmers drawn from upper cultivator castes, began in the 1970s to demand greater price support, loan write-offs, and subsidies for fertilizer and electricity for agricultural operations.[30] MGR's tactics in dealing with the TNAA, as with his response to reservations, rested on splitting the poorer peasantry from the movement's rich farmer leadership. His first two years in office witnessed some of the most violent activity by the TNAA. After the state government and the TNAA failed to reach a settlement in 1979 on the latter's demands for writing off unpaid loans, the MGR government decided to reduce electricity rates and write off loans for small farmers, agreeing only to reschedule loans for larger farmers.

Following the 1980 elections, however, the MGR government relented on reducing electricity rates for all farmers and electricity charges have since been reduced to virtually zero for agricultural operations. While this is one of the most frequently cited instances of populist excesses in Tamil Nadu, it should be emphasized first, that it was not necessitated by the electoral logic of the situation, and second, as we will see, that it has not come at the expense of fiscal prudence.

MGR's efforts to contain empowerment constituencies are themselves, in part, an expression of his efforts to target distributional benefits to the most excluded groups. While, in principle, subsidies for farmers are not zero-sum—except to the extent that they undermine the state's finances—reservations for backward classes clearly are, since the inclusion of relatively less backward groups tends to restrict the access of the more backward. Nonetheless, it is in the area of welfare measures that MGR's principal contribution lay.

[29] Here it should be noted that the expansion of reservations to 69 per cent in Tamil Nadu, recently sanctioned by Parliament, came about because of the MGR government's decision to preserve reservations for 'most backward.'

[30] The following account is drawn principally from Nadkarni (1987: 60–7, esp. 65–7).

Policies 2: Protection Policies as a Substitution Tactic

We have seen that a major difficulty faced by the Dravidian movement both as a cultural nationalist party and as a movement of the backward castes has been that these issues have not had immediate relevance for the majority of voters. Welfare and social reform policies played an important role in winning electoral support since at least the 1930s, first for the Congress and then for the ADMK. Indeed, Tamil Nadu has been something of a pioneer in these areas in the Indian context, with all parties promoting welfare schemes.

The general pattern is as follows: Congress in the 1930s first introduced issues with an indirect social insurance content; in the 1950s and 1960s, the Kamaraj administration introduced some important general social welfare policies; the Karunanidhi government of the 1960s and 1970s added to these some selective measures aimed at specially targeted populations, mostly introduced after MGR left the party; under the MGR regime there was a marked shift in favour of more broad-based measures aimed at women and vulnerable occupational groups that had been associated with MGR's image as protector in the past. The second Karunanidhi government of 1989–91 sought in fact to cut back on some of these while substituting a few more highly visible and selective measures—and lost. In the areas of social insurance, prohibition, and food and nutrition policy, MGR built on initiatives undertaken by the Kamaraj government.

Although, as in most places, social insurance in Tamil Nadu is strongest for the organized sector, Tamil Nadu has long been noted for measures aimed at providing minimum levels of social insurance to the 'poor-in-general' (Guhan 1989: 9–13). The first such measure was a pension programme for the destitute elderly introduced by the Kamaraj government in 1962, to which the DMK government of the 1970s added disability payments for the handicapped, a contributory social security programme for weavers, and monthly pensions for destitute widows in the 1970s (Guhan 1989: 9–13). This period, following MGR's defection, also saw Karunanidhi initiate a number of highly visible charitable measures, such as opening free eye clinics and distributing cycle-drawn rickshaws to rickshaw-pullers (Forrester 1976).

As is common, the effort has been to define some of the poor as deserving of special assistance (Skocpol 1992), but the definition of these groups has been broader under MGR, with special emphasis on women and the very poor. Thus the MGR administration introduced accident relief programmes for fishermen, sewage workers and other low status occupational groups. Even more notable is the greatly expanded eligibility of women for pensions: besides lowering the age of eligibility for old-age pensions from 65 to 60, the MGR government extended pensions to abandoned wives over the age of 30 and lowered the age of eligibility for widows to 40.

Apart from these formal social security measures, the regime greatly expanded the use of *ad hoc* disaster relief provided from the chief minister's relief fund, as well as from party funds. Both facts have been tied to the prevalence of kickbacks in the MGR regime, a subject to which I will turn shortly. In addition, the concern evident for poor women in these changes was, of course, the ostensible source of his two most famous policies— prohibition and the Noon Meal Scheme.

That MGR's approach to poverty was paternalistic rather than empowering comes out most clearly in the twists and turns of liquor policy under his regime. Tamil Nadu is not unique in presenting the prohibition of alcohol as a measure to aid poor women: the temperance movement in the United States made similar claims, while the issue has become increasingly popular in other Indian states. MGR's approach to prohibition, however, was distinctive in his willingness to delink this social welfare concern from a broader moral argument for it.

Prohibition was first introduced in the 1930s by a Congress ministry in accordance with Gandhi's wishes and was consistently supported by Tamil Nadu leaders, including E. V. Ramasami, Kamaraj, and Annadurai. During the early 1970s, Tamil Nadu was one of only two 'dry' states in the country. Shortly after the 1971 elections, however, prohibition was lifted by the Karunanidhi government in an effort to raise revenue from liquor taxes. This became one of the few identifiable policy differences between Karunanidhi and MGR in the period leading up to the 1972 split (Barnett 1976: 294–5). A promise to reintroduce prohibition formed an integral part of the ADMK's first manifesto. This promise was realized by the Congress government during the Emergency. Subsequently, however, Tamil Nadu witnessed repeated shifts in policy, often stimulated by the proliferation of illegal distilleries, associated deaths from adulterated illegal liquor, and the desire to recoup revenue. MGR himself lifted prohibition in 1981, only to reintroduce 'partial prohibition' in 1986. The Karunanidhi government lifted it again in 1989 only to have Jayalalitha campaign on a promise to reintroduce it in 1991. What is important, however, is that, especially under MGR, both the lifting and reimposition of prohibition were undertaken in ways that emphasized its importance as a social welfare issue, aimed at protecting the livelihoods of poor families and the physical security of poor women, rather than as a moral one. Two interesting patterns illustrate this: first, the periodic reimposition of prohibition is increasingly accompanied by attempts to preserve the access of the middle and upper classes to alcohol; second, the removal of prohibition tends to be accompanied by visible measures to compensate for the presumed loss of income to working class families.

The first tendency, preserving the access of the middle classes to alcohol, led to the liberal issuing of drinking permits on medical grounds in the 1970s and early 1980s, and the proliferation of 'permit rooms' (bars open only to those with permits). This class bias was made even more explicit in 1986, when the MGR government introduced 'partial prohibition'— only the production and sale of native or 'country' liquors favoured by the poor was prohibited, not the 'Indian Made Foreign Liquors' (IMFL) consumed by the elite. Indeed, throughout the 1980s, the granting of licences to distil IMFL was accompanied by charges of massive corruption.[31] The second principle, compensatory measures to offset the presumed welfare effects on the poor, was even more dramatic as it resulted in the most famous of MGR's welfare programmes, the Noon Meal Scheme.

As we have seen already, the politics of food have played an important and continuing role in Tamil Nadu politics, from the Kamaraj government's school lunch programme, introduced in 1956, to the DMK's promise to provide three measures of rice for one rupee. In part, this may be because of historically high levels of malnutrition in the state, which led to the involvement of international aid agencies by the late 1960s. During the MGR period, two important nutrition intervention programmes were initiated.[32]

The first of these, the Tamil Nadu Integrated Nutrition Project (TINP), was a World Bank-funded targeted nutrition intervention programme for weaning infants started in the early 1980s (Harris 1986: 2–3). It seeks to deliver vital nutrients to the infant at a critical stage of development at low cost. Still in effect, it has been widely hailed as a major policy success and held up as a model.

This is in sharp contrast to the far more ambitious and expensive

---

[31] See 'High and Dry!', *The Week*, 11–17 January 1987, pp. 26–7, for an account of this measure. Also 'Hooch Watch', *The Week*, 25 February 1990, pp. 18–19, and 'Prohibition: The Finishing Stroke', *Business India*, 16–29 April 1990, pp. 21–2, for overviews of prohibition in Tamil Nadu.

[32] This section draws on Vasantha Surya, 'Taming Hunger: Tamil Nadu's Nutritious Meal Scheme', *Frontline*, 20 January–2 February 1990; Harris (1986, 1991); Devadas (1986); interviews with public officials charged with the implementation of the programmes conducted in 1991; and conversations with C. Annadurai of Madras Institute of Development Studies.

programme with which the MGR regime is more commonly associated, the Chief Minister's Nutritious Noon Meal Programme or, as it is popularly known, the Noon Meal Scheme. Announced by MGR in 1982, the programme greatly expanded the coverage of the earlier school lunch programme by providing the service year-round, rather than just during the 200 days of the school year, and by including all children above the age of two rather than merely school-age children. In addition, the expanded programme involved a conscious effort to appeal to working class women. The Noon Meal Centres provide day-care facilities ('crèches' or *balwadis*) for working class women. Indigent widows and the elderly were also eligible for food at the Centres, and most importantly, by requiring that employees be poor women, the programme doubled as an employment programme (Harris 1986: 4).

That the funding for the programme in its initial years almost exactly matched the revenues from lifting prohibition may be a coincidence. Nonetheless, the link between the two measures was unmistakable: as Barbara Harris has pointed out, the Noon Meal Scheme virtually sought to compensate at the level of the household for calories lost by working class children and mothers to their fathers' drinking habits (1986: 170–1; 1991).

The programme has been extremely controversial politically, condemned as an instance of the developmentally dysfunctional character of MGR's populism and admired as an effort to provide for the poorest in society.[33] Among the criticisms is the expense of the programme— especially compared to the TINP, and the charge that it diverts food from the Public Distribution System (Annadurai 1988: 38–9). The short-lived Karunanidhi administration attempted to cut costs by, among other measures, eliminating the elderly and widows from the programme, in order to restore its status as a school lunch programme.

A case could be made, of course, that such measures would be beneficial to the poor in the long run by allocating funds to long-term developmental needs. I will not attempt to adjudicate this debate on the relative merits of the Noon Meal Scheme over other food enhancement strategies, except to observe that for this essay the real question is whether the general emphasis on the politics of food can be shown to have had an effect, at least enough to explain, voters' support for MGR.[34] I therefore turn to a consideration of development performance.

[33] Janaki Venkataraman, 'The Noon Meal Mess: Is There Hope?', *Aside: The Magazine of Madras*, 1–15 April 1987.

[34] See Devadas (1986) for an early positive assessment.

Development Performance

The success of the MGR regime is due in large measure to the relatively much better performance of the state during the 1980s both on general economic growth and on human development indices. Most surprisingly, in sharp contrast to the claims of most critics, when measured against the record of other large Indian states, Tamil Nadu's record on the dimensions of economic performance that critics imply were neglected—economic growth and investment in social infrastructure—is remarkably good.

The record on infrastructure is important to emphasize since arguments about the dysfunctional aspects of 'populist' subsidies focus on this issue. While power generation has, indeed, lagged, during the MGR period the state acquired by far the most extensive paved road network in the country.

TABLE 16

PERFORMANCE ON ROAD-BUILDING, TAMIL NADU AND
ALL-INDIA, 1982, 1988

	Roads (km)/ 1000 km2		Surfaced roads (km)/1000 km2		Roads (km)/ 1000 inhabitants		Surfaced roads (km)/1000 inhabitants	
	1982	1988	1982	1988	1982	1988	1982	1988
Tamil Nadu	784.0	1283.6	445.8	814.8	2.1	3.4	1.2	2.2
	(2)	(2)	(3)	(1)	(5)	(2)	(2)	(2)
All-India	453.3	575.9	207.8	270.1	2.2	2.8	1.0	1.3

SOURCE: Statistical Pocketbook of India, 1990. Figures in parentheses denote rank among 15 major states.

Additionally, between 1980 and MGR's death in 1987, Tamil Nadu experienced one of the better rates of growth in per capita income among the major states. Per capita state domestic product (SDP) increased from 92 per cent of the all-India average in 1980–1, placing Tamil Nadu sixth among major states, to slightly above the national average in 1987–8 (GOI 1990: 8–9). Two different estimates of compound annual growth in real per capita SDP both demonstrate that Tamil Nadu's growth rate accelerated during the 1980s.

TABLE 17

COMPOUND ANNUAL RATES OF GROWTH OF STATE DOMESTIC
PRODUCT, TAMIL NADU AND ALL-INDIA, 1970–92

	Ahluwalia's estimate (real SDP)		CMIE's estimate (Real SDP per capita)	
	1970/1– 1980/1	1980/1–1985/6	1970/1–1980/1	1980/1–1991/2
Tamil Nadu	2.8	6.9	0.05	2.92
All-India	3.7	5.0	0.96	3.00

SOURCES: Ahluwalia (1991:16); and CMIE (1989; 1994: Table 10.5).

It is, however, in its performance on social indicators that the MGR
government really shines. Here, figures on malnutrition rates show
interesting patterns: while the proportion of people who suffered no
malnutrition in Tamil Nadu did not diminish much over the period, the
proportion of those suffering from severe malnutrition fell dramatically,
especially when compared with other states.

TABLE 18

TRENDS IN MALNUTRITION LEVEL BY STATES

STATE	% normal		% with 'mild' malnutrition		% with 'moderate' malnutrition		% with 'severe' malnutrition	
	1975–9	1988–90	1975–9	1988–90	1975–9	1988–90	1975–9	1988–90
Andhra Pradesh	6.1	8.7	32.4	39.5	46.1	44.3	15.4	7.5
Gujarat	3.8	7.3	28.1	33.9	54.3	45.8	13.8	13.0
Karnataka	4.6	4.8	31.1	38.1	50.0	48.8	14.3	8.3
Kerala	7.5	17.7	35.7	47.4	46.5	32.9	10.3	2.0
Madhya Pradesh	8.4	17.7	30.3	27.4	45.1	38.9	16.2	16.0
Maharashtra	3.2	6.7	25.4	38.0	49.5	47.5	21.9	7.8
Orissa	7.5	8.1	35.9	34.6	41.7	46.6	14.9	10.7
Tamil Nadu	6.2	8.0	34.2	42.0	47.0	45.8	12.6	4.2

SOURCE: National Nutrition Monitoring Bureau, 1991: 55–70.

Even more impressive is the decline in infant mortality rates. Once among the highest in India, the Under Five Mortality Rate (U5MR) had declined to 59 deaths per 1000 by the 1990s, compared to a national average of 73, while a Capability Poverty Measure (computed on the basis of indicators of malnourishment) gave Tamil Nadu the second best ranking (Dev and Ranade 1997: 70–1). Similarly, a computation of the Human Development Index (HDI) for Indian states around 1987 placed Tamil Nadu among the handful of Indian states which were near or above the threshold for middle income states (Shiva Kumar 1991).

These scattered pieces of evidence do not prove conclusively that Tamil Nadu turned its developmental record around in the 1980s. Nor do they explain the improvement in macroeconomic indicators. They do suggest, though, that the poor of Tamil Nadu had sound material reasons to vote loyally for the ADMK, and that this may not have been the disaster that many have claimed it was.

In contrast to its reputation as an outsider to the mainstream of Indian politics, Tamil Nadu has been a pioneer, anticipating trends in the rest of the country. One obvious example is in the area of preferential quotas ('reservations'): the use of broad caste labels denoting 'the common people', including 'non-Brahmin' and 'backward class', the introduction of reservations for employment for these groups, and the subsequent conflicts over internal differentiation among backward classes were all anticipated in Tamil Nadu.[35] Equally important were the politicization of language by newly literate groups, and the first appearance in India of a farmers' movement organized around sectoral issues rather than distribution of land. On the other hand, a number of social insurance and other welfare measures which are becoming increasingly popular in other parts of India were pioneered in Tamil Nadu, first by Congress and then by the ADMK, prominent among them old age pensions and a universal school feeding programme.

These various measures, however, were the products of two very different styles of politics which result from an area in which Tamil Nadu *is* unique among Indian states: it has experienced two-party

---

[35] On this issue, 'the south' might actually be more accurate, since the earliest development of these issues was in multilingual Madras Presidency, and the princely state of Mysore experienced parallel developments. The first use of the term 'non-Brahmin' was, of course, in Bombay (Omvedt 1976) but this was before electoral politics got under way, and my understanding is that the party that lays claim to this legacy, the Peasants and Workers Party has never been a major force, in part because of the emergence of Maratha dominance within Congress (Lele 1981).

electoral competition for seventy years. Between 1917 and 1935, the Justice Party, a regional party representing well-to-do segments of agricultural and commercial caste groups, challenged the Indian National Congress for the support of politically articulate social groups within the British Indian province of Madras, the core of which was formed by the Tamil-speaking districts that now constitute Tamil Nadu. Contesting elections held under a very limited franchise, which the Congress usually boycotted, the Justice Party faded out of existence when the expansion of the franchise in 1935 led to decisive Congress victories. Twenty years later, however, a descendant of the Justice Party, the Dravida Munnetra Kazhagam (DMK) challenged Congress hegemony in the Tamil state and, in 1967, succeeded in permanently displacing Congress from state power. The DMK, in turn, split in 1972 and the state has since been characterized by a contest between the DMK and the ADMK.

These facts make Tamil Nadu an ideal case to test the hypercompetition model of political violence because it is often presented as an extreme case of the pitfalls of Indian party competition. Like arguments that Indian parties are incoherent collections of personalistic factions, regional parties of Tamil Nadu have been treated as so ideologically indistinguishable that their record in office can be treated as that of a single party (Washbrook 1989). Likewise, authors making the argument that 'competitive populism' has led to 'demand overload' often point to the Tamil Nadu case as paradigmatic: in most accounts electoral competition in the state has led to the steady expansion of preferential quotas for the backward classes, subsidies for farmers and other fiscally wasteful handouts, while reversing the developmental gains of the preceding Congress party administration and leaving untouched the structural inequities that sustain poverty.

The argument that the DMK and ADMK are merely personal factions of a single Dravidian movement ignores the fact that the latter's emergence replicates a critical feature of similar splits in the history of the movement since 1916: attempts to unite the majority of Tamils against a common enemy by addressing them as a single category repeatedly failed because, first, some newly mobilized groups viewed themselves as relatively *more* dispriviledged and, second, because the poorest voters responded to other parties' promises to address their basic needs.

More importantly, it is increasingly becoming clear that the MGR government's record on delivering material benefits in the form of growth and poverty alleviation was considerably better than that of most Indian states, suggesting that the absence of political violence in the state is ultimately the result of at least some of the attributes of good government, themselves the product of competition. As parties in the rest of India adjust to a competitive environment it is not impossible that they will likewise develop stable constituencies and programmes to serve them. This is an aspect of institutionalization that results from increasing competition that students of Indian politics would do well to consider.

The Rise and Fall of Democracy in Jammu and Kashmir, 1975–1989

Sten Widmalm*

Why did democracy in Jammu and Kashmir give way to armed struggle? What in the late 1970s looked like the democratization of the northernmost state of India had, by the end of the 1980s, become a small-scale civil war, causing indescribable suffering resulting in more than 20,000 casualties. The questions are: what gave rise to violent separatism in Jammu and Kashmir (JK) and could it have been averted?

Indian, Kashmiri and Pakistani nationalists have portrayed this tragedy as the inevitable outcome of trying to merge incompatible identities. In India, Pakistan is frequently denounced as the orchestrator of the 'insurgency movement', while the Pakistani side describes the uprising in 'Indian-Occupied Kashmir' (IOK) as a reaction against the suppression of the Kashmiris' wish to join Pakistan. In the West the conflict is often vaguely described as part of the spread of global ethnic conflict and the Islamization of Asia. It will be argued here, however, that the salience of incompatible identities should be regarded as an outcome of an earlier and distinctly political conflict in JK—a struggle for power between elites in the state and the central government. Viewing events from this perspective necessitates looking beyond ethnicity as an explanatory factor and focusing more closely on the development of political institutions and the decisions made by the political elite in JK and New Delhi during the crucial period 1975 to 1989.[1] Naturally socio-economic conditions in the region have to be considered as well. Furthermore, although democracy is often seen as an obstacle to integration, this story reinforces the claim, made, for example, by Robert Dahl, that it can be regarded as a vital component in the nation-building process (Dahl 1971: 43). Let us begin

---

* Field research in India and Pakistan was funded by the Swedish International Development Agency (SIDA). A complete version of this study was presented as a dissertation at the Department of Government, Uppsala University, in the spring of 1997. The dissertation also contains comparisons with developments in Tamil Nadu and West Bengal.

[1] For example Walker Connor (1993, 1994) and Donald Horowitz (1985) emphasize ethnicity as an independent variable which explains violent separatism.

with a quick glance in the rear view mirror in order to examine some important factors that rendered the foundations for democracy in JK so fragile; then we shall proceed to the events surrounding the replacement of democracy by violence in the 1980s.

DEMOCRACY IN JAMMU AND KASHMIR ON A DETOUR

Considering the traumatic events of the partition and the incomplete nature of the settlement at the time of accession, it is quite understandable why so many authors emphasize historical roots when trying to explain the conflict in JK (see, for example, Rizvi 1992: 49–51; Cheema 1992: 94–7; Varshney 1992: 194; Lamb 1991, 1994). But it should also be stressed that no other state in India had to wait as long for democracy. The poor record of democracy in JK was characterized by the constant rigging of elections and by various forms of central government intervention which prevented the development of fair and autonomous political competition between parties.

While elections were held in most parts of the country from 1952 onwards, the first Vidhan Sabha (state legislative assembly) elections in JK were held only in 1962, while the first Lok Sabha (national assembly) elections did not take place until 1967. It also appears that most elections held in JK before the mid-1970s were fraudulent in various ways. In the constituent assembly elections of 1951, candidates belonging to the regional Kashmiri opposition party, the JK National Congress (NC), won all seventy-five seats. The journalist and Congress (I) politician, M. J. Akbar, speculates that the results were accepted only because of the clearly widespread support for Sheikh Abdullah (Akbar 1991: 138–42; see also Ganai 1984: 16; Verma 1994: 38–42; Varshney 1992: 212; Lamb 1991: 192–3). The Praja Parishad Party, an opposition party dominated by landowning Hindus in Jammu, had no choice but to accept the illegal rejection of their candidates.

Equally corrupt electoral practices were to plague the state for the following twenty-five years, although they were employed mainly by the central government under Congress party rule. Rigging, however, was not the only factor that hindered democratic development. The wars in 1947, 1965 and 1971 made JK the most sensitive border state in India; as a result, the Congress-led central government viewed any political opposition in the state with increasing suspicion and used various means to curtail its freedom. Although Jawaharlal Nehru had been a close friend of Sheikh Abdullah, the leader of the NC, distrust crept in during the early 1950s amidst fears of the secession of JK. At this time NC leaders were divided on the question of accession. Before Independence, Bakshi Ghulam Muhammad had been one of the closest aides to Sheikh Abdullah, but by the 1950s the two leaders were pulling in different directions. Strengthened by the popularity following extensive land reforms, Sheikh Abdullah began increasingly to advocate far-reaching provisions to guarantee the autonomy of the state. Although plans for making JK an 'Eastern Switzerland' may not have been considered viable, and the option of joining feudal Pakistan was quickly rejected, Abdullah's policies were often interpreted by the central government as disloyalty to the Indian Union. Bakshi Ghulam Muhammad, on the other hand, supported a more comprehensive form of integration of JK with India. Consequently, he was rewarded for his position by increased support from the central government, whereas Sheikh Abdullah was arrested in 1953. While Abdullah was in jail, Bakshi Ghulam Muhammad was installed as prime minister of JK. In 1964 Sheikh Abdullah was released, but only a year later he was again arrested and detained for thirty months on suspicion of supporting a separatist agitation (Akbar 1991: 159–69).[2] Amendments that further integrated the constitution of JK with that of the rest of India were passed during the 1950s and 1960s, and the NC was practically converted into a regional branch of the Congress party (see Puri 1993: 31). These events were a major cause of frustration in the Valley and the turmoil they created was used by Pakistan to justify its military attack on India in 1965 after the Hazratbal crisis (Lamb 1991: 258–60, chap. 12). Nevertheless, the frustration did not necessarily translate into sympathy for Pakistan. Instead, much of the political opposition and its discontent were channelled through the Plebiscite Front founded by Mirza Afzal Beg in 1955, and after the Shimla Accord of 1972, it was used to resurrect the 'old' NC with Sheikh Abdullah as its leader.[3] Finally, in 1977, the first free and fair elections were held in JK, with the NC and the Congress party contesting as political equals. After a long detour, JK was finally on the road to democracy.

[2] After the release of Sheikh Abdullah in 1964 it looked, for a while at least, as if the Kashmir problem would be solved. Jawaharlal Nehru developed friendly relations with Sheikh Abdullah, who was sent to Pakistan to investigate the possibility of negotiations on the Kashmir question. Tragically, Nehru died before any agreement was reached between India and Pakistan. Sheikh Abdullah was released from prison in 1968, but excluded from the state from January 1971 to June 1972 (Verma 1994: 48–9).

[3] This should not be confused with Amanullah Khan's Plebiscite Front that became the Kashmir National Liberation Front, and later the Jammu and Kashmir Liberation Front (JKLF). According to Lamb it is possible to regard Amanullah Khan's organization as an 'informal offshoot' of Beg's Plebiscite Front. See Lamb (1991: 292).

THE DEMOCRATIC BREAKTHROUGH OF 1977

Indira Gandhi and Sheikh Abdullah are often given credit for initiating the democratization process in JK in 1975.[4] A different picture, however, is painted by some others including Balraj Puri, a former NC member, and Bhim Singh of the local Panthers Party in JK, who emphasize the role of Morarji Desai, who was prime minister when elections were held in the summer of 1977.[5] Trying to find a base for support in the north after its defeat in the Lok Sabha election in March 1977, the Congress (I) increased its efforts to capture votes in JK. Desai, however, took important steps to strengthen security in JK so that fair elections could be held. According to Bhim Singh, 'Morarji Desai openly declared that anyone who would attempt to pursue some form of rigging would be severely punished, and this was quite effective.'[6] The NC secured a majority in the assembly with 47 seats out of 75. The Janata Party and Congress (I) won 13 and 11 seats respectively, while the Jamaat-e-Islami finished with only 1.

It seems that in order for democracy to reach JK, the Indian National Congress first had to be removed from power at the centre. From the perspective of Jawaharlal Nehru and Indira Gandhi, the sensitive border state was not yet ready for democracy. Building Indian nationalism and expanding democracy at the same time tended to be regarded as incompatible goals; this reasoning appears to have been applied to the case of JK in particular. An autonomous political opposition was regarded as a hindrance to integration and development, and in the view of the

---

[4] For example, Akbar argues that Indira Gandhi and Sheikh Abdullah set the state on course for democracy as early as in 1975 (Akbar 1991: 192).

[5] Interviews with the former National Conference member Balraj Puri, 18 November 1994, Bhim Singh of the local Panthers Party in Jammu and Kashmir, 27 October 1994, and B.K. Nehru, 14 November 1994.

[6] Interview with Singh, 27 October 1994, New Delhi. Most of the Kashmiris interviewed who are active in politics, including many of those who are today critical of the central government, agree that the 1977 elections were free and fair. Interview with Bilal Ahmad Lodhi, JK High Court, 21 November 1994, Srinagar; interview with Abdul Ghani Lone (10 November 1994, New Delhi), who also supports Singh's view on the role of Morarji Desai. This view on the 1977 election is also supported by journalists writing on JK politics, for example Askari Zaidi of the *Times of India*: interview with Zaidi, 7 November 1994, New Delhi. Also see Puri (1993: 33); Akbar (1991: 192); Varshney (1992: 218). The Maulana Abbas Ansari, who is an important political and religious leader in Jammu and Kashmir, and his supporters (who have cooperated politically with the Jamaat-e-Islami) are among the few who claim that elections in 1977 were not carried out in a fair manner (interview, 22 November 1994, Srinagar).

Congress party, nation-building had to be given priority over democratization. Nevertheless, Balraj Puri, who has provided some of the most valuable analyses of the conflict, suggests that in the case of JK this argument can be proved wrong. He emphatically points out that with free and fair elections, a natural process of integration of JK with India had been initiated.[7] Therefore, beginning with the democratization process in the mid-1970s, 'there ... [were] ten years in Jammu and Kashmir with no fundamentalism, no secessionism and no communalism'. Of course, the region was not without problems during this period. The point is, however, that the situation was at least manageable and that, for a time, democracy worked. The level of violence and political turbulence in the early 1980s was insignificant compared with that of today and it would seem that these political conditions did indeed breed integration.[8] Further evidence of this comes from what may be considered an unexpected source—namely Amanullah Khan, the leader of the separatist JKLF.

The JKLF provides 'the third position' in this conflict, by advocating that JK should become an independent state.[9] It was founded in the mid-1960s by Amanullah Khan and Maqbool Butt, but did not become a significant political force in the Valley until the mid-and late-1980s. The question here is: why did the JKLF wait until 1988 to get organized to launch an effective separatist campaign in the Valley? Khan's position on the status of JK did not change much over the years. The demand for independence had been part of his platform since he began his organized activities in Karachi in the early 1960s. So could he have launched the offensive in the Valley earlier than he did? His own comments on these questions shed some light on the process of integration and the political climate in JK at the time.

The JKLF leadership was well aware of the need for local support before the organization could hope to become better established in the Valley, that is 'there had to be some fertile soil'.[10] 'Therefore', Khan explains, 'some boys were sent from England to IOK [Indian-Occupied

---

[7] B.K. Nehru also supports this argument in the interview recorded in 1994. As mentioned earlier, Puri's observation is in line with Dahl's (for example 1971: 43) writings on this topic.

[8] The assessment of the level of violence is based on interviews with Puri (1994); Singh (1994); B.K. Nehru (1994); newspaper cuttings from the period 1975–92; and, to some extent, statistics provided by the Ministry of Home Affairs published in Wirsing 1994.

[9] The other two most common positions on the future of Jammu and Kashmir are that it should either accede to Pakistan or remain with the Indian Union.

[10] Interview with Amanullah Khan, 6 February 1994, Rawalpindi.

Kashmir] to survey if the sentiments could be used for armed struggle.'[11] This was in 1983 and clearly conditions were not found favourable for launching a militant campaign:

They returned and gave me the answer that there was no chance of starting a movement at this time. Everybody in the area was busy. Some were dreaming of the accession to Pakistan, but most people were busy getting on with their daily lives and businesses.[12]

This observation shows that when democracy was functioning in a relatively peaceful JK; the demand to change the political status of the state was neither heard nor supported.[13] Bhim Singh of the Panthers Party endorses this impression of the general mood of the early 1980s, explaining that the minds of all politicians were set on competing within the framework of democracy.[14] Moreover, religious divides did not predicate political behaviour during this period. In the late 1970s, for example, it seems that political 'understandings' and some collaboration developed between the NC and a faction of the Rashtriya Swayamsevak Sangh (RSS).[15] In 1981 and 1982, the NC supported the Bharatiya Janata Party (BJP) in the Jammu Municipality.[16] In other words, political parties drawing most of their support from the Hindu population cooperated with a party mainly relying on a Muslim vote bank.[17] In addition, few of the political arguments in the mainstream debate during this period invoked religion as a source of legitimacy. This allows us to interpret the political climate as quite secular.

To sum up, there was evidently something akin to ethnic peace in JK in the late 1970s and early 1980s, in spite of the state's historically disputed status and the mix of different language and religious groups. Developments and popular sentiment in the area during this period show that democracy

---

[11] Ibid. In Pakistan and among separatists in India, it is a frequently used name for the part of Jammu and Kashmir that is *de facto* controlled by India.

[12] Ibid.

[13] B.K. Nehru, for example, says that Jammu and Kashmir was already a mismanaged state at that time, but it was peaceful (interview with Nehru, 1994). Also see Puri (1993: 50); Akbar (1991: 192); Varshney (1992: 218).

[14] Interview with Singh, 1994.

[15] See 'RSS, NC Link in Poll?', *Patriot*, 8 November 1978; 'RSS Faction Backs Sheikh', *Patriot*, 9 January 1979; 'Pro-Sheikh RSS Man Defeated', *Patriot*, 8 March 1979. The Rashtriya Swayamsevak Sangh and the Bharatiya Janata Party are political organizations that can be described as Hindu-dominated and, to different degrees, Hindu-chauvinistic.

[16] 'BJP, NC May End Alliance,' *Hindustan Times*, 8 January 1982.

[17] This contradicts Donald Horowitz's hypothesis that cross-cutting alliances are ruled out in ethnic two-party systems. See Horowitz (1985: 342–49).

was at least possible and valued. In this case the period of democracy in JK seems also to have aided integration and the nation-building process in India. Forces disloyal to the nation state project may always be present in a democracy, but the available evidence suggests that they attract little support and that the level of violence remains low as long as political freedoms remain intact and institutions are fairly stable. Nor is there any evidence in the events described above that the mix of religious identities per se created the conflict that escalated in the late 1980s.[18] So what went wrong? What factors explain such an early demise of democracy in JK?

THE DECLINE OF DEMOCRACY IN JAMMU AND KASHMIR 1983–1989

When Sheikh Abdullah passed away in 1982, he left a dual legacy for his son Farooq Abdullah who took over the party leadership. On the positive side, JK was a state where religion and the status of the region had not yet become the only or the primary dimensions of polarization. Sentiments in JK favoured peaceful development. On the other hand, institutional structures in the state were weak and this made the newly introduced democracy in JK vulnerable.

Even if economic development was rapid in JK in the 1970s and until the mid-1980s, this seems to have been in spite of, rather than because of, the state government.[19] Paradoxically, even though state funds grew and the central government increased its financial support for the region, the state's debt burden increased and development projects became more inefficient.[20] This culminated in accusations of financial irresponsibility

[18] The position that ethnicity is in itself a cause of conflicts is supported, for example, by Brian Barry (1975: 502–3); van den Berghe (1978: 404–5); and Connor (1994: 195–209). For a related discussion of primordial and instrumental views on the role of ethnicity see Brass (1991: 69–108); Hardin (1995: 142–50).

[19] See Swaminathan S. Aiyar, 'Korean Miracle in Kashmir?', *Hindustan Times*, 27 August 1981, for a discussion on economic growth and public administration in Jammu and Kashmir. For example, between 1970 and 1979 net domestic product increased more in Jammu and Kashmir than in Punjab, Maharashtra and Haryana. It should be noted, however, that the total level of production in Punjab, Maharashtra and Haryana was considerably higher than in Jammu and Kashmir to begin with.

[20] See Balraj Puri, 'Kashmir's Declining Development', *Nagpur Times*, 2 July 1979. For a discussion of the problems of a large state in an economically underdeveloped society see Hadenius (1992: 135–7); for general arguments and hypothesis testing, and for a more specific discussion of empirical evidence from India, (see Kohli, 1990b: 383–403).

against Sheikh Abdullah and his administration, and it was also alleged that he had exploited the situation to increase the wealth of his own family.[21] To cut a long story short, the younger Abdullah took over a state apparatus that can be characterized as quite large but unfortunately thoroughly 'soft'.[22] The state government continued to function in terms of client relationships rather than undertaking genuine development projects.

Even the leadership came to Farooq Abdullah under less than ideal circumstances: he inherited a popular but internally fractured party. Some of the trouble had started back in 1978, when Mirza Afzal Beg was expelled from the NC after forty years of friendship with and political struggle alongside Sheikh Abdullah. The latter seems to have followed the same political strategy as Indira Gandhi, allowing the centralizing tendencies inherent in dynastic rule to assert themselves instead of building a strong and internally democratic apparatus, firmly anchored in local organizations. Distrusting Beg, Sheikh Abdullah rejected him and began to look for a successor. The choice was between his son, Farooq Abdullah, whom he considered too young and inexperienced, and his son-in-law Ghulam Mohammed Shah, whom he thought excessively eager to take over party leadership and rather arrogant.[23] Shah was shocked by Sheikh Abdullah's decision ultimately to let Farooq Abdullah succeed him; later he was further provoked by Farooq Abdullah's decision to remove *his* nephew Ghulam Mohiuddin Shah from the post of party General Secretary.[24] Consequently, after the death of Sheikh Abdullah, the NC was torn by internal rivalry and was, simultaneously, under constant attack from outside forces.

In its determination to heal the wounds of its defeat in the 1977 election, the Congress party had decided to recapture JK at almost any cost. Initially, as the new leader of the NC, Farooq Abdullah was quite receptive to the idea of cooperating with the Congress (I), although some tension had

[21] Interview with Askari Zaidi, 1994. See also, for example, 'JK Govt Encouraging Pro-Pak elements: MP', *Times of India*, 23 March 1982, on charges of corruption against Sheikh Abdullah's ministry. Swaminathan S. Aiyar, however, argues in 'Korean Miracle in Kashmir?', 1981, that corruption declined in the public administration when Sheikh Abdullah was chief minister.

[22] The term 'soft state' originates from Gunnar Myrdal's *Asian Drama* (1968), and it is further developed in Hans Blomkvist's *The Soft State: Housing Reform and State Capacity in Urban India* (1988).

[23] Sheikh Abdullah shared this opinion with B.K. Nehru. Interview with B.K. Nehru 1994.

[24] Instead, the position was given to Sheikh Nazir Ahmed, Sheikh Abdullah's adopted son. See 'Twin Challenges to Kashmir C.M', *The Hindu*, 9 December 1982. Ghulam Muhammed Shah resigned from Sheikh Abdullah's cabinet in August 1982.

developed during discussions on the Resettlement Bill initiated by Sheikh Abdullah before his death.[25] The Resettlement Bill granted the right to return to those who had emigrated to Pakistan from JK, but had been subjects of the state before May 1954. Eventually it created a rift between the two parties. While the Congress (I) accused the NC of aiming only to increase its vote bank through the Bill, the NC charged Congress (I) with curtailing the constitutional rights of former citizens of the state. Not altogether surprisingly, negotiations on an electoral alliance broke down in April 1983. In addition, there was a seat equation that the two parties were unable to resolve. Congress (I) demanded between 15 and 23 of the 75 seats in the state, which Farooq Abdullah considered to be too many. Moreover, in *My Dismissal*, Farooq Abdullah explains that the alliance was avoided because of the fear that the NC could be marginalized.[26] Shortly after negotiations broke down, both parties declared they were contesting all the seats separately.

Campaigning was fierce and the Congress (I) took a firm stand against the Resettlement Bill. Although some early signs of communal politics are visible in this election, it should also be pointed out that the main political issues were still formulated along secular lines.[27] Political argumentation still sought legitimacy in principles of rights rather than in religion. Indeed, both the BJP and the Jamaat-e-Islami, parties respectively defining themselves as Hindu and Muslim, were wiped out in the election. This time, the Congress (I) and the NC competed on a more equal basis and as primary rivals. Ultimately the former received 26 of the total of 76 seats, while the latter won 46 seats. Only three seats went to others, all independent candidates, indicating a strong two-party polarization.

Nonetheless, the election was violent and plagued by an increased level of malpractice.[28] The Congress (I) office was set on fire in May while, a

[25] See, for example, 'Sheikh Abdullah's Dangerous Game', *The Hindu* (Gurgaon), 4 June 1982.

[26] As Ashutosh Varshney points out, if this conviction was true in 1983, it was tragically forgotten in 1986 when the party did join hands with the Congress (I) for the 1987 elections—with devastating results. Varshney (1992: 220).

[27] Varshney points out that the Congress party increasingly made use of communal messages in this election campaign (1992: 219). For important contributions and observations in connection with this discussion, see 'Awami Alliance May Cost Dr Abdullah Dearly in Jammu', *Statesman*, 30 May 1983; K.K. Katya, 'Rules of the Game', *Hindustan Times*, 30 May 1983; K.R. Sundar Rajan, 'Communalism in Kashmir', *Tribune*, 30 May 1983.

[28] See 'Election Rules Being Violated in Kashmir' *Statesman* (Delhi), 20 May 1983; 'Repoll Ordered in Two Polling Stations', *Statesman* (Delhi), 6 June 1983;

month prior to the polls, the NC was accused of planning to rig the elections. Almost 70 per cent of the electorate participated, but polling had to be suspended at several stations; the Chief Electoral Officer immediately ordered repolling in two of them. Admittedly this does demonstrate that at least some watchdog institutions were at work and it is likely that they helped to raise the legitimacy of the election. After the elections, there was an inquiry into polling in the Doda constituency, while the Congress (I) demanded repolling in eighteen constituencies and, together with the People's Conference, protested against the NC's manipulation of the electoral process. In spite of all these irregularities, however, the electoral victory of Farooq Abdullah and the NC was eventually largely accepted by the political opposition and the media. Or, as one paper put it, 'when everything is said, the popular mandate is beyond doubt. Sheikh Abdullah's mantle has truly fallen on his son who owes no thanks to any favours from any quarter.'[29] Democratic credibility, however, had begun to be undermined by electoral fraud and institutional decline; events in the following years accelerated the process.

The Fatal Dismissal

The blow that put a definite halt to the democratization process in JK came on 2 July 1984, when Farooq was told by the new Governor Jagmohan[30] that his party had lost its majority in the state following the defection of thirteen members of the legislative assembly (MLAs), twelve belonging to the NC and one independent. This group soon proposed to form a new government with outside support from the Congress (I). This provoked an angry reaction and was criticized as not only unconstitutional but also undemocratic. Jagmohan had asked Farooq Abdullah to step down without a vote of confidence, a test of his support on the floor of the assembly, and the central government was accused of having plotted the dismissal. During Indira Gandhi's leadership, the Congress (I) seemed willing to strike against all non-Congress state governments—regardless of whether or not they had been democratically elected. Disillusionment

---

'Doda Poll Officer Replaced', *Statesman* (Delhi), 8 June 1983; 'Cong-I Urges Repoll in 18 Constituencies', *Indian Express* (Delhi), 9 June 1983; Brij Bhardwaj, 'Protest against Poll "Rigging" in JK', *Hindustan Times*, 11 June 1983.

[29] Brij Bhardwaj, 'Protest against Poll "Rigging" in JK', *Hindustan Times*, 11 June 1983.

[30] Jagmohan, a BJP MP, is one of India's best-known civil servants and has twice served as Governor of Jammu and Kashmir.

with democratic institutions and contempt for the central government began to be apparent in JK after the dismissal of Farooq Abdullah and ensuing political developments. We should therefore look more closely at why this happened. Even if the road to democracy was bumpy and the bureaucracy and political parties were plagued by corruption, JK had been heading towards democracy until this fatal change of direction took place. Why did Farooq Abdullah have to be dismissed at such cost to the political development of JK?

The course of events was as follows: late on the evening of 1 July 1984, Jagmohan was informed that a group of MLAs in the NC, led by Ghulam Mohammed Shah and Devi Das Thakur, a High Court lawyer and former state finance minister, planned to withdraw support to Farooq Abdullah and form a new government with the support of Congress (I) (Jagmohan 1994: 276). With Thakur's help, Shah was about to take his revenge and seize the highest office in the state. The following morning, Jagmohan delivered the news to Farooq Abdullah; but rather than support the defectors and install Shah as chief minister, Jagmohan suggested to Farooq Abdullah that governor's rule could be imposed since the NC had lost its majority (Jagmohan 1994: 284–5; Abdullah 1985: 1–4). After a cabinet meeting, Abdullah responded in writing that 'democratic traditions require that the question of loss of confidence should always be tested on the floor of the House' and that Jagmohan should summon the legislature for this purpose (Jagmohan 1994: 290–2). Jagmohan claims that 'the surcharged atmosphere' at the time did not allow the assembly to convene and that he was disappointed by Abdullah's unwillingness to accept the option of governor's rule. When Jagmohan contacted Indira Gandhi at 11 am.on 2 July, however, she expressed her support for governor's rule. Shah and Thakur, naturally, were unhappy about this unexpected turn of events.[31] But then, according to Arun Nehru, a relative of the Nehru–Gandhi family who was working closely with Rajiv Gandhi and Indira Gandhi at the time, the Cabinet Sub-Committee on Political Affairs overruled the option, arguing, 'let there be a split in the National Congress—Shah will not last a year.'[32] At 3 pm this decision was delivered to Jagmohan who argues that he therefore had no choice but to swear Shah into office. Almost immediately, Jagmohan was widely castigated in the media for uncritically carrying out the orders of the central government when he should have allowed Abdullah to seek a vote of confidence in the

---

[31]Interview with Jagmohan, 16 December, 1994.

[32]Arun Nehru claims that he was in favour of Governor's rule. Interview with Arun Nehru, 1994.

assembly. In his defence, Jagmohan argues that this charge is baseless in that, when arguing for governor's rule, he had opposed the central government, which instead demanded that Shah be installed (Jagmohan 1994: 293). But there is a good deal to be said in Jagmohan's defence against his critics.

It was clear that the central government and, in particular, Indira Gandhi, had decided that Abdullah had to be removed from power. Since either of the options considered by Jagmohan—imposing governor's rule or putting Shah in charge—fulfilled this objective, it may still be argued that he was going along with the central government rather than opposing it, as he claims. Important evidence of this declared intention is found in several places. Even before the spring of 1984 it was common knowledge that Indira Gandhi wanted to remove Abdullah from office, but the following information suggests that a scheme to do this was hatched only a few months after the 1983 election. To begin with, this news item from September 1983 concerning political developments in JK shows that a surprising alliance had been made.

These developments were preceded by what seemed like the re-emergence of Mr. G. M. Shah, the Chief Minister's brother-in-law, in the political field after a long silence which appeared to suggest retirement from the power game.... It is now clear that Mr. Shah's silence over a period of some three months was a strain which he could not bear endlessly. He has decided to join hands with a former political enemy, Mr. D. D. Thakur, in what looks like an attempt to destabilize the Government and to overthrow Farooq Abdullah. The attitude of Mr. Thakur will not surprise many. Although he was close to Sheikh Abdullah and supported Farooq Abdullah for the leadership of the party, he was known for some time to be drifting away from the latter.[33]

The report suggests that the new alliance between Shah and Thakur was mainly an affair at the state level motivated by the wish to overthrow a common political enemy, but the plan actually originated in higher spheres, namely the central government and the prime minister. Thakur explains what happened behind the scenes and how Indira Gandhi called him in to discuss the removal of Farooq Abdullah from power immediately after the elections.

She said 'How do you go about Kashmir' and then I said that 'This is one of the ways which we can do.' [Indira Gandhi said] Can you do it?' I said 'Yes I am capable of doing it.' [Indira Gandhi said] 'But who is the horse that it is that you are going to flog then?' I said 'G. M. Shah.' '[Indira Gandhi said] but you are not pulling on well with him, how do you do it?' I said 'I'll surrender, I'll win him

[33] See 'Revolt in the Making', *Tribune*, 2 September 1983.

over'... And then I went to Kashmir. Then I had a meeting with G. M. Shah at my son-in-law's house, where he came for the dinner.... And we planned the entire thing, and I came back and reported to her that this is the line of acting.[34]

After this meeting, Farooq Abdullah was under constant attack from two fronts. Shah and Thakur were set on splitting the party from the inside. By the spring of 1984 this had gone so far that Shah and Farooq Abdullah were holding separate party conventions.[35] On the outside, the pressure came from the central government, which accused Farooq Abdullah of being lenient with, and even encouraging, separatists from Pakistan and Punjab. On 13 October 1983, during the cricket match between the West Indies and India, members of the Jamaat-e-Tulba, the youth wing of Jamaat-e-Islami, waved their flags and threw rubbish onto the field. The central government openly expressed concern that Farooq Abdullah was losing control of the state. According to the historian Alastair Lamb, this event

was more than a clash of parties on a specific occasion or over a specific issue. There was being injected into the Vale of Kashmir what can only be described as the first phase of a general Islamic rebellion against the Hindu Domination of New Delhi. (Lamb 1991: 329.)

It is, however, debatable whether the cricket match incident should be interpreted as something as significant as the beginning of a general Islamic rebellion. It should be pointed out that both the Kashmir Liberation Front and the Jamaat-e-Islami had threatened violence when the first international cricket match in Kashmir was to be played in 1978. As Abdullah recalls, however, things were a bit different then:

I was the Chairman of the Jammu and Kashmir Cricket Association at the time, and with the backing of the State Government, we had to seek the intervention of the President of India, Shri Sanjiva Reddy, and the match was played without any incident. (Abdullah 1985: 44.)

In 1983 again, bringing the international cricket match to the disputed territory immediately served to provoke the Jamaat-e-Islami which had never accepted the accession. It is pertinent to point out another difference that may explain the strong reactions of the central government in 1984. In 1978 Sheikh Abdullah had been at peace with the central government, while in 1983 Farooq Abdullah was not.

After the incident in 1983, Indira Gandhi expressed serious concern

---

[34] Interview with Devi Das Thakur, 3 December 1994.

[35] Shah's convention elected Farooq Abdullah's sister and G.M. Shah's wife Khalida Shah as their official leader.

over developments in JK and the fact that Farooq Abdullah was not taking necessary and stern measures against the 'insurgents'.[36] More criticism of Farooq Abdullah—both implicit and explicit—followed. In January 1984, Indira Gandhi warned that she would not accept any anti-national activities in JK, a month after that Rajiv Gandhi predicted an invasion of JK by Pakistan, and a few weeks later Congress (I) members claimed that Farooq Abdullah was a member of the JKLF.[37] But events and evidence did not confirm these criticisms and charges. Farooq Abdullah could certainly be accused of political incompetence (see, for example, Akbar 1991) and corruption, but no proof was ever produced that he was a JKLF member, and contrary to Rajiv Gandhi's prediction Pakistan did not invade JK. The intentions of the central government are quite clear, however. Farooq Abdullah was officially portrayed by the Congress (I) as a threat to national security, who ought therefore to be ousted. Now, there was only one obstacle. B. K. Nehru, another relative of Indira Gandhi was the Governor of JK, and he was not willing to accede to the plans.

According to B. K. Nehru, the central government tried to persuade him to remove Farooq Abdullah 'everyday'.[38] B. K. Nehru, however, did not welcome the attempts of the central government to intervene and he remained good friends with Farooq Abdullah. Whenever the latter was uncomfortable about the recommendations of his personal advisor P. L. Handoo, he would meet B. K. Nehru and discuss his problems with him, sometimes over a drink. However this friendly relationship, did not stop Farooq Abdullah from putting B. K. Nehru in a difficult position. Just when he was being most severely criticized by the central government on the law and order situation in JK, Farooq Abdullah was summoned to a meeting with the prime minister in New Delhi on 24 January 1984. Tensions were high. NC supporters had clashed with members of the Congress (I) on several occasions during the past month, and finally, in one confrontation, six members of the Congress (I) had been killed.[39] Arun Nehru recalls how he tried to bring Farooq Abdullah 'in line', but without success.

[36] See for example 'Concern Over Srinagar Violence', *Hindustan Times*, 16 October 1983.

[37] See 'Mrs. Gandhi Hints at Strong Action', *Times of India*, 5 January 1984; 'Pakistan May Invade Kashmir: Rajiv', *Tribune* (Chandigarh), 7 February 1984; 'Dr. Abdullah was Member of Liberation Front', *Statesman* (Delhi), 28 February 1984.

[38] Interview with B. K. Nehru, 1994.

[39] See '63 Cong men Hurt in Lathi-Charge', *Hindustan Times*, 6 January 1984; 'Congress (I) to Continue Stir in Jammu-Kashmir', *The Hindu* (Gurgaw), 11 January 1984; 'Six Congressmen Killed in Firing', *Times of India*, 15 January 1984.

'Now, you listen,' I told Farooq. 'You listen when the PM speaks. Mrs. Gandhi had clearly said that it only takes one signature to get rid of Farooq.' So he begged for mercy, he was told to behave by Mrs. Gandhi, and he got a second chance and he went back, and the first thing he does when he comes home is to take a vote of confidence! This was his disaster and a most stupid thing to do.[40]

In *My Dismissal*, Farooq Abdullah explains that he thought there was a 'conspiracy to dismiss' him following the meeting in New Delhi (Abdullah 1985: 9). On 27 January, therefore, he took measures to protect his position by seeking a vote of confidence in the legislative assembly. His victory in this vote was quite popular in JK, but it certainly made his enemies all the more determined to remove him from power. At the same time, it also seems that Farooq Abdullah had lost some of the sympathy of his powerful ally B. K. Nehru, who was disappointed that Farooq Abdullah had demanded the vote in the assembly without advance notice—which was unconstitutional. Furthermore, it seems that B. K. Nehru had basically guaranteed New Delhi that there would be no further provocation by the state government. The vote of confidence that followed soon after Farooq Abdullah's return to JK was thus perceived as a breach of that 'understanding'. The upshot was that the central government decided it was time for a change of regime in JK. In other words, as Arun Nehru described it, 'a hostile government in a sensitive border state became unacceptable'. In April, the central government transferred B. K. Nehru to Gujarat and Jagmohan was sent in as the new Governor of JK. After that, Shah declared that 'the real NC' was to hold its convention on 23 May. Farooq Abdullah held a separate convention with his group of followers a few days later. This action by the 'splinter group' led by Shah and the High Court lawyer Thakur was instrumental in the High Court's ruling that the defection in July was legal. Meanwhile, on 28 June, the letter of defection was signed by the twelve MLAs. Arun Nehru was later accused of having bribed the defectors. To this he comments, '[T]hat was never needed. What more can somebody want than to become chief minister and these MLAs were happy to do it anyway.'[41] Thus Shah finally became chief minister and Thakur deputy chief minister, while all the defectors received portfolios in the new government.[42] The support from the central government was strong and the Union home minister declared that Jagmohan had 'not committed any unconstitutional impropriety' in

[40] Interview with Arun Nehru, 14 December 1994.

[41] Ibid.

[42] A list of defectors is provided in Jagmohan (1994: 281) and Abdullah (1985: 68–9). See also 'D. D. Thakur is Deputy C.M.', *Tribune*, 4 July 1984; 'Thakur Made Deputy CM of Kashmir: Shah Allocates Portfolios,' *Statesman*, 4 July 1984.

dismissing the Farooq Abdullah Ministry.[43] The *Indian Express* reported:

Replying to remarks that Mr. Farooq Abdullah should have been allowed to test his majority, the Home Minister said it was not necessary that the majority should be tested always on the floor of the House. Every case depends on its merits, Mr. [P. V. Narasimha] Rao said.[44]

Nevertheless, the new government clearly lacked legitimacy. In the media and among the political elite, the dismissal of Farooq Abdullah was widely regarded as unconstitutional and as a breach of democratic norms.[45]

The events of 1983 and 1984 mark the beginning of a drastic decline in democracy in JK, and it is important to note that what characterizes the conflict today has little to do with what initiated the conflict. There is no evidence to support the idea that the dismissal of Farooq Abdullah was the result of ethnic antagonism or religious sentiment, or a response to demands for a separate state or accession to Pakistan—the leading themes in the conflict today.[46] What appears to have initiated the conflict was the failure of political institutions and leaders in JK to handle pressure from an interventionist central government. It is, however, not yet quite clear why the government was so eager to get rid of Farooq Abdullah. The national security argument was, of course, important and was the official reason given; but there were two other levels of conflict. There was a conflict between the state and central governments, and there was personal friction between Farooq Abdullah and Indira Gandhi. Different observers attribute differing emphases to these as factors in the dismissal.

[43] See 'Farooq Govt. Dismissal Not "Unconstitutional" ', *Indian Express* (Delhi), 27 July 1984; 'Grave Situation was Developing in Kashmir: Rao', *Hindustan Times*, 27 July 1984.

[44] 'Farooq Govt. Dismissal Not "Unconstitutional" ', *Indian Express* (Delhi), 27 July 1984.

[45] See, for example, Puri (1993: 34); Varshney (1992: 219); Ganguly (1992); Ganguly and Bajpai (1994); 'Thakur Made Deputy CM of Kashmir: Shah Allocates Portfolios.', *Statesman*, 4 July 1984; *The Hindu* (Gurgaw), 4 July 1984; G.K Reddy. 'Office of Dignity or Proxy of Centre?', *The Hindu* (Gurgaw) 8 July 1984; K.K. Katyal. 'Srinagar Experiment & a Punjab Parallel'. *The Hindu* (Gurgaw), 9 July 1984; A.G. Noorani, 'The Coup in Kashmir', *Indian Express*, 10 July 1984. For an opposing view to this interpretation, see R.K. Mishra, 'Opposition Parties and Farooq Abdullah', *Patriot*, 11 July 1984; N.C. Menon, 'Kashmir: A Stitch in Time', *Hindustan Times*, 11 July 1984. Mishra and Menon argue that the removal of Farooq Abdullah was necessary in order to safeguard national security.

[46] In other words, there is no proof that the Congress (I) opposed Farooq Abdullah and the National Conference for religious reasons, that is because of the fact that the Congress (I) is Hindu dominated and the National Conference is Muslim dominated. Such a hypothesis could be expected if we applied the reasoning developed in, for example, Horowitz (1985), or Connor (1993; 1994).

The first perspective could be characterized as mainly political, and it recurs elsewhere as a reflection of the centralizing tendencies of the Indira Gandhi leadership (for example Brass 1994: 215–27, Varshney 1992: 219, 225; Kohli 1990b: 28–32). The deterioration in relations between the state and the centre can be traced back to Farooq Abdullah's decision in May 1983 to join an alliance of regional parties from all over India—the so-called Opposition Conclave—along with thirteen other important political leaders, under the leadership of the charismatic N. T. Rama Rao of the Telugu Desam, who had just won the election in Andhra Pradesh, and Rama Krishna Hedge, who had done the same in Karnataka with the Janata Dal. Their opposition to the Congress (I) united them. This was during the last leg of the election campaign in JK, but Farooq Abdullah took the time to attend the meeting and even promised to host the next meeting of the Conclave. Indira Gandhi expressed deep concern over Farooq Abdullah's joining what was perceived as a national anti-Congress (I)-alliance. Never before had the NC opposed the Congress (I) outside JK.[47] So, from this perspective, Indira Gandhi was mainly motivated by the desire to maintain her sphere of power—and the strategy was to destabilize any state government that could be considered a significant threat to Congress (I) dominance.[48]

According to other observers, the personal animosity between Farooq Abdullah and Indira Gandhi was the main factor behind the dismissal. Former prime minister Chandra Sekhar, who was also one of the leaders of the Conclave, explains that the relationship between the two leaders was 'complicated'.[49] Without wanting to elaborate on this, he only comments that 'one could say that socio-economic factors and such were not the only reasons behind the tense relations between the Centre and the State.'[50] B. K. Nehru, former governor of JK, provides a less enigmatic answer. He claims that the great enmity that

[47] This observation is made by Akbar (1991: 203). It is important to take notice that Farooq Abdullah turned to the Conclave shortly after the electoral cooperation between the Congress (I) and National Conference had broken down. Abdullah obviously felt he had to make some new friends outside his own state and he fulfilled his promise by hosting a meeting for the Conclave in Srinagar in October 1983. The theme of that meeting was state–centre relations, while the Conclave meeting that followed in Calcutta in January 1984 specifically focused on the problem of the central government trying to remove opposition governments in the states.

[48] On the misuse and use of President's rule in India (and governor's rule in the case of Jammu and Kashmir) see Kathuria (1990). Also see Deshta (1993).

[49] Interview with Chandra Shekar, 28 October 1994. This is also supported by interviews with B.K. Nehru, 1994, and Arun Nehru, 1994.

[50] Interview with Chandra Shekar, 1994.

developed between Indira Gandhi and Farooq Abdullah originated in 'the Iqbal Park incident' during the 1983 election campaign: when Indira Gandhi was addressing the crowd, a number of men undressed themselves to insult her.

This is something that happened, a lot of people did not notice, but she saw it, she never mentioned it, but I have a feeling that this was reported to her as being the doing of Farooq Abdullah. And that seems to have embittered her to such an extent that she simply could not think of Farooq remaining in office. Farooq is a gentleman—he would never dream of doing this. It was only his enemies who could....The real cause [of the hostility between Abdullah and Gandhi] was that she thought he had organized this personal insult to her. And to womanhood, she was a very strong feminist. Any insult to her was an insult to her personally. It was there the complete lack of contact started. And she decided to depose Farooq at whatever cost. I refused to do that because it was not only unconstitutional, but it was politically highly undesirable and dangerous. So, Jagmohan was sent to do it.[51]

Despite the impression he gives in *My Frozen Turbulence*, Jagmohan agrees that when he was appointed new governor to JK, he too was aware that Indira Gandhi wanted to remove Farooq Abdullah from his post of chief minister—although she never directly told him to do so.[52] Farooq Abdullah seems to have been set up to take the blame for the worst possible insult to Indira Gandhi, and he never had an opportunity to defend himself against the allegations. The story of the relationship between Farooq Abdullah and Indira Gandhi tragically ends here. In a parallel development, Indira Gandhi was fighting the Khalistan movement in Punjab, and only three months after Farooq Abdullah was deposed, she was assassinated by her Sikh bodyguards. Democratic credibility could have been restored at this point, but over the following five years the actions of the political elite both in New Delhi and JK steadily dispelled any hope of a continuation of democracy.

The Election Cartel: Consociationalism Taken Too Far

The new government of Ghulam Mohammed Shah lasted less than two years. He was soon considered a greater burden to the central government than Farooq Abdullah had been. As early as August 1984, Indira Gandhi

---

[51] Interview with B.K. Nehru, 1994. The interview with D.D. Thakur in 1994 also supports the argument that the Iqbal Park incident was important as the beginning of the conflict between Farooq Abdullah and Indira Gandhi.

[52] Interview with Jagmohan, 1994.

expressed her concern over the inability of Shah to handle the increasing level of violence in the state.[53] In June 1985 a clear rift had opened between Congress (I) and Shah's faction of the NC.[54] During this period there was an increase in reports of insurgency supported by Pakistan in the Valley and explicitly religiously defined political groups took root in the state. For example, the Islamic organizations the Jamaat-e-Tulba and the People's League increased their recruitment of young Kashmiris from the Valley, while the Hindu organization Shiv Sena established itself firmly in Jammu.[55] Gradually, but at an increasing rate, extremist parties became more success-ful in using region and religion as the basis for political mobilization.

Finally in March 1986, the Congress (I) withdrew support to Shah, and Jagmohan imposed Governor's rule. Just before the six-month term of governor's rule expired, Farooq Abdullah entered into an agreement to share power with the Congress (I) until new elections could be held. Given the political background of the two parties, it was an amazing alliance. In November this agreement was crowned by the decision of the central government to reinstall Farooq Abdullah as chief minister.[56] This period of frequent changes of loose alliances, governor's rule and central government intervention dramatically eroded Kashmir's democracy.

Even if alliances across ideological lines are made more often in India than in other democracies, the cooperation between the Congress (I) and the NC that gradually developed prior to the 1987 elections was too much even for the hardy Indian electorate to accept. Only a few days after it was clear that an alliance between Farooq Abdullah and the Congress (I) was in the making, a hitherto unknown organization called the Muslim United Front (MUF) called a strike in the Valley.[57] Later it transpired that the Jamaat-e-Islami, led by Ali Shah Geelani and several other Islamic political groups and leaders in the Valley, had forged this new but somewhat fragile political unit. Abdul Ghani Lone of the People's Conference, a so-called 'pro-autonomy party' in JK, had long ago declared the need to unite the

---

[53] See 'Centre's Concern over Law & Order in Kashmir', *Statesman* (Delhi), 19 August 1984. It seems from news cuttings from the 1980s that this allegation had some real substance, as for example in comparison to Indira Gandhi's accusations against the Farooq Abdullah Government in 1983–4.

[54] See 'Rift in Cong NC alliance', *Times of India*, 9 June 1985.

[55] See, for example, 'Fundamentalists "Recruit" Youths', *Tribune* (Chandigarh), 18 September 1985; 'Shiv Sena Gaining Strength in Jammu.' *Times of India*, 17 January 1986.

[56] See 'Bid to Reconcile NC(F), Cong (I)', *Tribune* (Chandigarh), 23 September 1986; 'NC-F May Form Govt With Cong-I Support', *Hindustan Times*, 25 September 1986; 'Farooq Sworn in as Chief Minister', *Statesman*, 7 November 1986.

[57] 'Anger that Envelops Kashmir Valley', *Statesman*, 28 September 1986.

opponents of the NC and Congress (I), and at last this had become reality.[58] It seems that the closer the Congress (I) and the NC drew together, the more groups became firmly aligned with the MUF. Finally it was clear that the Congress (I) and the NC had reached an agreement not to oppose each other's candidates in the coming election; the Congress (I) would put up candidates for thirty-one seats and the NC for forty-six.[59]

An election where the two major rival parties decide to form an alliance and work out a seat equation beforehand is surely unique; 'tactical alliance' is a totally inadequate description of the extraordinary pact that was made. The term 'tactical alliance' usually refers to a coalition or the cooperation of two parties which are considered to differ too much ideologically. This was certainly true of the NC–Congress (I) alliance, given the historical antagonism between the two parties. But there was something more. Tactical alliances are sometimes accepted by the electorate if there is a common enemy that both parties have to try to defeat but cannot defeat individually. In the case of JK in 1986–7, however, it was the main rivals in a two-party dominated system that merged, and the aim, it seems, was to try to create a political monopoly to capture all the seats in the election.[60] This was more than tactical: it was cynical, and rather than a 'tactical alliance' or an 'election coalition', it can only be labelled an 'election cartel', This differs from, for example, Arend Lijphart's Grand Coalition in that, in the cartel situation, the main opponents divide the constituencies and power *before* the elections (Lijphart 1977: 25–36; 1996: 258–68). It is, at the same time, also possible to see the cartel created in JK as an extreme form of consociationalism. In a recent article, Lijphart argues that consociationalism is one of the devices that have contributed to India's high democratic performance (Lijphart 1996: 258–68). Government by Grand Coalition is a solution which counters dangerous forms of political polarization and, in JK, some observers welcomed the cooperation between

[58] 'Tough Challenge for Cong-NC(F) Combine', *Times of India*, 14 November 1986.

[59] See 'Cong (I)–Farooq Pact on Assembly Seats?', *Tribune* (Chandigarh), 2 February 1987. Also see Butler et al (1996: 194).

[60] Actually, the effective number of components in the 1983 election was 3.2 if we look at the vote shares, and 2.5 if we count the seat shares (see Taagepera and Shugart (1989: 77–81) for the formulas used). Measurements based on the Herfindahl–Hirschman concentration index, however, are not without problems when describing systems where two parties are dominant, for example together they may receive around 70 per cent of the support of the voters, but a substantial share of the remaining support is spread out over a very large number of small parties and/or independent candidates.. Considering the poor support for parties other than the National Conference and the Congress (I) in 1983, it is more accurate simply to use the term 'two-party-dominant system'.

the Congress (I) and the NC in the hope that it would counter 'communalist and anti-nationalist elements'.[61] Inherent in the consociationalist theory is the idea that coalitions and elite cooperation smooth the effects of the bumpy interruptions that elections create in politics. The case of JK, however, illustrates what can happen if consociationalism is taken to such an extreme. 'Smoothing the effects of elections' can be taken only so far before the electorate considers it meaningless to go to the polling booth. This mark was passed in JK. When leaders such as Farooq Abdullah and Rajiv Gandhi, heading the dominating parties, decided to create a cartel, they were obviously displaying very little regard for the democratic ethos. The fact that democracy thrives on competition between parties, where the electorate makes the final judgment, was, it seems, either completely forgotten or ignored. And the contempt for the cartel was immense. The *Times of India* correspondent who was stationed in JK at the time relates an anecdote that reflects the disdain the cartel provoked:

When Rajiv was to announce the accord between the Congress (I) and the NC at a large meeting in Srinagar, high level Congress (I) representatives had to hide in the press tent since they were genuinely fearing that the rank and file members of the National Conference would beat them up if they were given the chance.[62]

If the goal was to gain a monopoly of the seats, the plan failed. It only ended up provoking support and incentives for more radical forces of political opposition. The MUF soon became the main adversary of the cartel.

The stage was thus set for elections in the spring of 1987. The electorate was quite confused and many people were upset by the new cartel. The atmosphere was tense and political sentiments were further agitated by the discontent expressed by extremist voices within the MUF and also the BJP. Nonetheless, democracy probably still had a chance at this stage. Although the possibility of stable democratic development had already been eroded by the increased polarization of Muslims and Hindus, and of the citizens of JK and the central government, many of the most extreme religious opposition parties and their followers clearly agreed that democracy was still the right model for political competition. This is proved by the fact that the MUF put all its efforts into the elections. There was still a channel through which discontent—in particular dissatisfaction with the NC and the Congress (I)—could be routed. This avenue, however, was soon to be blocked by the Congress (I) and the NC, who decided that a cartel was not enough to ensure them a victory.

[61] Editorial, 'Congress–NC Alliance', *Patriot*, 4 February 1987.
[62] Interview with V.K. Dethe, 7 November 1994, New Delhi.

'To Hell With the Democratic Process'

According to several observers, the 1987 state assembly elections represented a crucial turning point. Before we can accept this claim, however, we need to dig even deeper into what really happened. Quite apart from what has been said about the election cartel, how fair and free was the polling, in any case? To what extent were political opponents of the election cartel hindered from participating? At least some aspects of these questions require more detailed examination.

The 75 per cent electoral participation was higher than average.[63] Of the total of 76 seats, the NC won 40, the Congress (I) 26, the BJP 2, and the remaining 8 seats went to so-called independent candidates.[64] Amongst the independents we find four candidates who were competing under the MUF umbrella. This immediately permits us to draw one important conclusion—namely that, in comparison with the election result from 1983, the alliance between Congress (I) and NC provoked increased support for parties on the flanks which explicitly defined themselves as Hindu or Islamic. Besides this, the effect of the cartel on the proportion of seats in relation to votes is also important.

Although the Congress (I) and the NC won 87 per cent of the seats in the assembly, they obtained the support of only 53 per cent of the electorate. Almost 35 per cent of the votes went to the various independent candidates, but they won only 10 per cent of the seats. This may be compared with election results of 1983 when the combined number of votes for the Congress (I) and NC reached 78 per cent, giving them 95 per cent of seats in the assembly. In other words, the correlation between votes and seats was very much weaker in JK in the 1987 elections. So, before considering the question of fraud, it is necessary to take into account some of the advantages to large parties caused by the first-past-the-post system prevalent in India. The cartel created a monolithic giant and this efficiently increased the tendency inherent in majority systems to give large or regionally concentrated parties a higher proportion of seats in relation to votes than their smaller rivals. The timing of the creation of the cartel also had the effect of exaggerating the disproportionality, because a new opposition to the alliance had little chance to develop in time for the election. The unusually poor correlation between votes and seats may

---

[63] Participation was higher than the average for both the Vidhan Sabha and the Lok Sabha elections.

[64] Depending on what sources one uses, the number of seats for the Congress (I) was between 25 and 27, and the number of seats for National Conference was between 39 and 41. See Butler et al. (1991); and Election Commission of India (1987).

possibly have planted unfounded suspicion in the minds of those who were unaware of the peculiarities of the majority election system with single-member constituencies. All the same, this does not allow us to dismiss all of the allegations that have been made.

Abdul Ghani Lone began his political career with the Congress party but founded his own party, the People's Conference, in 1978. In 1987 he contested the Handwara constituency in JK, where his main opponent was Chowdry Muhammad Ramzan from the NC. According to Lone, the counting of votes was disrupted by the Deputy Inspector-General of Police, A. M. Watali, who had arrived at the regional counting office by helicopter on the orders of Farooq Abdullah. Both Lone and his lawyer Z. H. Shah were hindered when trying to observe the process, and Lone claims that there was interference with the returns. Lone therefore filed a petition with the High Court of JK claiming that the election results had been falsified by the Counting Supervisors on the orders of the NC. The ballot papers were then collected from the Handwara constituency and taken in sealed containers to the High Court in Srinagar. The judge in Srinagar, however, decided not to act on Lone's petition, although a recount could have been taken fairly quickly on the evidence available. There are several similar stories from the 1987 elections. After the counting of ballots was interrupted, petitions were filed, but courts did not take action. The exact extent of rigging is still difficult to assess, but some qualified estimates have been made. An anonymous source at the Indian Intelligence Bureau claimed that approximately thirteen seats may have been lost by the MUF because of electoral malpractice; the same source comments that this was quite unnecessary since the political opposition could never have formed a government with the support available.[65] The Congress (I) and NC cartel was almost unbeatable.

Despite the level of fraud, even fewer watchdog institutions reacted than in 1983—in fact there was almost no reaction. It seems that the alliance between the NC and the Congress (I) made state authorities very reluctant to act independently. The Election Commission appears to have been inactive at the time, while the High Court of JK, which had the opportunity to look into some of the allegations, failed to do so. Instead the machinery of justice was used to circumscribe the political freedom of opposition leaders. Shortly before the elections, charges were brought against eight MUF leaders for 'rousing religious sentiments of the people and demanding independence from the Indian Union'. The cases were filed under the

---

[65] Information given to the *Times of India* journalist Askari Zaidi. Interview with Zaidi, 1994.

controversial Terrorist and Disruptive Activities Prevention Act (TADA) by the aforementioned, A. M. Watali.[66] According to *India Today*, 'Starting about two weeks before the election, 600 opposition workers were arrested in areas where the MUF, independents and PC candidates were showing strength.'[67] Two days after the election at least five MUF leaders were arrested for 'anti-national activities'.[68] After the elections, the MUF demanded that the allegations of rigging be investigated, but no action on a wider scale was taken by the central government, the courts or the Election Commission. All complaints and suspicions of electoral fraud were left by the NC and the Congress (I) to hang in the air like a poisonous cloud— and the consequences were disastrous.

Abdul Ghani Lone who, until then, had competed through democratic institutions throughout his political career, is today a leading member of the separatist movement and he draws the following conclusions from his experience in the 1987 election:

> It was this that motivated the young generation to say 'to hell with the democratic process and all that this is about' and they said 'let's go for the armed struggle.' It was the flash-point. The thought was there, the motivation was there, the urge was there, the demand was there, and the opposition was there. The situation became ripe, and then a flash-point.[69]

Several young activists in the political opposition decided to join the armed struggle after the 1987 election. For example the JKLF leader Yasin Malik had been the election agent of Mohammed Yusuf Shah, and both later reappeared in politics as separatist leaders. Shah became known as a leader of the Hizbul Mujahedin and Malik is still one of the leaders of the JKLF in JK. It seems from available interview materials that the main reason for the decision to resort to armed conflict was disillusionment and frustration created by the progressive failure of the democratic system. This is to some extent confirmed by a study of the views and perceptions of militant separatists made by a team of psychiatrists and psychologists from the Indian Army, which revealed that violence was mainly seen as a means to fight a corrupt system, justified by 'a deep sense of alienation', rather than by Islamic fundamentalism or notions of holy war.[70] Furthermore,

[66] '8 MUF Men Charged Under Terrorist Act', *Indian Express*, 9 March 1987.

[67] Inderjit Badhwar, 'A Tarnished Triumph', *India Today*, 15 April 1987, p. 41. This articles is also quite detailed on other accounts of rigging in Jammu and Kashmir in 1987.

[68] 'Top MUF Leaders Arrested', *Hindustan Times*, 26 March 1987.

[69] Interview with Abdul Ghani Lone, 1994.

[70] Harinder Baweja, 'In the Mind of the Militant', *India Today*, 31 December 1994, pp. 120–2. It may be important, however, to make a distinction between those who

the idea that the events of the 1987 election increased these feelings of frustration finds support from another source, namely Amanullah Khan, the Pakistan-based chairman of the JKLF.[71]

As mentioned earlier, Khan considered launching an offensive in the Valley in 1983 but gave up because of lack of support. Three years later, he observed that the situation had changed radically and youth in the Valley were 'ready'.[72] He explains that after he had been deported from England under the most humiliating circumstances, he felt 'a strong need for vengeance against India' which had, in his opinion, demanded his deportation.[73] Again, some members of the organization tested the mood in the region and found that 'circumstances were ripe for an armed struggle'. By 1986 the contempt felt for the alliance and the political system was enormous—a situation, Khan argues, created mainly by the state and central governments. The revolt was nourished by frustration, corruption, and the betrayal of Kashmiriyat—the Kashmiri identity. He adds that 'the psychology of the youth is very important here. Young people have a strong urge to do something'. Discontent has to be channelled, he says, and if there is a 'cause' to pick up, many will do so willingly. He recalls that after 1986 there was no difficulty in finding young men to join the movement.

The 1987 election led Kashmiris from the Valley to cross the border into Pakistan and enrol for military training in numbers without previous parallel.[74] When the NC and Congress (I) managed to pass the JK Special Powers (Press) Bill in the legislative assembly, bringing almost full press censorship to JK, even the political opposition that had remained loyal to the democratic system in spite of the electoral malpractices of 1987 declared it had had enough. When protests to the state assembly against the perversion of democracy and press censorship had no effect, one member of the MUF wrote that it was time to 'arouse the sense of Jihad

---

were motivated in 1987–9 and those who joined the armed struggle after the outbreak of violence in 1990. Violence itself tends to create a different type of motivation from that given by the original grievance.

[71] At least until February 1996 when the JKLF split into two sections.

[72] Interview with Amanullah Khan, 1994.

[73] In 1984, five members of the JKLF were questioned about the Birmingham kidnapping and assassination of the Indian diplomat Ravindra Mahtre. In 1986 Amanullah Khan was deported to Pakistan after being acquitted on charges of storing chemicals for explosives at the JKLF office (which was at Khan's home at the time).

[74] See, for example, Inderjit Badhwar, 'Valley of Tears', *India Today*, 31 May 1989, p. 36.

and general sense of martyrdom amongst youths'.[75] In December 1989, the JKLF kidnapped Rubaya Sayeed, daughter of the union home minister Mufti Mohammed Sayeed; the central government agreed to the kidnappers' demand for the release of five separatist activists. This key event set the Valley on fire in January 1990 and, since then, JK has only moved further up the spiral of violence.

ALTERNATIVE EXPLANATIONS

Before the final discussion of the causes of the conflict in JK, some other factors that are frequently cited as responsible at least deserve mention: socio-economic conditions in the state and the role of foreign intervention.

JK is a poor state and harsh living conditions have naturally added fuel to the discontent and conflicts that developed in the 1980s.[76] Nevertheless it should be noted that the economy of JK did not do much worse than that of other Indian states in 1970–90.[77] Infant mortality was high in 1981 with seventy-two deaths per thousand live births; by 1989, it had fallen only slightly to sixty-nine. But at least nine other states fight mortality rates around one hundred, and in Karnataka and Himachal Pradesh the infant mortality rate even rose during this period. If we accept infant mortality as one of several indicators of living standards, there is no evidence of a rapid turn for the worse in JK before the conflict broke out. The same applies to other indicators. The income level rose steadily in JK from 1950 to 1986; but even when it peaked at Rs 683 in 1986, it was below the national average of Rs 772. Then a minor economic decline set in. This was caused, according to the political scientist Tara Singh Rekhi, by climatic conditions and the increased breakdown of law and order (Rekhi 1993: 121). What should be noticed here is that the level of violence increased rapidly during G. M. Shah's regime, that is before the decline in the economy; therefore the level of violence may not have been due to

[75] See M. Syed Shah, statement submitted to the Jammu and Kashmir Legislative Assembly on 25 October 1989. *RGPJ–794/87–4,000 Bks. of 25 lvs: Jammu and Kashmir Legislative Assembly Secretariat.*

[76] In particular this section on alternative explanations, and also the historical background, is more fully developed in the dissertation on which this chapter is based, see Widmalm (1997).

[77] The data on socio-economic development were gathered from Rekhi (1993); Butler et al (1991); Bose (1991); and Chandok and Policy Group (1990). It should also be added that in 1978 Jammu and Kashmir was the only state in India where crime rates fell drastically. See 'Crime Rate Falls in JK', *Hindustan Times*, 20 May 1979.

economic decline. Rekhi suggests that the reverse was true: economic decline seems to have been, at least to some extent, caused by increase in violence.

There is another aspect to the question that should also be mentioned. The conflict has also been fuelled by the social differences between Hindus and Muslims. The Pandits and the Dogras belong to the traditional elite in JK, and in particular Pandits, like Brahmins all over India, have been overrepresented in banks, private companies and salaried jobs in the public sector, in relation to their share of the population.[78] The columnist Prem Shankar Jha, who argues that this imbalance is the most important underlying cause of the conflict, also points out that if the problem were only the denial of democracy in JK, the fathers of the youth leading the uprising today would have revolted much earlier. In other words, if lack of democracy were a cause of the conflict in the 1980s, the 1950s and the 1960s would have produced an even more violent uprising, since there was less democracy then. There are several reasons to treat Jha's hypothesis with caution.

To begin with, Jha's own position can be criticized with the arguments he advances against the hypothesis of the denial of democracy. If inequalities between Pandits and Muslims were the real underlying reason, why did Muslims not revolt earlier against Hindus, for example during the 1950s or the 1960s when discrimination may in some respects have been even greater than during the 1980s?[79] Data on class differences, labour and religious affiliation are unfortunately quite scarce, but one conclusion may be drawn. There is no evidence yet available that discrimination against Muslims in JK increased significantly during the first half of the 1980s.[80]

---

[78] See Jha (1991: 34–7). Also, see Bose et al, (1990) for information on job discrimination against Muslims in Jammu and Kashmir. Pandit is a common term for the Kashmiri Brahmins, but it can also be a title of a learned person. Dogras is a common term for members of the Hindu business community in Jammu and Kashmir, although it should be remembered that its historical roots and connection to caste are more complicated.

[79] For example when Article 312 (which regulates the All India Services, the so-called 'steel frame' of the Indian bureaucracy) came to include Jammu and Kashmir in 1958, it was the decided that 50 per cent of the personnel would be recruited from the Union Public Service Commission and 50 per cent from the State Service. Implementation of this did not begin until 1968, however (see Bose et al. 1990: 661). It should be noted that Kadian mentions that during the time when Syed Mir Qasim was chief minister (1971–5), a large number of officers from the Central Services were brought into the state to replace officers from Jammu and Kashmir. However, no increase in discrimination against Muslims in particular is mentioned and unfortunately the sources of this information were left out in the presentation. See Kadian (1992: 136).

[80] In my interviews with people from Jammu and Kashmir, including several political leaders, no one brought such charges to my attention.

On the contrary, on a more general level of political life, the political influence of Muslims seems to have increased since democracy was introduced in the late 1970s. For example in 1987, representation in the state assembly was proportional to religious division in the state.[81] That there were stronger reactions when democracy was denied in the 1980s than in, for example, the 1950s when democracy was almost absent, is natural, since by then most people in JK knew more about what they were being denied. The period from the mid-1970s to 1984 was one of democratic progress, freedom of expression and the right to organize, unprecedented in the history of JK. Naturally, the absence of these freedoms was felt far more acutely when they were suddenly withdrawn than when they had never been experienced.[82] Moreover, to my knowledge, the authors that do refer to the scarce data available on recruitment to the public sector have never substantiated this hypothesis with interviews with separatists and leaders of their movement. Jha, for example, goes so far as to say:

In Kashmir militancy is not born out of poverty or economic deprivation, but of the despair of a small, select group of young people who form a new but disinherited middle class sector.... [A] class that was trained to wield power, but denied the opportunity to do so. (Jha 1991: 35.)

In my opinion, the problem is that this point, although expressed with conviction, has yet to be proved empirically. Most of the separatist leaders interviewed in this study have been religious leaders or professional politicians for most of their lives. Among the separatists in the field, so to speak, some were students who might fit Jha's hypothesis, but there were also workers and members of other social categories.[83] None of the members of separatist organizations interviewed mentioned discrimination in the public sector as the main source of discontent. According to these

---

[81] Verma (1994: 187–9). Actually there was even a slight overrepresentation of Muslims in the state assembly in the late 1980s. This can be compared to the extreme underrepresentation of women, which is more seldom mentioned in the 'discrimination debate'. For example after the 1987 election only one woman had a seat in the state assembly. See Verma (1994: 185).

[82] This phenomenon is known in psychology as *hysteresis* and is amply expressed by Bentham who said, 'It is worse to lose than simply not to gain.' For a discussion on this, and how hysteresis is confirmed in other areas of research, see Hardin (1982: 82–3).

[83] For example if we look at the present leadership of the JKLF, Yasin Malik, a former student, would most likely fit Jha's description, while Javed Mir, a former professional plumber, would not. In a study by Tara Singh Rekhi, which will be further discussed below, it is mentioned (in one sentence) that there were 96,400 educated unemployed in the state in 1990 (see Rekhi 1993:106), but no source quoted and all my attempts to verify this statement have failed.

sources, alienation and the motivation to resort to violence stemmed generally from what was seen as the betrayal of the rules of democratic fair play and, more specifically, from events during the 1987 election. These interviews covered most of the important leaders within the Hurriyat Conference—the umbrella organization for most of the separatist, or accessionist, organizations in JK today—the JKLF and one student organization, and also politically active lawyers and some of the cadres in militant organizations.[84] But this is naturally not enough. A more systematic study of the separatists, with a larger number of interviews, would be necessary before we could make more conclusive remarks about the relation between class, inequality, and the incentive to resort to violent separatism. One thing, however, is clear: Jha's observation is not supported by empirical data. Although it is safe to assume that inequality and discrimination along ethnic lines have created some resentment, the fact remains that when it comes to socio-economic conditions, the information currently available does not allow this to be accepted as the reason why violent separatism broke out in JK in the late 1980s.

I want to emphasize that the aim here is not to generally rule out the argument that poor socio-economic conditions can cause conflicts. Undoubtedly they can. The point is that poverty cannot be considered to lead automatically to violence or separatism. If it did, the Indian state would have collapsed a long time ago.

Finally, this discussion of possible causes of the JK conflict should be concluded by mentioning the hypothesis that the revolt was orchestrated by a foreign power, namely Pakistan. There is no doubt that the Government of Pakistan assists the uprising in JK by supplying arms and by allowing separatist organizations to establish bases in Pakistan from which to operate. The Afghanistan war has significantly contributed to the proliferation of arms in the region. What is more, some groups involved in the armed struggle, for example the Harkut-ul-Ansar, seem to get direct

---

[84] A more detailed discussion on these sources is found in Widmalm (1997); naturally, some of the members of militant organizations wished to be quoted anonymously. Some of the more important leaders and members of the separatist movement who were interviewed and who should be mentioned, however, are: Maulana Abbas Ansari, interviewed 22 November 1994, Srinagar; Shah-Keel Bakshi, 21 November 1994, Srinagar; Baskar Ahmed Bhatt, 24 February 1996, Srinagar; Syed Ali Shah Geelani, 24 February 1996, Srinagar; Amanullah Khan, 6 February 1994 and 24 March 1996, Rawalpindi; Zafar Khan 6 December 1993, Luton; Abdul Ghani Lone, 10 November 1994, New Delhi and 24 February 1996, Srinagar; Javed Mir 24 February 1996, Srinagar; Muhammad Shafiq Misgar, 24 February 1996, Srinagar; Shabir Shah, 21 November 1994, Srinagar.

encouragement from members of the Pakistani Parliament and administration. The question is still whether the violent uprising in JK and the breakdown of democracy can be *explained* by the Pakistan factor. Supporting an uprising is different from creating it.

According to several sources, the uprising in JK is part of a scheme concocted by the Pakistani government in order to capture JK and destabilize its arch enemy India. Several sources refer to this scheme as Operation Topac and allege that it was created by General Zia-ul-Haq. The first article on Operation Topac, however, appeared in the Indian Defence Review in 1989, and it was clearly admitted that the scenario presented in the article was 'Part fact, part fiction' (*Indian Defence Review,* July 1989). But after the article was published, and largely because of the hostility between India and Pakistan, it soon became widely accepted as factually based.[85] There is, however, no concrete evidence to support the view that the uprising in JK was, from the beginning, instigated by the Pakistani government. I agree with Robert Wirsing that we may never learn the whole truth about Pakistani involvement, but we have learned from the political process that took place in the 1980s, that the motivation and the spark that ignited the Valley in 1990 were primarily provided by internal conditions (Wirsing 1994: esp. 113–18). This does not imply that Pakistan's involvement can be overlooked. Though a more active involvement is hard to prove, we can easily show that leaders in Pakistan saw developments in JK during the end of the 1980s at least as gratifying.

For this essay, in-depth interviews with some of the central decision makers in the Pakistan intelligence services—the Army Intelligence and Inter-Services Intelligence Directorate (ISI)—were conducted with a focus on the question of Pakistani involvement in the Kashmir conflict. Using information from these sources is of course not without its problems.[86] Nevertheless, before dismissing them out of hand, I think we should first listen to what some of them had to say.

[85] See, for example, Kumar's *Kashmir—Pakistan's Proxy War* (year of publication not available); Peer Giyas Ud-Din (1992: 55–7); Maheshwari (1993: 13, 51–2); Nanda (1994: 300–3). Wirsing (1995: 114, 306, n. 1) makes several interesting observations on this issue.

[86] I think that this is what the author Jan Guillou has named 'the useful idiot'. A useful idiot is someone to whom the political elite can feed information that is close enough to the truth to be plausible, but still hides the real facts. The useful idiot enthusiastically channels the information to, for example, the media, believing he/she has made a scoop, while in fact he/she has only served as a useful instrument for the real power holders who have managed to divert attention from facts that, if they were disclosed, would attract much more attention. Undoubtedly this is a problem of which any researcher in the social sciences should be aware.

Lieutenant General Muhammad Asad Durrani, who was Head of Army Intelligence from 1988 to 1989 and of the ISI from August 1990 to March 1992, naturally denies the existence of Operation Topac, but adds that the reason for this is that the Government of Pakistan would have more to lose than to gain from such a scheme.[87] Durrani's long military record is reflected in his continued references to clear and rational cost–benefit calculations, in particular when discussing and evaluating various military strategies involving human life. Durrani claims that nothing really changed in the stance towards Kashmir when Benazir Bhutto replaced Zia. 'Pakistan had simply enough to think about at home to want to risk rocking the boat and get into trouble with India.' Regardless of whether we are dealing with uprisings in Pakistan or in India, according to Durrani, one part of the rules of the game that both countries play is that internal problems should always be blamed on the neighbour. Nevertheless, Durrani agrees that militant leaders have been allowed to move across the border into India and then back again; 'but this has always been so', he says, although he also agrees that the number of guns that were moved across the border increased with the war in Afghanistan.

Pakistan can take the honour of having thrown out the Russians, but the price was high and paid through the proliferation of arms in the country. And this became a problem for ourselves just as much for the Indians. Look at Baluchistan and Karachi.

Then he continues to argue against the idea of Operation Topac by referring to the weakness of the Pakistan Army compared to the Indian Army. 'Just look at the power equation. It's more than five to one. It's impossible.' The same line was taken by a colleague of Durrani's who was interviewed in Pakistan a few months later.

This source, who is closely associated with the Pakistani Intelligence Service, wished to be quoted anonymously and the only point that needs to be made is that had insurgency been planned in Kashmir, he would undoubtedly have known. Finally, after a long introductory discussion including the usual rhetoric on India–Pakistan relations and further assurances that I would not reveal my source, a somewhat more plausible view was delivered:

At that time the Afghan Jihad was very successful. But they [the Kashmiris] came to us for help. But we did not want a two-front war. The gains from such action were far too uncertain. There was also pressure from Azad Kashmir. There was a political demand that we should help the Kashmiris in India. So we turned a blind

[87] Interview with Muhammad Asad Durrani, 18 December 1995, Bonn.

eye to all that was happening there. But the discontent was already established. But we did not want to involve the Afghans in this. At the beginning we really tried to keep them out so they would not mix with the people from Kashmir, because then you could not know what would happen, but eventually the Kashmiris made their own contacts with the Afghans. What we did was that we turned a blind eye to the whole process and all that was happening along the border.

Then, like Durrani, this source explained that this type of passive support and blaming one's neighbour is just 'a part of the game between India and Pakistan'.

If these two versions of what happened are fairly close to the truth, it is, to say the least, distressing that the risk of war between the two nations that has grown from the fighting in JK and the exchange of fire across the border is considered only 'a part of the game'. But this attitude towards life-and-death issues is not uncommon among high-ranking officials and certainly not unique to Pakistan and India. None of my sources would admit that the Pakistani government ever had a plan to start an uprising in JK, and although they would be unlikely to reveal an insurgency plan even if there were one, these accounts are consistent with the hypothesis that the uprising was caused by factors internal to JK and, so far, there is no concrete evidence available for examination that supports that there was ever an Operation Topac. At present, therefore, investigation of Pakistani sources yields nothing to throw doubt on the argument that the reasons and the will for an armed uprising were created within India and JK in the 1980s, and that Pakistan only provided the support base.[88]

EXPLAINING VIOLENT SEPARATISM IN JAMMU AND KASHMIR

It seems that the factors that first gave rise to the conflict are quite different from the salient features of the conflict today, such as religious antagonism, the demand for secession or Pakistani intervention, and the level of deprivation in the state. When social scientists search for explanations for what happened in the past, their analysis far too often considers only the present.[89] This is particularly unfortunate when history is rewritten by nationalists and separatists and when less space is given to moderate

---

[88] It seems, however, that more active support has been given by the Pakistani government to separatist organizations, but at a later stage in the conflict. See Widmalm (1997).

[89] Within the field of history, however, this is a much debated topic—especially by those investigating the history of nationalism. See, for example, Hobsbawm (1990).

positions than historical accuracy would demand, which has been the case in JK. I hope that the story told here has demonstrated that what characterizes the conflict today should be regarded as its *outcomes* rather than its *causes*. Political violence in JK has its roots in the acts of the political elites and the weaknesses of institutions, both in the bureaucracy and in party organizations.[90]

Democracy was established in JK in 1977. In the 1970s and the early 1980s, the National Conference was a fairly stable organization as long as Sheikh Abdullah was alive, and policies were still pursued on a secular basis. An underlying weakness in the system, however, was that the most important parties were organized dynastically or nepotistically. In 1983, both the Congress (I) and the NC were struggling for support and trying to hold their poorly organized parties together. Region and religion began to play a bigger part in attracting political support, although the overall character of the political messages from the parties could still be described as mostly secular. In 1987, however, after the NC and the Congress (I) had formed their cartel, the political situation so deteriorated that political allegiances were defined and expressed in religious terms. During the elections, institutional watchdogs such as courts and the Election Commission were rendered toothless. Finally, by 1989, the political opposition relinquished its faith in the usefulness of competing within what was left of the democratic framework. Somewhat simplified, the course of development leading to the conflict in JK was as follows:

Political elite —> Deinstitutionalization —> Populism & Communalism —> Political Violence

This is by no means an either/or approach to the role of structures and actors in relation to political violence. The interplay is often unpredictable. We may observe that institutions and their character are essential in the guiding decisions of the political elite. Nonetheless, it should not be forgotten that the acts of the political elite may be the first crucial factor in the chain of events that may set political development on one of two tracks: towards either stability or violence.

The political elite in New Delhi and JK could have changed the direction of events on several occasions during the 1980s. Instead, short-term political expediency was favoured at the expense of democracy. Together with fragile and strongly hierarchical institutions led by charismatic leaders,

---

[90] Other analyses of causes of instability and violence in India point towards similar factors. See Rudolph and Rudolph (1987); Kohli (1990b); Brass (1991 and 1994).

populist policies were increasingly encouraged. The politics of identity, connected to region and religion, became more important in political mobilization than long-term socio-economic development based on universalistic values. When short-term gains in politics are given priority, respect for democratic institutions usually suffers, and in JK electoral malpractice increased. Consequently, cross-cutting cleavages in society were replaced by one dimensional affiliations and strong polarization. The final outcome was violent conflict between Kashmiri Muslims and the central government.

At the same time, these conclusions also indicate that political violence within democracies can be countered by functioning and well-organized institutions and by political freedom. For those who hope to restore a legitimate democratic system or avoid violent separatism, these observations are particularly valuable. Democracy can obviously aid the nation-building project, but this does not mean that it is an infallible prescription for nation building or peace. During the past two years, the central government tried to reinstall democracy in JK and, although polling for both the Lok Sabha and the Vidhan Sabha took place in 1996, stability has not ensued. But democracy is more than elections. Institutions such as courts, the police, the Election Commission, and public administration need serious reform if they are once more to function in an independent manner. Moreover, bringing peace to a conflict requires a diplomatic solution as well. Until that is accomplished, we can expect the authority of both the central government and the state government to be challenged by influential groups in the area by violent means. Whether or not the legitimacy of the rule of the Indian Union can be restored in JK is yet to be proved.

Community, Authenticity and Autonomy: Insurgence and Institutional Development in India's North-East

JYOTIRINDRA DASGUPTA

Reports from India's north-eastern states—Arunachal Pradesh, Assam, Manipur, Meghalaya, Mizoram, Nagaland, and Tripura—rarely deal with the positive aspects of their institutional development processes. The national media mainly concentrates on the disquieting stories of unrest, insurgence and violence. The negative portrait of this region offered by both the press and scholarly studies in India and abroad must be distressing for the people of the north-eastern region.[1]

This chapter suggests that an excessive preoccupation with violence and a narrow reading of the implications of insurgent violence on the part of observers are responsible for a substantial misunderstanding of the north-eastern political processes. As a result, the positive aspects of community formation, the linkage of communities in wider political institutions as parts of the north-eastern administration and representative systems, and the contribution of these processes to the national system remain largely unexplored. The history of insurgence is rarely narrated in the context of an equally long history of peace, social collaboration, political reconciliation, democratic participation, and innovations in institution building and sustenance. Even the received narrative of violence is deeply flawed due to its frequent inability to attend to the possible rationality of forced desperation, and its insensitivity to the long-term constructive implications of many anti-authority struggles.[2]

THEMES AND PROPOSALS

The purpose of this chapter is to draw attention to some selected aspects of political community formation based on ethnic or extraethnic solidarities,

[1] Some recent studies, such as Hazarika (1994), mainly produced by scholars from this region, are exceptions.

[2] Scholars of European history have less trouble in conceding a constructive role to collective violence in politics; 'Great shifts in the arrangements of power have ordinarily produced—and have often depended on—exceptional movements of collective violence' (Tilly 1969: 5).

its connection with collective political engagement or alienation in the
north-east, and the impact of these processes on the national systems of
political and economic development. We assume that theories of political
participation relevant to multiethnic and multicultural democracies like
India should go beyond the traditional liberal concerns of the individual
citizen's political engagement or alienation (Dasgupta 1995). Collective
expressions claiming to be the voices and terms of communal solidarity
need to be considered in addition to the individual voices (Kymlicka 1995:
172). The collective expression of ethnic voices may register wide variation
in defining a community's boundaries, its interests, or the legitimacy of
particular spokespersons over time. One theme of this chapter will be
concerned with these changing representations and their connection with
organized political mobilization. A related theme will explore the choice
of methods of articulating the voice or voices of the community. If there
is a plurality or a progressive proliferation of voices within a community,
the issue of methods used to resolve the differences is important to
examine. What accounts for the use of peaceful or violent methods and
the transition from one to the other? How do institutional lineages affect
such transition?

A third theme will call attention to the approaches of communities to
the issues of authoritative institutions at the local, state, and regional levels.
How is autonomy sought to be served by a community's capacity for internal
generation of economic resources? What kind of national or regional
cooperation processes are desired or pursued? What are the institutional
forms of linkage with the wider circles of authority within the national
federal structure? What implications do these issues have on the general
questions of national cohesion and human well-being in the country?
(Dasgupta 1970; 1990; 1994; P. Chatterjee 1993; Dreze and Sen 1996)

These items are tied together by several analytic concerns. I would like
to suggest that ethnic or other social divisions do not indicate why, how,
or when they will be politically translated to produce what consequences
for the polity and the nation. Much should depend on political constructions
of claims for solidarity and definition of interest in specific authority
settings. The structure of political competition within and among ethnic
groups or communities and the institutional treatment of group demands
are likely to have an important bearing on the outcome. The focus of this
chapter on the centrality of political relations, strategies and processing
will guard against unnecessary imputation of undeserved or negative
properties to the categories of ethnicity of ethnic communities. The analysis
would suggest that there is good reason to be wary of notions of necessary
dynamics, or of inherent dangers associated with ethnic communities or

divisions, especially in democratizing settings (Horowitz 1985: 53–4; 1994: 36). It is more important to ground ethnic categories in collective practices than to treat them as 'special realities' (Weber 1993: 130) carrying ominous signs in order to gain insight into their impact on the prospects of institutional development in a developing federal democracy.

I am not interested in evaluating the north-eastern outcome merely in terms of the degree of violence involved in the process or by the intensity of the conflict persisting after a period of institutional treatment. I would, in fact, like to advance the proposition that the structure of democratic participation offered by the systems of representation at the parliamentary, states (union territory at some stages) and local levels, and the institutional treatment involving innovative extension of federalized resource and power sharing systems may have significantly contributed to a constructive coordination of ethnic communities into a national network of development and democratization.

In the north-eastern cases, given the scarcity of resources and the extensive fragmentation of ethnic communities and their internal divisions, such coordinating efforts may, for many years to come, fall short of a comprehensive capacity to pre-empt many forces of resentment and resistance. These areas were not exactly the models of realms of peace and non-violence during the colonial times or even earlier. Nothing like modern media exposure or communication systems of the kind associated with these areas in our time had existed before their democratization and reorganization into states and other autonomous institutions in the federation. The reconstitution of the political space, modernizing linkages with the national economy, expanding opportunities for mobility and movement, and freedom of communication offer unprecedented incentives for competitive and at times conflictual gains through organized collective action (Misra and Misra 1996). Occasional reports of violent acts need to be read in the context of the general incidence of ordered governance, which, unfortunately, never makes news. Patient contextualization of this kind obviously goes against the grain of the media's or many other observers' selective attention. Not surprisingly, the fact that protests including violent acts may not be unrelated to reasonable success attained by federalizing and democratic institutions is rarely appreciated.

THE REGION: THE COMPOSITION OF STATES

Many interesting features add elements of distinction to the north-eastern cluster of states, societies, and cultures. Most of the states are very small in size and population (see Table 1). Assam, the largest of the set, recorded in the 1991 census a total population of 22 million, with a density of 284 people per square kilometer (Government of India 1991a). For comparison, it may be noted that neighboring West Bengal had 68 million people and a density rate of 766 (highest in India with a mean rate of 267 in 1991). Within the north-eastern zone, Mizoram and Arunachal Pradesh registered, for 1991, less than a million people each with the respective density rates of 33 and 10, the lowest in the country. Tripura's population was 2.7 million, followed by Manipur (1.8 million), Meghalaya (1.8 million) and Nagaland (1.2 million)— the last three with fairly low density rates (82, 78 and 73, respectively).

TABLE 1

INDIA'S NORTH-EASTERN STATES: SELECTED FEATURES
(RECENT PERIOD)

	Population Million 1991	% of nation 1991	Density sq./km 1991	Major language 1991	Major religion 1991	% of sched. tribes 1991
A. with low tribe %					(a)	
1. Assam	22.4	2.65	284	Assamese	Hindi (71%)	13
2. Manipur	1.8	0.22	82	Manipur	Hindi (60%)	34
3. Tripura	2.7	0.33	262	Bengali	Hindu (89%)	31
B. with high tribe %				(b)	(c)	
4. Arunachal	0.86	0.10	10	Various/ Local	Various/ Local	64
5. Meghalaya	1.8	0.21	78	Various/ Local	Christian (53%)	86
6. Mizoram	0.69	0.08	33	Various/ Local	Christian (84%)	95
7. Nagaland	1.2	0.14	73	Various/ Local	Christian (80%)	88
India	844		267			8

Notes: (a) Figures refer to 1971; (b) Implies a variety of mainly local languages; (c) Implies various local and national religious groups.

SOURCES: Census of India, 1991, *Series 4, Assam, Paper no. 1 of 1991, Guwahati, 1991, p. 25: CMIE,* (1994b: various tables)

Besides size, the composition of the population of these states (Table 1) is also distinctive. Most of these states have the nation's highest proportion of scheduled tribes. According to 1991 census reports, Mizoram, Nagaland, Meghalaya and Arunachal Pradesh had an overwhelming majority of tribal population (95, 88, 86 and 64 per cent, respectively) (CMIE 1994b). Manipur and Tripura had 34 and 31 per cent tribal population, respectively, while Assam registered 13 per cent. The corresponding national average was 8 per cent. Hindus constitute the most numerous religious category in Assam and Tripura and in some ways in Manipur as well, though not without casting some shadow of doubt on the validation of enumeration in this case. Major religious labels are not easily applicable in the tribal areas of the north-east or even elsewhere in the country. Most people in Arunachal Pradesh are not covered by the nationally prominent major religious categories. A variety of local religious traditions predominate. Mizoram, Nagaland and Meghalaya are enumerated as Christian majority states.

Nationally prominent or constitutionally recognized languages included in the eighth schedule do not enjoy the same importance in the north-east, though Assamese, Bengali and Manipuri dominate in Assam, Tripura and Manipur, respectively. The four other states use a variety of local languages for internal communication. English enjoys the status of official language in Nagaland, Mizoram and Meghalaya. The predominance of tribal identification in matters relating to ethnic community, religion, language and culture in the smaller states of this region should not imply an easy equation between tribalness and social backwardness. Some of the smaller states show a higher rate of urbanization (Mizoram and Manipur, for example) than the national average (Table 2). Mizoram ranked second in the nation in literacy rates in 1991 with 81 per cent literate compared to the national average of 52 per cent. Nagaland, Manipur and Tripura also scored above the national average and higher than rates registered by Punjab (57.1 per cent) and West Bengal (57.7 per cent) (Government of India, 1991b: 6). Manipur and Meghalaya have a positive record of female literacy and well-being which should be a matter of envy for most large states of India (Dreze and Sen 1996: 135–6, 176).

TABLE 2

RELATIVE LEVELS OF DEVELOPMENT: NORTH-EASTERN STATES

States	% Literate 1991 (India – 52.11)	% Urban 1991 (India – 25.7)	Index of real per capita state income 1991–2 (India – 100)
A. With low tribe %			
1. Assam	52.9	11.1	73.7
2. Manipur	59.9	27.5	96.52 (a)
3. Tripura	60.4	15.3	71.6 (a)
B. With high tribe %			
4. Arunachal Pradesh	41.6	12.8	96.02
5. Meghalaya	49.1	18.6	72.30
6. Mizoram	82.3	46.1	99.24
7. Nagaland	61.7	17.2	93.68

Comparison:
West Bengal— 93.11
Tamil Nadu— 87.83
Uttar Pradesh—69.40
Bihar—   50.23

Notes: (a) Older series; for approximate comparison.

SOURCES: GOI (1993); CMIE (1994b).

If the word 'tribal' conjures up a necessary image of relative economic underdevelopment, it may be instructive to note a few comparative indicators. If we consider the index of per capita state income (India = 100; 1991–2), the smaller states with the highest tribal concentrations come pretty close to 100 (ranging from 94 to 96). These figures are better than those for West Bengal and Tamil Nadu. Meghalaya, however, falls behind but stays close to less tribal Tripura and Assam, though all of them in the north-east still do better than the larger mainstream Hindi-speaking states such as Uttar Pradesh (Table 2).

The north-eastern states are then different in many ways from the rest of India, but not in the sense of significantly lagging behind the average 'mainstream' states. However, the strategic location of the region and the nature of the polity, economy and society of the neighbouring regions and countries have added a set of special concerns, problems and anxieties to its normal share. Thus the politics of this region has been deeply influenced by the influx of people from other regions as well as neighbouring countries like Myanmar and Bangladesh, notably the latter. The population of the north-eastern regions has grown at a substantially higher rate than that of the rest of India since the turn of the century. From 1901 to 1981, the region's population grew six times, while the national population increased less than three times (Sebastian 1986: 63–5). The highest rate of increase was registered in the decade following Independence, with Tripura bearing the brunt.[3] Tripura also has the longest boundary with Bangladesh. That this big rise in number was not due to natural increase is obvious. The rising tide of immigration from Bangladesh and other regions of India was widely perceived as a major problem of the region. However, the impact of immigration was perceived in different ways in different areas of the region. The perception and its political implications also varied within the same areas depending on the time and specific communities involved.

Community Crafting: Assamese Strategies

Political movements in favour of ethnic interests or autonomy have had a long history in the north-eastern region. Constitutional concessions and favourable responses from the federal and regional governments have also assumed interesting and innovative forms. What sort of community perceptions set the contexts for such autonomy movements, political responses, and their institutional products? Were these communities driven by an exclusively ethnic imperative or dynamics internal to them? Or to what extent were extensive coalitions of exclusive ethnic formations politically sought to be brought together in more inclusive wider *combinations* in the name of territorial or cultural communities? What makes these combinations work to accomplish what kind of political projects, and what makes them come apart, fade, dissolve, or reappear in different patterns of collaborations in different contexts and moments of history?

A plausible set of answers to these questions would require a rather long view.[4] Fortunately we already have a record of five decades of

[3] Between 1951 and 1961, the annual percentage rate of growth of population of the region was 3.5, Tripura's was 6, Nagaland's 5.6. For this period, India's rate was 1.96 (Sebastian 1986: 65; CMIE 1994b: Table 1.1).

[4] In order to understand community formation processes involving 'a multitude of realities,' one needs proper raw materials: a plentiful record of lived time 'to yield an experimental laboratory' comparisons, as Fernand Braudel would insist (1988: 8–19, 21).

collective *expression* of community perceptions and interests in this region. We also have a record of processing of demands and supports connected with them by the relevant political authorities at the regional and national levels. We can begin with community formation processes and problems in Assam, the largest state and historically the most important context of autonomy movements in the region.

The cultural lineage of Assam as well as its political history can be traced back to the classical Pragjyotisha and Kamarupa phases (Majumdar 1988b: 88 ff., 139–41). Political considerations by the Ahom rulers ensured a dynastic system for about six centuries. Originally from Burma, these rulers gradually adopted Sanskritic names and culture. Asom, as the country was named, was already a composite of diverse races, cultures, religions, and languages. Internal dissension within the later Ahom ruling system invited Burmese conquest in 1819. Burmese rule was replaced by British rule in 1826 (Majumdar 1988a: 96–144).

Henceforth, the shape of Assam and its composition were completely dominated by British colonial reason and administrative cunning until the very end of the rule. This involved a process of making Assam an appendage of the colonial province of Bengal until 1874, followed by its partition and reconstitution as a new administrative unit. By this time extensive areas of the Bengali-speaking population were incorporated in the new Commissioner's province. The British rulers always liked to draw a distinction between what they called 'Assam Proper' and 'a number of tribes and nations whose history must be separately considered' (Government of India 1907: 158). These 'tribes and nations' were divided into several categories and subcategories.[5] The redrawing of boundaries in 1906 and 1912 continued to add complexity to the already bewildering diversity of Assam's population.

From the perspective of the advocates of the Assamese community, the entire exercise of shuffling boundaries was perceived as a way of reducing their importance in their own homeland. This perception was mainly shared by Hindu Assamese speakers associated with the Brahmaputra Valley (S. Hazarika 1994: 45). They resented the prominence of the Bengali language officially allowed until 1872 and the importance accorded to Bengali people in education, administration, urban professions and employment. Later the British Cabinet Mission Plan of 1946 to group together Muslim-dominated Bengal with Assam in a three-tier constitutional system to avoid the outright formation of Pakistan was perceived by them as a way of

---

[5] Five broad divisions are mentioned: the northern, north–eastern, and southern 'Hill Tribes', the Nagas and Manipur (Government of India 1907: 158).

reducing Assam to a junior partner in a surrogate version of eastern Pakistan.[6]

If they accepted the plan to join the new group (Bengal and Assam), they could be at the mercy of the much more numerous Bengalis and be dominated by a combined majority of Bengali and Assamese Muslims. The Congress leaders of Assam had already had an unpleasant taste of a Muslim League ministry headed by S. M. Saadulla (from 1939 to 1946, with interruptions) which had encouraged large-scale Muslim migration from eastern Bengal (S. Hazarika 1994: 58). These Congress leaders had built their political career and support bases by hitting at Bengali Hindus for several decades. In the process, they had always counted on the support of the poorer Bengali Muslim settlers who were politically prepared to be enumerated as Assamese speakers to swell the size of the Assamese-speaking community (1994: 44–5). If the group plan was conceded, the same Muslim population of Assam could conceivably cross over to strengthen the vastly larger numbers of Muslims in Bengal to overwhelm the Hindu Assamese Congress or nationalist leadership and their community.[7]

It was at this juncture that the support of Bengali Hindus of Assam and Bengal to strengthen the anti-grouping position of the nationalist leaders of Assam within the province (as in the 1946 elections), and in the national negotiation process for transfer of power, was of crucial importance.[8] Equally important was the incentive that Mahatma Gandhi gave to Assamese Congress leaders to defy national organizational leaders of the Congress party as well as colonial rulers in order to assert their

---

[6] The plan was to divide British India into three sections of provinces: A, consisting of six Hindu-majority provinces; B, Punjab, NWFP and Sind; and C, comprising Bengal and Assam. For a brief discussion, see Pandey (1969: 175–84).

[7] The Cabinet Mission Proposal indicated that the relative number of elected representatives in Section C provinces was to be as follows:

Province	General (Mostly Hindus)	Muslim	Total
Bengal	27	33	60
Assam	7	3	10
Total	34	36	70

Total for British India = 292

See Majumdar (1988: 737–8).

[8] Nationalist leaders of Assam enjoyed overwhelming success during the 1946 elections, which indicated strong support registered by Bengali Hindu voters (see Weiner 1978: 110).

autonomy.[9] The strategic combination of forces worked and the grouping plan was dropped. In the course of Partition of the subcontinent in 1947, Assam remained with India but lost a large part of one Muslim-majority district (Sylhet), which went to East Pakistan as a result of a referendum.

Assamese Dissonance

If the partition substantially reduced the weight of the Bengali Muslim factor in Assamese politics, it, at the same time, made Bengali Hindus more vulnerable. The territorial tilt of the definition of Assam as a community, which briefly allowed room for Bengali Hindus during the crisis years, gave way to an ethno-linguistic Assamese exclusivism after Independence. A new wave of enforcement of the dominance of Assamese language in schools, universities, administrative offices, and communication systems was pursued to demonstrate that the Assamese were the effective masters in their own house. The major targets of attack once again were the Bengali Hindus, who already had many more attractive jobs than votes. Other targets included migrant business communities and labourers from northern and eastern India, who had still fewer votes but enjoyed more dominant capital or remunerative employment than their Assamese counterparts.[10]

Now that the Assamese leaders were politically secure, it was time to convert this security into the economic security of their own language-based sense of authentic community. Since most of the attractive jobs were in the public sector, policies enforcing Assamese and displacing other languages, including Bengali and tribal languages, could bring about highly rewarding results. Those who led the attack on 'outsiders' were newly educated younger people and their cultural mentors in a variety of organizations. Language issues were crucial for this social mobility and economic gain.

[9] Mahatma Gandhi's advice was, 'No one can force Assam to do what it does not want to do. ... It must become fully independent and autonomous' (Hazarika 1994: 343–5). Important leaders of national stature from Bengal like Subhas Chandra Bose and Sarat Chandra Bose (Congress) and Shyama Prasad Mookherjee (Hindu Mahasabha; later the founder of the Jana Sangh) also lent significant support to Assam's case for autonomy (75–6).

[10] Historically, according to one Assamese scholar, though Marwari and British business interests were perceived as the most conspicuous exploiters in the economic domain, 'The Assamese elite did not feel the pinch of their dominance as much as that of the Bengali's ... the former did not pose a socio-cultural threat to the Assamese as the Bengalis did.' Phukon (1988: 53).

It is interesting that the established or ruling party leaders in Assam, including the Congress and the Janata parties, did not lead the cleansing rhetoric. These were the senior leaders who knew the value of cultivating support from other regions for Assamese autonomy (Dasgupta 1990: 144–68). The leadership of aggressive agitation, including campaigns of violence, was provided by other groups. These included, especially during the late 1970s, the All Assam Students Union (AASU) and a coalition of eleven groups called the All Assam Gana Sangram Parishad (AAGSP), or the Assam popular movement front (Dutta 1988: 29–49). They were aided by famous literary authors represented by the Asom Sahitya Sabha (Assam Literary Association).

The collective expression of Assamese community interests thus assumed, at least at this stage, two different forms. Old and established political organizations were in some ways involved in the issues of the day. But their emotions were controlled. More recent organizations like AASU and combination of groups went for drastic action, but were not entirely averse to compromise. A third form, more militant and wedded to insurgent violence, emerged later from the margins of ambiguity associated with the second form. This will be examined later. The boundaries of the immediate issue—definition for the popular struggle—were not self-evident to all the participants of the Assam movement that continued for about six years, beginning in 1979. AASU and AAGSP leaders wanted to concentrate on the problem of 'foreigners' (Muslim immigrants from East Pakistan, later, Bangladesh) illegitimately inflating the electoral rolls, excluding them from such rolls and deporting them. Some leaders were eager to add the issue of 'outsiders' (Indians from other regions) as well, though the literary authors advised against it for the moment. Eventually, the illegal immigrants issue with special reference to the misuse of voter lists and land grabbing by 'foreigners' gained greater attention. The magnitude of the migrants' intrusion was stated to be such as to make the Assamese lose their majority![11] The sense of alarm was deep enough to draw substantial popular support from Assamese speakers, including the already established early Muslim settlers. A new regional party was formed in October 1985 to consolidate the groups engaged in the movement. This party, the Asom Gana Parishad (AGP), scored an impressive victory in the general election of December 1985 and installed Prafulla Mahanta as the chief minister, the youngest in Indian history. The electoral legitimation

[11] The fear of being swamped was hardly convincing; in 1971 Assamese speakers constituted 61 per cent of the population while the Muslim population was 24 per cent (Sen 1982: 182).

of the young movement leaders was not unreciprocated by them. Mahanta lost no time in declaring that the AGP's victory implied a victory of 'regionalism with a nationalist outlook'.[12]

That the AGP was serious about its national linkage and collaboration was clearly demonstrated when the federal government under Rajiv Gandhi's leadership showed its willingness to drop the earlier hard line in favour of constructive negotiation. That hard line had treated the young Assamese leaders with contempt and sought to manipulate Assamese politics by exploiting minority resentment.[13] The AGP's predecessors had reacted with rage, which led to a chain of violence that hit even non-immigrant Assamese Muslims very hard.[14] The Assam accord of 12 August 1985 saved the situation for both sides. For a change, responsive federal treatment of regional demands facilitated a transition from a vicious circle of cumulative violence to a process of mutual legitimation and cooperation between the central government and the AGP. The Assam accord also indicated that the central Congress party's earlier inability to concede the regional movement's legitimate right to represent its community's case was a major factor in inducing the chain of violence that vitiated the political and economic atmosphere of the entire region. It took a small concession to induct the AGP into the national institutional system. Within a few years it became a valued component of a nationwide coalition of regional and national parties (the National Front) that came to power, though briefly, in 1989.[15] Here was evidence dismissing the Congress canard that regional challenges mounted against itself may be regarded as threats to national integrity.

However, the transition from ethnic rage to a statesmanly exercise of governance was not easy for the young and inexperienced leaders of the AGP. Their cooperation with the national political groups, the pressure of

---

[12] *India Today*, 15 January 1986, p. 10.

[13] Congress leaders in Assam were eager to use illegal immigrants as their secure vote banks.

[14] The worst instance of violence was the Nellie massacre in 1983, when tribal groups who had lost land to Muslim immigrants from Bangladesh attacked the latter and in one day killed more than 1700 people. The chain of continued violence took a toll of more than 3000 people—mostly Bengali Muslims and Hindus. The violence began because Muslims had defied the AASU order to boycott the 1983 elections, which Indira Gandhi had forced on Assam. As Hazarika puts it, this election was 'bizarre and farcical: it would have been funny had it not been for the brutality and the killing'. (Hazarika 1994: 144).

[15] An AGP leader, during the 1989–91 National Front government, became India's cabinet minister in charge of 'Law and Justice', in addition to 'Steel and Mines'!

other issues and the craving for the prizes[16] offered by office and authority made them renege on most of their commitments to the Assamese community. At the same time, the collective alienation of non-Assamese-speaking tribal and other people gradually intensified. Even active supporters of Assamese nationalism soon veered away from the AGP and increasingly began to admire, endorse and support more militant organizations wedded to insurgency and violence, like the United Liberation Front of Assam (ULFA). ULFA, which was organized in 1979, had remained dormant for a few years but hit the headlines at about the time that the AGP began to grossly let down its supporters (Das 1994: 68–89). ULFA's brand of terror and brutal violence, however, soon bred its competition in the form of sub-Assamese insurgency. Besides there was growing mobilization of federal counterinsurgence resources that had to be taken seriously.

The Insurgents and Their Competition

It is indicative of the predominantly middle class nature of Assamese ethnic mobilization that the AGP and ULFA were dominated by educated young men who had a strong association with the student movement. The AGP was eager to try the gradualist methods of mass struggle and representation for ensuring Assam's autonomy within the federation. For ULFA, moderate representations of Assam's interests were of no use (Baruah 1994: 871). It stood for armed action, conspicuous brutality and exemplary violence. While the AGP had made a career of campaigning against Muslim migrants from Bangladesh, ULFA eagerly sought arms and military training from official and clandestine sources located in Pakistan (at times through middlemen in Bangladesh), Myanmar and China.[17] It developed close connections with several north-eastern insurgency groups. Any support was welcomed so long as it contributed to Assam's 'independence'. At times, though, some leaders were not averse to switching from the term 'independence' to 'self-determination' (Baruah 1994: 868).

---

[16] Having won power, many of these rebel young AGP leaders rushed for a stable settled life. 'Many of them got married quickly. Their wedding receptions were lavish ... expensive gifts ...were bestowed on the couples. One minister received as many as a dozen refrigerators and an equal number of television sets from businessmen' (Hazarika 1994: 150–1).

[17] The leaders of ULFA do not necessarily deny these connections; some openly admit them (Hazarika 1994: 70–82). The use of sources in China was supposed to be indirect, through other north-eastern insurgency groups straddling the borders of several countries close to the region.

ULFA's concept of Assamese community was also different, at least when it was originally elaborated. Its ideological premises were related to more comprehensive socio-economic structural and developmental issues than is characteristic of subnational movements, including insurgency groups in this region. Most statements of ULFA leaders indicate that their notion of Assam is more territorial than ethno-linguistically exclusive. This implies a more inclusive form; it indicates legitimate room for non-Assamese-speaking people (Baruah 1994: 869). In practice, these leaders work closely with insurgency groups connected with the communities in Nagaland and Manipur. At home, in Assam, ULFA has stayed away from the 'foreigners' issue although it did direct its rage against the federal government for not solving the illegal immigration problem. In fact, the federal government or the 'centre', according to the ideological statements of the organization, is deeply implicated in a process of colonial extraction of resources from and manipulative control on Assam. Again, the explanation of this internal colonialism is not ethnic domination; it is defined as a structural characteristic of capitalism operative in India (Das 1994: 29).

During the formative stages of the Assamese movement, its leaders noted with dismay that though at that time (1970s) the state supplied 60 per cent of India's crude oil production, it received less than 3 per cent of its value in the form of royalties from the federal government. It was a major producer of tea but its royalty earning was incredibly low (Dasgupta 1990: 165–7). So was the case with plywood. Even the regional capitalist class that developed in Assam after Independence was composed mainly of Marwari entrepreneurs (Bhattacharya 1994: 349–63). Assam's enrichment, in that sense, according to the movement's leaders, served investors from elsewhere rather than the region's population. The urban areas were dominated by 'outsiders'. The latter also supplied at that time (1970s) the majority of senior administrative personnel in the public services controlled by the central government. However, the connection between capitalism and interregional injustice or internal colonialism was rarely clarified by ULFA statements. They did not make clear the distinctions and connections between multinational, national, regional and indigenous (Assamese) capital. Neither was the relative productive contribution of non-migrant capital, labour and organization specified to indicate their fair share in the aggregate product of the state.

However, the major contribution of such structural discourse was to lend an intellectual legitimation to what turned out to be a brutal chain of extortion, intimidation, terror and murder to demonstrate that the 'boys' meant business. The targets, in the mid-1980s, were those declared as the enemies of Assam. Initially the acts of terror were aimed at politicians, bureaucrats and others suspected of committing 'crimes' against Assamese society. These crimes might include involvement in drug dealing, prostitution networks, alcohol brewing, teasing women, or exploiting people (Das 1994: 73 ff.). Instant punishments meted out to such offenders earned ULFA immediate popularity. It became almost legendary when it also demonstrated a simultaneous interest ensuring that rural development projects subsidized by the state actually delivered the goods to the proper beneficiaries. But its most spectacular success began in the late 1980s when it turned its guns mainly on migrant big businessmen and professionals, and made them pay incredibly large sums of money to ULFA leaders. Hundreds of prominent businessmen were killed and millions of rupees were levied on businesses of all kinds (Das 1994: 75 ff.). However, Assamese businessmen, including large tea garden owners, were exempted. Often, even ULFA leaders were surprised by the easy capitulation of migrant traders and industrialists. Most of these acts of terror and extortion took place while AGP leaders looked the other way. The Assamese people of the Brahmaputra valley applauded such terror because it supposedly served to recover Assam's wealth for its people. For others in the state, it was a grim situation in which even the administrative authorities were not beyond complicity.

ULFA's brazen terrorism was not perceived by non-Assamese people in the state as an anti-capitalist or prosocialist movement. It was recognized as the military arm of Assamese middle class chauvinism. Hindi-speaking businessmen, Muslim groups and tribal groups formed their own militant organizations to confront ULFA terrorists (Das 1994: 76–7). By the early 1990s severe factional strife divided ULFA leadership. But the most damaging attack on the organization came from the federal government. Two major armed operations in 1990 and 1991 broke the back of ULFA. This time, it was the turn of its leaders to capitulate. In 1992, the organization assured the Indian prime minister that it would abjure violence and operate within the rules of the Indian constitution. Some hardliners disagreed and escaped to Bangladesh. These leaders were willing to view the Bangladeshi migrants in a positive light. Understandably this strengthened the case of the gradualists (AASU and allied organizations) to brand them as anti-Assam (Hazarika 1994: 232–3). Despite the decline of the armed capability of hardliners and their significant loss of political standing, the incidents of terror including the kidnapping of wealthy and prominent individuals, collecting huge ransoms and other acts of violence have not entirely disappeared. Occasionally they are committed by some local committees, or sometimes by armed units that have formally surrendered before.

BODO AUTONOMY: COMMUNITY CLAIMS CONFRONTING ASSAM

In recent years, Assamese ethnic emotions have been challenged more often within Assam than in the rest of the country. Most of these challenges have emerged from tribal communities from the hill areas or the plains. Whenever Assamese leaders equated the territorial identity of multiethnic Assam with the ethno-linguistic identity of Assamese speakers of the Brahmaputra valley, they pushed the other ethnic groups to seek security through their own autonomous structures. The central government often aided their quest for self-governance. Thus Nagaland became a separate state in 1963, Meghalaya was created in 1971, and Mizoram obtained statehood in 1986. Apparently these departures did not turn out to be instructive. Those were hill areas for which the plains elite of Assam probably had little affection. But gradually, the plains tribals were also pushed to a state of bitter alienation, which finally exploded into violent insurgency. The largest part of this revolt is broadly known as Bodo separatism or simply the Bodo movement.

Interestingly, the Bodo movement is positively interested in Indian national cohesion. The ethnic rage in this case is directed mainly towards Assam. The term 'Bodo' refers to a group of closely related tribes including the 'pure' Boro language speakers who are called the Boro Kochari people.[18] The entire group is often referred to as the Bodo Kochari community by others. It is the most numerous single indigenous ethnic community in Assam. In 1980, according to its spokespersons, its number exceeded five million. Depending on definitions and counting sources, however, the actual figures may vary considerably for the Bodo group as a whole or its Boro component.[19]

A credible capacity to recall a community's early historical accomplishments can offer valuable political capital for its political leaders. On this count the Bodos have few rivals in the region. The Plains Tribals Council of Assam, in a memorandum to the President of India in 1967, reminded him that the Bodos have maintained their sovereignty 'from

---

[18] According to the leaders of the Bodo movement, out of the five million-strong Bodo community, the Boro people account for four million. Several other tribes in the group, notably the Sonowal and the Lalung people, number about 200,000 each. These are mid-1986 estimates. See All Bodo Students Union, 'Why Separate State', document submitted to the President of India, reprinted in Datta (1993: 268).

[19] In one of the most detailed language breakdowns by communities offered by the Census of India for 1971, the Bodo group figure comes to 1.2 million (Government of India 1972: LII).

time immemorial ... till their last king died in ... 1854' (Datta 1993: 122). The Bodos claim to be the earliest known inhabitants of Assam and also the earliest as well as the longest chain of rulers. They are quick to point out that when Assamese leaders trace their heritage from the Ahom era, they actually glorify invaders from an alien culture. They use the category 'artificial Assamese' to describe the present generation of Assamese ethnonationalists who represent the relatively upper formations of the Hindu caste structure. The latter, according to Bodo leaders, can be traced to migrants from northern India (1993: 122).

The Bodos assert that the Assamese people are, in fact, outsiders who have unleashed a 'deadly anti-tribal' policy to arbitrarily cleanse Assam of its genuinely original and authentic inhabitants (1993: 122). They accuse the Assamese government of conducting a deliberate policy of Assamization through an imposition of 'Assamese language and culture upon the tribals undemocratically (and) violating the Constitution of India' (1993: 222–4). Like the hill tribal people of the state, the Bodos and other plains tribal people deeply resent the imposition of Assamese language in part because it is not 'the aboriginal language of Assam' and because it violates the pluralism of the multiethnic society (1993: 225). Assamese belongs to the Indo-Aryan family of languages. Most of the tribal languages historically associated with Assam belong to the Tibeto-Burman cluster, which includes the Bodo group (1993: 225). Assamese language and literary history bear too close an affinity to their counterparts in Bengal and farther west in the eastern Hindi area to lend credence to their indigenous pretensions (Government of India 1972). Given such a perception on the part of the Bodos, it is understandable why they want a division of Assam, and a homeland free from Assamese political domination and exploitation connected with 'land, education, culture, and job opportunities' (Datta 1993: 225–38).

From Representation to Resistance: State Inducement for Insurgence

Bodo demands for community rights were expressed as early as 1929 when several memorandums were submitted to the British Statutory Commission on Constitutional Reforms (better known as the Simon Commission) that visited Assam (Datta 1993: 8–9). A convention of plains tribals held in 1933 gave birth to the All Assam Tribal League (AATL). It registered striking success in the 1937 elections. The leaders of the organization lent crucial support to the Congress organization and its leader

Bardoloi at a time when the latter needed it the most to save the integrity of Assam on the eve of Partition. However, Bardoloi disappointed the AATL when, as chairman of the Constituent Assembly's subcommittee dealing with north-eastern tribals, he chose to ignore the plains tribals. The latter felt betrayed again when the choice of Assamese as the official language of the state put all tribal language speakers in a severely disadvantageous position. Bodo leaders, through the Bodo Sahitya Sabha (BSS), campaigned to introduce the Bodo language as a medium of instruction in primary schools, and later in higher schools. But the realization of community rights seemed to call for much more than educational or literary mobilization.

The structure of political rivalry in Assam and the shifts in the federal government's strategies in the 1960s encouraged Bodo leaders to intensify their organizational efforts. The state of Nagaland was carved out of Assam in 1963. New Delhi was preparing for a reorganization of Assam. Bodo leaders formed the Plains Tribals Council of Assam (PTCA) in 1967 to fight for 'full autonomy in the predominantly plains tribal areas' in Assam (Bhuyan 1989: 113–14). The administrative form of such autonomy was not specified. By 1973, the autonomous region demanded was named Udayachal and it was to be a union territory. The senior leaders of the PTCA formed electoral alliances, first with the Janata Party and then with the AGP, and gradually moderated their demand to make the new unit an autonomous region within Assam. This enraged the younger leaders, who wanted a more radical organization to represent their community demands. The formation of Meghalaya as a state and Mizoram as a union territory in 1971, reflecting institutionalized autonomy for the hills tribals of the respective areas of Assam, gave new impetus to Bodo radicalism. The All Bodo Students Union (ABSU, formed in 1967) was already making progress as a more radical representative of the interests of the community. It gained more prominence with its demand for a separate state.

However, ABSU was eager to build a wide front of Bodo forces. It tried to unify various factions of the PTCA and its rivals. It took the initiative in forming a new party called United Tribal Nationalist Liberation Front (UTNLF) in 1984. The concept of the 'homeland' state elaborated by ABSU and the UTNLF implied the status of a union territory within the federation for the plains tribal people of Assam in the northern tract of the Brahmaputra valley. Demands were also made (a) on behalf of plains tribals located on the south bank of the Brahmaputra river for the creation of district councils under the provisions of the Sixth Schedule of the Indian constitution and (b) for the inclusion of Bodo-Kacharis of Karbi and Anglong districts within the scope of the Sixth Schedule of the Indian constitution (Datta 1993: 274; Misra and Misra 1996). There was no trace of violence, insurgency, or secessionism at the time in these movements for community autonomy. Bodo youth leaders had even worked closely with AASU during the movement for the eviction of foreigners and for Assam's greater autonomy. But the AGP's coming to power did not help the Bodo cause at all. By the late 1980s, ABSU took a harder line and sponsored popular movements for realizing its objectives through struggle. Traditionally the Bodo economy had been highly dependent on land. But debt, destitution and encroachment by non-tribals progressively pushing them to a precarious margin. Protective provisions for tribals introduced by the Congress government did not help them AGP rule made the situation worse (George 1994: 881).

Economic miseries were only one part of the story of Bodo distress. There was a strong sense of resentment against the language policy in Assam, which put Bodo and all non-Assamese-speaking communities at a grave disadvantage in matters of education, employment and cohesion of community. The relative standing of the rich Bodo language and literature was also declining, despite larger numbers in comparison with those hill tribes which had by the 1970s gained autonomy and become masters of their houses and thus able to confer new dignity and authority on their medium of communication. Bodo language demands were less ethnocentric than was common in the region, if not in the country as a whole. Bodos demanded that Hindi be the official language of Assam (Datta 1993: 161). The Bodo Sahitya Sabha (BSS—Bodo Literary Association) pursued a spirited campaign to promote Hindi as the official language and the Bodo language written in Roman script for Bodo schools. But both ABSU and the BSS consistently discovered that peaceful agitation and institutional processes yielded very little return.

A large-scale mass movement led by ABSU and the Bodo People's Action Committee (BPAC), beginning in 1987, continued to exert pressure on political authorities for about six years. This movement turned out to be more determined, militant and disruptive than previous ones. Frequently its youthful participants engaged in conspicuous violence and destruction of property, in violation of the peaceful pronouncements of its leaders. One could see an uncanny similarity with the Assamese movement, and ironically it was now mainly directed against the Assamese leaders of the AGP who at this time were in power. This time it was the burden of the regionalist AGP to unleash state terror to suppress a subregional popular movement that was seeking to gain regional autonomy. The hardliners among young Bodo activists chose to hit back. They formed an insurgent organization, the Bodo Security Force (BSF), which has gained prominence, especially since 1990, when the AGP government's negotiations with ABSU turned out to be highly unsatisfactory for Bodo leaders.[20]

The end of AGP rule in 1990 and the beginning of Congress rule in 1991 did not expedite the realization of an independent Bodoland state that the BSF wanted to carve out of Assam. If anything, the stalemate gave new impetus to insurgent violence committed by the BSF. Within a few years it became one of the most effective organizations to carry out insurgency operations in the region—not a mean distinction, given the reputation of other, more experienced, organizations in the north-east. Daring acts of kidnapping, extortion, murder and other forms of violence sent waves of alarm through the region. The BSF also developed working linkages with important insurgent groups like ULFA, the NSCN (National Socialist Council of Nagaland) and the UPMLA (United People's Manipur Liberation Army) operating in the region.[21] Its insurgency operations rendered a new sense of urgency to the Assam government as well as the joint leadership of ABSU and the BPAC to find a solution. Central government leaders including the prime minister facilitated the signing of an accord between the Government of Assam and Bodo leaders in early 1993. Unlike the other major accords in the region, however the central government itself was not a signatory (George 1994: 887–91).[22]

The Architecture of Autonomy: Institutional Construction

The Bodo Accord of 1993 did not concede either a state or a union territory to be carved out of Assam. Instead, it provided for a statutory structure of autonomy within the state of Assam in the form of the Bodoland Autonomous Council (BAC). The Council was equipped with its own legislative and executive organs. The Bodo administration was allocated thirty-eight subjects, including matters relating to educational, social, economic, ethnic and cultural affairs affecting the community. These

[20] Another group, much smaller, though of similar insurgent inclinations, was the Bodo Volunteer Force (BVP). This was often considered as the armed support group of ABSU. The BVP became less important after 1993. For later evolution of organizational changes and alignments see Gokhale (1997: 26–7).

[21] R. Banerjee, 'Return to Arms', *India Today* (international edition), 30 November 1992.

[22] All three parties—the central government, the state government and the movement leaders—were involved in the Assam, Mizo, and Tripura accords (George 1994: 888).

subjects implied more, ways of applying laws made by the state to suit the interests and needs of the Bodos rather than allowing them to make laws completely on their own. On matters relating to religion of the community, customary laws, and ownership and transfer of land within Bodoland, Bodo views were supposed to prevail (George 1994: 889). Law and order, however, were left in the jurisdiction of the state of Assam. Major aspects of general revenue matters still remained under the control of the state, though certain assurances regarding flow of funds from the federal government were also made. It was made clear that the BAC was to have control over 2700 villagers and not 4000 as Bodo leaders had originally demanded. The state government finally conceded that at least twenty-five tea gardens would remain under BAC control. The state also agreed to release all Bodo activists in jail. At the same time, nearly 2000 militant Bodos surrendered.[23] The movement was withdrawn.

However, BSF militants did not accept the accord. Popular support for the BSF declined but dramatic acts of violence continued through the mid-1990s. The leaders of the more popular organizations like ABSU and the BPAC also had their reservations about the terms of the Accord and the way it was implemented. But they were ready to give it a trial. They also had a sense of assurance, based on the course of negotiations with the federal government on the eve of the signing of the accord, that if the Assam leaders let them down central leaders might come to their aid. But the institutional structure of autonomy associated with the BAC and growing factionalism raised many difficult questions for Bodo leaders. The BAC was not meant for only one district. Its scope was unusually large; it was designed to cover contiguous areas of Bodo predominance cutting across seven districts. There are substantial numbers of non-Bodo people in many villages in the BAC, some where Bodos do not even constitute a majority. They may react to Bodos in power exactly as the latter had reacted to Assamese in power, or as Assamese had to central leaders. Bodo militants can make matters worse by punishing non-Bodo or non-tribal resenters who then can turn to the Assamese state for redress. Autonomy exercised by an ethnic community in an ethnically plural context especially calls for a kind of conciliary accommodation that is contrary to the militant mentality. This is what makes the institutional problem of sustaining autonomy so complex and challenging.

Nearly four years of experience of the working of the BAC suggests that there was good reason for Bodo people and popular organizations to be disappointed with the Accord. The ruling Congress party failed to

[23] *Sunday*, 18 July 1993, p. 56.

reciprocate the confidence of Bodo leaders in federalizing institutions for autonomy within that state. Vital provisions of the accord were violated.[24] Elections to the BAC were continuously delayed. The first nominated chairman soon resigned, following disagreement with the state government regarding the implementation of the accord. The changing course of the state ruling leaders' political fortunes left its mark on the working of the autonomous council management. It was not surprising that the second nominated chairman served Assam Congress leaders more than his own people.

When the AGP came to power in Assam in 1996, it used its allied Bodo organization, People's Democratic Front (PDF) to control the Council through a new chairman. Meanwhile, radical Bodo organizations stepped up their demands for larger territory and greater autonomy.[25] Popular resentment against what was perceived as Assam's arrogance aided the premium on violence that followed during later years. Moderate forces, despite their larger support demonstrated during the state legislative elections in 1996, failed to stem the alienating effects of manipulative politics.[26] Militant groups gained new areas of support for terrorist acts. The BLT, a newer organization, apparently engaged in the blowing up of trains and bridges by the beginning of 1997 to dramatize their demand for statehood within the federation.[27] Interestingly, part of this drama, which involved gruesome loss of lives and property, was also designed to score points in the internal turfwar within the fragmented organizational scene in Bodo politics.

It would be wrong to conclude that the threat to the sustainability of the institutions designed to satisfy the sense of autonomy of ethnic communities is mainly posed by gun-toting militants or uncompromising hardliners in the popular movements. As is evident from the discussion so far, a major problem of ensuring and enhancing autonomy lies with authorities situated successively above the autonomous units in terms of the formal ordering of power. In this specific case, the strategies of the Government of Assam and how they are overseen by federal institutions, including the judiciary

[24] T. Ray, 'The north-east: Accord and Discord', *Frontline*, 26 January (1996, pp. 36–7).

[25] The prominent organizations now are the People's Democratic Front (PDF), the National Democratic Front of Bodoland (NDFB), and the Bodoland Liberation Tigers (BLT). Along with the ABSU, these are also engaged in desperate turfwars among themselves. See N.A. Gokhale, 'Back to Turmoil', *Outlook*, 15 January (1997, pp. 26–7).

[26] The pro-AGP PDF succeeded in electing six members to the Assam legislative assembly in the 1996 elections.

[27] N. A. Gokhale, 'Back to Turmoil', *Outlook* , 15 January (1997, pp. 26–7).

and the armed forces, are likely to make a big difference. Only a few months before the signing of the Bodo Accord, the Assam government led by chief minister Hiteshwar Saikia of the Congress party took over the administration of the Karbi Anglong Autonomous District Council.[28] This Council, set up to serve the autonomy needs of the hill tribals of that area, was governed by a popular organization called the Autonomous State Demand Committee (ASDC), which commanded a three-fourths majority and was dismissed on charges of mismanagement. The ASDC argued that the charges were an outrage. Fortunately the High Court in Assam agreed with it and the dismissal was declared unconstitutional. The Council was restored. But the ASDC asked for better guarantees for the future from the federal government. Its demands were conceded. This victory also enhanced the powers of other hill people organized in the Council for the North Cachar hills in the state.[29] For once, the lower units exercising their autonomy under the shadow of higher ones were probably assured that their hard-won space was institutionally protected. Judicial umpiring of this kind also indicates a dimension of central institutions that is not easy to recognize when the observers' gaze is exclusively focused on the national legislature and bureaucracy.

NORTH-EASTERN FEDERALIZING PROCESSES: COUNCILS AND CASCADED AUTONOMY

Most observers of ethnic politics and autonomy movements in India have been preoccupied with the intensity and extension of demands from the very beginning of Independence. The literature expressing alarm and despondency has been prolific since those early years. Unfortunately very few observers have paid much attention to the fact that many institutional arrangements for processing those demands were also carefully designed during the very founding moments of the independent state. Besides processing demands, these institutions were also supposed progressively to convert demands into supports for the system through a system of cascading linkages joining together various units of the federal polity in a complex system of coordination. The notion of federalism implied in such an institutional design was one of a structure of cooperation among the centre, the regional governments and the subregional units for generating the

[28] N. A. Gokhale, 'An Uphill Task', *Sunday,* 18 July (1993, p. 69).
[29] See 'Karbi-Dimasa Accord Signed', *The Statesman Weekly,* 8 April 1995, and Misra and Misra (1996: 130–6).

desired process of a nationwide development of political, economic and human resources. This was not a mechanical reproduction of the standard division and balance of powers between the federal and regional governments associated with conventional federal arrangements in developed countries (Dasgupta 1994: 70–87).

The issues of autonomy, from this perspective, were not defined in the oversimplified terms of an absence of federal control over states. Rather, it was understood that a series of negotiated jurisdictions and their changing boundaries authorized by a federalizing process were to link the centre, the state, the autonomous councils and the scheduled areas in one connected series of coordinated efforts. The approach was one of sharing power with a productive purpose among connected units. It did not assume a continuing adversary relation between two parties, the centre and the states. What we have so far explored in terms of the complex autonomy management and conflict resolution processes involving the centre, Assam and subregions of Assam, including the restive fragments of the latter, would indicate how the units are supposed to negotiate, cohere and cooperate in order to optimize their own as well as the system's capabilities.

Like all dynamic institutional designs, the one for federalizing the Indian political system left a lot to gradual learning from practice. The design itself was not very parsimoniously inscribed in constitutional documents. The standard federal provisions are elaborated in the parts specifying the relations between the union government and the states, indicating the distribution of legislative, executive, judicial and financial powers, and administrative control during normal and extraordinary times. The units of the federation can be altered and reorganized by the federal government. The most prominent reorganization was in 1956 to meet local and language demands. For our purpose one of the most interesting uses of these flexible processes was associated with the extensive reorganization of states in the north-east: the state of Nagaland was conceded in 1963. A part of Assam was organized as an autonomous state (or 'substate') within the state of Assam as Meghalaya in 1969 (Basu 1994: 69–70). A large-scale change was brought about in that region when Meghalaya, graduating from 'substate', Manipur and Tripura became states. Mizoram and Arunachal Pradesh became union territories in 1971 and full-fledged states in 1987.

The status of an autonomous state within a state was a special concession to accommodate autonomy demands from tribal areas of Assam. In fact, a major innovation in crafting institutions to respond to autonomy demands without conceding the stature of states was incorporated in the Sixth Schedule of the constitution, which was meant to apply to the administration of tribal areas in Assam, Meghalaya, Tripura and Mizoram. The creation of autonomous *district councils* and *regional councils* was specified by this schedule of detailed provisions (Government of India 1991c: 139–51). Regional Councils were to be permitted within autonomous districts if different scheduled tribes happened to reside in the same district. The Sixth Schedule was to serve as a special 'self-contained code' for the governance of these tribal areas.

Besides special provisions for the protection of rights on land and for ensuring welfare of tribal and other designated disadvantaged segments of population in states outside of the north-eastern region were encoded in the Fifth Schedule of the constitution. These provisions, however, offered more protection than autonomy. The idea was mainly to oversee and compensate the measures followed by the states by means of extrastatal authority. They offered much less than what the north-east was granted. Given the fact that the tribal population of the rest of India was vastly larger, the differences in treatment left wide open the possibility for movements to reduce this gap. This possibility has already been explored in several areas. The Jharkhand movement has already succeeded in gaining a large territorial area of autonomy in the form of a General Council (established in 1994) for eighteen districts comprising the Jharkhand area of Bihar. In Madhya Pradesh, another state with a large tribal concentration, there is a strong movement for implementing tribal autonomy following the model of the Sixth Schedule. The north-east has certainly set a significant trend for the entire nation.

UPHILL DEVELOPMENT: INSTITUTIONAL PERFORMANCE AND PROBLEMS

During the post-colonial reorganization of the subcontinent in 1947, many hill tribal leaders expressed a variety of ideas of autonomy. These were not products of organized collective representations of their respective communities. The voices of the Nagas, Khasis, or Garos, to take some examples, were plural and not unambiguous (Sema 1986: 156 ff.; Pakem 1993: 146–56). The nationalist leaders of India at that moment were also not confident about principles and policies for developing and coordinating the hill tribes of the region. The Constituent Assembly relied heavily on a subcommittee set up for the region with Gopinath Bardoloi, two tribal members from the north-east, and two other members (Shiva Rao 1967: 683 ff.; Singh 1987: 111–15), and its recommendation for autonomous districts led to the institutional arrangements of the Sixth Schedule.

Autonomous democratic administrative systems were introduced in all six hill districts of Assam in 1952 (Hazarika 1978: 283–92). The basic objective was to introduce the new political institutions without disturbing the tribal ways of life connected with land, forests, agricultural practices and modes of settling disputes. Most of the members (75 per cent) of the Autonomous District Councils were to be democratically elected. The rest were to be nominated to ensure the participation of social workers, rural notables and other less represented parts of the population. The governor of the state was to be a key figure, connecting the district with the state and the federal government. His assent was needed to validate laws made by the Council.

The early history of the working of these autonomous councils indicates that except for the Naga Hills, the new system initially appeared to work within the constraints that usually accompany novel institutions in an unaccustomed context. Continued insurgency on the Naga Hills, however, brought the issues of secession and sovereignty greater prominence, despite the fact that the path of violence was strongly disputed by several tribes within the Naga group (Horam 1988: 23). The creation of the state of Nagaland in 1963 altered the context of the autonomous councils that were working in the other districts. Hopes were raised for elevating the status of autonomous units into near or full-fledged statehood. Meanwhile the ethnic exclusivism of Assamese leaders scared the tribal leaders to the point of discouraging them from playing a continued role within the state of Assam. The result was gradual progression from autonomous councils to full statehood. However, the creation of new states did not necessarily do away with the need for autonomous councils. Anytime a major tribal group was identified with a state, the latter was likely to contain less numerous tribes or groups who chose to value such councils as their symbol of autonomy. For example when the Mizos attained the union territory of Mizoram (before it became a state), three of the Regional Councils (subunits within the District Council) were elevated in 1972 to the status of District Councils (Prasad 1994: 18–19).

How have these organizations functioned? Let us limit our discussion of functions to the earlier phase of the experience in the Mizo Hills. The District Council had access to a wide range of legislative, executive, financial, and judicial powers. These included powers to make laws for the allotment, occupation and use of land; management of forests under its control; use of water resources; and the regulation of practices, including those related to agriculture, public health, social customs, money lending and non-tribal traders. Executive powers included the establishment and management of primary schools and the right to determine the language of education in primary schools. Among financial powers, those regarding assessment and collection of land revenue and tax on trades and professions were the most important. All the District Councils in Mizoram, including those of the pre-state formation phase, however, initially appeared unprepared to judiciously exercise many of these powers.

The leaders were more interested in consolidating their political positions in the community than in attending to the developmental needs of their own people. Their emotional expressions of the community's urgent needs made in public, or especially for outside audiences often stood in sharp contrast to gross financial irregularities. The expansion of numbers of unnecessary personnel mainly fed their own political support system. Until 1969, there was no audit system to check them. Even later some glaring problems persisted. Yet, no criticism of these practices from the state authority above them was regarded as legitimate. When these same leaders interfered with the language rights of minor tribes for educating their children in the Regional Council within the District Councils, it was not supposed to count as a violation of tribal rights (Prasad 1994: 23 ff.).

But the leaders of the Mizo District Council, especially in the 1960s, were eager to blame the Assam and the central governments for the relatively poor performance of their own representative institutions. They declared that only the status of statehood could solve their problems. This was the claim of the Mizo Union that ruled the council for nearly two decades. Its demand for a state, however, was peaceful and constitutional. But there was also the secessionist case for an independent state advocated by the Mizo National Front (MNF), which opted for insurgency (Lalthangliana 1994: 175–88). Then too MNF was convinced that the state would deliver the promised land. The weak performance records of Mizo representative institutions were of no relevance to their calculations.

INSURGENCY RHETORIC AND DEMOCRATIC CONSTRUCTION

The prose of north-eastern institutional construction had a hard time competing with the poetic promise of a prosperous state and authentic community offered by insurgent groups. The MNF had the added advantage of learning from the Naga insurgency movements that had earlier induced the formation of the state of Nagaland. Unlike the gradualist Mizo leaders who gave a fair trial to representative institutions embodied in the District Council, MNF leaders like Laldenga had the benefit of support from adjacent and distant countries. However, Laldenga and his supporters had proved their credentials for serving the community by demonstrating their organizing skills in the course of mobilizing the Mizo National Famine Front (MNFF) in 1960 for famine relief action. Laldenga was, at the time, an employee of the District Council. The MNFF was renamed MNF in 1961 and became a political party that did not do well in the subsequent local elections (Ray 1982: 133 ff.).

The MNF turned to insurgency and extensive violence from 1966 onward in support of an independent Mizoram. When MNF plans began to fail, Laldenga was willing to negotiate with Congress leaders at the centre in the late 1960s. The latter, for party reasons, did not reciprocate at that time, though they did so in 1975 and later to counter non-Congress leaders who were becoming more popular in District Council and electoral politics in Mizoram. The latter was made a union territory in 1972. Prime minister Indira Gandhi stealthily cultivated the MNF's support when a non-Congress ruling party in Mizoram was heroically struggling against insurgents and thus risking brutal reprisals. The Congress party won the 1984 elections with MNF support. Rajiv Gandhi signed the Mizo Accord in 1986 and Mizoram graduated to statehood in early 1987. A mellowed Laldenga became the interim chief minister and his party won the 1987 elections (Dua 1992: 103 ff.; Chatterjee 1990, 3: 540–2). The MNF thus became a regular participant in an institutional system which was by then weakened due to the manipulative practices of the national Congress leadership. The MNF lost in the 1989 elections. The Congress party won the 1989 and 1993 elections.

The Mizo story tells us that the transition from insurgency and brazen violence to benign constitutionalism need not be considered as either unnatural or surprising. Perhaps the surprise lies more in scholarly and bureaucratic expectations that ethnic oppositions are likely to constitute 'dangerous enemies' posing severe threats to democracy and well-ordered political systems (Horowitz 1994: 36). The north-eastern cases actually suggest that proper institutional processing of ethnic demands, including violent ones, can transform 'dangerous enemies' into constructive contributors to democratic processes. However, if the national or regional authorities use cynical, unscrupulous, or simply unintelligent ways of manipulating ethnicity or insurgency, then the state itself can become a dangerous enemy of the democratic system. The complicity of the state or of ruling parties in undermining democratic institutions could be clearly seen in the way the centre negotiated with the MNF, or the way Assam Congress leaders dealt with the Karbi Anglong Council (in 1992). On the other hand, the positive sense of cooperation for national and democratic objectives demonstrated by the leaders and organizations involved in sustaining constitutional government in all the north-eastern states, and especially in Nagaland, Meghalaya, Mizoram, Manipur and Tripura for so many decades, has not been duly recognized.

The role of national institutions and organizations in the political and economic life of the north-east is worth noting. By 1997, when so many large states and the centre in India have been ruled by regional parties or coalitions of national and regional parties, it so happens that almost all the north-eastern states have continued to be controlled by national secular parties like the Congress and the Communist Party of India, Marxist (CPI[M]).[30] It is rarely recognized that the smaller and newer states of the region need the collective resources of the nation more than most of the larger states. The combined operation of the federal system and national economic plans have made it possible for the smaller north-eastern states to have a considerably higher per capita plan outlay allocation than the national average for all the states. Thus when the average amount for India in 1990–1, for example, was Rs 288, Arunachal Pradesh got Rs 2288, Mizoram Rs 1786, Nagaland Rs 1318, Meghalaya Rs 1029, Manipur Rs 1000 and Tripura Rs 800. The comparable figure for Assam was Rs 276, and, outside the region, for West Bengal it was Rs 205 and for Kerala Rs 214 (CMIE 1990: Table 14.20). Two states of the region most often identified with insurgence and turbulence in the press and the literature were Nagaland and Mizoram. These were also the ones that registered some of the highest rates of agricultural development as recorded, for example, in rice production in the country during the decade 1983–93. During this period these states recorded compound annual rates of growth of rice production on the order of 5.15 and 7.93 per cent respectively, when the national average percentage rate was 3.71. In fact, Mizoram's rate was even higher than that of Punjab (6.19) (CMIE 1994a: 1). It may not be wrong to infer that these new states have found the federal linkage to be highly productive and have also demonstrated their own capacity to cooperate and perform in the field of development.

Thus it should be fair to conclude that ethnic labels do not indicate with what ideologies, programmes, or methods different communities will be associated. North-eastern ethnic labels are also cluster labels, and within

---

[30] As of early 1997, all the north-eastern states except Assam and Tripura are ruled by the Congress party. Assam has been ruled by the AGP since 1996. Tripura is ruled by the CPI(M). It is interesting to note that the tribal people do not necessarily vote for tribal political organizations when they compete with the national organizations. In the 1995 elections to the 30-member Tripura Tribal Autonomous District Council, the Left Front led by the CPI(M) captured 23 of the 24 elective seats. All the well-known tribal organizations including the Tripura National Volunteers (TNV) participated in the contest (*The Statesman Weekly*, 12 August 1995, p. 8).

one presumed or postulated community, there may be many communities.[31] If colonial history set some incentives for separatist directions of ethnic mobilization, later developments were strong enough to change their courses. The federal democratic framework and the mostly conciliatory, though occasionally manipulative, civil society leadership at the central, regional, and local levels offered modes of institutional processing that significantly affected the patterns of competition among and within ethnic communities in manners that provided scope for a nationwide process of institutional cooperation. Insurgency did not go away but increasingly the advocates of violence had to contend with the supporters of reasonable rivalry abjuring self-righteous violation of others' rights.[32]

Gradually the connection between participation in the representative system and the promise of development helped reduce alienation and violence. The role of prudent, if not always proper, treatment from the relatively higher authorities also proved to be important for frequently inducting insurgents into democratic institutions, and thus probably beginning a process of dis-alienation (Kuechler and Dalton 1990: 281). Some even appeared to enjoy the perquisites of power a little too much for public taste.[33] Whatever it was, at least the easy presumption of any

[31] As noted above, the label Naga refers to thirty-three tribes representing a complex variety of language, culture, tradition and ideology-based social and political divisions. Political divisions often cut across the social divisions. A. Z. Phizo, the father of Naga insurgency, belonged to the Angami tribe. His Naga National Council (NNC) began as a moderate organization, turning into a militant insurgent one in the early 1950s. Insurgency was opposed and democratic means were upheld by a strong group of non-Angami cluster of tribes. Many Angami militants later became moderates especially following the Shillong Peace Agreement of 1975. These leaders include Phizo's brother and daughter. In 1980, the militants formed the National Socialist Council of Nagaland (NSCN) with leaders from three other tribes. By the late 1980s the Tangkhuls and Semas became more prominent in the leadership of the NSCN. The details are covered in Hazarika (1994: 86 ff., 237 ff.). See also Anand (1980: 61 ff.) and, for a short recent account, Subir Ghosh, 'Insurgent Hearts Follow Naga Heads', *The Telegraph*, 27 July 1995. The Mizo cluster comprises at least nine prominent tribes including, for example, the Lushais and the Lakhers (Chatterjee 1990, 3: 517–28, 577–88).

[32] I am using the term 'reasonable' in the sense it is used by John Rawls (1993: 49): 'The Disposition to be Reasonable', implies 'taking into account' on the part of the people 'the consequences of their actions on others' well being.'

[33] See Hazarika (1994: 234) for a reference to 'comfortable life-style and easy money, especially among ministers in the MNF government which became the talk of Aizawl' (Mizoram's capital). That many insurgent leaders can use 'ill-gotten assets' for lavish luxury even before gaining political power was observed, for example, in Punjab in the late 1980s and the following years. See Asit Jolly, 'Relatives Lay Claim to Fortune of Top Punjab Militants', *The Asian Age* (Calcutta), 23 July, 1995.

close connection between north-eastern ethnicity and endangerment of Indian democracy was not easy to sustain.

I am not implying that federal and democratic institutions of the kind that obtain in India can always easily process ethnic demands or convert such demands into supportive resources by continuously incorporating those who presume to speak for their communities or their fragments.[34] Rather, it is suggested here that the narratives of violence and alarm that dominate our literature have a tendency to make us miss the role of an interlinked system of institutions that have engaged in at least two tasks that are probably unprecedented in world history.[35] One of them, of course, is the gigantic scale of processing and converting demands that can strain even the most advanced polity in the world. The second, and more important, is the task, mostly invisible to eyes that lack empathy, of pre-empting and preventing conflict by creating in advance ways of inducting people into processes of identification with national, developmental, civic, or other cooperative norms or values. The narratives of peace, civility, economic construction and democratic engagement that reflect how most people in India most of the time conduct their lives and contribute to national development need not be neglected simply because they do not pack much drama. I also want to indicate—and our story offers enough clues in that direction—that successful processing of ethnic demands can encourage new demands from those who were not able to speak out before. This demonstration effect need not be necessarily construed as a signal of danger. It can be seen as a signal of social mobility that makes it possible for successively less advantaged and less articulate segments of the population to seek their space of dignity in the wider system. The example of middle class beneficiaries of so many ethnic movements may encourage lower status groups to use subethnic or newly created ethnic labels to press their claims. Instead of straining the system, this can be seen as a process of

[34] What is the extent of popular incorporation that is appropriate to successful democratization in a developing or, for that matter, any country? How inclusive should the state or the civil society be to earn a properly democratizing label? The scholarly literature is quite unclear on these issues. A welcome recent analysis suggests that 'every historical step the state takes toward inclusion should produce a pattern of exclusions as well'. These exclusionary transitions may serve as seeds of further democratization. This positive evaluation of oppositional space and incomplete inclusion can aid our understanding of the rationality of sequential incorporation, which at particular moments may be or should be compatible with a reasonable extent of disaffection in developing democracies (Dryzek 1996: 486).

[35] Amitav Ghosh, 'Shadow Lines, The Story', *The Telegraph*, 24 July 1995, p. 10.

democracy 'working its way down' to tap new sources of strength from the deeper strata of society (Naipaul 1990: 517). This is how constructive constitutionalism can possibly seek to turn ethnic conflicts into positive resources for social change and egalitarian development.

The Rebirth of Shiv Sena in Maharashtra
The Symbiosis of Discursive and
Institutional Power

MARY FAINSOD KATZENSTEIN, UDAY SINGH MEHTA and USHA
THAKKAR*

In rally upon rally over the last half dozen years, Shiv Sena party supporters
have been exhorted to intone *'Garva se kaho hum Hindu hai'* ('Say with
pride that we are Hindu'). In Hindi, not Marathi. This incantation as a
centrepiece of Shiv Sena events would have been scarcely imaginable in
the early years of the Shiv Sena. Both the stress on a Hindu identity and
the use of Hindi in political sloganeering are indicative of a major shift in
the politics of regionalism in western India.

This turn to Hinduism is what seemed to underlie the outbreak of violence
in Bombay on a scale never before witnessed in the city. In the winter of
1992–3, Bombay experienced the worst Hindu–Muslim conflagration the
city has ever known. According to Human Rights Watch, over a thousand
people were killed and tens or perhaps hundreds of thousands fled the city
(1995: 26–7). It is a shift in which the once local, nativist party in Bombay,
the Shiv Sena, now finds itself the dominant political force in the state of
Maharashtra with a ready capacity to incite widespread violence, extract
rents, and shape public policy and legislative initiatives (including the
decision to first nullify and then renegotiate the Enron power project that
recently attracted global attention). This chapter attempts to understand the
role of religious nationalism in the ascendancy of the Shiv Sena.

The argument of this chapter is two-fold: first, that the Shiv Sena
effectively exploited a discursive opportunity to link its own locally
produced version of militant Hinduism with the politicized Hinduism that
has been rapidly spreading throughout north India since the mid-1980s;
but second, that the discourse of Hindu nationalism was only able to take

* The authors thank Anthony Anunziato and Ved Kayastha, Ernest L. Stern '56
Asia Curator, Kroch Library, Cornell, for their invaluable assistance in locating material;
Dinu Ranadive, Mrinal Gore and Pankaj Joshi for their generous help; and Amrita
Basu, Ronald Herring, Peter Katzenstein, Atul Kohli, Bijoy Mishra, Gail Omvedt, and
Sidney Tarrow for their very useful comments.

hold in Bombay and in Maharashtra due to the tightly structured and coercive character of Shiv Sena as an organization operating in a political milieu that was increasingly fractured and undirected. Clearly discourses count. As long as the Shiv Sena continued to focus on local, nativist issues alone, its political appeal beyond the metropolitan reach of Bombay city was limited. And yet, its turn to the ideology of Hindutva would have been of less far-reaching implications were it not for the party's organizational strengths (including its capacity to intimidate) and the incapacity of other party and state institutions to respond.

The linking of religion with nationalism, by itself, but particularly in a form that vilifies a population whose 'difference' has deep historical roots, is likely to exert immense mobilizational power, both electoral and on the streets. Hindu nationalism on its own, however, can neither account for the devastation in Bombay during the winter of 1992–3 nor for the Shiv Sena's electoral successes of the 1990s. The discourse of religious nationalism derives its power in part from a transposition of language, ideology and rhetoric that heightens the politics of identity. But the power of discourse also depends crucially on the capacity or incapacity of organizations to make any particular set of competing discursive claims 'stick'. In the case of Shiv Sena, Hindutva and Maharashtra, this has everything to do with the Sena's organizational wizardry and coercive practices and with the weakened institutional structures in the state of Maharashtra.

DISCOURSE AND ORGANIZATION

A few words about terminology: discourse refers, in this article, to language and symbolic actions. Discourse is meaning-making work. It consists of the explanations people offer for their actions and the interpretations they attach to the actions and words of others. It is true that the links between what is understood, said and done are plainly not direct. People often act in ways that contradict what they say they will do and the same set of words and actions are often interpreted in contradictory ways by different groups or individuals. The justification, however, for taking seriously the expressive or discursive dimension of human sociability is that in admittedly complex ways, linguistic acts of interpretation shape how people feel, think, report their interests and imagine the choices they have for their actions.

Much recent work on discourse is inspired by the pioneering work of Michel Foucault. With Foucault, we prefer the term discursive to ideological, in part to avoid weighing (when such an evaluation is not the project of our chapter) the truth claims of one set of beliefs over another. But we also refer to discourses rather than ideologies in order to suggest that what may be at work here is not just an attachment to particular political 'positions' on Hinduism and Islam but also a deployment of a whole set of expressive acts (the wearing of saffron cloth and holy beads, the lavish spending at the time of religious festivals).

Foucault uses the term discourse in a way that makes it synonymous with institutional or disciplinary systems (1972: 171–3). The reason for this conflation of language and institutions within the notion of discourse relates to the subtle ways in which he sees the powers of institutions as deeply imbricated in modes of expression and categorization. The boundaries between discourse and institutions are indeed fuzzy. Nevertheless we believe the distinction of speech acts and institutional arrangements to be both possible and analytically productive.

We understand institutions as constituted by both discursive and organizational practices. Institutions are value-embedded organizations (Scott 1995; Powell and DiMaggio 1991). Organizations operate according to a set of rules, based on structures, that serve particular ends. But institutions are more than organizations. Institutions are associated with a set of particular norms or values, while organizations operate to perform particular functions. The Indian Administrative Service (IAS), for instance, is both an organization and institution. It is the former in the sense that it recruits personnel through a highly competitive examination process, trains these recruits, and assigns them to staff the administrative services of both centre and state bureaucracies. But the IAS is an institution in the sense that, as the 'steel frame of India', it has long been identified with old-school patrician integrity, dedication to political impartiality, and correct bearing and conduct.

Different organizational arrangements privilege the discursive acts of some groups over others. Attention to discourse takes seriously what people think, what they say, what they write, and the corresponding symbolic expressions. Concurrent attention to organizations precludes confining this interpretative analysis to what people say they mean, slighting the power laden and sometimes coercive organizational processes that transmit this meaning-making work to others. This broadly Weberian orientation is what informs this chapter.

When people use and manipulate a certain set of symbols and words as distinct from some other set that they earlier used, one can speak of discursive change and at least provisionally conclude that this change represents some transformation of individual and collective self-understanding and at least a disposition to altering strategies and interests.

Of course, changes of interests and strategies can, and often are, motivated by new organizational practices that have implications for intersubjective understandings. In these situations the boundaries of discursive and organizational practices can be blurred. In the present context, however, our contention is that the empirical examples used in this chapter are often outside these intersecting domains. Frequent references linking patriotism to religion is a discursive practice; the extortion of funds from businesses as protection money is an organizational practice. Both have implications for the institution of electoral politics in Maharashtra.

BACKGROUND

Although there is disagreement over the reasons for Shiv Sena's ascendancy, there is little dispute over the basic chronology of political events that preceded the party's emergence as a statewide political force. Maharashtra has been a Congress party stronghold for decades. The Congress had dominated state politics continuously from the period prior to the formation of the unilingual state of Maharashtra in 1960 until 1995. Congress chief ministers reigned, supported by strong majority governments straight up to 1995, broken only by a two-year hiatus in 1978–80. Congress dominance in Maharashtra survived numerous challenges: the passionate and sometimes violent Samyukta Maharashtra Movement in the 1950s which demanded a separate state for Marathi speakers (Phadke 1979; Joshi 1995); the claims for autonomy from the Vidarbha and Marathwada regions of the state; the state's strong Dalit (ex-untouchable) movement (Omvedt 1993; Zelliott 1992); a vibrant rural peasant movement that drew attention to urban–rural divisions; significant infighting within the party that was marked by a rapid turnover of chief ministers throughout the 1980s; and an economy that underwent inflationary swings and that has consistently suffered from high levels of unemployment and underemployment despite strong periods of growth (Lele 1995: 1520–28; Joshi 1995; Sardesai 1995). Given the multiple disruptive elements that might have undermined Congress dominance over the decades, why did Congress suffer a reversal only in 1995 and why was the Shiv Sena–BJP alliance the political entity that succeeded in outdistancing the Congress in state elections? This question is part of the puzzle this chapter explores.

The Shiv Sena was formed in 1966 in Bombay; it contested municipal elections two years later, winning one-third of the seats in the municipal corporation. From its beginning, the party made its imprint on local politics by championing the economic interests of Maharashtrians whose jobs, the party claimed, were being usurped by outsiders, particularly south

Indians, living in Bombay. As a sons-of-the soil movement, the Shiv Sena had made Maharashtrian-centric politics its first priority, followed closely by an anti-Communist stance and, only in third place, the championing of a patriotism that demonized 'anti-national' Muslims.

From its inception, the Shiv Sena won a reputation for violence. Its attack on the Communist Party office in Parel in 1967, Shiv Sainiks' role in the murder of Communist MLA Krishna Desai, its assaults on Udipi (south Indian) restaurants and street hawkers, its involvement in the 1971 Bhiwandi riots and in Belgaum border clashes were all early demonstrations of the party's readiness to utilize extreme methods of political action. At the same time, the party pursued a populist program—providing services in local neighborhoods and slums and courting the loyalties, particularly of Marathi-speaking male youth.

During this early period, the party was able to establish a firm place for itself on the Municipal Corporation with party members securing the mayorship on at least four different occasions during the 1970s. But until the 1990s, the Shiv Sena was never a significant political presence outside the Bombay–Thane municipalities. The party rebounded onto the political scene in 1985, winning 70 seats on the Municipal Corporation, up from the 21 seats it had won in 1978 (Thakkar 1995: 265). From the mid-1980s, the party underwent an ideological makeover, reordering its agenda to emphasize themes of Hindu nationalism. The Shiv Sena chief, Bal Thackeray, stepped up his anti-Muslim diatribe, urging his followers to take up a holy war or *dharm yuddh*;[1] Shiv Sena-sponsored Hindu festivals and celebrations became more lavish and elaborate; the party reached out to try to create an alliance of Hindu-minded parties calling a meeting in 1994 of seven Hindu parties. The party continued to play, moreover, a self-proclaimed part in the increasing numbers of communal conflagrations spanning the 1984 Bhiwandi riots and the ravages of Bombay in 1992–3 (Engineer 1989: 15–18; 1995: 3267–8). In anticipation of the 1990 election, the Shiv Sena entered into a seat adjustment with the BJP, whose image as the champion of Hindu nationalism was by now well-honed throughout northern India. In 1990, the Shiv Sena–BJP alliance won 94 seats in the state assembly, up from the 16 seats they (together) controlled in 1985. With the 1995 state assembly election, the Shiv Sena–BJP combine secured 138 seats, eclipsing Congress, whose seat tally fell to 80 seats from 141 in 1990.[2]

[1] Sudheendra Kulkarni, 'The Ominous Entry of Shiv Sena in Rural Areas', *Mainstream*, 7 March 1987, p. 13.

[2] Lekha Rattanani and Smruti Koppikar, 'Storming the Citadel', *India Today*, 31 March 1995, p. 44; M. Rahman with Lekha Rattanani, 'Savagery in Bombay', *India*

In the 1996 parliamentary elections, the Shiv Sena continued its electoral climb, winning 15 seats, up from four in the previous round.

Explanations of Shiv Sena's resurgence fall into three broad approaches. First, some accounts emphasize *societal* shifts—pointing to the economic duress and rising aspirations of Maharashtrian youth that have accompanied the rapid urbanization of Maharashtra in the last decade (Vora 1996) and the penetration of capitalism into the countryside (Lele 1995). In a related vein, others emphasize the process of democratization in which caste and class groups beyond the traditionally dominant Maratha caste have become politicized by and available to competing party elites (Hansen 1995). Societal accounts also stress the continued competition between Maharashtrians and non-Maharashtrians in the private and public sectors (Sadhu 1988).

A second set of explanations focuses on *institutional and organizational factors* such as the sudden access to resources gained by Shiv Sena's 1985 victory in the municipality which permitted the party to control rents, taxes, and contracts during a period in which Bombay real estate was booming (Sardesai 1995: 132); similarly some point to the party's service functions, running ambulance services, responding to local grievances.[3] This focus on organization also notes the disarray of the Congress party, the voter's disillusionment at the party's reputation for corruption,[4] and the alienation of Muslim voters who were an important vote bank for the party in Maharashtra (Vora 1996; Palshikar 1996).

A third set of accounts allude to *ideological or discursive forces*. Almost all analyses of Shiv Sena's resurgence describe the turn in Bombay politics towards 'saffronization' and the playing of the 'Hindu Card' as an explicit part of Shiv Sena's ascendancy, although the religious nationalist rhetoric is rarely the subject of very extensive analysis, and although it is often unclear how much weight the analysis assigns to Shiv Sena's Hindutva appeal.[5]

Today, 31 January 1995, p. 35; see also M. Rahman, 'Primed for Battle', *India Today*, 15 February 1995.

[3] 'Sena Strength Spreading', *Onlooker*, 16–30 September 1989, pp. 21–5.

[4] 'Congress(I) Losing Ground', *India Today*, 15 February 1995.

[5] Analyses of individual-level surveys are being undertaken by Nandita Aras, a doctoral student in political science at Columbia University. Surveys under the supervision of Yogendra Yadav and V. B. Singh at the Centre for the Study of Developing Societies in Delhi should also be able to shed light on the extent to which voter support for Shiv Sena has been augmented or diminished by the alliance's turn to Hindu nationalism.

In this chapter, we acknowledge the importance of looking at the socio-economic underpinnings of Hindutva and of political identities generally. Indeed, that was the approach taken by one of the authors in an account of Shiv Sena's earlier years (Katzenstein 1979). But at the same time, our preference for the second and third approaches (institutions and discourse) is premised on the argument that economic and social disruptions—whether precipitated by industrialization, urbanization, and/or the penetration of capitalism—can explain feelings of anomie, identity loss, and availability for political mobilization, but that these socio-economic changes cannot explain why people search out the political solutions offered by the 'right' rather than those proffered by more moderate, centrist forces or by the left. To understand this, we must turn to organizations and to discourse. We see Shiv Sena's resurgence as reflecting the weakened conditions of organizations that compete with the Shiv Sena's and BJP's mobilizational capacities and as reflecting, too, the power of a newly ascendant national discourse. Maharashtra, after all, is not an independent country, and the discourse of Hindutva is a meeting ground for the mutually constitutive process by which identities, both local and national, are created.

CREATING HINDUTVA: THE POWER OF DISCOURSE

If there were ever a location that seems to suggest how politics is reshaped when a new (or in this case a new-old) discourse catches on, Bombay and its environs in the 1990s are it. We are not dismissing the importance of economic interest: Shiv Sena's emergence in the mid-1960s rode a wave of very overt economic and social discontent among Maharashtrians. Although Maharashtrians had won their own state a half decade earlier, no instant amelioration in the job position of Marathi-speakers materialized, and the economic successes of non-Marathi-speaking ethnic groups in Bombay, particularly in white collar jobs and in the commercial sectors of the economy, were undeniable. Newly aroused Maharashtrian aspirations in the face of the apparent economic success of other groups provided an ideal 'cause' for a political party to champion.[6] This was in the 1960s.

[6] The dominance of 'outsiders' was the subject of weekly exposés, starting in 1965, of *Marmik*, the Marathi weekly started by the then cartoonist, Bal Thackeray. In the early years before the 1966 founding of Shiv Sena, *Marmik*'s pages dwelled on the dangers of Communists ('Lalbhai') and of Pakistani infiltrators. But it was not until *Marmik* drew attention to the presumed economic injustices suffered by Maharashtrian white collar job aspirants that the magazine's circulation soared and the Shiv Sena took off. By 1966, *Marmik*'s circulation had doubled reaching a readership that probably comprised nearly half of the literate Maharashtrian population in the city above the age of 15 (Katzenstein 1979: 51).

In the l990s, however, the Shiv Sena capitalized on an opportunity that was more discursive than material. The absence of any major change in the economic or social conditions structuring Hindu–Muslim relations could not be more striking. Indeed, the Sena did not claim (nor would it have rung true) that Muslims were taking jobs or educational places or housing away from Maharashtrians as the Sena had claimed about south Indians in the l960s.[7] No exposés about Muslim economic encroachment, similar to the 1960s' lists of south Indian company employees, ran in the pages of *Saamna,* the Shiv Sena's daily. Rather, there were at best vague allusions to the burden that must be borne by the taxpayer who has to support the allegedly rising numbers of illegal (Bangladeshi) immigrants and to Muslim (Bangladeshi) hawkers who crowd the roads and to the thousands who occupy scarce space, preying on urban services in an already overcrowded city. Muslims were not portrayed as traders whose wily ways were suspect or as privileged professionals who dominated the higher rungs of the city's white collar occupations. Muslims were—according to the Sena's creed—seditious. It was their presumed lack of political identification with the Indian nation rather than their societal position that was the subject of the Shiv Sena's diatribes.

This is not to downplay the economic dislocations that make Maharashtrians susceptible to the scapegoating in which the Shiv Sena and other parties have engaged. According to one report, the numbers of registered job seekers in the Bombay–Thane belt rose from 160,000 to 3.5 million between 1961 and 1990, with higher proportions of educated unemployed (between 3 and 4 per cent) than were registered in many other urban areas of India (Sainath 1993).[8] But even as these processes of economic change are unsettling, they cannot on their own explain the pull towards a political agenda of religious nationalism. These economic conditions cannot by themselves explain (a) why Muslims are targeted or (b) why leftist political organizations in Maharashtra have been less successful at responding to the frustrations of educated youth.[9]

[7] On the mythology of Muslim minorities being 'pampered', see Rahul Pathak with Vivian Fernandes, 'Nailing the Big Lie', *India Today,* 31 January 1993, p. 42.

[8] The State Directorate of Economics and Statistics records unemployment (job seekers listed with the employment exchange registry) as growing from 250,000 in 1985–6 to 330,000 in April 1994. The consumer price index for agricultural labourers also rose sharply between the end of the 1980s and the mid-1990s. See 'Maharashtra; Mixed Record, Negative Image', *India Today,* 31 January 1996, p. 47. It is interesting, too, that Maharashtra has a higher percentage of people living in urban areas (39 per cent) than is true elsewhere. The average in India generally is 26 per cent (Vora 1996: 172).

[9] The leftist alliance of Samyukta Maharashtra Samiti in the 1950s did not frame

Shiv Sena's turn to Hindutva and the demonization of Muslims in the 1990s was traceable, then, less to economic conditions than to discursive possibilities. By the mid- to late 1980s, a number of events heightened the salience of religious identities. The Shah Bano case (which raised the issue of whether a Muslim divorced woman claiming support was entitled to a hearing under the uniform civil code) had become a political football stirring Hindu–Muslim tensions throughout north India as had the Ramjanmabhoomi Mandir (temple)–Babri Masjid (mosque) dispute. Video and tape recordings of the speeches of Hindu nationalist leaders were widely disseminated. In the second half of the 1980s, the discourse of Hindutva had made its presence felt throughout north India.

The responsiveness to Shiv Sena's exploitation of this new discourse seemed to surprise even Sena leaders themselves. As Sudhir Joshi, a long time Sena leader exclaimed: 'We don't know how it happened. But the Sena is getting a tremendous response from people from all walks of life. They seem to have caught on with our concept of Hindu rashtra (state).'[10]

The sense of satisfaction among Shiv Sena leaders that, at long last, their appeal to Hindu nationalist loyalties had gotten a hearing among the Maharashtrian populace was transparent. As Thackeray commented, 'Earlier, Hindutva was regarded as narrow-minded and the Sena was called communal for projecting this feeling.' Now, to paraphrase the Sena chief, its power is recognized and this kind of nationalism is considered legitimate.[11]

If the 1980s' construction of Hindutva ('Hindu-ness'; Hindu nationalism) was the first time after Independence that Hinduism was linked to nationalism, one of the cognitive mechanisms by which this was accomplished in Shiv Sena's writings was through the demonization of 'anti-national Muslims'. Over and over in the pages of *Saamna* as well as in speeches by Thackeray and by some of the other party leaders, the denigration of Muslims is repeated in phraseologies that invoke the real or imagined *political* identities and claims of the minority and majority communities.

— how can Congress pamper this minority community?

— what right do *burkha*- (long garment with headpiece which entirely covers the wearer) clad women have to vote?[12]

---

their demand for a separate state in 'mere' class politics terms. They also engaged in ethnic stereotyping, if less overt and extreme than the rhetoric and actions of the Hindu Mahasabha/Shiv Sena and other parties on the right.

[10] Uma Keni Prabhu, 'Shiv Sena Riding the Tiger', *Bombay*, 7 August 1988, p. 13.

[11] 'Strategic End to Thackeray Drive', *Times of India*, 26 February 1990, p. 6.

[12] See 'No Polls If Burkha-clad Exercise Franchise, Says Thackeray', *Indian*

— why should Muslims be exempt from a uniform civil code?

— how can Muslims loyal to Pakistan be tolerated?

Again and again, Shiv Sena conjures up images of Muslim treachery and betrayal. In inflammatory language, the Sena depicts anti-national Muslims as destroyers of temples, as murderers of the police, and as threats to the Indian state. In Thackeray's words (from *Saamna*):

Muslims revolt in their own areas. They beat Hindus, demolish temples and attack the police. The government is appeasing these traitors. It is learnt that Pakistan has manufactured seven bombs. But the bomb that has been made in India with the blessings of Pakistan is more dangerous. Now Pakistan need not cross the borders for launching an attack on India. Twenty-five crore (ten million) Muslims loyal to Pakistan will stage an insurrection. One of these seven bombs made by Pakistan lies hidden in Hindustan. (Women, Law, and Media 1994: Annexure H.)

Using the practised semantic formula of its Maharashtrian xenophobic days, the Shiv Sena insists it is not anti-Muslim, just against anti-nationalist Muslims. In earlier days, the Sena also used to insist that, as a movement, it was not against non-Maharashtrians, only against those who did not 'share the joys and sorrows' of Maharashtrian, a definition, however, that was of little comfort to the Udipi restaurant owner whose establishment was about to be burned by marauding youths or the Tamil clerk whose job the Sena claimed belonged to a Maharashtrian (Katzenstein 1979: 26). Asked to define or describe Muslims who are known to be anti-nationalist, Thackeray invariably talks of Muslims who have 'their heart in Pakistan'.[13] How are these Muslims to be identified from others who may be loyal citizens of India? Repeatedly Thackeray's answer summons up the sports stadium.[14] Anti-national Muslims are those who set off firecrackers of victory when Pakistan defeats India in the stadiums of Bombay.[15]

Express, 13 March 1994. The article quotes Thackeray: ' "In the ensuing elections if the Election Commission allows burkha-clad women of minority community to exercise their franchise, then Sena will not allow elections to be held, not only in Maharashtra, but in the entire country," Thackeray thundered.'

[13] Thackeray typically says things such as 'an ordinary peace-loving Muslim has nothing to fear'. Those who 'have their heart in Pakistan' will not be spared. See 'Sena Pledges Probe into Pawar's Conduct', *Times of India*, 31 January 1995, p. 5.

[14] Thackeray, in a 'populist' measure designed to attract wide attention, demanded the cancellation of a one-day international cricket match between India and Pakistan to be held at the Wankhede stadium, threatening to organize a Bombay Bandh if the Cricket Association did not cancel the match. The chief minister, S. Naik, initially firm in his stand against Thackeray's threat, then began to soft-peddle. Eventually the Pakistan team declined to play and the match was cancelled. See Rajdeep Sardesai's and Prakash Joshi's article in the *Times of India*, 27 October 1991, as well as the extensive coverage the incident received between 23 October and the end of the month.

[15] Namita Bhandare, 'Courting Trouble', *Sunday*, 16–22 April 1995, p. 24. In a

As in its earlier days when the Sena would cite its support of individual south Indians, such as General Cariappa, the Sena's candidate for parliament, as evidence that the party was not xenophobic, the Sena now defends its record by referring to its patronage of individual Muslims. An interview with Sabir Shaikh, the one Muslim in the Sena–BJP state cabinet, is indicative of what such endorsement requires: calling himself 'a Hindustani and therefore a Hindutvavadi (supporter of Hindutva)', Shaikh says that 'Hindutva has nothing to do with religion; it is the culture of India'. Shaikh has been with the Sena since its founding, claiming to have been drawn to the party because of its championing of Maharashtrians. 'I am an Indian first, Maharashtrian second, and Muslim last,' Shaikh explains. After twenty-nine years with the Sena, Shaikh says, he is still Muslim and still proud of his religion. As if by rote, Shaikh responds to an interviewer's query about how he can live with the virulence that the Sena is directing against Muslims by saying, canonically, that the Shiv Sena is only against anti-national Muslims. His definition: 'One who bursts crackers when Pakistan wins against India in a cricket match.' When asked how many Muslims actually do this, Shaikh says that it may be less than 1 per cent, but the point is that the other 99 per cent do not come out in opposition to this practice.[16] These conversations reveal Shiv Sena's use of the standard technique of social control—the distinction between the 'good Negro' and 'bad Blacks'—between the well-behaved and compliant, on the one hand, and the obstreperous, on the other hand. Good Muslims are those who are personally known to Shiv Sena leaders as being patriotic, those who denounce 'bad' Muslims, or those who are vocal in their declarations of patriotism.

This demonization of anti-national Muslims is one of four definitional pillars in the construction of Shiv Sena's version of Hindutva. A second pillar is built on the connection between Hinduism and militancy and a distinction between weak and strong proselytes of nationalism. Hindu nationalism, for the Sena, must be a militant nationalism. Non-violence is

---

typical interview, Thackeray will make exceptions for individual Muslims. 'My inner voice', he says, for instance, 'tells me that Sunjay Dutt is not involved in the bomb blasts.' Why? Because Thackeray knows Dutt's parents personally and knows they are loyal Indian patriots. Thackeray also repeatedly comments that he is not anti-Muslim. 'I am willing to cooperate and help solve their problems. But I would like them to come forward and join the national mainstream. It is not in the interests of any religious group to have large numbers of aliens staying in their midst.' Thackeray insists he is only against Muslim 'traitors', 'A traitor is a traitor whichever religion he belongs to. If I were the Prime Minister, I would gun down a Hindu, a Muslim, or a Sikh if it is proved that he is a traitor. What is wrong with that?' (S. Balakrishnan, 'I'm Not Opposed to Muslims, Says Thackeray', *Times of India*, 31 March 1995).

[16] 'A Suitable Hindutvavadi', *Times of India*, 26 March 1995, p. 15.

weakness, not strength. Bal Thackeray, who has rarely been contradicted by other Sena leaders in this regard, is a vehement critic of Gandhian non-violence. To Thackeray, Gandhi's non-violence and supposed appeasement of Muslims is anathema. This highly masculinist rhetoric no doubt pulls young men towards the Sena. It is not surprising that, by one report, a full *two-thirds* of all Shiv Sena–BJP supporters are male (Palshikar 1996: 175).[17]

The paragon of a political leader, it follows, is represented by Shivaji, known for his martial exploits against the Muslim rulers of the north. Thackeray's admiration for Adolph Hitler is also widely cited in interviews. When asked by a reporter for the *Illustrated Weekly of India* whether Hitler really exemplified his model of a nationalist leader, Thackeray demurs about the extremes to which Hitler went but speaks admiringly of Hitler's love of nation.[18] Gandhi, for Thackeray, is just one leader, not even to be acknowledged as the father of the Indian nation. A true national leader, for Thackeray, is one who will 'inject militancy, into the Hindu blood*' (19 February 1989, p. 33).

To this self-educated Sena leader, whose economic circumstances precluded the possibility of attending university, it is action, rather than

[17] In a speech at an election rally at the Alkha Talkies square in Pune, Thackeray commented on Gandhi's assassination: 'We are proud of Nathuram. He saved the country from second partition. Nathuram was not a hired assassin. He was genuinely infuriated by Mahatma Gandhi's betrayal of the nation. Killing of any person is necessarily an evil act and it should be condemned. But we must find out the reasons behind such incidents. Mahatma Gandhi betrayed the nation. He had said he would lay down his life before allowing the division of the country. But ultimately he did nothing to stop the partition. Moreover, he insisted on giving Rs. 55 crore to Pakistan at a time when the country was ravaged. . . . ' ('Thackeray Lauds Godse', *Indian Express*, 17 May 1991.)

[18] See 'The Tiger Roars Again', *The Illustrated Weekly of India*, 19 February 1989, pp. 30–3. One interviewer asked Thackeray whether he had changed his mind over the years about Hitler as a model. Thackeray replied: 'Yes, I haven't changed my mind. Hitler wanted his country to come up and he thought, "What are the reasons?" He found corruption was the main thing. Then he asked, "Who are the people doing it?" It was the Jews, yes the Jews. Now I like some Jews, they have a warrior-like thing. Even the girls are sitting in the trenches and fighting against the enemy. I want that spirit in my country. But Hitler found that not only were they the corrupt people but they also didn't behave. He realized "that if I don't drive them out, then my country won't come up." You may condemn that kind of act—even I would condemn. It is not the only way; this gas chamber and all, I don't like. But you may drive them out—things like that. It is all right. But don't blame the man. He wanted to bring his country up and he knew what were the evils.' (Vir Sanghvi , *The Weekly Interview*: Bal Thackeray, 'I Still Believe in Dictatorship', *Illustrated Weekly of India*, 19 February 1984, pp. 30–3).

* 'The Tiger Roars Again', *The Illustrated Weekly of India*, 19 February 1989, pp. 30–3.

reflection that seems to be life motivating. In his younger days, Thackeray saw few Hindi films, but he used to

be mad after cowboy pictures. Every week, my brother and I would go to Aurora cinema and see a cowboy picture.... I like action, everything should have action. Yes—John Wayne, Gary Cooper and gun-fights. I like gun-fights. Perhaps, it might have influenced me.[19]

Action gets prime attention in the pages of *Saamna*. Reporting on the Ayodhya crusade, the *Saamna* asks:

How does our Shiv Sainik appear as he is marching towards Ayodhya? Like the roaring lion spreading terror, with the gait of an intoxicated elephant, like the assault of a rhino which reduces to powder a rocky mountain, like the manoeuvres of a leopard: Our infinite blessings to these Hindu warriors who are marching towards Ayodhya (5 December 1992, p. 1).

If this second pillar of Hindutva for the Shiv Sena, then, is militancy, the third pillar is patriotism. Hindutva, in Shiv Sena's vista, is about religious nationalism, with 'nationalism' the operative word. But the nation which Shiv Sena reconstructs from the historical past is one that is free of Muslim rule rather than one that is unburdened from the yoke of Western colonialism. There is very little talk in rallies or in the pages of *Saamna* of British colonialism or of present-day exploitation by the West. Shiv Sena leaders have travelled little outside India and none were educated abroad. Bal Thackeray was in his fifties before he ventured abroad. And when he did, he travelled briefly to London and then to Disneyland. 'You know I had always dreamt of going to Disneyland. It is fantastic.'[20]

Whether because of or in spite of this limited experience of life abroad, there is little animus in Shiv Sena speeches and publications when it comes to questions about the imposition of Western values. Chief minister Manohar Joshi was counselled by Thackeray against wearing suit and tie on his recent trip to the United States but it was one of the rare situations in which Joshi could openly joke about not acquiescing to the wishes of the Senapati, indicating the relative insignificance of this stricture.[21] The Sena's sponsorship of the Michael Jackson extravaganza in Bombay, which was intended to raise Rs 40 million for the Sena's 'non-profit' trust, the Udyog Sena, destroyed any semblance of the Sena critique of the assault

[19] Vir Sanghvi, 'I Still Believe in Dictatorship', *Illustrated Weekly*, 19 February 1984, p. 31.
[20] Ibid., p. 30.
[21] See Nirmal Mitra, 'Chief Minister Indulges in His Native Marathi', *India Abroad*, 30 June 1995, p. 12. News articles comment on the chief minister and the Sena party

on Indian culture by the decadent West (Menezes 1966: 20). (The Sena–
BJP combine has given more serious attention to reclaiming the 'authentic'
name of Mumbai after Mumbadevi, the goddess traditionally worshipped
by fisherfolk of Bombay.) But such examples aside, there is surprisingly
little talk about Western colonization and unwelcome influence. In all the
recent discussions of the Enron power project contract, in fact, the Sena's
opposition has been formulated as one about overpricing and the faulty
procedures of negotiating a contract without open bidding. Missing is the
strong rhetoric about national autonomy and freedom from foreign control
that attended the Janata's ouster of Coca-Cola and IBM in the late 1970s.

Religion is a fourth pillar of Shiv Sena's conceptualization of Hindutva,
but its importance is less scriptural or doctrinal than ritualistic. On occasion,
a speech by a Sena leader will invoke religious texts and a Sena leader
will be accompanied on the dais by a religious ascetic. Pramod Navalkar,
one of the Sena leaders with a more outwardly spiritual bent, has brought
Hindu holy men to address Sena gatherings. In rallies and on the occasion
of electoral victories, Thackeray typically appears in saffron (or other)
draped robes of an ascetic—recently with wooden holy beads and wrist
bands (*rudrakshas*). It is telling, however, that after the death of his wife
and son in 1996, Thackeray removed his beads and banished all pictures
and statues of gods from his residence. According to one report that cites
an editorial by Thackeray in *Saamna*, Thackeray has declared himself an
atheist.[22] It is significant that Thackeray's declaration seems to have caused
no stir among Shiv Sena subscribers to the party's brand of religious
nationalism.

Where religion seems mostly to count is in its performative and
ritualistic role: the local *shakhas* (literally, branches; RSS training meeting)
are intensely involved in the annual Bombay Ganesh or Ganapati ritual,
Ganesh Chaturthi (fourth day of a lunar fortnight). On this festival day,
when the image of Ganapati is marched to the sea, Shiv Sainiks and Sena
flags are visible in every neighbourhood. In some ways this event has
become a Sena festivity and, as we shall discuss below, an important means
to raise funds for party activity. Recently, and even more significantly, the
Sena has organized *Maha Aartis* (a grand version of the Hindu ritual of
worship performed at sunset) in the streets. These convocations are partly
in response to Muslim *namaz* (literally, prayers; in this context,
congregational prayers held in mosques). During the 1992–3 violence,

---

in the legislature operating by remote control. Manohar Joshi says his relationship to
Thackeray is like father to son.

[22] 'Uneasy Lies the Head', *The Telegraph*, 20 July 1996.

Maha Aartis were explicit tools by which youthful crowds were incited to act collectively, leading to the rampages and violent assaults against Muslim residents (see chapter by Jaffrelot in this volume for more details on the instrumental use of religious rituals to incite riots).

It is difficult to characterize the Sena's cultural vision of Hinduism as either reformist or conservative. Sudhir Joshi, one of the more modern-minded Sena leaders, tends to emphasize the forward-looking cast of Hinduism:

The Hinduism of the four Varnas [ritual rank] is not acceptable to us, being regressive. We do not believe in a religion on that basis. What we are talking about is a Hinduism that is rational, reformist, practical and evolving. We reject *Sati* and its propagandists. We reject even dowry as a barbarism.[23]

But this reformist voice is not the dominant line enunciated by Thackeray. Although the Sena in recent elections has sought support from particular Dalit communities (Chamars, Dhors and Bhangis), it has targeted the projects of other (better off) Dalits, largely ex-Mahars, criticizing the effort to rename Marathwada University as Ambedkar University and the publication of Ambedkar's writings in which the Sena considered his comments on Rama and Krishna to be offensive (Lele 1995: 1526). Thackeray sees neo-Buddhist Dalit activists as anti-Hindu and therefore uses a rhetorical style similar to that which he deploys when he talks of Muslims: 'Today is the anniversary of Ambedkar. We won't be tolerant. Is over, burnt. If anyone stands against Hindus, we'll burn them to ashes' (Patwardhan 1994). Indeed the Shiv Sena on more than a few occasions has targeted Dalit neighbourhoods during the binges of violence led by Sena youth.

To summarize: The importance of discursive change should not be underestimated. This transposition from an organization that protested the incursion of non-Maharashtrians into Bombay to one that speaks, principally, about the restoration of a Hindu political order should, rightly, be named as what it is—a major discursive gyration. The discursive handiwork of Shiv Sena is now visible in the form of a four-pillar doctrine of Hindutva built on Muslim demonization, the militancy of Hinduism, a political nationalism defined by regional rather than global enemies, and the restitution of specified religious rituals. What should be recognized to be at work here are not the rumblings of new economic or societal tectonic formations creating new fault lines to which political elites must respond

[23] Mahesh Vijapurkar, 'Shiv Sena: the Hindu Card', *Frontline*, 21 January 1989, p. 100.

but the recreation of existing meanings in response to new ideological or discursive opportunities.

DEPLOYING HINDUTVA: THE POWER OF INSTITUTIONS

It would perhaps be wrong to claim, however, that this new discourse was, by itself, responsible for the Shiv Sena's recent political success or for the unprecedented eruption of communal violence in Bombay in 1992–3. To look to the discourse of Hindu nationalism alone would leave us unable to explain why the BJP could not expect to supplant Shiv Sena, but was rather compelled to join hands in an electoral alliance. Discourse alone cannot explain why Hindu–Muslim hostilities, which have long been present in Bombay, in Maharashtra, and elsewhere in India, should erupt in such particularly virulent form at this time. To answer these questions, we must turn to the adroit organization-building that Shiv Sena can boast and to the concomitant infirmity, at least for the present, of the local Congress party and of state institutions. Central to this discussion is Shiv Sena's determination to use coercive and terrorizing tactics and the inability or unwillingness of the government to respond.

A modern day Machiavelli might advise his ruler that political success requires the creation of institutions that will secure (1) enough riches to rule, (2) influence over the modes of popular communication, (3) firm control over the ruler's own party or power base and (4) the capacity to deliver something of what the populace perceives its needs to be. By these criteria, Shiv Sena has demonstrated mastery in the craft of party building.

(1) The Shiv Sena has clearly accumulated vast coffers of funds—no small feat for a party that has been, for most of its political life, not in power, but in opposition. Almost no hard information exists in print about the source of these funds, but there is enough anecdotal commentary to allow some picture to be sketched. According to numerous commentaries, the Congress party was itself responsible in the early days of the Sena for building up the party coffers, hoping that the Shiv Sena would prove a strong counteractive force to the leftist unions. The close relations between Congress and Shiv Sena, Sainath claims, won the Sena the epithet of Vasant Sena (alluding to the alleged links between the then chief minister Vasant Rao Naik and the Shiv Sena). Similar observations were routinely made about the support the Sena was supposed to have received from industrial houses in Bombay that shared Congress party interests in seeing leftist unions weakened. In recent years, what has been widely recognized is the huge intake of funds the Sena secures from its control over real estate in Bombay—said to be among the highest priced urban real estate outside

Japan. Part of this control has been secured through the Sena's victory in municipal elections, giving the party access to the municipal budget, which, as others have commented, is larger than the revenue coffers of many states. This control ranges from the capacity of the Shiv Sena to collect a few rupees from stall owners (protection money) to its ability to tithe large corporations that wish to gain access to office or factory space. What seem to be absolutely routine party practices are the neighbourhood collections for 'religious festivals' by party *shakhas* and the extortion of security money. The role of coercion here is key: whether it is the Shiv Sena's ability to approach a business owner after the riot with a demand for Rs 50,000 as payment for having prevented the business from being destroyed, or whether it is a demand for several rupees from a small time Muslim trader, extortion is a primary vehicle by which party coffers are filled.

(2) The Shiv Sena's media clout reflects the confluence of the party's organizational acumen and its terrorist tactics. Absolutely crucial to the party's early successes was the broadcasting of employee lists in the party's own paper, *Marmik*. Critical to the dissemination of Hindutva has been the capacity of the party to spread its message through its own daily newspaper, *Saamna*, first published in 1989 in Marathi and then expanded into a Hindi edition in 1993. *Saamna* is said to have an enormous circulation of between 150,000 to 300,000 copies.[24] This circulation depends on a highly sophisticated distribution network, which provides for papers to be sold at regular news outlets as well as on railway platforms and street corners. Here too, the Sena's coercive organizational apparatus is fundamental to the party's capacity to broadcast its party doctrine. By utilizing tactics of intimidation against rival Marathi papers—and less directly against the English language dailies—the Sena has endeavoured (with no small effect) to stifle its critics. Some of the large circulation Marathi papers are no cause of worry to the Shiv Sena. But several Marathi dailies such as *Mahanagar*, which has been directly critical of the Shiv Sena, have been the target of frighteningly violent assaults. The *Mahanagar* offices have been repeatedly ransacked and journalists beaten. In 1993, a counterdemonstration to protest Sena's tactics was planned, and a procession was taken out by a group of sympathetic journalists near the Shiv Sena's Dadar headquarters. As the procession disbanded, four members of the procession were injured, one receiving a skull fracture. Specific journalists have been individually targeted for intimidation.[25] The home of Haroon Rashid of the weekly

[24] Lekha Rattanani, 'Paper Tiger', *India Today*, 28 February 1995, p. 28.
[25] V. K. Ramachandran, 'The Press Protest', *Frontline*, 8 October 1993, pp. 109–10.

Blitz was attacked and all his possessions were burned including 3000 books and the diaries he had been safeguarding for the purpose of later compiling an autobiography. The effect of this incident and of Shiv Sena's terrorist tactics more generally have been an understandable self-censoring by the media.[26]

(3) The multilayer institutional structure of Shiv Sena and the party's close control over its own organization are renowned. The party is run autocratically. There are no internal party elections and votes are never taken. There are four institutional components to the party: the newspapers (*Saamna* and *Marmik*); the *shakhas* or branch offices; the employment organization; and the Sena unions. The neighbourhood *shakhas* (220 in Bombay) are connected to informal networks, mostly of young men, who are linked through family, school, neighbourhood, and athletic clubs or *mandals*. The party also has another layer of organization, the *Sthaniya Lokadhikar Samiti* (SLS), variously described as a cultural club and employment exchange. The SLS, reportedly, has 325 units spread throughout the state.[27] Although there is now talk of others (Bal Thackeray's son and nephew) being trained to succeed the Sena domo, control over party, and to an extent, governmental affairs, is tightly managed by Bal Thackeray himself. No major party positions are reached without consultation with Thackeray, including policy decisions that are now taken by the Sena–BJP combine in the state legislature. In a recent row, the Sena chief minister signed a memorandum of understanding with the Hinduja business group regarding a feasibility study for a new Bombay international airport. Done without Thackeray's approval, the signing angered the Sena chief who made his ire known in *Saamna*. The story was then picked up by the English press. According to a *Times of India* report, 'Mr. Thackeray sent an unambiguous message that the latter's commitment to the Sena is more important than his brief as the chief executive of the state.'[28] Leadership control over the ranks is said to be less efficacious now than in earlier years. Rajdeep Sardesai aptly describes the Sena:

---

of which were done. Although Muslim leaders also objected to aspects of the film, similar editorial changes were apparently not made. Recently, too, a paper in Aurangabad, *Lokmat*, was attacked, allegedly by Shiv Sena workers because of its critique of a Sena leader. Four employees were injured, machines were destroyed and files torched. See 'Four Employees of *Lokmat* Hurt in Shiv Sena Attack', *Times of India*, 10 June 1995, p. 1.

[26] The controversy over the film *Bombay* has also been revealing. Thackeray was allowed to review the film and make recommendations for editorial changes a number

[27] 'Native Appeal', *India Today*, 28 February 1995, p. 29.

[28] 'Anti-Joshi Remarks Upset Alliance', *Times of India*, 29 June 1995, p. 13.

Although on the surface it seems as if Thackeray is in total control of his 'boys', the fact is that many of them are now doing their own thing within their respective spheres of influence. Thackeray's charisma may still be an important mobilizing factor, but a number of new recruits to the Sena are only using the Thackeray name to start their own private enterprises. Many of them are youth in the under–35 group who have little commitment to the party as such. (Sardesai 1995: 133.)

Gerard Heuze, too, notes the decline of what he rightfully says is the still much-underestimated social service function of the *shakhas* and its replacement by a sort of gangster/underworld element more interested in the prosperity to be won from trading in contraband and illicit goods than in service to neighbourhood and community (Heuze 1995).

(4) Part of Shiv Sena's appeal has always been rooted in the way the *shakhas* provide a place for youth to be engaged in activities, whether in service to the community or in party campaign issues. The neighbourhood-based programmes for women (the crèches, income-generating projects like food preparation, and cultural festivals like *haldi-kumkum*) are specifically aimed at mobilizing women locally (Banerjee 1995: 223).[29] It is also the case that local corporators and even state legislators are electable, based to a large extent on whether they are perceived as serving the interests of people in the constituency. Newspaper coverage of the 1995 campaign for the most part reported the prevalence of many of the same issues of daily living that overwhelm much of the low income Bombay electorate. In Worli, a Bombay neighbourhood, the news account reviews the competing claims between Shiv Sena and Congress candidates about who has done more for the constituency in terms of spending funds on housing, 'beautification', and opposing the sale of mill land.[30] Only in a few accounts does the report indicate that issues such as education, water, sanitation, and roads were forced into the background by the legacy of the 1992–3 riots. In one of these accounts, the Sena candidate (half-heartedly supported by the BJP, according to newspaper coverage) had been earlier arrested under the National Security Act during the riots and later had been held for alleged extortion.[31] Whether the Shiv Sena's past reputation

---

[29] The journalist Teesta Setalvad recounts an interesting anecdote about a woman who returned to Bombay after being employed in Saudi Arabia as a domestic worker. The woman, exploited by her employers, approached a feminist organization in the city for help. The feminist group was unable to galvanize either the Indian government or the Saudi Arabian embassy to assist the woman. When the woman approached Shiv Sena, their women's wing, the Mahila Aghadi, went to the employer's house, 'threatened him with his life', and recovered her back wages (1995: 239).

[30] Meena Menon, 'Straight Contest in Worli and Naigaum', *Times of India*, 9 February 1995, p. 5.

[31] Anil Singh, 'Dharavi Constituency May Witness Triangular Contest', *Times of India*, 5 February 1995, p. 5.

at the local level for being committed 'social workers' will be eclipsed by a reputation for gangsterism is likely to have a significant effect on electoral contests in the future.

The Shiv Sena, organizationally, appears to be something of a contradiction. On the one hand, it depends heavily on the magnetism and autocratic style of a single leader. On the other hand, it is constituted of a complex, multilayered set of institutions that are sufficiently dispersed so as not to be fully accountable to the party leadership. On the one hand, the party has had a reputation for being less corrupt than the Congress (as we shall discuss). On the other hand, the party is widely known for its fear-inducing and extortionist practices. On the one hand, Sainiks at the local level have been seen as active party workers with a commitment to social service; on the other hand, there are wide reports of criminal elements pervading the party ranks. Corruption charges against the Sena brought by Anna Hazare, accusations that the involvement of the Sena caused the death of Ramesh Kini, the emerging criticism of Thackeray in several of the Marathi papers during the last months of 1996, and the reported increase in gangsterism at the *shakha* level of the Sena organization indicate that the party's organizational coherence may be faltering. But at least to date, as we shall explore in the next section, these contradictions have not obstructed Shiv Sena's expansion both in the realm of elections and as a party that commands ever widening notice.

THE ELECTIONS AND THE 1992–1993 CONFLAGRATION

It would be impossible to understand the 1992–3 post-Ayodhya tragedy or the Sena–BJP victory in the 1995 elections as a function of either discursive power or institutional processes alone. Only as discourse and institutions operating together can these two events be understood.

What characterized at least the second round of violence in January 1993 were inflammatory communalist words of the Shiv Sena and the presence of youthful activists at the sites of the violence. The translations of *Saamna* editorials presented as court documents make patent the explosive character of the Sena's language. From the 9 January 1993 editorial:

The Hindu does not lose heart in misery adversity or confrontation. On the contrary, he retaliates. . . . We cannot be silent peace keepers. . . . Those Muslims who have put this nation on auction, are appeased by Government in self surrender. But we are not prepared to let the pigeons of peace fly in the sky. Our brethren are dying in agony for no reason. The Hindus have to write their future right now. We must keep the fire burning. The night is dominated by the enemy. (Women, Law and Media, 1994, Exhibit)

From the 14 January 1993 editorial: 'Although we have stopped our *dharm yuddh* , everything will depend on how the government tackles anti-nationals. . . . Everyone knows their place now' (Sainath). But to see the riots as the result of verbal provocations alone underplays the importance of institutional contexts. Neither the state nor the Congress party has been prepared to apply punitive measures either in the form of closing down the Sena's journals, by jailing the Sena leadership, or by, it seems, the deploying of punitive police powers to curb the rioters. Although numerous proceedings have been initiated against Bal Thackeray and others in Shiv Sena, no court or legislative actions had restricted Thackeray or *Saamna*'s use of inflammatory language. On 27 September 1994, the Bombay High Court dismissed a public interest petition filed by J. B. D'Souza and Dilip Thakore asking for a court direction to the Government of Maharashtra to prosecute Bal Thackeray and Sanjay Raut, executive editor of *Saamna*. In January 1995, the Supreme Court also dismissed the special leave petition against the High Court ruling, precipitating a harsh critique from several eminent lawyers and retired judges, including H. M. Seervai, Nani Palkhivala and Soli Sorabjee.[32] During the winter session of 1994, the privileges committee of the Maharashtra legislative assembly proposed that Thackeray be punished by a short jail sentence for an objectionable article, but the session lapsed before any action could be taken. During the riots themselves, moreover, the lower echelons of the police were seen as partial to the Sena.[33] The government leadership was criticized for playing politics (as confusion arose as to the role of union defence minister Sharad Pawar and chief minister Suddhakarao Naik). Caught between the critiques of Muslims and the Shiv Sena, the state remained indecisive. The lesson here seemed to be that Shiv Sena could issue directives and action would follow, but that the judiciary and the government were immobilized by ambivalence as to how to proceed. The provocation of the Sena's language thus was supported by the weakness of institutional controls.

The Sena's march to dominance in the state assembly in alliance with the BJP in 1995 is similarly a result of both Hindu nationalist appeals and institutional processes. As Rajdeep Sardesai astutely recounts, the Sena came back from its 1975–85 exile with a strong showing in the 1985 municipal elections, thanks largely to infighting within the Congress party.

[32] The recently-founded Bombay journal, *Communalism Combat*, edited by Javed Anand and Teesta Setalvad, has tracked these issues carefully.

[33] M. Rahman with Lekha Rattanani, 'Savagery in Bombay', *India Today*, 31 January 1995; M. Rahman, 'Primed for Battle', *India Today*, 15 February 1995.

Its electoral forays beyond Bombay were facilitated by its efforts to broaden its caste base and by the role played by Chhaggan Bhujbal before he left the Sena for the Congress, but its use of Hindutva appeals was absolutely key. The Sena's first major victory outside the Bombay area was in Aurangabad in 1988, where the party fought the election utilizing the language of *dharm yuddh*. The Sena's alliance with the BJP in anticipation of the 1990 assembly elections reflected the party's recognition that the Ramjanmabhoomi momentum had caught popular attention. The acceptance of a Hindu nationalist framework within a significant section of the population is most evident in the fact that despite Shiv Sena's self-proclaimed participation in the Bombay riots of 1992–3, Bombay voters returned the Sena-led alliance in 1995 with a thumping victory, electing it from 30 out of 34 seats in the metropolis.

But institutional factors were clearly critical in the 1995 election. As Rajendra Vora rightly observes, the Sena–BJP alliance gained forty-four seats (over 1990) by virtue of a mere rise of 2.64 per cent of the popular vote. As Vora remarks, the single most important factor in the Congress party's loss of seats was the presence in many of the 288 constituencies of rebel Congress candidates (Vora 1996: 171–2). In the 1995 election, factionalism within the Congress ranks, the attack on the Congress for corruption and for links with the underworld, and disillusionment among some of the traditional Congress constituencies were a significant part of the Shiv Sena–BJP victory.[34]

Some observers of the recent Bombay/Maharashtra events might contend that to reduce the narrative of Shiv Sena to any single story is problematic. Although the Shiv Sena may appear to trade in Hindu–Muslim hostilities, other narratives might also be told: about urban anomie; about the death of the Nehru era and the quest for new identities; about the crisis of capitalism diverted into inter-community violence; about Congress party factionalism; and about a multiplicity of caste, class and ethnic issues encased in a patina of politicized religious identities. Still other observers might argue that this turn to Hindutva is in a sense no different from previous waves of group confrontations (Samyukta Maharashtra, sons-of-the-soil politics), and that their volatility and capacity for destruction

---

[34] The Jalgaon sex scandal also played a role in discrediting the Congress. In the MARG poll, corruption issues seemed to be where the anti-Congress sentiment most directly focused. A number of reports also comment on Muslim alienation from Congress, perceiving Congress to have been ineffective protectors of Muslims during the 1992–3 violence. See, for instance. Gunvanthi Balaram, 'Sena Nominee May Romp Home in Mahim', *Times of India*, 4 February 1995, p. 5; 'W. Maharashtra Only Hope for Congress', *Times of India*, 8 February 1995, p. 15.

will depend on the strengths, first and foremost, of state institutions. While we agree with these observations, our position is that discourses differ in their mobilizational and violence-generating capacities, and that the discourse of religious nationalism needs to be taken particularly seriously. When political leaders call for a *dharm yuddh* and when shortly thereafter Muslims (in large numbers) and Hindus (in smaller numbers) die at each others' hands, we need to take people at their word and measure them by their deed. This means taking seriously both what people say they mean as well as the institutional processes that translate those interpretations into action.

A few years ago, a *Washington Post* article described Bal Thackeray as 'a man who rules Bombay the way Al Capone ruled Chicago: through fear and intimidation'.[35] The analogy is apt yet lacking. Central to the distinction between the two is that in Bombay in the 1990s, fear and intimidation have been married to a populist discourse—one that elevates the interlacing of religious identity and militant nationalism.

The spread of Hindu nationalism in and beyond Bombay to Maharashtra has depended on the deployment of both discursive and institutional power working symbiotically. Shiv Sena rose to power on its sons-of-the-soil appeal and, in the early years, built a highly effective array of institutions. On its own, however, this well-organized system of local institutions (its job bureaus, unions, its cartoon weekly, and the *shakhas* whose service functions have been key to the party's mobilizational efforts), together with the system of intimidation already in place, were not enough to afford the party more than a limited role in Bombay city politics. By the mid-1970s, the party's political fortunes had stalled. When Shiv Sena shifted its ideological emphasis, however, from a Maharashtrian ethnic appeal to a pan-Hindu religious appeal—linking the party to the already expanding discourse of Hindutva, the party's electoral successes soared.

And yet it would be misleading to see Shiv Sena's success as testimony to this transposition of discourse alone. Were that the case, the BJP might well have been able to reap the full benefits of Hindutva without having had to join hands with Shiv Sena. Shiv Sena's organizational strength—the patronage politics its local organizational units perform and its capacity to support party activities through its extortionist net spread across Bombay's real estate, provided the party with an advantage denied to the BJP. It would be similarly problematic to see the Bombay conflagration of 1992–3 or the 1995 electoral success of the Shiv Sena–BJP combine as

---

[35] John W. Anderson, 'The Flames That Lit an Inferno', *Washington Post*, 11 August 1993, p. A14.

a 'triumph' of religious nationalism pure and simple. To understand these events requires an analysis of the capacities and incapacities of both state and party institutions: neither the judiciary nor the Congress government has been ready to utilize even a modicum of constitutional or police powers, in marked contrast to the violence perpetrated against the Naxalite left some years ago. The displacement of the Congress party by the Shiv Sena–BJP alliance in the state assembly in 1995 was also rooted in institutional causes. The divisions within the Maharashtrian Congress, the party's own reputation for corruption, its incapacity to present itself as the defender of the powerless and its consequent loss of some of its traditional Muslim and low caste constituencies were all critical to the party's recent ouster.

Discourse and organizations interact in numerous ways that bear further exploration: it seems likely, for instance, that the cry of *dharm yuddh* helps to legitimate extortionist pressures on Bombay business owners and shop managers; that the turn to Hindu nationalism alleviates the pressure on Shiv Sena's *shakhas* and its SLS branches to 'deliver' real goods in the form of housing improvements, jobs and resources; and that the institutional character of democratic politics (the competition between BJP and Shiv Sena) pushes the Sena to outdo its Hindu nationalist rival by claiming a greater militancy of thought and action. Such speculation about the intersection of organizational and discursive power aside, our claim is straightforward: what we have endeavoured to demonstrate is that both discursive and organizational power are both independently significant and mutually reinforcing. Without the turn to a discourse of Hindu nationalism, the party would have continued to be a local, Bombay political entity of little interest beyond the limits of the metropolis. The converging of Hindutva as a discourse with a set of particular organizational conditions—the Shiv Sena's capacity to deliver services as well as to terrorize and the presently weakened condition of other state and party institutions—has established a new political regime. Within this new framework, there are many possible eventualities, but none that, in the near future, are likely to eclipse the voice of Hindu nationalism.

Conclusion:
Reflections on Community Conflicts and
the State in India*

AMRITA BASU

An important contribution of recent historical and anthropological scholarship on community identities is to analyse how identities are constructed and how these constructions influence their enactment. Such arguments have been made about caste and 'communal' categories and conflicts (See, for example, Brass 1997, Dirks 1992, Pandey 1990 and 1992 and Tambiah 1996). Political theorists and philosophers have contributed to dismantling old categories by exploring the diverse meanings, possibilities and limits of secularism in India (Bhargav 1994, Bilgrami 1994, Chatterjee 1994). Given these important methodological and theoretical developments which focus on the construction of community identities, are there distinctive contributions that students of Indian politics can make to the study of community conflicts? The chapters in this volume provide several important responses to this question.

Political scientists (though not political theorists) generally remain committed to *explaining* the growth of community conflicts. Indeed if recent critical scholarship on community identities signals a warning about the dangers of parsimonious causal analysis, the chapters in this collection identify dangers of prematurely abandoning the project of explaining how, why and with what consequences community conflicts have grown in India. One of their underlying assumptions is that, however much we have learned about community conflicts at the local level, we have yet to establish satisfactory generalizations about the conditions under which they emerge and subsequently decline or flourish. Furthermore all of the authors link their quest for explanation with comparison of the national and state levels and highlight regional differences within India.

Related to this emphasis on a comparative approach is an emphasis on the explicitly political dimensions of community conflicts. How broadly the authors define the domain of the political varies, from Kohli, who

* I am grateful to Mark Kesselman and Atul Kohli for helpful comments on this chapter.

accords primacy to the character and actions of the state, to Katzenstein, Mehta and Thakkar, who examine both discourses and institutions. However they concur that the precise forms and timing of community conflicts do not mechanically result from socio-economic changes. Similarly accounts focusing exclusively on societal changes have been unable to identify the relationships between community conflicts at the state and national levels. In brief, the authors agree that the political underpinnings of community conflicts are of central importance.

Attention to political influences provides a highly effective vantage point from which to critique what has been termed primordialism and is captured by the phrase 'ancient hatreds'. (For critiques of primordialism see Appadurai 1993, Fox 1996, Rudolph and Rudolph 1987 and van der Veer 1994.) Most of the authors reject a primordialist perspective and emphasize the constructed character of community identities. In Kohli's account, ethnic self-determination movements can be interpreted as a variant of power conflicts. Both Jaffrelot and Hasan argue that Hindu nationalism is a political and not a religious movement. Parikh, who gives most credence to a primordialist perspective, still contends that 'riots are difficult to attribute to affective attachments alone' and that 'sustained violence can only be explained through the analysis of institutional, especially political factors'. To Katzenstein, Mehta and Thakkar, the Shiv Sena's shift from ethnic to religious themes represents an effective strategy to extend its influence from the regional to the national level. Dasgupta argues that violent insurgency in the north-eastern states results from the manipulation of ethnic identities by the state and political parties. Widmalm similarly argues that conflict in Kashmir did not stem from incompatible identities, but rather from tensions between political elites in the state and central governments.

THE STATE AND COMMUNITY CONFLICTS

There are, however, some important differences in the ways the essays conceptualize the relationship between the state and community conflicts. One of the most significant concerns the importance they accord to the state as opposed to other social and political forces. Kohli provides the most forceful argument about the connections between state actions and community conflicts. He argues that leadership strategy and the institutionalization of state power are the major determinants of the causes and outcomes of ethnic self-determination movements in multicultural democracies. In his reading, given scarce political power and economic resources, it is inevitable that ethnic movements will emerge, but just as inevitably that they will decline if they obtain substantial concessions from the state.

To what extent does the pattern that Kohli identifies characterize the states that have experienced ethnic conflict in recent years? The actions of the state and political leaders have been crucial determinants of the intensity of community mobilization. At the national level, Congress party strength eroded as a result of its centralization and personalization of power, its manipulation of electoral processes and the rise of new social forces that it could not accommodate. At the state level, although Congress had dominated Maharashtrian politics since 1960, it was steadily weakened by factionalism, corruption, and a loss of Muslim and lower caste support. Thus, as Katzenstein, Mehta and Thakkar note, in the 1995 legislative assembly elections, Congress found itself unable to compete with the Shiv Sena's organizational strength, institutional control and financial resources. In Uttar Pradesh, Zoya Hasan argues, the collapse of the Congress system was critical to the BJP's growth. She argues that local Congress leaders capitulated to the Hindu nationalist campaign that the Vishwa Hindu Parishad (VHP) launched after 1984 through a series of *yatras* throughout the state. The Ramjanmabhoomi movement revealed and exacerbated a crisis within the Congress party.

In both Kashmir and the north-eastern states, Congress under Indira Gandhi's intransigent leadership hardened the positions of ethnic movements, which thereby contributed to a spiralling cycle of violence by ethnic groups and the state. In Kashmir, democratic institutions were being established in the late 1950s when Nehru was Prime Minister. By the early 1980s, however, Indira Gandhi at the centre and Sheikh Abdullah in Kashmir undermined democratic institutions by centralizing and personalizing leadership. The progressive erosion of political institutions became evident in the 1987 elections and continued in their aftermath. Similarly, the worst violence occurred in the north-east in the early 1980s when Indira Gandhi refused to concede the Asom Gana Parishad (AGP) the right to represent the Assamese community. In contrast, Rajiv Gandhi's willingness to sign the Assam Accord in 1985 helped to revitalize political institutions and restore political order.

Although the authors emphatically agree that the state's character and actions are critical to understanding community conflicts, they part company when analysing other forces that explain the emergence, growth, transformation and decline of such conflict. Widmalm considers the role of the state the most decisive determinant of whether Kashmir would experience democracy; he accords much less importance to religious beliefs, economic disparities and historical memories. Dasgupta and

Katzenstein, Mehta and Thakkar accord less importance than Widmalm and Kohli to state actions and more attention to the organization and activities of ethnic and 'communal' parties and movements. Their accounts suggest that community mobilization is often the expression of contest and negotiation among communities. Paradoxically, groups that express the most xenophobic identities often do so in order to undermine competing expressions of community identity.

Dasgupta shows that crucial determinants of the intensity of community mobilization in the north-east were the number and variety of ethnic communities and their complicated interrelationships. Whenever Assamese leaders equated the territorial identity of multiethnic Assam with the ethno-linguistic identity of the Assamese speakers of Brahmaputra valley, other groups reacted by demanding autonomy. For example the Bodos were aggrieved by the Assamese language policy, which disadvantaged them and all other non-Assamese-speaking communities with respect to education and employment. In 1987 they launched a movement against the ruling AGP, demanding that it make Hindi the official language of Assam. Paradoxically, the Bodo autonomy movement brought about a closer relationship between the state and central government. In this case the causal arrows were the reverse of the scenario that Kohli describes, for inter-ethnic conflict was in part responsible for a more accommodating state policy.

Katzenstein, Mehta and Thakkar supplement a focus on the state by highlighting the importance of Hindu nationalist discourses. They argue that an exclusive focus on political institutions cannot explain the transformation of an ethnic 'sons-of-the-soil' movement into a religious nationalist one. Additionally, a discursive shift had occurred by the second half of the 1980s. Many of the Shiv Sena's key themes, including Muslim demonization, political nationalism and the restoration of religious rituals, found expression in the growth of Hindu nationalism at the centre and resonated in Maharashtra as a result of institutional changes in the character of the Shiv Sena and the Congress party.

In a similar vein, Arun Swamy identifies two distinct discourses underlying party competition in Tamil Nadu: empowerment populism of the Dravida Munnetra Kazhagam (DMK) and protection populism of the Anna Dravida Munnetra Kazhagam (ADMK). Employing different rhetorical styles and cultural symbols, each party appealed to different conceptions of underprivilege. The contrasts between these discourses enabled the two parties to develop stable constituencies and programmes, and thereby institutionalize their gains. In analysing the appeals of the ADMK's protection populism, Swamy deciphers the cultural symbols that captured the public imagination when M.G. Ramachandran (MGR) and Jayalalitha appeared on screen. But what made these appeals meaningful to women, an important part of their constituency, were relatively high levels of women's labour force participation and their increased social and economic vulnerability. In Tamil Nadu, as in Maharashtra, certain discourses became meaningful in the presence of particular institutional possibilities and socio-economic conditions.

The chapters by Hasan, Parikh and Swamy all suggest that expressions of caste and cultural or religious nationalism are mutually interdependent. These reciprocal influences are strikingly evident in the agitations around 'mandal' and 'masjid'. As both Hasan and Parikh show, the BJP's decision to organize the Ramjanmabhoomi campaign was significantly influenced by the growing power of Other Backward Classes (OBCs), and their further politicization as a result of the government's implementation of the Mandal Commission recommendations. The BJP's electoral victory in UP in 1991 and its nationwide growth were closely related to the success of the Ramjanmabhoomi movement. However, in the aftermath of the temple conflagration, lower caste mobilization continued to grow and resulted in the BJP's electoral defeat in UP in 1993 and its inability to create a governing coalition in 1996.

The counterpart to the dialectic between communal and caste politics in UP is the dialectic between ethnic nationalism and class politics in Tamil Nadu. Arun Swamy argues that there was long-standing tension between the DMK's attempts to represent Tamils and the poor. In 1972 this tension gave rise to the ADMK, which shifted attention from opposition to Brahminical and north Indian domination to pro-poor populism. Tensions between cultural nationalism and pro-poor populism have fuelled party competition in Tamil Nadu.

There have been numerous debates among students of politics as to the extent of state autonomy *vis-à-vis* societal forces, the sources of its autonomy, and the boundaries between the state and civil society (Jessop 1990, Kohli 1990b, Migdal, Kohli and Shue 1994, Mitchell 1991, and Evans, Rueschemeyer and Skocpol 1985). Rather than rehearse these arguments, it may be more useful to suggest how diverse characterizations of the state influence scholarly interpretations of community conflicts.

By focusing on the role and character of the state in community conflicts, Kohli is able to identify some broad patterns concerning the rise and decline of community conflicts. It is probably not coincidental that his is the only chapter in the book that compares several Indian states while making broad generalizations about national patterns. However, by focusing on the interaction between states and ethnic self-determination movements, Kohli is less equipped to assess movements in relation to civil society, on the one hand, and their structures, ideologies and strategies as movements, on the other.

We need more research that transcends the depiction of community movements exclusively as products of state actions, thereby ignoring the complicated ways in which such movements mirror tensions within civil society that are likely to persist irrespective of state actions. But nor is it productive to view community movements as wholly coterminous with civil society, given that they are usually dominated by political elites whose interests are at variance with the communities they claim to represent. Katzenstein, Mehta and Thakkar point in this direction when they argue that the Shiv Sena's success in Maharashtra grows out of a complex web of elements which include its organizational structure, use of the media, substantial resources and immersion in the daily lives of local communities. Both they and Dasgupta suggest that the very questions of leadership and accountable institutions that Kohli raises about the state should also be asked of community movements.

Not surprisingly, the authors who focus on political upheaval and violence, namely Jaffrelot and Katzenstein, Mehta and Thakkar, analyse both discourses and institutions. Hindu nationalists' ability to engage in mass mobilization by appealing to anti-Muslim sentiments reveals the power of cultural symbols, ideas and networks to anger, energize, terrify and empower 'ordinary' people. A focus on discourses complicates the study of community conflicts by suggesting that the collapse of political institutions may be both cause and effect of broader political and cultural changes. Furthermore discursive changes may have important implications even when unaccompanied by institutional changes. Movements which fail to achieve their formal demands may nevertheless deeply affect community relations in ways that only become evident at some future point. For example, although the Hindu–Muslim violence that accompanied the Hindu nationalist campaign around Ayodhya has subsided and the BJP has moderated its stance, Hindu nationalism has arguably influenced the discourse and agenda of Indian politics in ways that will have far-reaching implications for years to come (Basu 1996).

COMMUNITY CONFLICTS AND DEMOCRACY

Several of the chapters assess the implications of community conflicts for democracy. But they differ in their evaluation of their severity and consequences. At one end of the spectrum is Dasgupta, who argues that 'the narratives of peace, civility, economic construction and democratic engagement ... reflect how most people in India most of the time conduct their life and contribute to national development'. At the other end of the spectrum are Katzenstein, Mehta and Thakkar, who argue that narratives of violence and anti-Muslim xenophobia underlie the Shiv Sena's growth in Maharashtra. In contrast to Dasgupta's prognosis, they anticipate that the strident voice of militant Hindu nationalism is likely to endure.

Kohli paints a less optimistic picture than Dasgupta but contends that even when the Indian state has suffered its most serious setbacks, it has still been strong enough to prevent secession. He concludes that Indian democracy can accommodate the demands of ethnic self-determination movements. Where Kohli considers the institutionalization of power a key determinant of political stability at the national level, Swamy denies its importance in the southern states. He argues that despite corrupt, populist leadership, which is often associated with deinstitutionalization, political parties in Tamil Nadu have managed to maintain political stability and deliver material benefits to underprivileged groups.

Differences in the authors' normative and analytic perspectives may help explain their divergent assessments of the implications of community conflicts for democracy. However, equally important are differences in the character of state governments, political parties and social movements that they analyse. Consider, for example, the varied forms of populism that the chapters describe. The populist appeals of the Shiv Sena and the BJP in its militant phase vilify Muslims in order to unify Hindus across class, caste and regional lines. By contrast, the populism of the ADMK in Tamil Nadu actually caters to the material interests of women and the poor. Thus competitive populisms in Tamil Nadu strengthen the connection between electoral performance and responsiveness of political parties to underprivileged groups. By contrast, party competition between the BJP and the Congress in north India has tended to diminish attention to the class interests of the poor. Indeed the power and danger of Hindu nationalism lies in its ability to mask its commitment to upper class and caste interests through its appeals to religion. The attempt to forge unity among Hindus by fostering antipathy to Muslims is likely to generate violence for it must overcome socio-economic divisions among Hindus. Similarly, the DMK's strategy of attempting to unite Tamils against a common enemy failed because some newly mobilized Tamils regarded themselves as more disadvantaged than others.

One reason that Hindu chauvinism is far more dangerous than the chauvinism of ethnic minorities is that Hindus constitute the large majority of the population whereas the ethnic groups that have demanded rights to self-determination form minorities within the national context. (Note that in states where ethnic movements have been organized by groups that form majorities, they have often demonstrated intolerance towards ethnic minorities.) In fact, as Katzenstein, Mehta and Thakkar assert, the Shiv Sena adopted the discourse of religion over that of ethnicity precisely to extend its appeal beyond the regional level. In 1966, when the Shiv Sena established a strong base in Maharashtra, the Akali Dal spearheaded a movement for a Punjabi-speaking state and attained power for the first time in the Punjab. A year later the DMK ousted the Congress party from power in Tamil Nadu. However, given differences among mobilized ethnic groups, the demands they voiced and the political contexts of particular states, there was no single discourse of ethnicity in the 1960s comparable to the discourse of Hindu nationalism in the 1990s.

By broadening the definition of community conflicts to comprise caste, ethnic and religious nationalist movements, their very different implications for democracy become evident. Religious nationalist movements employ methods and seek objectives that are most inimical to democracy; although caste conflicts may generate violence, lower caste struggles to achieve greater power and representation may contribute to creating a more democratic and inclusive society. The methods and objectives of ethnic movements are diverse, particularly in recent years when they have acquired a religious tint, but ethnic self-determination movements have generally contributed to democracy by enhancing cultural pluralism and strengthening state governments *vis-à-vis* the centre.

Hindu nationalist mobilization, the major form of religious politics that India has experienced, has undermined democratic processes. The movement that Hindu nationalist groups launched around the destruction of the mosque in Ayodhya fostered extensive Hindu–Muslim violence which, in turn, weakened already frayed institutions, deepened biases of the civil service and accentuated a leadership crisis in the state. Most importantly, Hindu nationalism seeks objectives which are inimical to democracy, above all in seeking to undermine minority rights. That the BJP has been inconsistent in its commitment to these principles reflects a strategic choice rather than a durable ideological shift, for it has not renounced its connection to the RSS or to its earlier positions. Jaffrelot shows that even though the incidence of riots has declined in recent years, they remain an ever present possibility, for riots have become intertwined with elections and an important means for the BJP to make inroads into new regions and constituencies. Even more dangerous is the recent trend towards state complicity in communal violence.

In contrast, lower castes have broadened the parameters of democracy by demanding greater rights and opportunities. The violence associated with caste conflict is usually instigated by the upper castes to prevent subordinate groups from acquiring greater power. Lower castes have not retaliated with comparable campaigns of hatred. Nor do they conceive of their identities in an exclusionary fashion. Lower caste movements are strengthened by forming coalitions with other groups which seek to challenge under-representation and inequality. Indeed, over the past decade, lower caste consciousness has been one of the major antidotes to the growth of Hindu nationalism. By contrast, Hindu nationalist mobilization rests precisely on drawing rigid and immutable boundaries between Hindus and Muslims. Its proclivity for violence is closely associated with its bigotry. Where caste-based reforms would foster a more equitable system, Hindu nationalism would do the opposite.

Ethnic movements have more complicated and mixed implications for democracy than caste and religious nationalist movements. Ethnic self-determination movements can be violent and exclusionary, as has been true of certain phases in the history of the DMK in Tamil Nadu, the United Liberation Front in Assam and the Jammu and Kashmir Liberation Front. However, government intransigence heightens violent, exclusionary tendencies. When the centre has demonstrated a responsiveness to their demands, these movements have moderated their stance. Ethnic movements which have been concerned with the devolution of power and resources bear a striking resemblance to social movements active around women's rights, environmental protection and civil liberties. This similarity is often overlooked because ethnic identities are assumed to be primordial.

One reason that Hindu nationalism is so destructive of democracy is that it is often unwilling to yield to state concessions. Indeed the key ingredient for the growth of religious nationalism has been an accommodating state. Nehru's refusal to negotiate with states which framed their appeals in religious terms curtailed religious appeals by political parties and ethnic self-determination movements. However, once Nehru overcame his initial reluctance to reorganize state boundaries along linguistic lines, his attitude towards the demands of ethnically based regional movements was quite conciliatory. By contrast, Indira Gandhi hardened her stance towards ethnic movements while making concessions to Hindu nationalism during her last years in office. Not only did this encourage the BJP to make Hindu appeals but it induced several ethnic movements that had previously organized along regional lines—in the Punjab, Kashmir and Maharashtra—to express their demands in increasingly religious terms.

The language of appeasement, which the BJP employs to refer to the Congress party's stance towards Muslims, describes the stance of political leaders towards the BJP since the mid- 1980s. First Indira Gandhi, then ironically the left-of-centre V.P. Singh, who needed BJP support to form a government in 1991, and most importantly Narasimha Rao, all made significant concessions to Hindu nationalists, both institutionally and discursively. Accordingly, the BJP grew. In the abstract it would seem that an accommodating, conciliatory state would be highly desirable in India. But the context, nature and timing of state concessions have very different implications for democracy. Whereas the state strengthens democratic processes by conceding rights to ethnic self-determination, it erodes democracy by accommodating groups that employ the discourse of secularism to undermine minority rights.

Why have state concessions pacified ethnic self-determination movements but not religious nationalists? The demands of ethnic self-determination movements generally focus on territory, resources and power. These are finite demands which the state can meet. By contrast, the BJP's principal objective is to attain power in New Delhi, a demand that the state cannot satisfy. Indeed the BJP's interests are best served by intransigence in face of the concessions made by the ruling party. Moreover religious appeals are an excellent method of generating electoral fervour. This implies that the BJP sometimes unleashes forces that it cannot fully control. How to respond democratically to undemocratic demands is a challenge that the state will continue to confront. How it meets that challenge will significantly influence the fate of Indian democracy in the years to come.

Glossary

aarti	Hindu ritual of worship performed at sunset
akhara	gymnasium, generally attached to a temple, where one practises weight lifting and wrestling
alim	Islamic scholar (pl. *ulema*)
Arya Samaj	Hindu reformist organization
asthi	bone
Bande Mataram	Hail to the Motherland
bhakti	devotion
burkha	long garment with headpiece which can cover the wearer from head to foot
chaturthi	fourth day of a lunar fortnight
crore	ten million
dalit	Untouchable
darshan	viewing; sight
dharm yuddh.	holy war
dharma	religion; theology; piety; righteousness
Durga Puja	festival in honour of the Hindu goddess Durga
firangis	foreigners
Ganesh	Hindu god, usually associated with success
gopis	milkmaids; in the Mahabharata, they are Krishna's lovers
gulal	coloured powder used during Holi
Hindutva	'Hindu-ness'; Hindu nationalism
Holi	Hindu festival marking the end of the winter season which people celebrate by throwing colour at each other
kalash	urn
Kali	Hindu goddess
kar sevak	volunteer worker

lakh	one hundred thousand
lathi	stick
maidan	large open space
mangalsutra	the necklace received by a woman upon marriage, and meant to be worn at all times
Marwaris	caste of Hindu merchants from Marwar, Rajasthan
Muharram	first month of Muslim calendar; month of mourning, particularly for Shias, since tenth Muharram marks the death anniversary of Hasan and Hussain, grandsons of the Prophet Muhammad
namaz	literally, prayers; also congregational prayers held in mosques
parikrama	ritual circumambulation
puja	Hindu ceremony of worship
rais	nobleman, notable, magnate
Ram *dal*	a group celebrating Ram during the festival of this god
Ram *Jyoti Yatra*	pilgrimage of light in honour of Ram
Ram Shilan Puja	literally, worship of the Ram bricks
Ramjanmabhoomi	the birthplace of Ram
rath	chariot used in Hindu festivals
Rath Yatra	traditionally, the Hindu festival of Jagannath during which his image is taken in a chariot for a bath in the sea; also the name used by VHP and BJP for their chariot procession from Somnath to Ayodhya in 1990
rudhraksha	a kind of dried fruit which is used as a bead
sadhu	ascetic
Sangh Parivar	the 'family' of the RSS, that is the Hindu nationalist combine
shakha	literally, branch; RSS training meeting
shila	brick

Shiv Jayanti	festival celebrating the anniversary of Shivaji
shuddhi	ritual purification
smarta	pertaining to the Smrita and especially the traditional codes of Hindu law, such as the Dharmashatra; by extension, 'the orthodox *par excellence*'
taziya	replica of cenotaphs of Hasan and Hussain taken out in a procession on the occasion of the Muslim festival of Muharram
ulema	Islamic scholars
varna	caste (Brahmin, Kshatriya, Vaishya and Shudra)
Vidhan Sabha	state legislative assembly
yajna	sacrifice
yatra	procession; pilgrimage

References

ABDULLAH, FAROOQ, 1985. *My Dismissal—As Told to Sati Sahni*. New Delhi: Vikas Publishing House.

ADVANI, L. K., 1979. *The People Betrayed*. Delhi: Vision Books.

AHLUWALIA, ISHER JUDGE, 1991. *Productivity and Growth in Indian Manufacturing*, Delhi: Oxford University Press.

AHMAD, AIJAZ, 1994. 'Nation, Community, Violence', *South Asia Bulletin: Comparative Studies in South Asia, Africa and the Middle East* 14: 24–32.

AKBAR, M. J., 1985. *India: The Siege Within: Challenges to a Nation's Unity*. Harmondsworth, Middlesex: Penguin Books.

———, 1988. *Riot After Riot: Reports on Caste and Communal Violence in India*. New Delhi: Penguin Books.

———, 1991. *Kashmir behind the Vale*. New Delhi: Viking.

ALLEN, DOUGLAS (ed.), 1992. *Religion and Political Conflict in South Asia*. New Delhi: Oxford University Press/ Westport: Greenwood Press.

ANAND, VIJAY K., 1980. *Conflict in Nagaland: A Study of Insurgency and Counter-Insurgency*. Delhi: Chanakaya.

ANDERSEN, WALTER K. and SRIDHAR K. DAMLE, 1987. *The Brotherhood in Saffron: The Rashtriya Swayamsevak Sangh and Hindu Revivalism*. New Delhi: Vistaar.

ANNADURAI, C., 1988. 'The Public Distribution System in Tamil Nadu: An Interim Assessment', *Bulletin, Madras Institute of Development Studies* 18 (1).

APPADURAI, ARJUN, 1993. 'Numbers in the Colonial Imagination', in Carol Beckenridge and Peter van der Veer (eds), *Orientalism and the Post Colonial Predicament: Perspectives on South Asia*. Philadephia: University of Pennsylvania Press.

ARNOLD, DAVID, 1977a. 'The Politics of Coalescence: The Congress in Tamil Nadu, 1930–37', in D.A. Low (ed.), *Congress and the Raj: Facets of the Indian Struggle, 1917–47*. New Delhi: South Asia Books.

———, 1977b. *The Congress in Tamil Nadu: Nationalist Politics in South India, 1919–1937*. New Delhi: Manohar.

ASIAN SURVEY. 1993. Issue on 'South Asia: Responses to the Ayodhya Crisis', 33 (July).

BABB, LAWRENCE A. and SUSAN WADLEY (eds), 1994. *Media and the*

Transformation of Religion in South Asia. Philadelphia: University of Pennsylvania Press.

BAKER, CHRISTOPHER J. and D. A. WASHBROOK (eds), 1975. *South India: Political Institutions and Political Change, 1880–1940.* Delhi: Macmillan.

BAKER, DAVID E. U., 1979. *Changing Political Leadership in an Indian Province: The Central Provinces And Berar, 1919–1939.* Delhi: Oxford University Press.

BAKKER, HANS, 1986. *Ayodhya.* Groningen: Forsten.

BANERJEE, ASHISH, 1990. ' "Comparative Curfew": Changing Dimensions of Communal Politics in India', in Veena Das (ed.), *Mirrors of Violence: Communities, Riots and Survivors in South Asia.* Delhi: Oxford University Press.

BANERJEE, SIKATA, 1995. 'Hindu Nationalism and the Construction of Women: The Shiv Sena Organises Women in Bombay', in Tanika Sarkar and Urvashi Butalia (eds), *Women and the Hindu Right.* New Delhi: Kali for Women.

BANU, ZENAB, 1989. *Politics of Communalism: A Politico-Historical Analysis of Communal Riots in Post-Independence India with Special Reference to the Gujarat and Rajasthan Riots.* Bombay: Popular Prakashan/ London: Sangam.

BARNETT, MARGUERITE R., 1976. *The Politics of Cultural Nationalism in South India.* Princeton: Princeton University Press.

BARRY, BRIAN, 1975. 'Political Accommodation and Consociational Democracy', *British Journal of Political Science* 5 (4).

BARUAH, SANJIB, 1986. 'Immigration, Ethnic Conflict and Political Turmoil: Assam, 1979–1985', *Asian Survey* 26 (11).

——, 1994. 'The State and Separatists Militancy in Assam: Winning a Battle and Losing a War?', *Asian Survey* 34 (10).

BASU, AMRITA, 1994. 'When Local Riots Are Not Merely Local: Bringing the State Back in, Bijnor, 1988–1992', *Economic and Political Weekly*, 1 October.

——, 1996. 'Mass Movement or Elite Conspiracy? The Puzzle of Hindu Nationalism', in David Ludden (ed.), *Contesting the Nation: Religion, Community and the Politics of Democracy in India.* Philadelphia: University of Pennsylvania Press, Delhi: Oxford University Press.

——, forthcoming. *The Lotus and the Trishul: The Bharatiya Janata Party and the Growth of Hindu Nationalism.*

BASU, DURGA D., 1994. *Introduction to the Constitution of India.* New Delhi: Prentice-Hall of India.

BASU, KAUSHIK and SANJAY SUBRAHMANYAM (eds), 1996. *Unravelling the Nation: Sectarian Conflict and India's Secular Identity*. Delhi: Penguin Books.

BASU, TAPAN, PRADIP DATTA, SUMIT SARKAR, TANIKA SARKAR and SAMBUDDA SEN, 1993. *Khaki Shorts and Saffron Flags*. New Delhi: Orient Longman/ London: Sangam.

BAYLY, C. A., 1973. 'Patrons and Politics in Northern India', *Modern Asian Studies* 7 (3).

———, 1975. *The Local Roots of Indian Politics: Allahabad 1880–1920*. Oxford: Clarendon Press.

BÉTEILLE, ANDRÉ, 1965. *Caste, Class and Power: Changing Patterns of Stratification in a Tanjore Village*. Berkeley and Los Angeles: University of California Press.

BHARGAV, RAJEEV, 1994. 'Giving Secularism Its Due', *Economic and Political Weekly*, 9 July.

BHARTI, I., 1989. 'Bhagalpur Riots and Bihar Government', *Economic and Political Weekly*, 2 December.

BHATNAGAR, SATYAVAN and PRADEEP KUMAR (eds), 1988. *Regional Political Parties in India*. New Delhi: Ess Ess Publications.

BHATTACHARYA, JAYANTA B., 1994. *Studies in the Economic History of Northeast India*. New Delhi: Har Anand.

——— (ed.), 1982. *Social Tension in Northeast India*. Calcutta: Research India.

BHATTACHARYA, NEELADRI, 1991. 'Myth, History and the Politics of Ramjanmabhoomi', in S. Gopal (ed.), *Anatomy of a Confrontation: The Babri Masjid–Ramjanmabhoomi Issue*. New Delhi and New York: Viking.

BHUYAN, B. C., 1989. *Political Development of the Northeast*, vol. 1. New Delhi: Omsons.

BILGRAMI, AKEEL, 1994. 'Two Concepts of Secularism: Reason, Modernity and Archimedean Ideal', *Economic and Political Weekly*, 9 July.

BJORKMAN, JAMES W. (ed.), 1988. *Fundamentalism, Revivalists and Violence in South Asia*. New Delhi: Manohar /Riverdale, MD: Riverdale Co..

BLOMKVIST, HANS, 1988. 'The Soft State: Housing Reform and State Capacity in Urban India'. Ph.D. diss., Uppsala University, Uppsala.

BOSE, ASHISH, 1991. *Population of India: 1991 Census Results and Methodology*. Delhi: B.R. Publishing Corporation.

BOSE, P. K., 1981. 'Social Mobility and Caste Violence: A Study of the Gujarat Riots', *Economic and Political Weekly*, 18 April.

BOSE, SUGATA and AYESHA JALAL (eds), 1997. *Nationalism, Democracy and Development: State and Politics in India*. New Delhi and New York: Oxford University Press.

BOSE, SUMANTRA, 1997. *The Challenge in Kashmir: Democracy, Self Determination and a Just Peace*. New Delhi: Sage.

BOSE, TAPAN, DINESH MOHAN, GAUTAM NAVLAKHA AND SUMANTA BANERJEE, 1990. 'India's "Kashmir War"', *Economic and Politcal Weekly*, 31 March.

BRASS, PAUL R., 1990. 'The Punjab Crisis and the Unity of India', in Atul Kohli (ed.), *India's Democracy: An Analysis of Changing State–Society Relations*. Princeton, NJ: Princeton University Press.

———, 1991. *Ethnicity and Nationalism: Theory and Comparison*. New Delhi: Sage Publications.

———, 1993. 'The Rise of the BJP and the Future of Party Politics in Uttar Pradesh', in H. Gould and S. Ganguly (eds), *India Votes: Alliance Politics and Minority Governments in the Ninth and Tenth General Elections*. Boulder: Westview Press.

———, 1994. *The Politics of India since Independence*, 2nd edn. Cambridge: Cambridge University Press.

———, 1997. *Theft of an Idol: Text and Context in the Representation of Collective Violence*. Princeton: Princeton University Press.

BRAUDEL, FERNAND, 1988. *The Identity of France*, vol. 1: *History and Environment*. London: Collins.

BREMAN, JAN, 1993. 'Anti-Muslim Pogrom in Surat', *Economic and Political Weekly*, 17 April.

BRENNAN, LANCE, 1994. 'The State and Communal Violence in UP: 1947–1992', *South Asia* 17.

BROWN, JUDITH M., 1985. *Modern India: The Origins of an Asian Democracy*. Delhi: Oxford University Press.

BUTLER, DAVID, ASHOK LAHIRI and PRANNOY ROY, 1991. *India Decides: Elections 1952– 1991*. New Delhi: Living Media Books.

———, 1996. *India Decides: Elections 1952–1995*. New Delhi: Living Media Books.

CASHMAN, RICHARD I., 1975. *The Myth of the Lokamanya: Tilak and Mass Politics in Maharashtra*. Berkeley and Los Angeles: University of California Press.

CHAKRAVARTI, UMA and NANDITA HAKSAR, 1987. *The Delhi Riots: Three Days in the Life of a Nation*. New Delhi: Lancer International.

CHAKRAVARTI, UMA, PREM CHAUDHURY, PRADIP DATTA, ZOYA HASAN, KUMKUM SANGARI and TANIKA SARKAR, 1992. 'Khurja Riots 1990–91: Understanding the Conjuncture', *Economic and Political Weekly*, 2 May.

CHANDHOK, H. L. and THE POLICY GROUP, 1990. *India Database: The Economy*. New Delhi: Living Media Books.

CHANDRA, SUDHIR, 1996. 'Of Communal Consciousness and Communal Violence: Impressions From Post-Riot Surat', in J. Mcguire, P. Reeves and H. Brasted (eds), *Politics of Violence: From Ayodhya to Behrampada*. New Delhi: Sage.

CHATTERJEE, PARTHA, 1993. *The Nation and Its Fragments: Colonial and Post-Colonial Histories*. Princeton: Princeton University Press.

————, 1994. 'Secularism and Toleration', *Economic and Political Weekly*, 9 July, 1768–77.

CHATTERJEE, SUHAS, 1990. *Mizoram Encyclopedia*, 3 vols. Bombay: Jaico.

CHATTERJI, MANINI, 1994. 'The BJP: Political Mobilization for Hindutva', *South Asia Bulletin: Comparative Studies of South Asia, Africa and the Middle East* 14 (1).

CHATTOPADHYAY, DILIP KUMAR, 1990. *History of the Assamese Movement since 1947*. Calcutta: Minerva Associates.

CHATURVEDI, SITARAM, 1972. *Madan Mohan Malaviya*. Delhi: Government of India.

CHEEMA, PERVAIZ I., 1992. 'Pakistan, India and Kashmir—A Historical Review', in Raju G. C. Thomas (ed.), *Perspectives on Kashmir: The Roots of Conflict in South Asia*. Boulder: Westview Press.

CHIBBER, PRADEEP and SUBASH MISRA, 1993. 'Hindus and the Babri Masjid: The Sectional Basis of Communal Attitudes', *Asian Survey* 33 (7).

CHIRIYANKANDATH, JAMES, 1992. 'Tricolour and Saffron: Congress and the New Hindu Challenge', in S.K. Mitra and J. Chiriyankandath (eds), *Electoral Politics in India: A Changing Landscape*. New Delhi: Segment Books.

CMIE (Center for Monitoring the Indian Economy), 1989. *Basic Statistics Relating to the Indian Economy*, vol. 2: *States* (September). Bombay.

————, 1990. *Basic Statistics Relating to the Indian Economy*, vol. 2: *States* (September). Bombay.

————, 1994a. *Basic Statistics Relating to the Indian Economy*, vol. 2: *States* (September). Bombay.

————, 1994b. *Basic Statistics Relating to the States of India* (September). Bombay.

Connor, Walker, 1993. 'Beyond Reason: "The Nature of the Ethnonational Bond" ', *Ethnic and Racial Studies* 16 (3).

————, 1994. *Ethnonationalism: The Quest for Understanding*. Princeton: Princeton University Press.

DAHL, ROBERT A., 1971. *Polyarchy: Participation and Opposition*. New Haven: Yale University Press.

DALE, STEPHEN F., 1975. 'The Mapilla Outbreaks: Ideology and Social Conflict in Nineteenth Century Kerala', *Journal of Asian Studies* 35 (1).

DAS, SAMIR K., 1994. *ULFA: United Liberation Front of Assam: Analysis.* Delhi: Ajanta Publications.

DAS, VEENA (ed.), 1990. *Mirrors of Violence: Communities, Riots and Survivors in South Asia.* Delhi: Oxford University Press.

DASGUPTA, JYOTIRINDRA, 1970. *Language Conflict and National Development: Group Politics and National Language Policy in India.* Berkeley: University of California Press.

——, 1990. 'Ethnicity, Democracy and Development', in Atul Kohli (ed.), *India's Democracy: An Analysis of Changing State–Society Relations,* 2nd ed. Princeton: Princeton University Press.

——, 1994. 'Developmental Federalism', in N. K. Choudhary and S. Mansur (eds), *The Indira–Rajiv Years.* Toronto: University of Toronto.

——, 1995. 'India: Democratic Becoming and Developmental Transition', in L. Diamond, J. J. Linz and M. Lipset (eds), *Politics in Developing Countries,* 2nd edn. Boulder: Lynne Rienner.

DATTA, P. K., 1993. 'VHP's Ram: The Hindutva Movement in Ayodhya', in Gyanendra Pandey (ed.), *Hindus and Others.* Delhi: Penguin Books.

DATTA, P. S. (ed.), 1993. *Autonomy Movements in Assam: Documents.* New Delhi: Omsons.

DATTA, RAY. B. (ed.), 1986. *The Patterns and Problems of Population in North–East India.* New Delhi: Uppal Publishing.

DAVID, C. R.W., 1983. *Cinema as Medium of Communication in Tamil Nadu.* Madras: Christian Literature Society.

DAVIS, RICHARD A., 1996. 'The Iconography of Rama's Chariot', in David Ludden (ed.), *Contesting The Nation: Religion, Community and the Politics of Democracy in India.* Philadelphia: University of Pennsylvania Press, Delhi: Oxford University Press.

DAVIS, NATALIE Z., 1975. *Society and Culture in Early Modern France.* Cambridge: Polity Press, 1987.

DESHTA, SUNIL, 1993. *President's Rule in the States: Constitutional Provisions and Practices.* New Delhi: Deep and Deep Publications.

DEUTSCH, KARL, 1961. 'Social Mobilization and Political Development', *American Political Science Review* 56(4).

DEV, S. MAHENDRA and AJIT RANADE, 1997. 'Poverty and Public Policy: A Mixed Record', in Kirit S. Parikh (ed.), *India Development Report 1997.* Delhi: Oxford University Press.

DEVADAS, RAJAMMAL P., 1986. 'Nutritional Outcomes of a Massive Feeding Programme in Tamil Nadu', in *Proceedings of the Nutrition Society of India,* no. 32. Hyderabad: National Institute of Nutrition.

DHARMAVEER, DR. B.S. MOONJE *Commemoration Volume,* 1972. Nagpur: Birth Centenary Celebration Committee.

DICKEY, SARAH, 1993. 'The Politics of Adulation: Cinema and the Production of Politicans in South India', *Journal of Asian Studies* 52 (2).

DIRKS, NICHOLAS, 1992. 'Castes of Mind', *Representations* 37 (Winter).

DRÉZE, JEAN and AMARTYA K. SEN, 1996. *India: Economic Development and Social Opportunity.* Delhi: Oxford University Press.

DRYZEK, JOHN S., 1996. 'Political Inclusion and the Dynamics of Democratization', *American Political Science Review* 90 (3).

DUA, B. D., 1992. 'Problem of Federal Leadership', in S. Roy and W. E. James (eds), *Foundations of India's Political Economy.* New Delhi: Sage.

DUBEY, S. M. (ed.), 1978. *North-East India.* Delhi: Concept Publishing.

DUTT, R. C. (ed.), 1989. *Challenges to the Polity: Communalism, Casteism and Economic Challenges.* New Delhi: Lancer in association with India International Centre.

DUTTA, A., 1988. 'Growth and Development of a Regional Political Party', in S. Bhatnagar and P. Kumar (eds), *Regional Political Parties in India.* New Delhi: Ess Ess Publications.

DUTTA, P. K., 1990. 'War over Music: The Riots of 1926 in Bengal', *Social Scientist*, June–July.

ELECTION COMMISSION OF INDIA, 1987. *Report on the General Elections to the Legislative Assemblies of Haryana, JK, Kerala, Mizoram, Nagaland and West Bengal, 1987—Statistical.* New Delhi: Election Commission of India.

ELST, KOENRAAD, 1990. *Ram Janmabhoomi vs. Babri Masjid: A Case Study in Hindu–Muslim Conflict.* New Delhi: Voice of India.

———, 1991. *Ayodhya and after: Issues before Hindu Society.* New Delhi: Voice of India.

ENGINEER, ASGHAR ALI, 1982. 'The Guilty Men Of Meerut', *Economic and Political Weekly*, 6 November.

———, 1984. *Communal Riots in Post Independence India.* Hyderabad, India: Sangam.

———, 1986. 'Gujarat Burns again', *Economic and Political Weekly*, 3 August.

———, 1988. 'Meerut, Shame of the Nation', in Asghar Ali Engineer (ed.), *Delhi–Meerut Riots: Compilation, Documentation and Analysis.* Delhi: Ajanta.

———, 1989. 'Anatomy of Shiv Sena's Growth', *Mainstream*, 3 September.

———, 1990. 'Communal Riots in Recent Months', *Economic and Political Weekly*, 6 October.

———, 1991. 'Making of the Hyderabad Riots', *Economic and Political Weekly*, 9 February.

ENGINEER, ASGHAR ALI, 1992. 'Benares Rocked by Communal Violence', *Economic and Political Weekly*, 7 March.

———, 1993. 'Bastion of Communal Amity Crumbles', *Economic and Political Weekly*, 13 February.

———, 1994. 'Communal Violence and the Role of Law Enforcement Agencies', *South Asia Bulletin: Comparative Studies of South Asia, Africa and the Middle East* 14.

———, 1995a. 'Communalism and Communal Violence—1994', *Economic and Political Weekly*, 4 February.

———, 1995b. 'Communalism and Communal Violence in 1995', *Economic and Political Weekly*, 23 December.

———, 1996. 'Bhagalpur Riot Inquiry Commission Report', *Economic and Political Weekly,* 15 July.

———, 1997. 'Communalism and Communal Violence, 1996', *Economic and Political Weekly*, 15 February.

——— (ed.), 1988. *Delhi–Meerut Riots: Compilation, Documentation and Analysis.* Delhi: Ajanta.

——— (ed.), 1991. *Secular Crown on Fire: The Kashmir Problem.* Delhi: Ajanta Publications.

EVANS, PETER, DIETRICH RUESCHEMEYER and THEDA SKOCPOL (eds), 1985. *Bringing the State Back in.* Cambridge: Cambridge University Press.

FORRESTER, DUNCAN, 1976. 'Factions and Film Stars: Tamil Nadu Politics since 1971', *Asian Survey* 16 (3).

FOUCAULT, MICHEL, 1972. *Archeology of Knowledge.* New York: Pantheon.

FOX, RICHARD, 1996. 'Communalism and Modernity', in David Ludden (ed.), *Contesting the Nation: Religion, Community and the Politics of Democracy in India.* Philadelphia: University of Pennsylvania Press.

FRANKEL, FRANCINE R., 1990. 'India's Democracy in Transition', *World Policy Journal,* August.

FRANKEL, FRANCINE R. and M. S. A. RAO (eds), 1989. *Dominance and State Power in Modern India,* vol. 1. New York and Delhi: Oxford University Press.

——— (eds), 1990. *Dominance and State Power in Modern India,* vol. 2, New York and Delhi: Oxford University Press.

FREITAG, SANDRIA, 1980. 'Religious Rites and Riots: From Community Identity to Communalism in North India, 1870–1940'. Ph.D diss., University of California, Berkeley.

———, 1990. *Public Arenas and the Emergence of Communalism in North India.* Delhi: Oxford University Press.

FREITAG, SANDRIA, 1996. 'Contesting In Public: Colonial Legacies and Contemporary Communalism', in David Ludden (ed.), *Contesting The Nation: Religion, Community and the Politics of Democracy in India*, Philadelphia: University of Pennsylvania Press, Delhi, Delhi: Oxford University Press.

FRYKENBERG, ROBERT, 1991. 'Hindu Fundamentalism and the Structural Instability of India', in Martin Marty and R. Scott Appleby (eds), *Fundamentalisms Observed*. Chicago, IL: University of Chicago Press.

GABORIEAU, M., 1985. 'From Al'beruni to Jinnah', *Anthropology Today* 1 (3).

GANAI, ABDUL JABBAR, 1984. *Kashmir: National Conference and Politics*. Srinagar: Mehraj-ud-din for Gulshan Publishers.

GANGULY, SUMIT, 1992. 'The Prospects of War and Peace in Kashmir', in Raju G. C. Thomas (eds), *Perspectives on Kashmir—The Roots of Conflict in South Asia*. Boulder: Westview Press.

———, 1993. 'Ethno–Religious Conflict in South Asia', *Survival* 35 (June).

GANGULY, SUMIT and KANTI BAJPAI, 1994. 'India and the Crisis in Kashmir', *Asian Survey* 34 (5).

GEETHA, V. and S. V. RAJADURAI, 1990. 'Communal Violence in Madras: A Portent?', *Economic and Political Weekly,* 22 September.

———, 1993. 'Two Swords in a Scabbard: Crisis in DMK', *Economic and Political Weekly*, 6 November.

GEORGE, S. J., 1994. 'The Bodo Movement in Assam', *Asian Survey 34* (10).

GHOSH, S. K., 1987. *Communal Riots in India: Meet the Challenge Unitedly*. New Delhi: Ashish Publishing House.

GHURYE, G. S., 1968. *Social Tensions in India*. Bombay: Popular Prakashan.

GIYAS UD-DIN, PEER, 1992. *Understanding the Kashmiri Insurgency*. Jammu: Jay Kay Book House.

GOLD, DANIEL, 1991. 'Organized Hinduism: From Vedic Truth to Hindu Nation', in Martin Marty and R. Scott Appleby (eds), *Fundamentalisms Observed*. Chicago, IL: University of Chicago Press.

GOPAL, SARVEPALLI (ed.), 1991. *Anatomy of a Confrontation: The Babri Masjid–Ramjanmabhoomi Issue*. New Delhi and New York: Viking.

GORDON, R., 1975. 'The Hindu Mahasabha and the Indian National Congress—1915 to 1926', *Modern Asian Studies* 9 (2).

Government of India (GOI), 1907 (reprinted 1984). *North and North–eastern Frontier Tribes of India*, compiled in the Intelligence Branch, Division of the Chief of Staff, Army Headquarters. Reprint 1984 Delhi: Cultural Publishing House.

———, 1972. *Census of India 1971, Language Handbook on Mother Tongue in Census*. New Delhi: Register General, Annexure I.

Government of India (GOI), 1980. *Report of the Backward Classes Commission*, Parts I & II.

——, 1991a. *Census of India*, 1991, Series 4, Assam, paper no. 1 of 1991, Guwahati.

——, 1991b. *Census of India*, 1991, Series 18, Nagaland, paper no. 1 of 1991, Kohima.

——, 1991c. *The Constitution of India*. New Delhi.

——, 1993. *India 1991*. New Delhi: Publications Division.

GRAHAM, BRUCE D., 1990. *Hindu Nationalism and Indian Politics: The Origins and Development of the Bharatiya Janata Sangh*. Cambridge and New York: Cambridge University Press.

GROVER, VERINDER (ed.), 1995. *The Story of Kashmir: Yesterday and Today*, 3 vols. New Delhi: Deep & Deep Publications.

GUHAN, S., 1989. Social Security Initiatives in Tamil Nadu, 1989. Working Paper no. 96, Madras Institute of Development Studies.

GUPTA, DIPANKAR, 1982. *Nativism in a Metropolis: The Shiv Sena in Bombay*, Delhi: Manohar Press.

GUPTA, GIRI RAJ (ed.), 1978. *Cohesion and Conflict in Modern India*. Durham: Carolina Academic Press.

GUPTA, SURENDRA K. and INDIRA B. GUPTA, 1990. *Conflict and Communications: Mass Upsurge in Assam*. New Delhi: Har-Anand Publications in association with Vikas Publishing House.

HADENIUS, AXEL, 1992. *Democracy and Development*. Cambridge: Cambridge University Press.

——, 1994. 'The Duration of Democracy: Institutional vs. Socio-Economic Factors', in David Beetham (ed.), *Defining and Measuring Democracy*. 36 SAGE Modern Politics Service.

HANSEN, THOMAS BLOM, 1995. 'Democratisation, Mass-Politics and Hindu Identity: The Communalisation of Bombay', paper prepared for the workshop on Political Culture and Religion in the Third World, ECPR Joint Session, Bordeaux, April–May.

HARDGRAVE, ROBERT L., 1971. 'The Celluloid God: M.G.R. and the Tamil Film', *South Asian Review* 4 (July).

——, 1973. 'Politics and the Film in Tamil Nadu: The Stars and the DMK', *Asian Survey* 13 (3)

——, 1977. 'The Mapilla Rebellion, 1921: Peasant Revolt in Malabar', *Modern Asian Studies* 11(1).

——, 1979. 'The Dravidian Movement and Tamil Politics', in Robert L. Hardgrave (eds), *Essays in the Political Sociology of South India*. Delhi: Usha Publications.

HARDIN, RUSSEL, 1982. *Collective Action.* Baltimore: Johns Hopkins University Press.

———, 1995. *One for All: The Logic of Group Conflict.* Princeton: Princeton University Press.

HARRIS, BARBARA, 1986. 'Meals and Noon Meals in South India: Food and Nutrition Policy in the Rural Food Economy of Tamil Nadu State', Development Studies Occasional Paper No. 31, School of Development Studies, University of East Anglia.

———, 1991. 'The Give and Take of Calories: Tamil Nadu's Food and Nutrition Policies and Village Food Energy Economy during Drought in the Early Eighties', in C.T. Kurien, E.R. Prabhakar and S. Gopal (eds). *Economy, Society and Development: Essays and Reflections in Honour of Malcolm S. Adiseshiah.* New Delhi: Sage Publications.

HARRISON, SELIG S., 1960. *India: The Most Dangerous Decades.* Princeton: Princeton University.

HASAN, MUSHIRUL, 1994. 'Minority Identity and Its Discontents: Ayodhya and Its Aftermath', *South Asia Bulletin: Comparative Studies of South Asia, Africa and the Middle East* 14: 24–40.

HASAN, ZOYA, 1989. 'Power and Mobilisation: Patterns of Resilience and Change in Uttar Pradesh Politics', in Francine R. Frankel and M. S. A. Rao (eds), *Dominance and State Power in Modern India: Decline of a Social Order.* Delhi: Oxford University Press.

———, 1991. 'Changing Orientation of the State and the Emergence of Majoritarianism in the 1980s', in K. N. Panikkar (ed.), *Communalism in India: History, Politics and Culture.* New Delhi: Manohar.

———, 1994a. 'Party Politics and Communal Mobilization in Uttar Pradesh', *South Asia Bulletin: Comparative Studies of South Asia, Africa and the Middle East* 14: 42–52.

———, 1994b. 'Shifting Ground: Hindutva Politics and Farmers' Movement in Uttar Pradesh', *Journal of Peasant Studies,* 21 April.

HAZARIKA, N., 1978. 'The Working of the Autonomous District Councils', in S. M. Dubey (ed.), *North-East India.* Delhi: Concept Publishing.

HAZARIKA, S., 1994. *Strangers in the Mist.* New Delhi: Viking.

HERRENSCHMIDT, OLIVIER, 1989. *Les Meilleurs Dieux Sont Hindous.* Paris: L'Age d'homme.

HEUZE, GERARD, 1995. 'Cultural Populism: The Appeal of the Shiv Sena', in Sujata Patel and Alice Thorner (eds), *Bombay: Metaphor for Modern India.* Bombay, New Delhi and Oxford: Oxford University Press.

HOBSBAWM, ERIC J., 1990. *Nations and Nationalism since 1780: Programme, Myth, Reality.* Cambridge: *Canto,* Cambridge University Press.

HORAM, M., 1988. *Naga Insurgency.* New Delhi: Cosmos Publications.

HOROWITZ, DONALD L., 1985. *Ethnic Groups in Conflict*. Berkeley: University of California Press.

———, 1994. 'Democracy in Divided Societies', in Larry Diamond and Marc F. Plattner (eds), *Nationalism, Ethnic Conflict and Democracy*. Baltimore: Johns Hopkins University Press.

HUMAN RIGHTS WATCH, 1995. *Playing the 'Communal Card': Communal Violence and Human Rights*. New York: Human Rights Watch.

HUNTINGTON, SAMUEL, 1968. *Political Order in Changing Societies*. New Haven, CT: Yale University Press.

Indian Defence Review Research Team, 1989. 'Op Topac: The Kashmir Imbroglio', *Indian Defence Review*, July: 35–48.

IRSCHICK, EUGENE F., 1969. *Politics and Social Conflict: The Non-Brahman Movement and Tamil Separatism*. Berkeley: University of California Press.

———, 1986. *Tamil Revivalism in the 1930s*. Madras: Cre-A.

JAFFRELOT, CHRISTOPHE, 1996. *The Hindu Nationalist Movement and Indian Politics, 1925 to the 1990s*. New Delhi: Viking/London: Hurst/New York: Columbia University Press

JALAL, AYESHA, 1995. *Democracy and Authoritarianism in South Asia: A Comparative and Historical Perspective*. Cambridge: Cambridge Press.

JESSOP, BOB, 1990. *State Theory: Putting Capitalist States in Their Place*. University Park: Penn State University Press.

JHA, PREM SHANKAR, 1991. 'Frustrated Middle Class—Roots of Kashmir's Alienation', in Asghar A. Engineer (ed.), *Secular Crown on Fire: The Kashmir Problem*. Delhi: Ajanta Publications.

JOG, N. G., 1979. *Lokamanya Bal Gangadhar Tilak*. New Delhi: Government of India.

JOSHI, RAM, 1995. 'Politics in Maharashtra—An Overview', in Usha Thakkar and Mangesh Kulkarni (eds), *Politics in Maharashtra*. Delhi: Himalaya.

KADIAN, RAJESH, 1992. *The Kashmir Tangle: Issues and Options*. New Delhi: Vision Books.

KAKAR, SUDHIR, 1990. 'Some Unconscious Aspects of Ethnic Violence in South Asia', in *Mirrors of Violence: Communities, Riots and Survivors in South Asia*. Delhi: Oxford University Press.

———, 1996. *The Colors Of Violence: Cultural Identities, Religion and Conflict*. Chicago: University of Chicago Press.

KARANDIKAR, S. L., 1957. *Lokamanya Bal Gangadhar Tilak: The Hercules and Prometheus of Modern India*. Poona.

KATHURIA, HARBIR SINGH, 1990. *President's Rule in India 1967–89*. New Delhi: Uppal Publishing House.

KATZENSTEIN, MARY FAINSOD, 1979. *Ethnicity and Equality: The Shiv Sena*

Party and Preferential Policies in Bombay. Ithaca and London: Cornell University Press.

KELKAR, N. C., 1967 [1928]. *Life and Times of Lokamanya Tilak*. Translated from Marathi by D. V. Divekar. Delhi: Aupama Publications.

KESAVAN, M., 1990. 'Communal Violence and Its Impact on the Politics of North India: 1937–39', *Occasional Papers on History and Society* (Second Series). New Delhi: Nehru Memorial Museum and Library.

KOHLI, ATUL, 1987. *The State and Poverty in India: The Politics of Reform*. Cambridge and New York: Cambridge University Press.

———, 1990a. 'State–Society Relations in India's Changing Democracy', in Atul Kohli (ed.), *India's Democracy: An Analysis of Changing State–Society Relations*, 2nd ed. Princeton: Princeton University Press.

———, 1990b. *Democracy and Discontent: India's Growing Crisis of Governability*. Cambridge: Cambridge University Press.

———, 1993. 'Democracy amidst Economic Orthodoxy: Trends in Developing Countries', *Third World Quarterly* 14 (4).

———, 1994. 'Centralization and Powerlessness: India's Democracy in a Comparative Perspective', in Joel Migdal, Atul Kohli and Vivienne Shue (eds), *State Power and Social Forces: Domination and Transformation in the Third World*. Cambridge: Cambridge University Press.

KOLODNER, ERIC, 1995. 'The Political Economy of the Rise and Fall (?) of Hindu Nationalism', *Journal of Contemporary Asia* 25 (2).

KUECHLER, MANFRED and RUSSELL J. DALTON, 1990. 'New Social Movements and the Political Order: Inducing Change for Long-term Stability?', in R. J. Dalton and M. Kuechler (eds) *Challenging the Political Order*. New York: Oxford University Press.

KUMAR, D. P., nd. *Kashmir—Pakistan's Proxy War*. New Delhi: Har-Anand Publications.

KYMLICKA, WILL, 1995. *Multicultural Citizenship*. Oxford: Clarendon Press.

LALTHANGLIANA, 1994. 'Mizo National Front Movement', in R. N. Prasad (ed.), *Autonomy Movements in Mizoram*. New Delhi: Vikas.

LAMB, ALASTAIR, 1991. *Kashmir: A Disputed Legacy 1846–1990*. Hertingfordbury: Roxford Books.

———, 1994. *Birth of a Tragedy: Kashmir 1947*. Hertingfordbury: Roxford Books.

LELE, JAYANT, 1981. *Elite Pluralism and Class Rule: Political Development in Maharashtra, India*. Toronto: Toronto University Press.

———, 1995. 'Saffronisation of Shiv Sena', *Economic and Political Weekly*, 24 June.

LIETEN, G. K., 1994. 'On Casteism and Communalism in Uttar Pradesh', *Economic and Political Weekly*, 2 April.

LIETEN, G. K., 1996. 'Hindu Communalism: Between Caste and Class', *Journal of Contemporary Asia* 26 (2).

LIJPHART, AREND, 1977. *Democracy in Plural Societies*. New Haven: Yale University Press.

———, 1996. 'The Puzzle of Indian Democracy: A Consociational Interpretation', *American Political Science Review* 90 (2).

LUDDEN, DAVID (ed.), 1996. *Contesting the Nation: Religion, Community and the Politics of Democracy in India*. Philadelphia: University of Pennsylvania Press.

MADAN, D. P., nd. *Report of the Commission of Inquiry into the Communal Disturbances at Bhiwandi, Jalgaon and Mahad in May 1970*, vol. 1. np.

MAHESHWARI, ANIL, 1993. *Crescent over Kashmir: Politics of Mullaism*. New Delhi: Rupa & Co.

MAJUMDAR, R. C., 1988a. *The History and Culture of the Indian People, vol. 9: British Paramountcy and Indian Renaissance*, Part 1. Bombay: Bharatiya Vidya Bhavan.

———, 1988b. *The History and Culture of the Indian People, vol. 3: The Classical Age*. Bombay: Bharatiya Vidya Bhavan.

MALHOTRA, JAGMOHAN, 1994. *My Frozen Turbulence in Kashmir*. New Delhi: Allied Publishers Ltd.

MALIK, DEEPAK, 1994. 'Three Riots in Varanasi, 1989–90 to 1992', *South Asia Bulletin: Comparative Studies of South Asia, Africa and the Middle East* 14.

MANIVANNAN, R., 1992. '1991 Tamil Nadu Elections—Issues Strategies and Performance', *Economic and Political Weekly*, 25 January.

MASSELOS, JIM, 1993. 'The City as Represented in Crowd Action: Bombay 1893', *Economic and Political Weekly,* 30 January.

———, 1996. 'The Bombay Riots of January 1993: The Politics of Urban Conflagration', in J. Mcguire, P. Reeves and H. Brasted (eds), *Politics of Violence: From Ayodhya to Behrampada*. New Delhi: Sage.

MATHEW, G., 1982. 'Politicization of Religion. Conversions to Islam in Tamil Nadu', *Economic and Political Weekly*, 19 June.

———, 1983. 'Hindu–Christian Communalism: An Analysis of Kanyaku-mari Riots', *Social Action,* October.

MENEZES, SAIRA, 1966. 'Sena's History Reversed', *Outlook,* November.

MICHAEL, S. M., 1986. 'The Politicization of the Ganapati Festival', *Social Compass* 33.

MIGDAL, JOEL, ATUL KOHLI and VIVIENNE SHUE (eds), 1994. *State Power and*

Social Forces: Domination and Transformation in the Third World. New York: Cambridge University Press.

MISRA, T. and U. MISRA, 1996. 'Movements for Autonomy in India's North-East', in T. V. Sathyamurthy (ed.), *Region, Religion, Caste, Gender and Culture in Contemporary India.* Delhi: Oxford University Press.

MITCHELL, TIMOTHY, 1991. 'The Limits of the State: Beyond State Theories and Their Critics', *American Political Science Review* 85 (1).

MITRA, SUBRATA K., 1990. 'Between Transaction and Transcendence: The State and the Institutionalisation of Authority in India', in Subrata K. Mitra (ed.), *The Post-Colonial State in Asia: The Dialectics of Politics and Culture.* New York and London: Harvester.

———, 1995. 'The Rational Politics of Cultural Nationalism: Subnational Movements of South Asia in Comparative Perspective', *British Journal of Political Science* 25 (1).

MITRA, SUBRATA K. and JAMES CHIRIANKANDATH (eds), 1992. *Electoral Politics in India: A Changing Landscape.* New Delhi: Segment Books.

MOON, PANDEREL, 1944. *Strangers in India.* London: Faber and Faber.

MYRDAL, GUNNAR, 1968. *Asian Drama.* New York: Pantheon.

NADKARNI, M. V.. 1987. *Farmers' Movement in India.* New Delhi: Macmillan.

NAIPAUL, V. S., 1990. *India, A Million Mutinies Now.* New York: Viking.

NANDA, K. K., 1994. *Conquering Kashmir: A Pakistani Obsession.* New Delhi: Lancer Books.

NANDY, ASHIS, SHIKHA TRIVEDI, SHAIL MAYARAM and ACHYUT YAGNIK, 1995. *Creating a Nationality: Ramjanmabhoomi Movement and Fear of the Self.* New Delhi and New York: Oxford University Press.

NEHRU, JAWAHARLAL, 1960. *A Bunch of Old Letters: Written Mostly to Jawaharlal Nehru and Some Written by Him.* Bombay: Asia Publishing House.

NOORANI, A. G., 1987. 'Amnesty Reports on Meerut Killings', *Economic and Political Weekly*, 12 December.

OMVEDT, GAIL, 1976. *Cultural Revolt in a Colonial Society: The Non-Brahmin Movement in Western India, 1873-1930.* Bombay: Scientific Socialist Education Trust.

———, 1990. 'Hinduism and Politics', *Economic and Political Weekly*, 7 April.

———, 1993. *Reinventing Revolution: New Social Movements and the Socialist Tradition in India.* Armonk, NY: Sharpe.

PADGAONKAR, DILIP, 1993. *When Bombay Burned: Reportage and Comments on the Riots and Blasts from the Times of India.* New Delhi: UBSPD Publishers' Distributors.

PAGE, DAVID, 1982. *Prelude To Partition: Indian Muslims and The Imperial System of Control*, 1920–1932. New York: Oxford University Press.

PAKEM, B. (ed.), 1993. *Regionalism in India.* New Delhi: Har-Anand.

PALSHIKAR, SUHAS, 1996, 'Capturing the Moment of Realignment', *Economic and Political Weekly.* 13 January.

PANDE, B. N. (ed.), 1985. *A Centenary History of the Indian National Congress, 1885–1985,* 2 vols. New Delhi: All-India Congress Committee (I).

PANDEY, B. N, 1969. *The Break-up of British India.* New York: Macmillan.

PANDEY, GYANENDRA, 1978. *The Ascendency of Congress in Uttar Pradesh.* Delhi: Oxford University Press.

———, 1990. *The Construction of Communalism in Colonial North India.* Delhi: Oxford University Press.

———, 1992. 'In Defence of the Fragment: Writing About Hindu–Muslim Riots in India Today', *Representations,* 37 December.

——— (ed.), 1993. *Hindus and Others: The Question of Identity in India Today.* New Delhi and New York: Viking.

PANDIAN, M. S. S., 1991. '*Parasakthi*: Life and Times of a DMK Film', *Economic and Political Weekly*, Annual Number (March).

———, 1992. *The Image Trap: M. G. Ramachandran in Film and Politics.* New Delhi: Sage Publications.

PANIKKAR, K. N., 1991. *Communalism in India: History, Politics and Culture.* New Delhi: Manohar.

PARIKH, SUNITA, 1997. *The Politics of Preference: Democratic Institutions and Affirmative Action in the United States and India.* Ann Arbor: University of Michigan Press.

PARMANAND, 1985. *Mahamana Madan Mohan Malaviya.* Benares: Benares Hindu University.

PATEL, S., 1985. 'Violence with a Difference', *Economic and Political Weekly*, 7 July.

PATEL, SUJATA and ALICE THORNER (eds), 1995. *Bombay: Metaphor for Modern India.* Bombay: Oxford University Press.

PATWARDHAN, ANAND, 1994. *Father Son and Holy War.* New York: First Run/ Icarus Films.

PHADKE, Y. D., 1979. *Politics and Language.* Bombay: Himalaya Publishing House.

PHUKON, GIRIA, 1988. 'Genesis of Asom Gana Parishad', in S. Bhatnagar and P. Kumar (eds), *Regional Political Parties in India.* New Delhi: ESS ESS Publications.

PINCH, WILLIAM, 1990. 'Being Vaishnav, Becoming Kshatriya: Culture, Belief and Identity in North India 1806–1940', Mimeograph, Department of History, University of Virginia.

POWELL, WALTER W. and PAUL J. DIMAGGIO, 1991. *The New Institutionalism in Organizational Analysis.* Chicago: University of Chicago Press.

PRAKASH, I., 1938. *A Review of the History and Work of the Hindu Mahasabha and the Hindu Sangathan Movement.* New Delhi: Akhil Cheratiya Hindu Mahasabha.

PRASAD, K.V. EASWARA, 1995. 'Social Security for Destitute Widows in Tamil Nadu', *Economic and Political Weekly*, 15 April.

PRASAD, R. N. (ed.), 1994. *Autonomy Movements in Mizoram.* New Delhi: Vikas.

PRESLER, FRANKLIN A., 1987. *Religion under Bureaucracy: Policy and Administration for Hindu Temples in South India.* Cambridge: Cambridge University Press.

PRICE, PAMELA G., 1989. 'Kingly Models in Indian Political Behavior: Culture as a Medium of History', *Asian Survey* 29 (6).

PURI, BALRAJ, 1993. *Kashmir: Towards Insurgency.* Hyderabad: Orient Longman.

RADHAKRISHNAN, P., 1989. 'Ambasankar Commission and Backward Classes', *Economic and Political Weekly*, 10 June.

———, 1990. 'Backward Classes in Tamil Nadu, 1872–1988', *Economic and Political Weekly*, 10 March.

———, 1993. 'Communal Representation in Tamil Nadu, 1850–1916: The Pre-Non-Brahmin Phase', *Economic and Political Weekly*, 31 July.

RAJGOPAL, P. R., 1987. *Communal Violence in India.* New Delhi: Uppal Publishing House.

RAMACHANDRAN, S. (ed.), 1975. *Anna Speaks: At the Rajya Sabha, 1962–66.* Madras: Orient Longman.

RAMASWAMY, SUMATHI, 1993. 'En-gendering Language: The Poetics of Tamil Language Identity', *Comparative Studies in Society and History* 35 (4).

RAWLS, JOHN, 1993. *Political Liberalism.* New York: Columbia University Press.

RAY, A., 1982. *Mizoram: Dynamics of Change.* Calcutta: Pearl.

RAY, ASWINI K., 1994. 'Regional Politics of East Pakistan and Kashmir', *Journal of Peace Studies* 1 (2).

———, 1996. 'Recalling Bhagalpur—Aftermath of 1989 Riots', *Economic and Political Weekly*, 4 May.

REKHI, TARA SINGH, 1993. *Socio Economic Justice in Jammu and Kashmir.* New Delhi: Ideal Publications.

RIZVI, GOWHER, 1992. 'India, Pakistan and the Kashmir Problem, 1947–1972', in Raju G. C. Thomas (ed.), *Perspectives on Kashmir —The Roots of Conflict in South Asia.* Boulder: Westview Press.

ROBB, P., 1986. 'The Challenge of Gau Mata. British Policy and Religious Change in India, 1880–1916', *Modern Asian Studies* 20 (2).

ROBINSON, FRANCIS, 1973. 'Municipal Government and Muslim Separatism in the United Provinces, 1833 to 1916', *Modern Asian Studies* 7(3).

—— (ed.), 1989. *The Cambridge Encyclopedia of India, Pakistan, Bangladesh, Sri Lanka, Nepal, Bhutan and the Maldives.* Cambridge: Cambridge University Press.

ROKKAN, STEIN, 1975. 'Dimensions of State Formation and Nation-Building: A Possible Paradigm for Research on Variations within Europe', in Charles Tilly (ed.), *The Formation of National States in Europe.* Princeton: Princeton University Press.

——, 1987. *Stat, Nasjon, Klasse.* Oslo: Universitetsforlaget.

RUDOLPH, LLOYD I., 1961. 'Urban Life and Populist Radicalism: Dravidian Politics in Madras', *Journal of Asian Studies* 20.

RUDOLPH, LLOYD I. and SUSANNE H. RUDOLPH, 1987. *In Pursuit of Lakshmi.* Chicago: University of Chicago Press.

——, 1993. 'Modern Hatred', *The New Republic* 203 (12).

SADHU, ARUN, 1988. 'Not by Jobs Alone', *Free Press Journal,* 6 January.

SAINATH, P., 1993. Video of talk delivered after 1992–1993 riots. Sainath is a journalist with *Blitz.* Available with Mary Katzenstein, Department of Government, Cornell University.

SAXENA, N. S., 1990. *Communal Riots in India.* Noida: Trishul.

SARAF, MUHAMMAD YUSUF, 1979. *Kashmiris Fight for Freedom,* vol. 2. Lahore: Feroz Sons Ltd.

SARDESAI, RAJDEEP, 1995. 'The Shiv Sena's New Avatar: Marathi Chauvinism and Hindu Communalism', in Usha Thakkar and Mangesh Kulkarni (eds), *Politics in Maharashtra.* Delhi: Himalaya.

SARKAR, SUMIT, 1996. 'Indian Nationalism and The Politics of Hindutva', in David Ludden (ed.), *Contesting The Nation: Religion, Community and The Politics of Democracy In India.* Philadelphia: University of Pennsylvania Press, Delhi: Oxford University Press.

SCOTT, W. RICHARD, 1995. *Institutions and Organizations.* Thousand Oaks, CA.: Sage.

SEBASTIAN, A., 1986. 'Migrants in North Eastern Region of India', in B. Datta Ray (ed.), *The Patterns and Problems of Population in North-east India.* New Delhi: Uppal Publishing.

SEMA, H., 1986. *Emergence of Nagaland.* New Delhi: Vikas.

SEN, S., 1982. 'Social Tension in North-East India in Retrospect', in J. B. Bhattacharya (ed.), *Social Tension in North-East India*. Calcutta: Research India.

SETALVAD, TEESTA, 1995. 'The Woman Shiv Sainik and Her Sister Swayamsevika', in Tanika Sarkar and Urvashi Butalia (eds), *Women and the Hindu Right*. Delhi: Kali for Women.

SHAH, GHANSHYAM, 1991. 'Tenth Lok Sabha Elections: BJP's Victory in Gujarat', *Economic and Political Weekly*, 21 December.

————, 1994. 'The BJP and Backward Castes in Gujarat', *South Asia Bulletin: Comparative Studies of South Asia, Africa and the Middle East* 14.

SHAKIR, MOIN (ed.), 1989. *Religion, State and Politics in India*. Delhi: Ajanta.

SHARMA, SHALENDRA D., 1991. 'India's Precarious Democracy: Between Crisis and Resilience', *Contemporary South Asia* 3.

SHIVA KUMAR, A. K., 1991. 'UNDP's Human Development Index: A Computation for Indian States', *Economic and Political Weekly*, 12 October.

SHIVA RAO, B., 1967. *The Framing of India's Constitution*, vol. 3. Bombay: N. M. Tripathi.

SINGH, ANITA INDER, 1987. *The Origins of the Partition of India, 1936–1947*. Oxford: Oxford University Press.

SINGH, B. P., 1987. *The Problem of Change*. New Delhi: Oxford University Press.

SINGH, BALBIR, 1982. *State Politics in India*. New Delhi: Macmillan.

SINGH, V. B. and SHANKAR BOSE, 1988. *State Elections in India: Data Handbook on Vidhan Sabha Elections, 1952–85*, vol. 5. New Delhi: Sage Publications.

SKOCPOL, THEDA, 1992. *Protecting Soldiers and Mothers: The Political Origins of Social Policy in the United States*. Cambridge, MA: Belknap Press of Harvard University Press.

SONTHEIMER, GUNTHER D. and HERMANN KULKE (eds), 1989. *Hinduism Reconsidered*. New Delhi: Manohar.

SPODEK, HOWARD, 1987. 'From Gandhi to Violence: Ahmedabad 1985 Riots in Historical Perspective', Unpublished paper.

SUBRAMANIAN, NARENDRA, 1993. 'Ethnicity, Populism and Pluralist Democracy: Mobilization and Representation in South India, Tamil Nadu'. Unpublished Ph.D. diss., Massachusetts Institute of Technology.

SUNDARAM, V. A. (ed.), 1942. *Benares Hindu University 1916–1942*. Benares: R. Pathak.

SURESH, V., 1992. 'The DMK Debacle: Causes and Portents', *Economic and Political Weekly*, 17 October.

SWAMY, ARUN R., 1996a. 'The Nation, the People and the Poor: Sandwich Tactics in Party Competition and Policy Formation, India, 1931–1996'. Unpublished Ph.D. diss., University of California, Berkeley.

———, 1996b. 'Sense, Sentiment and Populist Coalitions: The Strange Career of Cultural Nationalism in Tamil Nadu', in Allison K. Lewis and Subrata Mitra (eds), *Subnational Movements in South Asia*. Boulder: Westview Press.

TAAGEPERA, REIN and MATHEW SOBERG SHUGART, 1989. *Seats and Votes: The Effects and Determinants of Electoral Systems*. New Haven: Yale University Press.

TAMBIAH, S., 1996. *Leveling Crowds: Ethnonationalist Conflicts and Collective Violence in South Asia*. Berkeley: University of California Press.

TAYLOR, DAVID and MALCOLM YAPP, 1979. *Political Identity In South Asia*. London: Curzon Press.

THAKKAR, USHA, 1995. 'The Commissioner and the Corporators: Power Politics at Municipal Level', in Sujata Patel and Alice Thorner (eds), *Bombay: Metaphor for Modern India*. Bombay: Oxford University Press.

THANDAVAN, R., 1987. *All-India Anna Dravida Munnetra Kazhagam: Political Dynamics in Tamil Nadu*. Madras: Tamil Nadu Academy of Political Science.

The Statesman Weekly. 1995. 'Karbi–Dimasa Accord Signed', 8 April.

THOMAS, RAJU G.C. (ed.), 1992. *Perspectives on Kashmir—The Roots of Conflict in South Asia*. Boulder: Westview Press.

TILLY, CHARLES, 1969. 'Collective Violence in European Perspective', in Hugh D. Graham and Ted R. Gurr (eds), *Violence in America: Historical and Comparative Perspectives*, vol. 1. Washington D.C.: Superintendent of Documents, US Government Printing Office.

TURNER, VICTOR, 1974. *Dramas, Fields and Metaphors : Symbolic Actions in Human Society*. Ithaca and London: Cornell University Press.

VAN DEN BERGHE, PIERRE, 1978. 'Race and Ethnicity: A Sociobiological Perspective', *Ethnic and Racial Studies* 1 (4).

VAN DER VEER, PETER, 1987. 'God Must Be Liberated! A Hindu Liberation Movement in Ayodhya', *Modern Asian Studies* 21(2).

———, 1994a. *Religious Nationalism: Hindus and Muslims in India*. Berkeley: University of California Press.

———, 1994b. 'Hindu Nationalism and the Discourse of Modernity', in Martin Marty and R. Scott Appleby (eds), *Accounting for Fundamentalism: The Dynamic Characteristics of Movements*. Chicago: University of Chicago Press.

VAN DER VEER, PETER, 1996. 'Writing Violence', in David Ludden (ed.), *Contesting The Nation: Religion, Community and The Politics of Democracy in India.* Philadelphia: University of Pennsylvania Press, Delhi: Oxford University Press.

VARSHNEY, ASHUTOSH, 1991. 'India, Pakistan and Kashmir: Antinomies of Nationalism', *Asian Survey* 31 (11).

———, 1992. 'Three Compromised Nationalisms: Why Kashmir Has Been a Problem', in Raju G. C. Thomas (ed.), *Perspectives on Kashmir—The Roots of Conflict in South Asia.* Boulder: Westview Press.

———, 1993. 'Contested Meanings: India's National Identity, Hindu Nationalism and the Politics of Anxiety', *Daedalus,* 122 June.

VARMA, HARNAM S., RAM ABHILASH SINGH and JAY SINGH, 1993. 'Power Sharing: Exclusivity and Exclusion in a Mega State', Paper presented at the All-India Sociological Conference, December.

VERMA, P. S., 1994. *Jammu and Kashmir at the Political Crossroads.* New Delhi: Vikas Publishing House.

VIDAL, D., G. TARABONT and E. MEYER, 1994. *Violences et non-Violences en Inde, Purushartha,* n. 16. Paris: EHESS: 261–87.

VORA, RAJENDRA, 1996. 'Shift of Power from Rural to Urban Sector', *Economic and Political Weekly,* 13 January.

WASHBROOK, DAVID, 1973. 'Country Politics: Madras 1880 to 1930', *Modern Asian Studies* 7 (3).

———, 1989. 'Caste, Class and Dominance in Modern Tamil Nadu: Non-Brahmanism, Dravidianism and Tamil Nationalism', in Francine Frankel and M.S.A. Rao (eds), *Dominance and State Power in Modern India: Decline of a Social Order,* vol. 1. Delhi: Oxford University Press.

WEBER, MAX, 1993. Cited in H. Liebersohn. 'Weber's Historical Concept of National Identity', in H. Lehmann and G. Roth (eds), *Weber's Protestant Ethic: Origins, Evidence, Contexts.* Cambridge: Cambridge University Press.

WEINER, MYRON, 1967. *Party-Building in a New Nation.* Chicago, IL: University of Chicago Press.

———, 1978. *Sons of the Soil, Migration and Ethnic Conflict in India.* Princeton: Princeton University Press.

———, 1989. *The Indian Paradox: Essays in Indian Politics.* New Delhi: Sage.

WIDMALM, STEN, 1997. 'Democracy and Violent Separatism in India: Kashmir in a Comparative Perspective'. Ph.D. diss., Uppsala University, Department of Government.

WIRSING, ROBERT G., 1994. *India, Pakistan and the Kashmir Dispute.* London: Macmillan.

Women, Law and the Media Workshop. 'Shifting Boundaries', 22–8 October 1994. Organized by the Centre for Feminist Legal Research in

Association with the Asia Pacific Forum on Women, Law and Development, Annexure H. New Delhi: Jamia Hamdard.

WOOD, C., 1987. *The Moplah Rebellion and Its Genesis*. New Delhi: People's Publishing House.

YAGNIK, ACHYUT and ANIL BHATT, 1984. 'The Anti-Dalit Agitation in Gujarat', *South Asia Bulletin* 4: 45–60.

YOUNG, CRAWFORD, 1993. *The Rising Tide of Cultural Pluralism: The Nation-State at Bay?* Madison, WI: University of Wisconsin Press.

ZELLIOTT, ELEANOR, 1992. *From Untouchable to Dalit: Essays on the Ambedkar Movement*. Delhi: Manohar.

Name Index

Subject Index

5/2388

28-8-2001

Rajdani 13hrs.

~~Monday~~   9.10 am.   10.10 p.m.

Weds & Sat.

BA.   ~~Mon~~
           Tues   To Bhub. arrive 10.30
           Wed   In Bhub
           Thur evening to Delhi
           Friday. Nirulas
           Sat.